HACCP & SANITATION

in restaurants and food service operations

A Practical Guide
Based on the
FDA Food Code
With Companion CD-ROM

By Lora Arduser and Douglas Robert Brown

HACCP & SANITATION IN RESTAURANTS AND FOOD SERVICE OPERATIONS: A PRACTICAL GUIDE BASED ON THE FDA FOOD CODE WITH COMPANION CD-ROM

By Lora Arduser and Douglas Robert Brown

Published by **ATLANTIC PUBLISHING GROUP, INC**

ATLANTIC PUBLISHING GROUP, INC • 1210 S.W. 23rd Place • Ocala, FL 34474-7014

800-814-1132 • www.atlantic-pub.com • sales@atlantic-pub.com

SAN Number :268-1250

Member American Library Association

Library of Congress Cataloging-in-Publication Data

Arduser, Lora.
   HACCP & sanitation in restaurants and food service operations : a practical guide based on the FDA food code with companion CD-ROM / by Lora Arduser and Douglas Robert Brown.
       p. ; cm.
   Includes index.
   ISBN 0-910627-35-5 (alk. paper)
   1. Food service--Sanitation. 2. Food service employees--Health and hygiene. 3. Food handling. 4. Food service management. I. Title: HACCP and sanitation in restaurants and food service operations. II. Brown, Douglas Robert, 1960- III. Title.

   TX911.3.S3A73 2005
   363.72'96--dc22

                              2005002849

                 10 9 8 7 6 5 4 3 2 1

WARNING DISCLAIMER

This book is designed to provide information in regard to the subject matter covered. It is sold with the understanding that the publisher and author are not engaged in rendering legal, accounting or other professional services. If legal or other expert assistance is required, the services of a competent professional should be sought.

It is not the purpose of this manual to reprint all the information that is otherwise available to the author and/or publisher but to complement, amplify and supplement other texts.

Every effort has been made to make this manual as complete and as accurate as possible. However, there may be mistakes, both typographical and in content. Therefore, this text should be used only as a general guide and not as the ultimate source of information.

The purpose of this manual is to educate and entertain. The author and the publisher shall have neither liability nor responsibility to any person or entity with respect to any loss or damage caused or alleged to be caused directly or indirectly by the information contained in this book.

Cover and interior design by Meg Buchner of Megadesign • www.mega-designs.com • e-mail: megadesn@mchsi.com
Book production design by Laura Siitari of Siitari by Design • www.siitaribydesign.com

TABLE OF CONTENTS

CHAPTER 1   HAZARDS TO FOOD SAFETY

CHAPTER 2   FACTORS AFFECTING FOOD-BORNE ILLNESS

CHAPTER 3   FOOD SAFETY REGULATIONS

CHAPTER 4   FOLLOWING THE FLOW OF FOOD:
PURCHASING, RECEIVING AND STORAGE

CHAPTER 5 FOLLOWING THE FLOW OF FOOD: PREPARING, HOLDING, SERVING AND REHEATING

CHAPTER 6 HACCP

CHAPTER 7   FACILITY PLAN

GLOSSARY

APPENDIX

HACCP PRODUCTS SECTION

HACCP TEST

INDEX

INTRODUCTION

According to the FDA, it is estimated that up to 76 million people get a food-borne illness each year. Since people don't go to the doctor for mild symptoms, the actual number of illnesses can't be known, but 5,000 people a year die from food-borne illness in the United States and many others suffer long-term effects.

Almost all of this sickness and death could have been prevented with the proper procedures that are taught in this comprehensive book. If these numbers don't upset you, realize that a food-borne outbreak in your establishment can put you out of business. If the business survives, it will be severely damaged, even after the lawsuits are resolved. If you do not have proper sanitation methods and a HACCP program in place, you need them today.

Take a look at this headline from CNN as an illustration of what can happen during a food-borne illness outbreak: *Hepatitis Outbreak Spreads Fear*, Saturday, November 15, 2003, Posted: 6:40 PM EST (2340 GMT)

PITTSBURGH, Pennsylvania (AP) – The nation's biggest known outbreak of hepatitis A is causing such a panic that people are lining up by the thousands for antibody shots and no longer eating out. A third person died Friday and nearly 500 others who ate at a Chi-Chi's Mexican restaurant have fallen ill in the outbreak that has prompted the Centers for Disease Control and Prevention to send assistance.

Health investigators are focusing on whether contaminated produce—perhaps scallions—caused the outbreak at the restaurant in the Beaver Valley Mall, about 25 miles northwest of Pittsburgh.

"We're very concerned. It's very serious and we've sent a team of people out there to assist," said CDC spokesman David Daigle.

Health officials Friday met with worried shoppers at the mall to try to squelch rumors that the virus was spreading out of control to other restaurants in the region. State Rep. Mike Veon attended a news conference at the mall and ate a sandwich he bought there.

Officials at the mall said sales at the food court were off by as much as 40 percent and sales throughout the mall were down up to 25 percent.

This book is based on the FDA Food Code and will teach food service managers and employees every aspect of food safety, HACCP and sanitation, from purchasing and receiving food to properly washing the dishes. They will learn time and temperature abuses; cross-contamination; personal hygiene practices; biological, chemical and physical hazards; proper cleaning and sanitizing; waste and pest management; and the basic principles of HACCP (Hazard Analysis of Critical Control Points).

This book also explains what safe food is and how to provide it; and it covers bacteria, viruses, fungi and parasites; various food-borne illnesses; safe food-handling techniques; purchasing and receiving food; storage; preparation and serving; sanitary equipment and facilities; cleaning and sanitizing of equipment and facilities; pest-management program; accident-prevention program; crisis management; and food safety and sanitation laws. The companion CD-ROM contains all the forms and posters needed to establish your HACCP and food-safety program.

HAZARDS TO FOOD SAFETY

According to the Food Code, food-borne illness in the United States is a major cause of personal distress and preventable death and is an avoidable economic burden. The Council for Agricultural Science and Technology estimated 6.5 to 33 million people become ill from microorganisms in food, resulting in as many as 9,000 needless deaths every year. The Centers for Disease Control and Prevention (CDC) have consistently stated that where reported, food-borne outbreaks were caused by mishandling of food; most of the time the mishandling occurred within the retail segment of the food industry where ready-to-eat food is prepared and provided to the public for consumption.

Because many foods are agricultural products and have started their journey to your door as animals and plants, raised in the environment, they may contain microscopic organisms. Many foods contain nutrients that make them a place where microorganisms can live and even grow. Some of these organisms are pathogens, which means that under the right conditions and in the right numbers, they can make someone who eats them ill. Raw animal foods such as meat, poultry, fish and eggs often carry bacteria, viruses or parasites that can be harmful to humans.

Because foods are from the environment, they can contain objects such as stones that could cause injury. Food may be contaminated naturally, for example, from the soil in which it is grown or because of harvest, storage or transportation practices. Some foods undergo further processing and at times, despite best efforts, become contaminated. These inherent hazards, along with the hazards that may occur in your establishment, such as metal fragments from grinding, can lead to injury, illness or death.

Food-borne illness is caused by eating contaminated food. A food-borne disease outbreak occurs when two or more people experience similar symptoms from eating the same food. There are many foods that can be culprits in a food-borne illness outbreak or occurrence. Some of the ones we are most familiar with are hamburgers, hot dogs, luncheon meats, chicken and oysters, but other foods can also harbor bacteria. Strawberries, green onions, ice cream and dry cereal can also cause food-borne illness if not properly processed and handled.

Food can be contaminated whether it is made from scratch or prepackaged. However, the main culprit of contamination is bacteria. It is estimated that bacteria is responsible for 90 percent of food contamination, viruses cause approximately 6 percent, chemicals are responsible for 3 percent, and parasites cause approximately 1 percent.

Anyone can fall a victim to food-borne illness, but some members of the population are more susceptible than others. These include pregnant women, the elderly, the very young, and people with impaired immune systems due to AIDS, cancer, diabetes or medications that suppress their immune function. Whereas the general population may recover from an incident in a few days, people in this group are much more likely to die from a food-borne illness.

The main symptoms of food-borne illness are:

- Headache
- Fatigue
- Nausea
- Abdominal pain
- Fever
- Dehydration
- Diarrhea
- Vomiting

Food-borne illnesses are generally classified as food-borne infections, intoxication or toxin-mediated infection. Infections are caused by eating food that contain living disease-causing organisms. Intoxication is caused by eating food that contains a harmful toxin or chemical produced by bacteria or another source, and toxin-mediated infection is caused by eating a food that contains harmful organisms that will produce a toxin once it has been consumed.

A food-borne hazard is a biological, chemical or physical hazard that can cause illness when it is consumed in food.

Food hazards include biological concerns such as:

- Bacterial, parasitic or viral contamination
- Bacterial growth
- Bacterial, parasitic or viral survival
- Bacterial toxin production
- Bacterial, parasitic or viral cross-contamination

Physical objects:

- Stones
- Glass
- Metal fragments
- Packaging materials

Chemical contamination:

- Nonfood-grade lubricants
- Cleaning compounds
- Food additives
- Insecticides

More information can be found on the FDA's Web site at **www.cfsan.fda.gov/~mow/intro.html**.

BACTERIA

Bacteria is everywhere: in the air, in all areas of the restaurant and all over one's body. Most bacteria is microscopic and of no harm to people. Many forms of bacteria are actually beneficial, aiding in the production of such things as cheese, bread, butter, alcoholic beverages, etc. Only a small percentage of bacteria will cause food to spoil and can generate a form of food poisoning when consumed.

Bacteria exists in a vegetative state. The vegetative cells grow and reproduce like any other living organism. Some bacteria forms "spores." The spores help the bacteria survive in less than ideal environments that may not have enough food or the right amount of moisture or ideal temperature. This spore structure allows the bacteria to survive stresses such as cooking, freezing and high-salt environments. In other words, cooking, freezing or curing will not kill these bacteria. The spores themselves are not harmful (except to babies; the spore Clostridium botuinlum, which can be found in honey, can cause infant botulism). However, if the environmental conditions become suitable for bacterial growth, the spore will turn into a vegetative cell, and this cell can multiply and cause illness.

Bacteria need several things in order to reproduce. Many food service managers refer to these items as F-A-T-T-O-M:

Food
Acid
Temperature
Time
Oxygen
Moisture

Food. Most bacteria prefer high-protein or high-carbohydrate foods like meats, poultry, seafood, cooked potatoes and dairy products.

Acid. Most foods have a pH less than 7.0. Very acidic food like limes and lemons normally do not support bacterial growth. While most bacteria prefer a neutral environment, they are capable of growing in foods that have pHs between 4.5 and 9.0.

The quality known as "pH" indicates how acidic or alkaline (basic) a food or other substance is. The pH scale ranges from 0.0 to 14.0—7.0 being exactly neutral. Distilled water, for example, has a neutral pH of 7.0. Bacteria grow best in foods that are neutral or slightly acidic, in the pH range of 4.6 to 7.0. Highly acidic foods, such as vinegar and most fresh fruits, inhibit bacterial growth. Meats and many other foods have an optimal pH for bacterial growth. On the other hand, some foods normally considered hazardous, such as mayonnaise and custard filling, can be safely stored at room temperature if their pH is below 4.6.

Lowering the pH of foods by adding acidic ingredients, such as making sauerkraut from cabbage or pickles from cucumbers, may render them non-potentially hazardous. This is not a foolproof prevention method, however. For example, although commercially prepared mayonnaise has a pH below 4.6, adding mayonnaise to a meat salad will not inhibit bacteria. The moisture in the meat and the meat's pH are likely to raise the pH of the salad to a point where bacteria can multiply.

ACIDITY VS. ALKALINITY pH Levels of Some Common Foods	
Vinegar	2.2
Lemons	2.2
Cola drinks	2.3
Commercial mayonnaise	3.0
Grapefruit	3.1
Dill pickles	3.2
Orange juice	3.7
Pears	3.9
Tomatoes	4.2
Buttermilk	4.5
Carrots	5.0
White bread	5.1
Tuna	6.0
Green peas	6.0
Potatoes	6.1
Chicken	6.2
Corn	6.3
Steamed rice	6.4
Fresh meat	6.4
Milk	6.6

Temperature. Most disease-causing bacteria grow between the temperatures of 41° and 140°F. This is called the temperature danger zone. Some bacteria like Listeria monocytogenes, a bacteria that is often the culprit in food-borne illness related to processed luncheon meats, can grow at temperatures below 41°F.

Time. Bacteria only need about four hours to reproduce enough cells to cause a food-borne illness. This time is the total time the food item spends in the temperature danger zone.

Oxygen. There are aerobic bacteria and anaerobic bacteria, and these two types have different oxygen requirements. Aerobic bacteria must have oxygen in order to grow. Anaerobic bacteria, on the other hand, do not. These bacteria grow well in vacuum-packed or canned food items. Anaerobic conditions might also exist in the middle of large, cooked food masses, such as a large stockpot of stew or the middle of a large roast.

Moisture. The amount of water in a food that is available to support bacterial growth is called water activity. It is measured on a scale between 0.0 and 1.0; water activity must be greater than 0.85 to support bacterial growth. Dairy products, meats, fish, shellfish, poultry, egg, cut melons, pasta, steamed rice and sprouts all have water activity levels between 0.85 and 1.0.

Bacterial growth rate depends upon how favorable these six conditions are. Bacteria prefer to ingest moisture-saturated foods, such as meats, dairy products and produce. They will not grow as readily on dry foods such as cereals, sugar or flour.

Bacterial growth has four phases:

1. **Lag phase** – little or no growth occurs. This phase lasts a few hours at room temperature, but can be increased if foods are kept out of the temperature danger zone.

2. **Log phase** – bacteria double every 15 to 30 minutes.

3. **Stationary phase** – number of bacteria remains fixed because the new organisms being produced are equal to the number that are dying.

4. **Death phase** – bacteria die off rapidly because they lack the items necessary for their survival.

Bacteria will grow most rapidly when the temperature is between 85°F and 100°F. In most cases, the growth rate will slow down drastically if the temperature is hotter or colder than this. Thus, it is vitally important that perishable food items are refrigerated before bacteria have a chance to establish themselves and multiply. Certain bacteria can survive in extreme hot- and cold-temperature ranges. By placing these bacteria in severe temperatures, you will be slowing down their growth rate, but not necessarily killing them.

The greatest problem in controlling bacteria is their rapid reproduction cycle. Approximately every 15 minutes the bacteria count will double under optimal conditions. The more bacteria present, the greater the chance of bacterial infection. This is why food products that must be subjected to conditions favorable to bacteria are done so for the shortest period possible.

An important consideration when handling food products is that bacteria need several hours to adjust to a new environment before they are able to begin rapidly multiplying. Thus, if you had removed a food product from the walk-in refrigerator and had inadvertently introduced bacteria to it, advanced growth would not begin for several hours. If you had immediately placed the item back into the walk-in, the temperature would have killed the bacteria before it became established.

Bacterial forms do not have a means of transportation; they must be introduced to an area by some other vehicle. People are primarily responsible for transporting bacteria to new areas; the body temperature of 98.6°F is perfect for bacterial existence and proliferation.

A person coughing, sneezing or wiping their hands on a counter can introduce bacteria to an area. Bacteria may be transmitted also by insects, air, water and articles onto which they have attached themselves, such as boxes, blades, knives and cutting boards.

Dangerous Forms of Bacteria

An estimated 76 million cases of food-borne disease occur each year in the United States. The great majority of these cases are mild and cause symptoms for only a day or two. The most severe cases tend to occur in the very old, the very young, those who have an illness already that reduces their immune system function, and in healthy people exposed to a very high dose of an organism.

More precautions should be taken by high-risk groups such as:

- Pregnant women, the elderly and those with weakened immune systems are at higher risk for severe infections such as Listeria and should be particularly careful not to consume undercooked animal products. They should avoid soft French-style cheeses, pâtés, uncooked hot dogs and sliced deli meats, which have been sources of Listeria infections. Persons at high risk should also avoid alfalfa sprouts and unpasteurized juices.

- Persons with liver disease are susceptible to infections from a rare but dangerous microbe called Vibrio vulnificus, found in oysters. They should avoid eating raw oysters.

The most commonly recognized food-borne infections are those caused by the bacteria Campylobacter, Salmonella and E. coli O157:H7, and by a group of viruses called calicivirus, also known as the Norwalk and Norwalk-like viruses.

Campylobacter is a bacterial pathogen that causes fever, diarrhea and abdominal cramps. It is the most commonly identified bacterial cause of diarrheal illness in the world. These bacteria live in the intestines of healthy birds, and most raw poultry meat has Campylobacter on it. Eating undercooked chicken or other food that has been contaminated with juices dripping from raw chicken is the most frequent source of this infection.

Salmonella is also a bacterium that is widespread in the intestines of birds, reptiles and mammals. It can spread to humans via a variety of different foods of animal origin. The illness it causes, salmonellosis, typically includes fever, diarrhea and abdominal cramps. In persons with poor underlying health or weakened immune systems, it can invade the bloodstream and cause life-threatening infections.

E. coli O157:H7 is a bacterial pathogen that has a reservoir in cattle and other similar animals. Human illness typically follows consumption of food or water that has been contaminated with microscopic amounts of cow feces. The illness it causes is often a severe and bloody diarrhea and painful abdominal cramps, without much fever. In 3 to 5 percent of cases, a complication called Hemolytic Uremic Syndrome (HUS) can occur several weeks after the initial symptoms. This severe complication includes temporary anemia, profuse bleeding and kidney failure.

Calicivirus or Norwalk-like virus is an extremely common cause of food-borne illness, though it is rarely diagnosed because the laboratory test is not widely available. It causes an acute gastrointestinal illness, usually with more vomiting than diarrhea, that resolves within two days. Unlike many food-borne pathogens that have animal reservoirs, it is believed that Norwalk-like viruses spread primarily from one infected person to another. Infected kitchen workers can contaminate a salad or sandwich as they prepare it if they have the virus on their hands. Infected fishermen have contaminated oysters as they harvested them.

Some common diseases are occasionally food-borne, even though they are usually transmitted by other routes. These include infections caused by Shigella, hepatitis A and the parasites Giardia lamblia and Cryptosporidia. Even strep throats have been transmitted occasionally through food.

In addition to disease caused by direct infection, some food-borne diseases are caused by the presence of a toxin in the food that was produced by a microbe in the food. For example, the bacterium Staphylococcus aureus can grow in some foods and produce a toxin that causes intense vomiting. The rare but deadly disease botulism occurs when the bacterium Clostridium botulinum grows and produces a powerful paralytic toxin in foods. These toxins can produce illness even if the microbes that produced them are no longer there.

Other toxins and poisonous chemicals can cause food-borne illness. People can become ill if a pesticide is inadvertently added to a food or if naturally poisonous substances are used to prepare a meal. People have become ill after mistaking poisonous mushrooms for safe species or after eating poisonous reef fishes.

More information can be found on the FDA's Web site at **www.cfsan.fda.gov /~mow/intro.html**.

The following charts list many food-borne illness, symptoms and prevention.

BACTERIA		
Illness: Bacillus Cereus Gastroenteritis		**Agent:** Bacillus cereus
Onset: Diarrhea type: 8–16 hours Vomiting type: 30 minutes–6 hours	**Symptoms:** Diarrhea type: Abdominal cramps. Vomiting type: Vomiting, diarrhea, abdominal cramps.	**Source:** Diarrhea type: Meats, milk, vegetables. Vomiting type: Rice, grains, cereal.
Prevention: Properly heat, cool and reheat foods.		

Illness: Bacillus Salmonellosis		**Agent:** Salmonella spp.
Onset: 6–48 hours	**Symptoms:** Nausea, vomiting, abdominal cramps, headache, fever and diarrhea (may cause dehydration in infants and elderly).	**Source:** Raw poultry, poultry salads, raw meat, fish, dairy products, eggs, improperly cooked custards and sauces, tofu, sliced melon, sliced tomatoes.
Prevention: Cook poultry to 165°F for at least 15 seconds, cook other foods to proper minimum internal temperature, avoid cross-contamination, properly cool and refrigerate foods.		

Illness: Shigellosis		Agent: Shigella spp.
Onset: 1–7 days	Symptoms: Diarrhea (may be bloody), abdominal pain, fever, nausea, cramps, vomiting, chills, fatigue, dehydration.	Source: Cold salads (tuna, potato, chicken, shrimp), lettuce, raw vegetables, dairy products, poultry.
Prevention: Make sure employees practice good hygiene, avoid cross-contamination, properly cool foods.		

Illness: Listeriosis		Agent: Listeria monocytogenes
Onset: 1–3 weeks	Symptoms: Fever and diarrhea. In highly susceptible populations, may cause septicemia, meningitis and encephalitis. In pregnant women, it may result in stillbirth.	Source: Unpasteurized soft cheeses, hot dogs, deli meats, seafood, poultry, meat, raw vegetables.
Prevention: Only use pasteurized dairy products, avoid cross-contamination, wash vegetables, cook food to minimum internal temperatures.		

Illness: Staphyococcal Gastroenteritis		Agent: Staphylococcus aureus
Onset: 1–6 hours	Symptoms: Diarrhea, abdominal cramps, nausea, vomiting. In severe cases. May cause headache, changes in blood pressure and pulse, and muscle cramping.	Source: Foods reheated or held improperly, meat, poultry, eggs, dairy products, cream-filled pastries, cold salads.
Prevention: Have employees practice proper hand-washing technique, properly refrigerate and cool foods.		

Illness: Clostridium Perfringens Gastroenteritis		Agent: Clostridium perfringens
Onset: 8–22 hours	Symptoms: Diarrhea, nausea, abdominal pain.	Source: Meat, stews, beans.
Prevention: Practice proper time and temperature controls.		

Illness: Botulism		**Agent:** Clostridium botulinum
Onset: 12–36 hours	**Symptoms:** Fatigue, weakness, vertigo, blurred or double vision, difficulty speaking and swallowing, and dry mouth. Eventually leads to paralysis and death.	**Source:** Improperly canned foods, untreated oil and garlic mixtures, temperature-abused onions sautéed in butter, leftover baked potatoes, stews, MAP and sous vide foods.
Prevention: Do not serve home-canned products; practice careful time and temperature controls; sauté onions to order; properly cool leftovers.		

Illness: Campylobacteriosis		**Agent:** Campylobacter jejuni
Onset: 2–5 days	**Symptoms:** Fever, nausea, diarrhea (watery or bloody), abdominal pain, headache and muscle pain.	**Source:** Poultry, unpasteurized milk, unchlorinated water.
Prevention: Thoroughly cook foods to proper minimum internal temperature, do not use contaminated water sources.		

Illness: Hemorrhagic Colitis		**Agent:** Shiga toxin-producing Escherichia coli (includes O157:H7 and O157:NM)
Onset: 2–72 hours	**Symptoms:** Diarrhea, severe abdominal cramps and vomiting. May cause kidney failure in the very young.	**Source:** Undercooked ground beef, unpasteurized apple cider, lettuce, alfalfa sprouts, nonchlorinated water.
Prevention: Thoroughly cook ground beef to 155°F for at least 15 seconds, use pasteurized dairy and juice products, practice good hygiene, avoid cross-contamination.		

Illness: Vibrio Parahaemolyticus Gastroenteritis		**Agent:** Vibrio parahaemolyticus
Onset: Within 3 days	**Symptoms:** Diarrhea, nausea, vomiting, abdominal cramps, headache.	**Source:** Undercooked oysters or raw oysters, raw or partially cooked shellfish.
Prevention: Purchase seafood from approved suppliers, avoid cross-contamination, practice proper time and temperature control.		

Illness: Vibrio vulnificus Primary Septicemia		**Agent:** Vibrio vulnificus
Onset: Within 7 days	**Symptoms:** Fever, chills, hypertension, nausea, and skin lesions.	**Source:** Raw or partly cooked oysters.
Prevention: Purchase seafood from approved suppliers, avoid cross-contamination, practice proper time and temperature control.		

Illness: Yersiniosis		**Agent:** Yersinia enterocolitica
Onset: 18–36 hours	**Symptoms:** Diarrhea. Symptoms may seem like appendicitis.	**Source:** Tofu, unpasteurized milk, meat, oysters, fish, nonchlorinated water.
Prevention: Use pasteurized milk, avoid cross-contamination, cook foods to required minimum internal temperatures, only use a sanitary water supply.		

VIRUSES

Illness: Hepatitis A		**Agent:** Hepatovirus or Hepatitis A virus
Onset: 10–50 days	**Symptoms:** Sudden fever, fatigue, loss of appetite, nausea, abdominal pain, jaundice.	**Source:** Shellfish, salads, deli meats, fruit and fruit juice, milk products, vegetables, water, ice.
Prevention: Make sure employees practice good hygiene, get shellfish from approved sources, avoid cross-contamination, sanitize food-contact surfaces, use sanitary water sources.		

Illness: Norovirus Gastroenteritis		**Agent:** Norovirus
Onset: 24–48 hours	**Symptoms:** Watery diarrhea with cramps, nausea, mild fever.	**Source:** Salads and other ready-to-eat foods, sandwiches, bakery items, salad dressing, cake icing, contaminated raspberries, oysters and water.
Prevention: Make sure employees practice good hygiene, use sanitary water.		

Illness: Rotavirus Gastroenteritis		**Agent:** Rotavirus
Onset: 24–72 hours	**Symptoms:** Diarrhea, abdominal pain, vomiting and mild fever.	**Source:** Water, ice, ready-to-eat foods like salads.
Prevention: Make sure employees practice good hygiene, avoid cross-contamination, use sanitary water, cook foods to required minimum internal temperature.		

PARASITES

Illness: Trichinoisis		**Agent:** Trichinella spiralis
Onset: 2–28 days	**Symptoms:** Nausea, diarrhea, vomiting, fever and fatigue.	**Source:** Raw or undercooked pork products, raw and undercooked wild game.
Prevention: Cook pork and wild meat to required minimum temperature; wash, rinse and sanitize equipment; purchase meats from approved sources; have employees practice good hygiene.		

Illness: Yersiniosis		**Agent:** Yersinia enterocolitica
Onset: 18–36 hours	**Symptoms:** Diarrhea. Symptoms may seem like appendicitis.	**Source:** Tofu, unpasteurized milk, meat, oysters, fish, nonchlorinated water.
Prevention: Use pasteurized milk, avoid cross-contamination, cook foods to required minimum internal temperatures, only use a sanitary water supply.		

Illness: Anisakiasis		**Agent:** Anisakis simplex
Onset: 1 hour–2 weeks	**Symptoms:** Coughing, vomiting, abdominal pain, fever.	**Source:** Raw or undercooked seafood.
Prevention: Obtain seafood from approved sources, use only sashimi-grade fish that has been properly treated to eliminate parasites. If fish is to be eaten raw, it should be frozen to 44°F for 7 days.		

Illness: Giardiasis		**Agent:** Giardia duodenalis
Onset: 1–2 weeks	**Symptoms:** Gas, diarrhea, abdominal cramps, nausea, weight loss, fatigue.	**Source:** Contaminated water and ice and salads and vegetables washed with contaminated water.
Prevention: Use sanitary water supply, ensure employees are practicing safe hygiene.		

Illness: Toxoplasmosis		**Agent:** Toxoplasma gondii
Onset: 6–10 days	**Symptoms:** Enlarged lymph nodes in head and neck, severe headaches, sever muscle pain, rash.	**Source:** Contaminated water, raw or undercooked meat (pork, lamb, wild game and poultry).
Prevention: Cook meats to required minimum temperatures, make sure employees practice good hygiene.		

Illness: Intestinal Cryptosporidiosis		Agent: Cryptosporidium parvum
Onset: Within 1 week	**Symptoms:** Severe watery diarrhea.	**Source:** Water, salads, raw vegetables, milk, unpasteurized apple cider, ready-to-eat foods.
Prevention: Make sure employees practice good hygiene, wash produce, use sanitary water sources.		

Illness: Cyclosporiasis		Agent: Cyclospora cayetanensis
Onset: Within 1 week	**Symptoms:** Watery, explosive diarrhea, loss of appetite, bloating.	**Source:** Water, raw produce, fish, raw milk.
Prevention: Make sure employees practice good hygiene, wash produce, use sanitary water sources.		

INTOXICATION		
Illness: Ciguatoxin		Agent: Ciguatoxin
Onset: 30 minutes–6 hours	**Symptoms:** Vertigo, nausea, hot/cold flashes, diarrhea, vomiting, shortness of breath.	**Source:** Marine finfish.
Prevention: Purchase fish from an approved source.		

Illness: Scombrotoxin		Agent: Scombrotoxin
Onset: Few minutes to a half hour	**Symptoms:** Dizziness, facial rash or hives, burning feeling in mouth, shortness of breath, peppery taste in mouth, headache, itching, teary eyes, runny nose.	**Source:** Tuna, mahi mahi, bluefish, sardines, Swiss cheese, anchovies, mackerel.
Prevention: Purchase fish from an approved source, store fish between 32° and 39°F to prevent growth of histamine-producing bacteria.		

INVESTIGATING A FOOD-BORNE ILLNESS OUTBREAK

Once an outbreak is strongly suspected, an investigation begins. A search is made for more cases among persons who may have been exposed. The symptoms, time of onset and location of possible cases is determined, and a "case definition" is developed. The outbreak is systematically described by time, place and person. A graph is drawn of the number of people who fell ill on each successive day to show pictorially when it occurred. A map of where the ill people live, work or eat may be helpful to show where it occurred. Calculating the distribution of cases by age and sex shows who is affected. If the causative microbe is not known, samples of stool or blood are collected from ill people and sent to the public health laboratory to make the diagnosis.

To identify the food or other source of the outbreak, the investigators first interview a few persons with the most typical cases about exposures they may have had in the few days before they got sick. In this way, certain potential exposures may be excluded while others that are mentioned repeatedly emerge as possibilities. Combined with other information, such as the likely sources for the specific microbe involved, these hypotheses are then tested in a formal epidemiological investigation. The investigators conduct systematic interviews about a list of possible exposures with the ill persons and with a comparable group of people who are not ill. By comparing how often an exposure is reported by ill people and by well people, investigators can measure the association of the exposure with illness. Using probability statistics, similar to those used to describe coin flips, the probability of no association is directly calculated.

For example, imagine that an outbreak has occurred after a catered event. Initial investigation suggested that hollandaise sauce was eaten by at least some of the attendees, so it is on the list of possible hypotheses. We interview 20 persons who attended the affair, 10 of whom became ill and 10 of whom remained well. Each ill or well person is interviewed about whether or not they ate the hollandaise sauce, as well as various other food items. If half the people ate the sauce, but the sauce was not associated with the illness, then we would expect each person to have a 50/50 chance of reporting that they ate it, regardless of whether they were ill or not. Suppose, however, that we find that all 10 ill people ate the hollandaise sauce, but none of the well persons reported eating hollandaise sauce at the event. This would be very unlikely to occur by chance alone if eating the hollandaise sauce were not somehow related to the risk of illness. In fact, it would be about as unlikely as getting heads ten times in a row by flipping a coin (that is 50 percent multiplied by itself 10 times over or a chance of just under 1 in 1000). So the epidemiologist concludes that eating the hollandaise sauce was very likely to be associated with the risk of illness. Note that the investigator can draw this conclusion even though there is no hollandaise sauce left to test in a laboratory. The association is even stronger if she can show that those who ate second helpings of hollandaise were even more likely to become ill, or that persons who ate leftover hollandaise sauce that went home in doggie bags also became ill.

Once a food item is statistically implicated in this manner, further investigation into its ingredients and preparation and microbiologic culture of leftover ingredients or the food itself (if available) may provide additional information about the nature of contamination. Perhaps the hollandaise sauce was made using raw eggs. The source of the raw eggs can be determined, and it may even be possible to trace them back to the farm and show that chickens on the farm are carrying the same strain of Salmonella in their ovaries. If so, the eggs from that farm can be pasteurized to prevent them from causing other outbreaks.

Some might think that the best investigation method would be just to culture all the leftover foods in the kitchen and conclude that the one that is positive is the one that caused the outbreak. The trouble is that this can be misleading because it happens after the fact. What if the hollandaise sauce is all gone but the spoon that was in the sauce got placed in potato salad that was not served at the function? Now, cultures of the potato salad yield a pathogen, and the unwary tester might call that the source of the outbreak even though the potato salad had nothing to do with it. This means that laboratory testing without epidemiological investigation can lead to the wrong conclusion.

Even without isolating microbes from food, a well-conducted epidemiological investigation can guide immediate efforts to control the outbreak. A strong and consistent statistical association between illness and a particular food item that explains the distribution of the outbreak in time, place and person should be acted upon immediately to stop further illness from occurring.

An outbreak ends when the critical exposure stops. This may happen because all the contaminated food is eaten or recalled, a restaurant is closed, a food processor shuts down or changes its procedures, or an infected food handler is no longer infectious or is no longer working with food. An investigation that clarifies the nature and mechanism of contamination can provide critical information even if the outbreak is over. Understanding the contamination event well enough to prevent it can guide the decision to resume usual operations and lead to more general prevention measures that reduce the risk of similar outbreaks happening elsewhere.

More information can be found on the FDA's Web site at **www.cfsan.fda.gov/ ~mow/intro.html.**

POTENTIALLY DANGEROUS FOODS

Some foods are more prone to supporting the rapid growth of bacteria. These foods are called potentially hazardous food, and special attention is paid to them by the FDA and food service operators when dealing with food safety. These foods generally are high in protein and have a pH above 4.5. Potentially hazardous foods include red meat, dairy products, shellfish, fish, raw eggs and poultry. In their Food Code, the FDA classifies the following as potentially hazardous foods:

- Foods of animal origin.

- Foods of plant origin that are heat treated or have raw seed sprouts.

- Cut melon.

- Garlic and oil mixtures.

Other foods that also are potentially hazardous are cooked potatoes and rice, refried beans and vegetables.

Ready-to-Eat Foods

The FDA Food Code classifies the following items are ready-to-eat:

- Raw fruits and vegetables that are washed.

- Fruits and vegetables that are cooked for hot holding.

- All potentially hazardous foods that are cooked then cooled.

- Bakery items.

- Spices, sugar and seasonings.

- Raw animal foods that are cooked or frozen.

- Thermally processed low-acid foods that are packaged in hermetically sealed containers such as smoked salmon.

- Dry, fermented sausages such as pepperoni and dry cured meats such as proscuitto ham.

These foods can become contaminate if they are not handled properly in the preparation process.

2

FACTORS AFFECTING FOOD-BORNE ILLNESS

Every restaurant employee and manager is responsible for preparing and serving quality and safe food products. Each employee and manager must be thoroughly familiar with basic food safety and sanitation practices. This chapter will describe the fundamental methods and procedures that must be practiced in order to control food contamination, the spread of infectious diseases and personal safety practices.

Management must provide employees with the training, knowledge and tools that will enable them to establish and practice proper food-handling and sanitation procedures.

Through the use of this section and under the guidance of your local department of health, you and your staff can obtain training and knowledge. First, the restaurant must be equipped with the proper tools, training and working conditions.

Employees will never establish good sanitation procedures if they do not first have the proper environment in which to practice them. Aside from what is required by law, management should provide training materials, proper training sessions or clinics, hand sinks at every station, hand and nailbrushes, labels for dating and rotation procedures, disposable towels, gloves, first-aid kits, germicidal hand soaps, employee bathrooms and lockers, scrub brushes, uniforms, hairnets, thermometers, test kits and quality, color-coded utensils.

Food service establishments may harbor all types of bacteria, bugs and animal pests. Restaurants can attract these health hazards with the three basic ingredients necessary to sustain life: food, water and warmth. Any environment that provides these three elements for an extended period of time will become host to these intruders. In order to eliminate contamination, all that is necessary is to make the living conditions unfavorable for these unwanted intruders.

FACTORS CONTRIBUTING TO FOOD-BORNE ILLNESS

According to the CDC, the most common reason food-borne illness occurs is because of food mishandling. This includes time and temperature abuse, poor personal hygiene, poor hand-washing technique, and cross-contamination. According the CDC's Surveillance for Food-borne Disease Outbreaks (1988-1992) these are the major factors:

Major Factors for Food-Borne Disease Outbreaks	
Use of leftovers	4%
Improper cleaning	7%
Cross-contamination	7%
Contaminated raw food	11%
Inadequate reheating	12%
Improper hot storage	16%
Inadequate cooking	16%
Infected people touching food	20%
Time between preparing and serving	21%
Improper cooling of foods	40%

CONTROLLING BACTERIA

Most bacteria can be controlled by:

- Good personal hygiene practice.

- Eliminating cross-contamination.

- Monitoring time and temperature.

- Employing a sanitation program.

The first step in controlling bacteria is to limit its access to the restaurant. Make certain that all products entering the restaurant are clean. Follow the prescribed bug-exterminating procedures to stop bacteria from being transported into the restaurant. Keep all food products stored and refrigerated as prescribed. Clean up any spills as you go along, making the environment unsuitable for bacteria to live. Keep all food refrigerated until needed, and cook it as soon as possible.

TIME AND TEMPERATURE CONTROL

One of the most critical things you can do to avoid contamination of food is to control time and temperature. Most disease-causing bacteria grows between 41° and 140°F. By properly cooking and reheating foods and storing cold foods below 41°F and hot foods above 140°F, you can control the growth of bacteria on these foods.

As previously mentioned, bacteria's growth rate is very quick. Bacteria can double in number every 15 minutes, generating over 1 million cells in just 5 hours. In the food service industry, the general principle is that bacteria needs 4 hours to grow in high enough numbers to cause food-borne illnesses—this includes the total time the food is in the temperature danger zone. By practicing proper storage, you can help prevent this bacterial growth.

Of course, you can't always keep food out of the temperature danger zone. You have to cook it, cool it, reheat it and prepare it. While engaged in these activities, you should try to minimize the time the foods are in the temperature danger zone. For example, while slicing deli meat, you shouldn't stop in the middle to take a break, unless you put the meat back in the refrigerator until you go back to work.

TEMPERATURE MEASUREMENTS

The temperature measurement is only as accurate as the device used. Regular calibration of the device is an important practice and a provision of the Food Code. Thermometers should have calibration instructions from the manufacturer and suggested calibration intervals.

Modern thermometers which measure temperature electronically, rather than the older bimetal types which rely on thermal expansion of two different metals, are recommended. In these instruments, a sensor is used to detect the temperature, and the signal is amplified and processed electronically. This device generally yields a faster response and provides greater overall accuracy because it does not drift out of calibration and is less likely to give variable readings.

A number of different sensor technologies are available, most of which are satisfactory for the temperature range needed in food temperatures. However, there are considerations other than temperature range that should be taken into account when selecting the best and most appropriate device for the specific application.

Thermometers scaled only in Celsius or scaled in Celsius and Fahrenheit must be accurate to 1°C. Thermometers that are only scaled in Fahrenheit must be accurate to 2°F. Thermometers that measure ambient air and water temperature in Celsius only or Celsius and Fahrenheit must be designed to be easily readable and accurate to 1.5°C. Ambient air and water measuring devices that are scaled only in Fahrenheit must be accurate to 3°F.

In a mechanically refrigerated or hot food storage unit, the thermometer must be located so it can measure the air temperature in the warmest part of a mechanically refrigerated unit and in the coolest part of a hot food storage unit.

Cold or hot holding equipment used for potentially hazardous food must include at least one integral or permanently affixed temperature measuring device that is located to allow easy viewing of the device's temperature display.

If it is not practical to place a thermometer in equipment to measure the ambient air surrounding the food, such as with calrod units, heat lamps, cold plates, bains-marie, steam tables, insulated food transport containers and salad bars, this is not required. All thermometers for food and water temperature measuring must be easily readable and they must have a numerical scale, printed record or digital readout in increments no greater than 1°C or 2°F in the intended range of use.

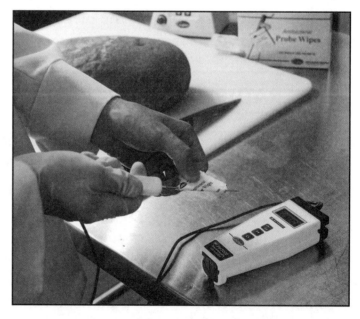

Reduce cross-contamination risks by using Antibacterial Probe Wipes. Available from Atlantic Publishing, Item # APW-TM. Call 1-800-814-1132 to order.

Cleaning and Sanitizing the Temperature Probe

Before internal food temperatures

are taken, the probe must be cleaned and sanitized. When taking a series of temperatures, it is particularly important to thoroughly clean and sanitize the probe between uses to prevent cross-contamination. Boiling water, sanitizers or alcohol swabs can be used to destroy any remaining pathogens on the probe before it is used.

Monitoring Procedures for Temperature Measurements

Some of the most important critical limits in a food operation involve the temperatures and times at which pathogen growth is limited or pathogens are destroyed. Establishments should monitor critical control points at a frequency that ensures that they are under control.

TEMPERATURE MEASURING DEVICES

Dial-Face Bimetallic

A bimetal bayonet-style thermometer is the most commonly used thermometer in food service establishments. It can be used at every stage of food preparation. It has a dial face scale with a range of -18° to 105°C (0° to 220°F). The dial face should be a minimum of about 1 inch in diameter and is usually available in larger sizes. The stem length should be a minimum of 127 mm (5 inches) and may need to be much longer to measure thicker foods. The stem of a bimetallic thermometer must be inserted into the food product at least 2 inches for it to properly measure the food's temperature.

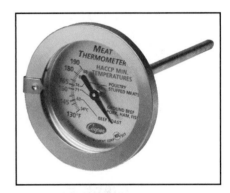

Meat Thermometer

Specific measurement instructions from the manufacturer of the instrument should be followed. The bimetal bayonet-style thermometer can accurately measure the temperature of relatively thick or deep foods such as beef roasts and stockpots. However, this instrument does not accurately measure the temperature of food less than 2 inches thick. The

Hanging Thermometer for Refrigerator or Dry Storage. Available from Atlantic Publishing, call 1-800-814-1132 to order.

thermistor and the thermocouple discussed below do not have these limitations. The recent food-borne illness outbreaks associated with inadequate cooking of eggs and hamburger patties have shown that it is very important to be able to accurately determine the temperatures associated with these products as well.

Thermistor

This device uses the temperature sensitivity of a semiconductor junction as the sensor. The advantages are a fast response time at a very low cost. Disadvantages include nonlinearity and a limited upper temperature range, typically 300°C (572°F). The accuracy and response time of a thermistor lend themselves very well to food temperature measurement.

Thermocouple

This device provides a digital readout of the temperature and has interchangeable probes. It relies on the voltage generated by the junction of two dissimilar metals. The advantages of this type of thermometer are a relatively rugged construction and a wide temperature range. Disadvantages include higher cost, lower sensitivity and non-linear output, which require a built-in reference. This technology has been used in food preparation for a number of years and has performed very well.

Infrared Thermometers

These thermometers quickly register surface temperatures, which facilitate general food safety by allowing the scanning of numerous food temperatures over a short period of time. However, you need to check its accuracy frequently.

It measures the temperature without actually touching the food, which decreases the potential for cross-contamination. It operates much like a radar gun and requires the user only to aim at the target food, pull the trigger, and read the displayed temperature.

This type of thermometer is intended only for measuring surface temperatures of food products and should not be used to measure and verify critical internal temperatures such as cooking temperatures.

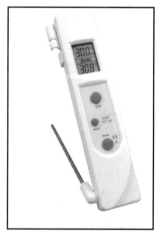

Infrared Thermometer. Available from Atlantic Publishing, Item # TTT-03 call 1-800-814-1132 to order.

Infrared thermometers are usually constructed of a high-strength, solvent-resistant plastic and measure invisible infrared energy being emitted from a target object. All objects emit infrared energy. The hotter the object is, the more active its molecules are and the more infrared energy it emits. An infrared thermometer houses optics that collect the radiant infrared energy from the object and focus it onto a detector. The detector converts the energy into an electrical signal, which is amplified and displayed as a temperature reading.

T-Sticks

These devices measure only one temperature, changing color when the temperature is reached. They are used to monitor food temperatures and sanitizing temperatures in dishwashing machines.

T-stick Disposable Thermometer. Available from Atlantic Publishing, call 1-800-814-1132 to order.

PERFORMANCE—THERMOCOUPLES, THERMISTORS AND INFRARED THERMOMETERS

Sensors used for food temperature measurement should be encased in a metal sheath. Unfortunately, the disadvantage of a sheath is that it increases response time. As the thickness and length of the probe increase, response time increases dramatically. A food probe with a maximum diameter of 4 mm (0.150 in) is the best compromise.

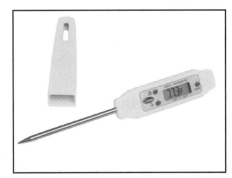

Digital Pen-Style Thermometer. Available from Atlantic Publishing, Item # DPT-TM, call 1-800-814-1132 to order.

Smaller diameters show similar response times for a wide variety of probe materials, including stainless steel. A usable response time for food measurement should be less than 6 seconds time constant (TC). Probes thicker than 4 mm show a response TC of 8 to 10 seconds and should be used only for hot grease and surface measurements.

A second factor in response time is placement of the sensor within the probe. The actual sensor element should be placed no more than 1 mm (0.04 in) from the tip of the sheath. If the sensor is not firmly against the end of the probe, response time decreases dramatically. As an example, if the sensor is placed 1 mm (0.5 in) from the tip, the response time can be as high as 20 seconds.

Most types of electrical-based thermometers can effectively measure the internal temperature of thin foods. Depending on construction, basically all are capable of at least 0.5°C (2°F) accuracy over the required temperature range. The limiting factor for effective temperature measurement is the physical characteristics of the probe that is inserted into the food. Thick metal walls and improper placement of the sensor can lead to erroneous readings. The bimetal bayonet-style thermometer may be suitable for measuring internal temperatures of thick foods.

As we stated earlier, infrared thermometers do not measure internal temperature, but register surface temperature only. Typical applications are at a salad bar where surface temperatures will likely be higher than internal product temperatures or a hot buffet line where surface temperatures will likely be cooler than internal product temperatures.

Dataloggers

Dataloggers are devices that record temperature over time. The measurements may be stored on a circular chart, printed out, or stored electronically for later reporting or downloading to a computer. These devices are primarily used for ambient or product-specific cold holding or cooling, but may also be used for cooking or smoking operations, hot holding, or special applications such as CIP systems.

The instrument may be either an analog or digital type. Proper calibration procedures should also be followed.

The records generated from these devices should indicate date, time and source of reading and should be signed by the individual responsible for the device at that time.

Time/Temperature Integrators/Indicators

Time/Temperature Integrators or Indicators (TTI) are simple label-like devices that continuously monitor cumulative time and temperature of food products. Some of these devices are threshold-sensitive or change in appearance when a certain threshold for temperature or time is reached. The appearance changes only if the threshold has been breached.

Other devices will record the full history of the temperature and time profile. Some are coupled with bar code-like readers, which download information to computers. These devices and the computer software are calibrated to mimic actual changes in the product over the range of temperatures and times encountered.

TTIs are not widely used now, but industry and public health officials agree that there are widespread potential benefits. Applications would include Reduced Oxygen Packaging (ROP) products such as sous vide or vacuum-packaged foods and some fresh products which are temperature-sensitive, such as milk and seafood.

CALIBRATION PROCEDURES

Calibration of Sensor Thermometers

Before you use a thermometer you must calibrate it. Bimetallic thermometers should be calibrated before their initial use, at regular intervals, if dropped, if used to measure extreme temperatures, and whenever you question their accuracy.

Calibrations should include both the instrument and any interchangeable probes used with that instrument. Each piece should be separately identified in the calibration records with serial numbers or agency equipment numbers.

The thermometer should be calibrated against a thermometer, which has been certified, by the National Institute of Standards and Technology (NIST).

ICE POINT METHOD

There are two methods for calibrating dial-face thermometers: **ice point** and **boiling point**.

Ice Point Method. Break up ice into very small pieces and pack into an insulated container. Stir this with cold water into a very thick slurry. Place the sensor at the very center of the container to a depth of at least 50 mm (2 in) and frequently agitate the slurry. Wait until the temperature stabilizes, about three minutes, and adjust the needle to 0.5°C from 0°C when calibrating a Celsius thermometer or 2°F from 32°F when calibrating a Fahrenheit thermometer.

Boil Point Method. Bring a 25-cm (>10 in) deep container of water to a rolling boil on a stove or other source of constant heat. Carefully insert the probe in the boiling water until the sensor is located in the approximate center of the container with at least 76 mm (3 in) of water below it. Wait for the temperature to stabilize at 212°F and adjust the needle. It should be 0.5°C from 100°C when calibrating a Celsius thermometer or 2°F from 212°F when calibrating a Fahrenheit thermometer. The altitude above sea level should be considered when using this method; check with your local health department if you have questions.

BOILING POINT METHOD

Adjustments to some of the instruments are possible to bring them back into calibration. Others should be returned to the manufacturer since field adjustments are not possible. Some instruments are not adjustable and should be replaced.

PERSONAL HYGIENE

Personal hygiene is the best way to stop bacteria from contaminating and spreading into new areas. Hands are the greatest source of contamination. Hands must be washed constantly throughout the day. Every time an individual scratches her head or sneezes, she is exposing her hands to bacteria and will spread it to anything she touches, such as food, equipment and clothes. Hand and nailbrushes, antibacterial soaps and disposable gloves should be a part of every restaurant, even if not required by law. Proper training and management follow-up is also critical.

Every employee must practice good basic hygiene:

*   Short hair and/or hair contained in a net.

*   Clean shaven or facial hair contained in a net.

- Clean clothes/uniforms.

- Clean hands and short nails.

- No unnecessary jewelry.

- A daily shower or bath.

- No smoking in or near the kitchen.

- Hand washing prior to starting work, periodically and after handling any foreign object: head, face, ears, money, food, boxes or trash.

An employee who has the symptoms of the common cold or any open cuts or infections should not go to work. By simply breathing, he may be inadvertently exposing the environment to bacteria. Although it is rarely practiced in the food industry, all employees should be required to have a complete medical examination as a condition of employment. This should include blood and urine tests. A seemingly healthy individual may unknowingly be the carrier of a latent communicable disease.

Hand washing is perhaps the most critical aspect of good personal hygiene in food service. Employees should wash their hands after the following activities:

- Smoking (hands come in contact with mouth).

- Eating (hands come in contact with mouth).

- Using the restroom.

- Handling money.

- Touching raw food (the raw food may contain bacteria).

- Touching or combing their hair.

- Coughing, sneezing or blowing their nose.

- Taking a break.

- Handling anything dirty (touching a dirty apron or taking out the trash, for example).

Fingernails

Fingernails must be trimmed, filed and maintained. This addresses both the cleanability of areas beneath the fingernails and the possibility that fingernails or pieces of the fingernails may end up in the food due to breakage. Failure to remove fecal material from beneath the fingernails after defecation can be a major source of pathogenic organisms. Ragged fingernails present cleanability concerns and may harbor pathogenic organisms.

Jewelry

Jewelry such as rings, bracelets and watches may collect soil, and the construction of the jewelry may hinder routine cleaning. As a result, the jewelry may act as a reservoir of pathogenic organisms transmissible through food.

The term "jewelry" generally refers to the ornaments worn for personal adornment; medical alert bracelets do not fit this definition. However, the wearing of such bracelets carries the same potential for transmitting disease-causing organisms to food. In the case of a food worker who wears a medical information or medical alert bracelet, the EEOC has agreed that this requirement can be met through reasonable accommodation in accordance with the Americans with Disabilities Act by the person in charge and the employee working out acceptable alternatives to the bracelet worn at the wrist. An example would be wearing the bracelet high on the arm or secured in a manner that does not pose a risk to the food but provides emergency medical information if it is needed.

An additional hazard associated with jewelry is the possibility that pieces of the item or the whole item itself may fall into the food being prepared. Hard foreign objects in food may cause medical problems for consumers, such as chipped and/or broken teeth and internal cuts and lesions.

Outer Clothing

Dirty clothing may harbor diseases that are transmissible through food. Food employees who inadvertently touch their dirty clothing may contaminate their hands. This could result in contamination of the food being prepared. Food may also be contaminated through direct contact with dirty clothing. In addition, employees wearing dirty clothes send a negative message to consumers about the level of sanitation in the establishment.

Eating, Drinking or Using Tobacco

Smoking or eating by employees in food preparation areas is prohibited because of the potential that the hands, food and food-contact surfaces may become contaminated. Unsanitary personal practices such as scratching the head, placing the fingers in or about the mouth or nose, and indiscriminate and uncovered sneezing or coughing may result in food contamination. Poor hygienic practices by employees may also adversely affect consumer confidence in the establishment.

Food preparation areas such as hot grills may have elevated temperatures and the excessive heat in these areas may present a medical risk to the workers as a result of dehydration. Consequently, in these areas food employees are allowed to drink from closed containers that are carefully handled.

Discharges from the Eyes, Nose and Mouth

Discharges from the eyes, nose or mouth through persistent sneezing or coughing by food employees can directly contaminate exposed food, equipment, utensils, linens and single-service and single-use articles. When these poor hygienic practices cannot be controlled, the employee must be assigned to duties that minimize the potential for contaminating food and surrounding surfaces and objects.

Hair Restraints

Consumers are particularly sensitive to food contaminated by hair. Hair can be both a direct and indirect vehicle of contamination. Food employees may contaminate their hands when they touch their hair. A hair restraint keeps dislodged hair from ending up in the food and may deter employees from touching their hair.

Animals

Dogs and other animals, like humans, may harbor pathogens that are transmissible through food. Handling or caring for animals that may be legally present is prohibited because of the risk of contamination of food employee hands and clothing.

Preventing Contamination from Hands

Infected food employees are the source of contamination in approximately one in five food-borne disease outbreaks reported in the United States with a bacterial or viral cause. Most of these outbreaks involve enteric; i.e., fecal-oral agents. Because of poor or nonexistent hand-washing procedures, workers spread these organisms to the food. In addition, infected cuts, burns or boils on hands can also result in contamination of food. Viral, bacterial and parasitic agents can be involved.

Employees must wash their hands using the proper techniques. Workers should wash their hands with soap and warm water for 20 seconds. When working with food, they should wash gloved hands as often as bare hands.

The proper hand-washing method is as follows:

1. Remove any jewelry.

2. Turn water on as hot as you can stand it.

3. Moisten hands and forearms up to elbows.

4. Lather them thoroughly with soap.

5. Wash for at least 20 seconds, rubbing hands together, washing between fingers and up to the elbows.

6. Use a brush for under nails.

7. Rinse hands and forearms with hot water.

8. Dry hands and forearms with a paper towel.

Hand washing is such a simple yet very effective method for eliminating cross-contamination, you may want to use the following exercise in your training.

First, you'll need a fluorescent substance and a black light. (One possible source for these is Atlantic Publishing's Glo Germ Training Kit. See **www.atlantic-pub.com** or call 1-800-814-1132.) Using these materials you can show trainees the "invisible dirt" that may be hiding on their hands:

- Have employees dip their hands in the fluorescent substance.

- Tell employees to wash their hands.

- Have employees hold their hands under the black light to see how much "dirt" is still there.

- Explain proper hand-washing technique.

- Have employees wash their hands again, this time using the proper hand-washing technique.

- Have employees once again hold their hands under the black light.

Handling Dishware

Even employees with clean hands need to follow certain procedures when handling food and dishware:

- Use tongs, scoops or food-grade rubber gloves when picking up bread, butter pats, ice or other ready-to-eat foods.

- Pick up glasses from the outside, not with fingers inside the glass or on the rims. Cups must be picked up by the handles or bottoms; do not touch glass or cup rims with your bare hands.

- Pick up forks and spoons by the handles rather than the tines or bowls.

- Carry plates by the bottoms or edges; do not touch the eating surface. Do not stack dishes, cups and saucers in order to carry more.

- Wash your hands after handling soiled dishes.

- Wash your hands before you put on gloves. Also be aware that gloved hands become contaminated if a task is interrupted. Contaminated gloves should be removed and discarded, hands must be washed, and fresh gloves put on to resume the task.

- An employee may not use a utensil more than once to taste food that is to be sold or served.

Gloves. Multiuse gloves, especially when used repeatedly and soiled, can become breeding grounds for pathogens that could be transferred to food. Soiled gloves can directly contaminate food if stored with ready-to-eat food or may indirectly contaminate food if stored with articles that will be used in contact with food. Multiuse gloves must be washed, rinsed and sanitized between activities that contaminate the gloves. Hands must be washed before donning gloves. Gloves must be discarded when soil or other contaminants enter the inside of the glove.

Slash-resistant gloves are not easily cleaned and sanitized. Their use with ready-to-eat foods could contaminate the food.

Natural rubber latex gloves. Natural rubber latex gloves have been reported to cause allergic reactions in some individuals who wear latex gloves during food preparation, and even in individuals eating food prepared by food employees wearing latex gloves This information should be taken into consideration when deciding whether single-use gloves made of latex will be used during food preparation.

OBTAINING EMPLOYEE INFORMATION

The health department will take action when it has reasonable cause to believe that a food employee has possibly transmitted disease; may be infected with a disease in a communicable form that is transmissible through food; may be a carrier of infectious agents that cause a disease that is transmissible through food; or is affected with a boil, an infected wound, or acute respiratory infection. These actions would include:

- Securing a confidential medical history of the employee suspected of transmitting disease or making other investigations as deemed appropriate.

- Requiring appropriate medical examinations, including collection of specimens for laboratory analysis, of a suspected employee and other employees.

Based on the findings of the investigation, the health department may issue an order to the suspected food employee or permit holder instituting one or more of the following control measures:

- Restricting the employee.

- Excluding the employee.

- Closing the restaurant by summarily suspending a permit to operate.

Based on the findings of the investigation and to control disease transmission, the health department may issue an order of restriction or exclusion to a suspected employee or the permit holder without prior warning, notice of a hearing, or a hearing if the order:

- States the reasons for the restriction or exclusion that is ordered.

- States the evidence that the employee or permit holder shall provide in order to demonstrate that the reasons for the restriction or exclusion are eliminated.

- States that the suspected employee or the permit holder may request an appeal hearing by submitting a timely request.

- Provides the name and address of the health department representative to whom a request for an appeal hearing may be made.

Release of Food Employee from Restriction or Exclusion

The health department will release a food employee from restriction or exclusion under the following conditions:

- An employee who was infected with *Salmonella* typhi if the employee's stools are negative for S. typhi based on testing of at least three consecutive stool specimen cultures that are taken:

  - Not earlier than one month after onset.

  - At least 48 hours after discontinuance of antibiotics.

  - At least 24 hours apart.

If one of the cultures taken is positive, repeat cultures are taken at intervals of one month until at least three consecutive negative stool specimen cultures are obtained.

- An employee who was infected with *Shigella* spp. or Shiga Toxin-Producing *Escherichia coli* if the employee's stools are negative for *Shigella* spp. or Shiga Toxin-Producing *Escherichia coli* based on testing of two consecutive stool specimen cultures that are taken:

  – Not earlier than 48 hours after discontinuance of antibiotics.

  – At least 24 hours apart.

- An employee who was infected with hepatitis A virus if:

  – Symptoms cease.

  – At least two blood tests show falling liver enzymes.

3

FOOD SAFETY REGULATIONS

While most food safety laws are created by federal agencies such as the Department of Environmental Health or the Department of Agriculture, these laws are enforced by state and local agencies, including the local health department.

HEALTH DEPARTMENT

It's a good idea to work closely with your local health department. In large cities the health department is usually the city health department. In smaller towns you may work with the county or state health department. Many food service managers view their local health department as the enemy, thinking only of the inspections conducted by the department. However, the health department is a good source of information for food service managers. For example, your local health department can provide you with a copy of the food safety regulations and standards that apply to your type of operation.

The health department is also responsible for issuing food service permits. (You cannot operate a food service establishment without a valid permit issued by your local authority.)

You should apply for the permit long before you actually open because the permit process does take some time. Often the health department might want to see blueprints and specs if you are opening a new building or doing extensive remodeling.

The number of inspections conducted by health departments will vary dependent on the risk a food establishment poses. In determining how many times a facility will be inspected a year, the health department authorities will look at the facility's sanitation history, number of meals served, number of potentially hazardous items on the menu, and number of critical violations that have been documented.

Low-risk operations are generally inspected every six months. Higher-risk operations may be inspected four or more times a year.

Access—Reasonable Times After Due Notice

After the health department presents official credentials and provides notice of the purpose of and an intent to conduct an inspection, the person that is in charge must allow the health department official to determine if the establishment is in compliance with the Food Code by allowing access to the establishment, allowing inspection, and providing information and records specified in the Code and to which the health department is entitled according to law. This access must be given during the food establishment's hours of operation and other reasonable times.

If a person denies access to the health department, the department official shall inform the person that:

1. The permit holder is required to allow access to the health department.

2. Access is a condition of the acceptance and retention of a food establishment permit to operate.

3. An order issued by the appropriate authority allowing access, hereinafter referred to as an inspection order, may be obtained according to the law.

After doing this the official will make one final request for access.

If after the health department official presents credentials and provides notice as specified above, explains the authority upon which access is requested, and makes a final request for access, the person in charge continues to refuse access, the health department official shall provide details of the denial of access on an inspection report form.

If denied access for an authorized purpose and after complying with the above actions, the health department may issue, or apply for the issuance of, an inspection order to gain access.

INSPECTION AND CORRECTION OF VIOLATIONS

The health department will inspect a food operation at least once every six months. It may increase the interval between inspections beyond six months if:

- The food establishment is fully operating under an approved and validated HACCP (pronounced hassip) plan.

- The food establishment is assigned a less frequent inspection frequency based on a written risk-based inspection schedule that is being uniformly applied throughout the jurisdiction and at least once every six months if the establishment is contacted by telephone or other means by the health department to ensure that the establishment manager and the nature of food operation have not changed.

- The establishment's operation involves only coffee service and other unpackaged or prepackaged food that is not potentially hazardous such as carbonated beverages and snack food such as chips, nuts, popcorn and pretzels.

The health department may conduct more frequent inspections based upon its assessment of a food operation's history of compliance and the establishment's potential as a vector of food-borne illness by evaluating:

- Past performance, for nonconformance with critical Food Code or HACCP plan requirements.

- Past performance, for numerous or repeat violations of noncritical Food Code or HACCP plan requirements.

- Past performance, for complaints investigated and found to be valid.

- The hazards associated with the particular foods that are prepared, stored or served.

- The type of operation including the methods and extent of food storage, preparation and service.

- The number of people served.

- Whether the population served is a highly susceptible population.

Documenting Information and Observations

The health department official shall document the following on an inspection report form:

- Administrative information about the establishment's legal identity, street and mailing addresses, type of establishment and operation, inspection date, and other information such as type of water supply and sewage disposal, status of the permit, and personnel certificates that may be required.

- Specific factual observations of violative conditions or other deviations from the Food Code that require correction by the permit holder, including:

  1. Failure of the person in charge to demonstrate the knowledge of foodborne illness prevention and the application of HACCP principles.

  2. Failure of employees and the person in charge to demonstrate their knowledge of their responsibility to report a disease or medical condition.

  3. Nonconformance with critical items of the Food Code.

  4. Failure of the appropriate employees to demonstrate their knowledge of, and ability to perform in accordance with, the procedural, monitoring, verification and corrective action practices required by the health department.

  5. Failure of the person in charge to provide records required by the health department for determining conformance with a HACCP plan.

  6. Nonconformance with critical limits of a HACCP plan.

The health department official also shall specify on the inspection report form the time frame for correction of the violations.

Issuing Report and Obtaining Acknowledgment of Receipt

At the conclusion of the inspection, the health department official will provide a copy of the completed inspection report and the notice to correct violations to the person in charge and request a signed acknowledgment of receipt.

If the person in charge refuses to sign the report, the health department will:

1. Inform the person who declines to sign an acknowledgment of receipt of inspectional findings that:

   - An acknowledgment of receipt is not an agreement with findings.

   - Refusal to sign an acknowledgment of receipt will not affect the permit holder's obligation to correct the violations noted in the inspection report within the time frames specified.

   - A refusal to sign an acknowledgment of receipt is noted in the inspection report and conveyed to the health department's historical record for the food establishment.

2. Make a final request that the person in charge sign an acknowledgment receipt of inspectional findings.

The health department will treat the inspection report as a public document and make it available for disclosure to someone who requests it.

Ceasing Operations and Reporting

An owner or permit holder must immediately discontinue operations and notify the health department if an imminent health hazard may exist because of an emergency such as a fire, flood, extended interruption of electrical or water service, sewage backup, misuse of poisonous or toxic materials, the onset of an apparent food-borne illness outbreak, gross unsanitary occurrence or condition, or other circumstance that may endanger public health.

If operations are discontinued because of an imminent health hazard, the establishment cannot reopen unless the owner has approval from the health department to resume operations.

At the time of an inspection, the establishment owner must correct a critical violation of the Food Code and implement corrective actions for a HACCP plan provision that is not in compliance with its critical limit.

Considering the nature of the potential hazard involved and the complexity of the corrective action needed, the health department may agree to or specify a longer time frame, not to exceed ten calendar days after the inspection, for the permit holder to correct critical Food Code violations or HACCP plan deviations.

VERIFICATION AND DOCUMENTATION OF CORRECTION

After observing at the time of inspection a correction of a critical violation or deviation, the health department will enter the violation and information about the corrective action on the inspection report.

After receiving notification that the permit holder has corrected a critical violation or HACCP plan deviation, or at the end of the specified period of time, the health department will verify correction of the violation, document the information on an inspection report, and enter the report in the health department's records.

The permit holder must correct noncritical violations by a date and time agreed to or specified by the health department but no later than 90 calendar days after the inspection. (The health department may approve a compliance schedule that extends beyond these time limits if a written schedule of compliance is submitted by the permit holder and no health hazard exists or will result from allowing an extended schedule for compliance.)

FEDERAL AGENCIES INVOLVED WITH FOOD SAFETY

The primary federal agencies involved with food safety are the Food and Drug Administration (FDA), the U.S. Department of Agriculture (USDA), and the Environmental Protection Agency (EPA). Other agencies that play a role in food safety include the CDC, the National Marine Fisheries Services, Occupational Safety and Health Administration (OSHA), the Federal Trade Commission (FTC) and the Consumer Product Safety Commission.

The USDA is responsible for inspecting domestic and imported meats, poultry and processed meats. The agency maintains a list of approved facilities for meat and poultry processing, and it conducts voluntary grading services for red meats, eggs, poultry, dairy products and fruits and vegetables.

The USDA develops grade standards for processed fish products, and the National Marine Fisheries Service provides voluntary inspection services for processed fish products and maintains a list of approved fish processors.

The CDC is responsible for protecting public health through disease prevention. This agency is involved in food-borne illness investigations and prepares statistical reports on food-borne illness outbreaks.

The EPA regulates the use of toxic substances, such as pesticides and sanitizers, and monitors compliance. OSHA enforces health standards and work-related safety regulations.

The FTC enforces laws concerning food-related marketing practices and advertising.

Food and Drug Administration

The federal agency whose work this book focuses on is the Food and Drug Administration. The FDA touches the lives of virtually every American every day. It is the FDA's job to see that the food we eat is safe and wholesome, the cosmetics we use won't hurt us, the medicines and medical devices we use are safe and effective, and that radiation-emitting products such as microwave ovens won't do us harm. Food and drugs for pets and farm animals also come under FDA scrutiny. The FDA also ensures that all of these products are labeled truthfully with the information that people need to use them properly.

The FDA is one of our nation's oldest consumer protection agencies. Its approximately 9,000 employees monitor the manufacture, import, transport, storage and sale of about $1 trillion worth of products each year. It does that at a cost to the taxpayer of about $3 per person.

First and foremost, the FDA is a public health agency, charged with protecting American consumers by enforcing the Federal Food, Drug and Cosmetic Act and several related public health laws. To carry out this mandate of consumer protection, the FDA has some 1,100 investigators and inspectors who cover the country's almost 95,000 FDA-regulated businesses. These employees are located in district and local offices in 157 cities across the country.

These investigators and inspectors visit more than 15,000 facilities a year, seeing that products are made right and labeled truthfully. As part of their inspections, they collect about 80,000 domestic and imported product samples for examination by FDA scientists or for label checks.

If a company is found violating any of the laws that the FDA enforces, the FDA can encourage the firm to voluntarily correct the problem or to recall a faulty product from the market. A recall is generally the fastest and most effective way to protect the public from an unsafe product.

When a company can't or won't correct a public health problem with one of its products voluntarily, the FDA has legal sanctions it can bring to bear. The agency can go to court to force a company to stop selling a product and to have items already produced seized and destroyed. When warranted, criminal penalties— including prison sentences — are sought against manufacturers and distributors.

About 3,000 products a year are found to be unfit for consumers and are withdrawn from the marketplace, either by voluntary recall or by court-ordered seizure. In addition, about 30,000 import shipments a year are detained at the port of entry because the goods appear to be unacceptable.

The FDA publishes the Food Code, a model that assists food control jurisdictions at all levels of government by providing them with a scientifically sound technical and legal basis for regulating the retail and food service segment of the industry. Local, state, tribal and federal regulators use the FDA Food Code as a model to develop or update their own food safety rules and to be consistent with national food regulatory policy. The FDA's Food Code is intended to help state health departments develop regulations for a food service inspection program. The Food Code is not actual law, it is basically the FDA's advice on how to regulate the food system to ensure safety. Some states may adopt the Code in its entirety and others may just use it as a basis for their own code.

It also serves as a reference of best practices for the retail and food service industries (restaurants, grocery stores and institutions such as nursing homes) on how to prevent food-borne illness. Many of the over one million retail and food service establishments apply Food Code provisions to their own operations.

Between 1993 and 2001, the Food Code was issued, in its current format, every two years. With the support of the Conference for Food Protection, the FDA has decided to move to a four-year interval between complete Food Code revisions.

The next complete revision of the Food Code will be published in 2005. During the four-year interim period, a Food Code Supplement that updates, modifies or clarifies certain provisions is being made available.

The main areas on which the Food Code focuses are:

- Food handling and food preparation.

- Personnel.

- Equipment and utensils.

- Cleaning and sanitizing.

- Services (water, sewage, plumbing, waste disposal and pest management).

- Construction and maintenance.

- Compliance procedures.

The Food Code addresses controls for risk factors and establishes five key public health interventions to protect consumer health. Specifically, these interventions are:

- Demonstration of knowledge.

- Employee health controls.

- Controlling hands as a vehicle of contamination.

- Time and temperature parameters for controlling pathogens.

- Consumer advisory.

The following is a partial listing of the types of businesses that are usually considered part of the retail food industry. There are many situations which may include more than one type of operation.

Partial Listing of Retail Food Industry Businesses	
Back-country guided trips for groups	Health care facilities
Bakeries	Interstate conveyances
Bars and taverns	Mail order foods
Bed and breakfast operations	Markets
Cafeterias	Meal services for home-bound persons
Camps – recreational, children's, etc.	Mobile food cards
Casinos	Panel institutions
Child and adult day care	Restaurants
Church kitchens	Chains
Commissaries	Ethnic specialities
Community fund raisers	Fast food
Convenience stores	Full service
Fairs	Independent operations
Food banks	Road-side stands
Grocery stores with specialized departments	Schools
Deli	Snack bars
In-store prepared foods	Temporary outdoor events
Produce	Vending machines

Consider also the following characteristics that retail food establishments share.

The industry has a wide range of employee resources, from highly trained executive chefs to entry-level front-line employees. Employees may have a broad range of educational levels and communication skills. It may be difficult to conduct in-house training and to maintain a trained staff because employees may speak different languages or there may be high employee turnover.

Many establishments are start-up businesses operating without benefit of a large corporate support structure and having a relatively low profit margin and perhaps less capital to work with than other segments of the food industry.

There is an almost endless number of production techniques, products, menu items and ingredients used. Suppliers, ingredients, menu items or specifications may change frequently.

Milestones in U.S. Food and Drug Law History

From the beginnings of civilization people have been concerned about the quality and safety of foods and medicines. In 1202, King John of England proclaimed the first English food law, the Assize of Bread, which prohibited adulteration of bread with such ingredients as ground peas or beans. Regulation of food in the United States dates from early colonial times. Federal controls over the drug supply began with inspection of imported drugs in 1848. The following chronology describes some of the milestones in the history of food and drug regulation in the United States. — May 3, 1999

1820	Eleven physicians meet in Washington, D.C., to establish the **U.S. PHARMACOPEIA**, the first compendium of standard drugs for the United States.
1848	**DRUG IMPORTATION ACT** passed by Congress requires U.S. Customs Service inspection to stop entry of adulterated drugs from overseas.
1862	**PRESIDENT LINCOLN** appoints a chemist, Charles M. Wetherill, to serve in the new Department of Agriculture. This was the beginning of the Bureau of Chemistry, the predecessor of the Food and Drug Administration.
1880	**PETER COLLIER**, chief chemist, U.S. Department of Agriculture, recommends passage of a national food and drug law, following his own food adulteration investigations. The bill was defeated, but during the next 25 years, more than 100 food and drug bills were introduced in Congress.
1883	**DR. HARVEY W. WILEY** becomes chief chemist, expanding the Bureau of Chemistry's food adulteration studies. Campaigning for a federal law, Dr. Wiley is called the "Crusading Chemist" and "Father of the Pure Food and Drugs Act." He retired from government service in 1912 and died in 1930.
1897	**TEA IMPORTATION ACT** passed, providing for Customs inspection of all tea entering U.S. ports, at the expense of the importers.
1898	Association of Official Agricultural Chemists (now AOAC International) establishes a **COMMITTEE ON FOOD STANDARDS** headed by Dr. Wiley. States begin incorporating these standards into their food statutes.
1902	The **BIOLOGICS CONTROL ACT** is passed to ensure purity and safety of serums, vaccines and similar products used to prevent or treat diseases in humans. Congress appropriates $5,000 to the Bureau of Chemistry to study **CHEMICAL PRESERVATIVES AND COLORS** and their effects on digestion and health. Dr. Wiley's studies draw widespread attention to the problem of food adulteration. Public support for passage of a federal food and drug law grows.

Milestones in U.S. Food and Drug Law History

1906	The original **FOOD AND DRUGS ACT** is passed by Congress on June 30 and signed by President Theodore Roosevelt. It prohibits interstate commerce in misbranded and adulterated foods, drinks and drugs. The **MEAT INSPECTION ACT** is passed the same day. Shocking disclosures of unsanitary conditions in meat packing plants, the use of poisonous preservatives and dyes in foods, and cure-all claims for worthless and dangerous patent medicines were the major problems leading to the enactment of these laws.
1907	First **CERTIFIED COLOR REGULATIONS**, requested by manufacturers and users, list seven colors found suitable for use in foods.
1911	In **U.S. v. JOHNSON**, the Supreme Court rules that the 1906 Food and Drugs Act does not prohibit false therapeutic claims but only false and misleading statements about the ingredients or identity of a drug.
1912	Congress enacts the **SHERLEY AMENDMENT** to overcome the ruling in U.S. v. Johnson. It prohibits labeling medicines with false therapeutic claims intended to defraud the purchaser, a standard difficult to prove.
1913	**GOULD AMENDMENT** requires that food package contents be "plainly and conspicuously marked on the outside of the package in terms of weight, measure or numerical count."
1914	In **U.S. v. LEXINGTON MILL AND ELEVATOR COMPANY**, the Supreme Court issues its first ruling on food additives. It ruled that in order for bleached flour with nitrite residues to be banned from foods, the government must show a relationship between the chemical additive and the harm it allegedly caused in humans. The court also noted that the mere presence of such an ingredient was not sufficient to render the food illegal. **THE HARRISON NARCOTIC ACT** requires prescriptions for products exceeding the allowable limit of narcotics and mandates increased recordkeeping for physicians and pharmacists who dispense narcotics.
1924	In **U.S. v. 95 BARRELS ALLEGED APPLE CIDER VINEGAR**, the Supreme Court rules that the Food and Drugs Act condemns every statement, design or device on a product's label that may mislead or deceive, even if technically true.
1927	The Bureau of Chemistry is reorganized into two separate entities. Regulatory functions are located in the **FOOD, DRUG AND INSECTICIDE ADMINISTRATION**, and nonregulatory research is located in the **BUREAU OF CHEMISTRY AND SOILS**.

Milestones in U.S. Food and Drug Law History

1930	**McNARY-MAPES AMENDMENT** authorizes FDA standards of quality and fill-of-container for canned food, excluding meat and milk products. The name of the Food, Drug and Insecticide Administration is shortened to **FOOD AND DRUG ADMINISTRATION (FDA)** under an agricultural appropriations act.
1933	The FDA recommends a complete revision of the obsolete **1906 FOOD AND DRUGS ACT**. The first bill is introduced into the Senate, launching a five-year legislative battle.
1937	**ELIXIR OF SULFANILAMIDE,** containing the poisonous solvent diethylene glycol, kills 107 persons, many of whom are children, dramatizing the need to establish drug safety before marketing and to enact the pending food and drug law.
1938	**THE FEDERAL FOOD, DRUG AND COSMETIC (FDC) ACT of 1938** is passed by Congress, containing new provisions: • Extending control to cosmetics and therapeutic devices. • Requiring new drugs to be shown safe before marketing—starting a new system of drug regulation. • Eliminating the Sherley Amendment requirement to prove intent to defraud in drug misbranding cases. • Providing that safe tolerances be set for unavoidable poisonous substances. • Authorizing standards of identity, quality and fill-of-container for foods. • Authorizing factory inspections. • Adding the remedy of court injunctions to the previous penalties of seizures and prosecutions. Under the **WHEELER-LEA ACT**, the Federal Trade Commission is charged with overseeing advertising associated with products otherwise regulated by the FDA, with the exception of prescription drugs.
1939	**FIRST FOOD STANDARDS** issued (canned tomatoes, tomato puree and tomato paste).
1940	**THE FDA TRANSFERRED** from the Department of Agriculture to the Federal Security Agency, with Walter G. Campbell appointed as the first Commissioner of Food and Drugs.
1941	**INSULIN AMENDMENT** requires the FDA to test and certify purity and potency of this life-saving drug for diabetes.

Milestones in U.S. Food and Drug Law History

1943	In **U.S. v. DOTTERWEICH**, the Supreme Court rules that the responsible officials of a corporation, as well as the corporation itself, may be prosecuted for violations. It need not be proven that the officials intended or even knew of the violations.
1944	**PUBLIC HEALTH SERVICE ACT** is passed, covering a broad spectrum of health concerns, including regulation of biological products and control of communicable diseases.
1945	**PENICILLIN AMENDMENT** requires FDA testing and certification of safety and effectiveness of all penicillin products. Later amendments extended this requirement to all antibiotics. In 1983 such control was found no longer needed and was abolished.
1948	**MILLER AMENDMENT** affirms that the Federal Food, Drug and Cosmetic Act applies to goods regulated by the Agency that have been transported from one state to another and have reached the consumer.
1949	The FDA publishes **GUIDANCE TO INDUSTRY** for the first time. This guidance, "Procedures for the Appraisal of the Toxicity of Chemicals in Food," came to be known as the "black book."
1950	In **ALBERTY FOOD PRODUCTS CO. v. U.S.**, a court of appeals rules that the directions for use on a drug label must include the purpose for which the drug is offered. Therefore, a worthless remedy cannot escape the law by not stating the condition it is supposed to treat.

OLEOMARGARINE ACT requires prominent labeling of colored oleomargarine, to distinguish it from butter.

DELANEY COMMITTEE starts congressional investigation of the safety of chemicals in foods and cosmetics, laying the foundation for the 1954 Miller Pesticide Amendment, the 1958 Food Additives Amendment and the 1960 Color Additive Amendment. |
| 1951 | **DURHAM-HUMPHREY AMENDMENT** defines the kinds of drugs that cannot be safely used without medical supervision and restricts their sale to prescription by a licensed practitioner. |
| 1952 | In **U.S. v. CARDIFF**, the Supreme Court rules that the factory inspection provision of the 1938 FDC Act is too vague to be enforced as criminal law.

FDA CONSUMER CONSULTANTS are appointed in each field district to maintain communications with consumers and ensure that the FDA considers their needs and problems. |

Milestones in U.S. Food and Drug Law History

1953	**FEDERAL SECURITY AGENCY** becomes the Department of Health, Education and Welfare (HEW).
	FACTORY INSPECTION AMENDMENT clarifies previous law and requires the FDA to give manufacturers written reports of conditions observed during inspections and analyses of factory samples.
1954	**MILLER PESTICIDE AMENDMENT** spells out procedures for setting safety limits for pesticide residues on raw agricultural commodities.
	First large-scale **RADIOLOGICAL EXAMINATION OF FOOD** carried out by the FDA when it received reports that tuna suspected of being radioactive was being imported from Japan following atomic blasts in the Pacific. The FDA begins monitoring around the clock to meet the emergency.
1955	**HEW SECRETARY OVETA CULP HOBBY** appoints a committee of 14 citizens to study the adequacy of the FDA's facilities and programs. The committee recommends a substantial expansion of FDA staff and facilities, a new headquarters building, and more use of educational and informational programs.
	The biologics control function in the National Institutes of Health is reorganized into the **DIVISION OF BIOLOGICS CONTROL** within the FDA, after polio vaccine thought to have been inactivated is associated with about 260 cases of polio.
1958	**FOOD ADDITIVES AMENDMENT** enacted, requiring manufacturers of new food additives to establish safety. The Delaney proviso prohibits the approval of any food additive shown to induce cancer in humans or animals.
	The FDA publishes in the Federal Register the first list of **SUBSTANCES GENERALLY RECOGNIZED AS SAFE (GRAS)**. The list contains nearly 200 substances.
1959	**U.S. CRANBERRY CROP** recalled three weeks before Thanksgiving for FDA tests to check for aminotriazole, a weed killer found to cause cancer in laboratory animals. Cleared berries were allowed a label stating that they had been tested and had passed FDA inspection, the only such endorsement ever allowed by the FDA on a food product.

Milestones in U.S. Food and Drug Law History

1960	**COLOR ADDITIVE AMENDMENT** enacted, requiring manufacturers to establish the safety of color additives in foods, drugs and cosmetics. The Delaney proviso prohibits the approval of any color additive shown to induce cancer in humans or animals. **FEDERAL HAZARDOUS SUBSTANCES LABELING ACT**, enforced by the FDA, requires prominent label warnings on hazardous household chemical products.
1962	**THALIDOMIDE**, a new sleeping pill, is found to have caused birth defects in thousands of babies born in Western Europe. News reports on the role of Dr. Frances Kelsey, FDA medical officer, in keeping the drug off the U.S. market, arouse public support for stronger drug regulation. **KEFAUVER-HARRIS DRUG AMENDMENTS** passed to ensure drug efficacy and greater drug safety. For the first time, drug manufacturers are required to prove to the FDA the effectiveness of their products before marketing them. The new law also exempts from the Delaney proviso animal drugs and animal feed additives shown to induce cancer but which leave no detectable levels of residue in the human food supply. **CONSUMER BILL OF RIGHTS** is proclaimed by President John F. Kennedy in a message to Congress. Included are the right to safety, the right to be informed, the right to choose, and the right to be heard.
1965	**DRUG ABUSE CONTROL AMENDMENTS** are enacted to deal with problems caused by abuse of depressants, stimulants and hallucinogens.
1966	The FDA contracts with the National Academy of Sciences/National Research Council to evaluate the **EFFECTIVENESS OF 4,000 DRUGS** approved on the basis of safety alone between 1938 and 1962. **CHILD PROTECTION ACT** enlarges the scope of the Federal Hazardous Substances Labeling Act to ban hazardous toys and other articles so hazardous that adequate label warnings could not be written. **FAIR PACKAGING AND LABELING ACT** requires all consumer products in interstate commerce to be honestly and informatively labeled, with FDA enforcing provisions on foods, drugs, cosmetics and medical devices.

Milestones in U.S. Food and Drug Law History

1968	**FDA BUREAU OF DRUG ABUSE CONTROL** and Treasury Department Bureau of Narcotics are transferred to the Department of Justice to form the Bureau of Narcotics and Dangerous Drugs (BNDD), consolidating efforts to police traffic in abused drugs. **REORGANIZATION** of federal health programs places the FDA in the Public Health Service. The FDA forms the **DRUG EFFICACY STUDY IMPLEMENTATION (DESI)** to implement recommendations of the National Academy of Sciences investigation of effectiveness of drugs first marketed between 1938 and 1962. **ANIMAL DRUG AMENDMENTS** place all regulation of new animal drugs under one section of the Food, Drug and Cosmetic Act—Section 512—making approval of animal drugs and medicated feeds more efficient.
1969	The FDA begins administering **SANITATION PROGRAMS** for milk, shellfish, food service and interstate travel facilities and for preventing poisoning and accidents. These responsibilities were transferred from other units of the Public Health Service. The **WHITE HOUSE CONFERENCE ON FOOD, NUTRITION AND HEALTH** recommends systematic review of GRAS substances in light of the FDA's ban of the artificial sweetener cyclamate. President Nixon orders the FDA to review its GRAS list.
1970	In **UPJOHN v. FINCH**, the Court of Appeals upholds enforcement of the 1962 drug effectiveness amendments by ruling that commercial success alone does not constitute substantial evidence of drug safety and efficacy. The FDA requires the first **PATIENT PACKAGE INSERT**: oral contraceptives must contain information for the patient about specific risks and benefits. The **COMPREHENSIVE DRUG ABUSE PREVENTION AND CONTROL ACT** replaces previous laws and categorizes drugs based on abuse and addiction potential compared to their therapeutic value. **ENVIRONMENTAL PROTECTION AGENCY** established; takes over FDA program for setting pesticide tolerances.

Milestones in U.S. Food and Drug Law History

1971	**PHS BUREAU OF RADIOLOGICAL HEALTH** transferred to the FDA. Its mission: protection against unnecessary human exposure to radiation from electronic products in the home, industry and the healing arts. **NATIONAL CENTER FOR TOXICOLOGICAL RESEARCH** is established in the biological facilities of the Pine Bluff Arsenal in Arkansas. Its mission is to examine biological effects of chemicals in the environment, extrapolating data from experimental animals to human health. Artificial sweetener **SACCHARIN**, included in the FDA's original GRAS list, is removed from the list pending new scientific study.
1972	**OVER-THE-COUNTER DRUG REVIEW** begun to enhance the safety, effectiveness and appropriate labeling of drugs sold without prescription. **REGULATION OF BIOLOGICS** — including serums, vaccines, and blood products—is transferred from the NIH to the FDA.
1973	**THE U.S. SUPREME COURT** upholds the 1962 drug effectiveness law and endorses FDA action to control entire classes of products by regulations rather than to rely only on time-consuming litigation. **LOW-ACID FOOD PROCESSING** regulations issued, after botulism outbreaks from canned foods, to ensure that low-acid packaged foods have adequate heat treatment and are not hazardous. **CONSUMER PRODUCT SAFETY COMMISSION** created by Congress; takes over programs pioneered by the FDA under 1927 Caustic Poison Act, 1960 Federal Hazardous Substances Labeling Act, 1966 Child Protection Act, and PHS accident prevention activities for safety of toys, home appliances, etc.
1976	**MEDICAL DEVICE AMENDMENTS** passed to ensure safety and effectiveness of medical devices, including diagnostic products. The amendments require manufacturers to register with the FDA and follow quality-control procedures. Some products must have pre-market approval by the FDA; others must meet performance standards before marketing. **VITAMINS AND MINERALS AMENDMENTS** ("Proxmire Amendments") stop the FDA from establishing standards limiting potency of vitamins and minerals in food supplements or regulating them as drugs based solely on potency.

Milestones in U.S. Food and Drug Law History

1977	**SACCHARIN STUDY AND LABELING ACT** passed by Congress to stop the FDA from banning the chemical sweetener but requiring a label warning that it has been found to cause cancer in laboratory animals.
1980	**INFANT FORMULA ACT** establishes special FDA controls to ensure necessary nutritional content and safety.
1982	**TAMPER-RESISTANT PACKAGING REGULATIONS** issued by the FDA to prevent poisonings such as deaths from cyanide placed in Tylenol capsules. The Federal Anti-Tampering Act passed in 1983 makes it a crime to tamper with packaged consumer products. The FDA publishes first **RED BOOK** (successor to 1949 "black book"), officially known as Toxicological Principles for the Safety Assessment of Direct Food Additives and Color Additives Used in Food.
1983	**ORPHAN DRUG ACT** passed, enabling the FDA to promote research and marketing of drugs needed for treating rare diseases.
1984	**FINES ENHANCEMENT LAWS** of 1984 and 1987 amend the U.S. Code to greatly increase penalties for all federal offenses. The maximum fine for individuals is now $100,000 for each offense and $250,000 if the violation is a felony or causes death. For corporations, the amounts are doubled. **DRUG PRICE COMPETITION AND PATENT TERM RESTORATION ACT** expedites the availability of less costly generic drugs by permitting the FDA to approve applications to market generic versions of brand-name drugs without repeating the research done to prove them safe and effective. At the same time, the brand-name companies can apply for up to five years' additional patent protection for the new medicines they developed to make up for time lost while their products were going through the FDA's approval process.
1985	**AIDS TEST FOR BLOOD** approved by the FDA in its first major action to protect patients from infected donors.
1986	**CHILDHOOD VACCINE ACT** requires patient information on vaccines, gives FDA authority to recall biologics and authorizes civil penalties.
1987	**INVESTIGATIONAL DRUG REGULATIONS REVISED** to expand access to experimental drugs for patients with serious diseases with no alternative therapies.

Source: **www.fda.gov/opacom/backgrounders/miles.html**; January 13, 1998, *New Stamp Honors the First Comprehensive National Food and Drug Law.*

Food Manager Certification

Certification shows that managers are knowledgeable in food safety. Manager certification is required in some states or localities. Check with your local health department to see if it is required in your state or log onto the National Restaurant Association's Web site at **www.restaurant.org**.

Food protection manager *certification* occurs when individuals demonstrate through a certification program that they have met specified food safety knowledge standards.

Food protection certification program accreditation occurs when *certification organizations* demonstrate through an accreditation program that they have met specified program standards.

Accreditation is a conformity assessment process through which organizations that certify individuals may voluntarily seek independent evaluation and listing by an accrediting agency based upon the certifying organization's meeting program accreditation standards. Such accreditation standards typically relate to such factors as the certifying organization's structure, mission, policies, procedures, and the defensibility of its examination processes. These standards are intended to affirm or enhance the quality and credibility of the certification process, minimize the potential for conflicts of interest, ensure fairness to candidates for certification and others, and thereby increase public health protection.

Program accreditation standards known to be relevant to food protection manager certification programs include those contained in the *Standards for Accreditation of Food Protection Manager Certification Programs* available from the Conference for Food Protection.

Allowing food protection managers to demonstrate their required food-safety knowledge "through passing a test that is part of an accredited program" is predicated on the fact that their credentials have been issued by certifying organizations that have demonstrated conformance with rigorous and nationally recognized program standards.

Responsibility

Designation of a person in charge during all hours of operation ensures the continuous presence of someone who is responsible for monitoring and managing all food establishment operations and who is authorized to take actions to ensure that the Code's objectives are fulfilled. During the day-to-day operation of a food establishment, a person who is immediately available and knowledgeable in both operational and Code requirements is needed to respond to questions and concerns and to resolve problems.

Knowledge

The designated person in charge who is knowledgeable about food-borne disease prevention, HACCP principles and Code requirements is prepared to recognize conditions that may contribute to food-borne illness or that otherwise fail to comply with Code requirements, and to take appropriate preventive and corrective actions.

There are many ways in which the person in charge can demonstrate competency. Many aspects of the food operation itself will reflect the competency of that person. A dialogue with the person in charge during the inspection process will also reveal whether or not that person is enabled by a clear understanding of the Code and its public health principles to follow sound food safety practices and to produce foods that are safe, wholesome, unadulterated and accurately represented.

The Food Code does not require reporting of uninfected cuts or reporting of covered, protected infected cuts/lesions/boils since it requires no bare-hand contact with ready-to-eat food.

Presently there are a wide variety of industry management training and certification programs being offered by regulatory agencies, academic institutions, food companies, industry groups and third-party organizations. Most certification programs share a common desire to have the food manager certificate they issue universally recognized and accepted by others, especially by the increasing number of regulatory authorities that require food manager certification.

Certification programs vary significantly in focus and primary mission of sponsors, organizational structures, staff resources, revenue sources, testing mechanisms, policies toward applicants and employers of food managers, and policies pertaining to such things as public information, criteria for maintaining certification and the need for recertification. Where courses are offered, they vary in scope, content, depth and duration, quality of instructional materials, qualifications of instructors, and instructional approach (classroom, on-the-job, PC-based, home study, etc.). Where testing is a program component, varying degrees of attention are given to test construction and test administration as they relate to nationally accepted standards (reliability, validity, job analysis, subject weighting, cut scores, test security, etc.).

Manager's Responsibilities

According to the Food Code, the restaurant owner and/or manager needs to ensure that a manager or supervisor is on the premises during all hours of operation. This person also must have demonstrated knowledge of food-borne illness prevention, HACCP principles, and the Food Code requirements. The manager/supervisor needs to demonstrate this knowledge by:

- Complying with the Code.

- Being certified in food safety through an accredited program such as the ServSafe program offered through the National Restaurant Association.

- Responding correctly to the inspector's questions

The areas of knowledge the manager/supervisor should have include:

- Describing the relationship between the prevention of food-borne disease and the personal hygiene of an employee.

- Explaining the responsibility of the manager for preventing the transmission of food-borne disease by an employee who has a disease or medical condition that may cause food-borne disease.

- Describing the symptoms associated with the diseases that are transmissible through food.

- Explaining the relationship between maintaining the time and temperature of potentially hazardous food and the prevention of food-borne illness.

- Explaining the hazards in consuming raw or undercooked meat, poultry, eggs and fish.

- Knowing the food temperatures and times required for the safe cooking of potentially hazardous food, including meat, poultry, eggs and fish.

- Stating the required temperatures and times for the safe refrigerated storage, hot holding, cooling and reheating of potentially hazardous food.

- Describing the relationship between the prevention of food-borne illness and:

  - Cross-contamination.

  - Hand contact with ready-to-eat-food.

  - Hand washing.

  - Maintaining the establishment in clean condition and good repair.

- Explaining the relationship between food safety and providing equipment that is sufficient in number and capacity, and properly designed, constructed, located, installed, operated, maintained and cleaned.

- Explaining correct procedures for cleaning and sanitizing utensils and the food-contact surfaces of equipment.

- Identifying the source of water used and measures taken to ensure that it remains protected from contamination such as providing protection from backflow and precluding the creation of cross connections.

- Identifying poisonous or toxic materials in the establishment and the procedures necessary to ensure that they are safely stored, dispensed, used and disposed of according to law.

- Identifying critical control points in the operation and explaining steps taken to ensure that the points are controlled in accordance with the requirements of the Code.

- Explaining the details of how the manager and employees comply with the HACCP plan.

- Explaining the responsibilities, rights and authorities assigned by this Code to the employees, manager and health department.

The manager is responsible for ensuring employees understand what they need to do to keep their customers safe from food-borne illnesses.

The following is a list of things the manager should do.

- Ensure operations are conducted in an establishment deemed proper by the health code. For example, if you buy your desserts from a private vendor and your local health code does not allow for desserts that are sold to the public be prepared in a private home, you need to make sure your vendor is using a space that meets the requirements of your health code.

- Make sure non-employees are not in the food preparation, storage or dishwashing areas.

- Make sure all your employees, vendors and suppliers that come into your food prep areas are complying with the Food Code requirements.

- By routinely monitoring them, make sure employees are properly washing their hands.

- Make sure employees are inspecting foods as they receive them to determine that they are from approved sources and delivered that are at the required temperatures.

- Ensure employees are properly cooking potentially hazardous foods through daily oversight of the employees' routine monitoring of the cooking temperatures using appropriate temperature measuring devices that are properly scaled and calibrated.

- Ensure employees are using proper methods to rapidly cool potentially hazardous foods.

- Make sure that customers who order raw or partially cooked ready-to-eat foods of animal origin are informed of its hazards.

- Make sure employees are properly sanitizing equipment and utensils through routine monitoring of solution temperature and exposure time for hot water sanitizing, chemical concentration, pH, temperature, and exposure time for chemical sanitizing.

- If you have a buffet area, be sure customers are informed to use clean tableware when they return to the buffet for refills.

- Be sure employees prevent cross-contamination of ready-to-eat foods, such as salad, by properly using suitable utensils such as deli tissue, spatulas, tongs and single-use gloves.

- Make certain employees are properly trained in food safety as it relates to their assigned duties.

Employee Health

The Food Code specifies that the manager and/or owner is responsible for requiring applicants and food employees to report certain symptoms, diagnoses, past illnesses, high-risk conditions and foreign travel as they relate to diseases transmitted through food by infected workers. The employee is personally responsible for reporting this information to the person in charge.

An employee who comes into work sick is a potential health hazard for your customers. Unfortunately, many restaurant employees will come to work sick simply because they can't afford to miss the pay, they don't have any sick time or they can't find someone to fill in. As a manager consider policies you could implement to alleviate this issue. This is the first step in protecting the health of your employees and customers.

According to the Food Code, when you offer someone a job, you should require that person to provide you with information on his or her health pertaining to diseases that may be transmittable through food. In addition, an employee should report any illness he or she has to the supervisor so the supervisor can make a decision on whether or not this illness is likely to be one that can be transmitted through contact with food.

Disease or Medical Condition

According to the Food Code, the owner of an establishment must require applicants to whom a conditional offer of employment is made and employees to report information regarding their health which are related to disease that are transmissible through food to their manager or the owner. This information must be reported so that the manager and/or owner can prevent the likelihood of food-borne disease transmission.

The following conditions could lead to an employee or applicant passing an illness on to others through food:

- If an employee or applicant is diagnosed with an illness due to:

    - *Salmonella* typhi

    - *Shigella* spp

    - *Shiga* Toxin-Producing *Escherichia* coli

    - Hepatitis A virus

- If an employee has symptoms associated with an acute gastrointestinal illness such as:

    - Fever

    - Vomiting

    - Jaundice

    - Sore throat with fever

    - Diarrhea

- An infected lesion containing pus such as a boil or infected wound that is open or draining and is:

    - On the hands or wrists, unless an impermeable cover such as a finger cot or stall protects the lesion and a single-use glove is worn over the impermeable cover.

    - On exposed portions of the arms, unless the lesion is protected by an impermeable cover.

    - On other parts of the body, unless the lesion is covered by a dry, durable, tight-fitting bandage.

- Had a past illness from:

  - *S. typhi* within the past three months.

  - *Shigella* spp. within the past month.

  - Shiga Toxin-Producing *Escherichia coli*, within the past month.

  - Hepatitis A virus.

An employee or applicant is also at high risk of passing on a food-borne illness if he or she meets the following criteria:

- An employee could cause a risk of an outbreak of *S. typhi*, *Shigella* spp., Shiga Toxin-Producing *Escherichia coli*, or hepatitis if he or she has been at an event such as a family meal, community supper or festival where there was food implicated in the outbreak; if he or she consumed food at such an event; or if he or she consumed food at the event prepared by a person who is infected or ill with the infectious agent that caused the outbreak.

- If an employee lives in the same household as a person who is diagnosed with a disease caused by *S. typhi*, *Shigella* spp., Shiga Toxin-Producing *Escherichia coli*, or hepatitis A virus.

- An employee who lives in the same household as a person who works in a setting where there is a confirmed disease outbreak caused by *S. typhi*, *Shigella* spp., Shiga Toxin-Producing *Escherichia coli*, or hepatitis A virus.

- If an employee has traveled out of the United States or to a United States' territory within the last 50 calendar days to an area that is identified as having an epidemic or endemic disease caused by *S. typhi*, *Shigella* spp., *E. coli* O157:H7, or hepatitis A virus based on information published by the CDC, such as the document titled *Health Information for International Travel*.

The manager, supervisor or person in charge is required to exclude an employee from the establishment if he or she is diagnosed with an infectious agent listed above (*S. typhi, Shigella* spp., *Escherichia coli*, or hepatitis A virus).

The person in charge is required to notify the health department of a food employee or a person who applies for a job as a food employee who is diagnosed with or is suspected of having an illness due to *Salmonella* typhi, *Shigella* spp., *Escherichia coli*, or hepatitis A virus.

If the food establishment serves the general public (rather than a high-risk population such as the dining facility of a nursing home), the manager/owner will need to restrict employees from working with exposed food; clean equipment, utensils and linens; and unwrapped single-service and single-use articles in a food establishment if the food employee is suffering from symptoms associated with an acute gastrointestinal illness such as diarrhea, fever, vomiting, jaundice or a sore throat with fever or a lesion containing pus such as a boil or infected wound.

An employee must be excluded from the establishment if an employee:

- Is not experiencing a symptom of acute gastroenteritis but has a stool that yields a specimen culture that is positive for *S. typhi, Shigella* spp., or *E. coli* O157:H7.

- Had a past illness from S. typhi within the last three months.

- Had a past illness from *Shigella* spp. or *E. coli* O157:H7 within the last month.

If an employee has jaundice, the employee must be excluded from the establishment or restricted if:

- The onset of jaundice occurred within the last seven calendar days (employee must be excluded).

- The onset of jaundice occurred more than seven calendar days before (the food employee must be excluded from a food establishment that serves a highly susceptible population, or restricted if the food establishment does not serve a highly susceptible population).

4

FOLLOWING THE FLOW OF FOOD: PURCHASING, RECEIVING AND STORAGE

According to the Food Code, restaurants will serve food that is safe, unadulterated and honestly presented.

In addition, food must be procured from sources that comply with the law. Food that is prepared in a private home may not be sold in a food service establishment, and packaged food must be labeled as specified in the law.

The flow of food, which is the path that food follows from receiving through serving, is important for determining where potentially significant food safety hazards may occur. Many different things can happen at each stage to compromise food safety. At each operational step in the flow, active management of food preparation and processes is an essential part of business operations. With a HACCP system, you set up control measures to protect food at each stage in the process.

The illustrations of food processes listed below are not intended to be all-inclusive; for instance, quick-service, full-service and institutional providers are major types of food service operations. Each of these has their own individual food safety processes. These processes are likely to be different from a deli in a retail food store.

Some operations may have all three types of processes or variations of the three. Identifying the food process flows specific to your operation is an important part of providing a framework for developing a food safety management system.

FOOD PROCESS WITH NO COOK STEP

Receive ⟶ Store ⟶ Prepare ⟶ Hold ⟶ Serve

As mentioned in the Introduction, the important feature of this type of process is the absence of a cooking step. Heating foods destroys bacteria, parasites and viruses and is often a critical control point (CCP). But since this particular food flow does not include cooking, there is no step that will eliminate or kill bacteria, parasites or viruses. An example is tuna salad that is prepared and served cold. Control in this process will focus on preventing:

Many salads are prepared and served cold.

- Bacterial growth (e.g., storage under refrigeration).

- Contamination from employees (e.g., restriction of employees ill with diarrhea, proper hand washing, preventing bare-hand contact with ready-to-eat foods, etc.).

- Cross-contamination from other foods (e.g., raw to ready-to-eat).

- Cross-contamination from soiled equipment (e.g., cleaning and sanitizing).

- Obtaining foods from approved sources (e.g., a supplier of raw fish for sushi that adequately freezes fish to control parasites).

You should also think about some other factors.

- Are there any ingredients or menu items of special concern?

- Is this a potentially hazardous food requiring specific temperature controls?

- How will it be served? Immediately? On a buffet?

- Does this food have a history of being associated with illnesses?

- Will this require a great deal of preparation, making preparation time, employee health and bare-hand contact with ready-to-eat food a special concern?

- How will an employee ill with diarrhea be restricted from working with food?

- Are you serving food to a population that is known to be highly susceptible to food-borne illness (e.g., residents of health care facilities, persons in child or adult day care facilities, etc.)?

FOOD PREPARATION FOR SAME-DAY SERVICE

Receive ➞ Store ➞ Prepare ➞ Cook ➞ Hold ➞ Serve

In this process, a food is prepared and served the same day. The food will be cooked and held hot until service, such as chili. Generally, the food will pass through the temperature danger zone only once before it is served to the customer, thus minimizing the opportunity for bacterial growth.

The preparation step may involve several processes, including thawing a frozen food, mixing in other ingredients or cutting or chopping. It is important to remember that added ingredients may introduce additional contaminants to the food. Cutting or chopping must be done carefully so that cross-contamination from cutting

Soups are often prepared for same-day service.

boards, utensils, aprons or hands does not occur. Control points at this operational step include good sanitation and hand washing.

During cooking, food will be subjected to hot temperatures that will kill most harmful bacteria, parasites and viruses that might be introduced before cooking, making cooking a CCP. It is the operational step where raw animal foods are made safe to eat, and, therefore, time and temperature measurement is very important. Temperature of foods during hot holding must be maintained until service so that harmful bacteria do not survive and grow.

COMPLEX PROCESSES

Receive ➞ Store ➞ Prepare ➞ Cook ➞ Reheat ➞ Hot Hold ➞ Serve

Failure to adequately control food product temperature is the one factor most commonly associated with food-borne illness. Foods prepared in large volumes or in advance for next-day service usually follow an extended process flow. These foods are likely to pass through the temperature danger zone several times. The key in managing the operational steps within the process is to minimize the time foods are at unsafe temperatures.

In some cases, a variety of foods and ingredients that require extensive employee product preparation may be part of the process. A sound food safety management system will incorporate standard operating procedures for personal hygiene and cross-contamination prevention throughout the flow of the food.

Foood prepared in large volumes usually follow a complex process.

Before you set up a management system for your operational steps, there are several factors you should consider. Multiple-step processes require proper equipment and facilities. Your equipment needs to be designed to handle the volume of food you plan to prepare. For example, if you use a process that requires the cooling of hot food, you must provide equipment that will adequately and efficiently lower the food temperature as quickly as possible. If you find that a recipe is too hard to safely prepare, you may want to consider purchasing pre-prepared items from a reputable source.

To assist food establishments in applying HACCP principles at the retail level, the FDA has issued a draft document entitled *Managing Food Safety: A HACCP Principles Guide for Operators of Food Service, Retail Food Stores, and Other Food Establishments at the Retail Level*. This document is available from the FDA and can be found on the FDA Web page at **http://vm.cfsan.fda.gov/~ear/retail.html**.

There are seven steps in the flow of food that we will take a closer look at in regard to food safety including possible contaminates at each stage and ways to avoid contamination at each stage. In order, we'll look at:

1. Purchasing and receiving.

2. Storing.

3. Preparing.

4. Cooking.

5. Serving and holding.

6. Cooling.

7. Reheating.

There are multiple hazards at, and specific preventative measures for, each step.

PURCHASING

Your responsibility for food safety in your establishment begins long before the food arrives and is prepared. You must purchase wholesome, safe foods to meet your menu requirements. Safety at this step is primarily the responsibility of your vendors, but it's your job to choose your vendors wisely.

Suppliers must meet federal and state health standards. They should use the HACCP system in their operations and train their employees in sanitation. Be sure to ask if they use a HACCP system.

You should also make sure that suppliers are getting their products from approved sources — ones that have been inspected and are compliance with the law. In addition, make sure your suppliers are reputable. Ask other operators about their experiences with a particular vendor.

Delivery trucks should have adequate refrigeration and freezer units, and foods should be packaged in protective, leak-proof, durable packaging. If it's possible, inspect their warehouses and trucks. Are the trucks clean and well maintained? Are they holding products at the proper temperatures?

Also make sure your supplier is shipping quality product. Look for broken boxes, dented cans and leaks for signs of unsafe packaging.

Let vendors know up front what you expect from them. Put food-safety standards in your purchase specification agreements. Ask to see their most recent Board of Health Sanitation Reports, and tell them you will be inspecting trucks on a quarterly basis. Also ask them to deliver your products when your employees will be able to put them into storage in a proper and timely manner.

Good vendors will cooperate with your inspections and should adjust their delivery schedules to avoid your busy periods so that incoming foods can be received and inspected properly.

Rejecting Shipments

You have the right to reject any shipments that do not meet your standards. Develop a company policy about returns, and make sure your suppliers and employees get a copy of it.

To reject a shipment from a supplier, you should take the following steps:

1. Keep the rejected product separate from those you are keeping.

2. Tell the delivery person what is wrong with the product.

3. Get a signed credit from the delivery person at the time of delivery before the product is taken away or thrown away.

4. Make a note of the rejection on your copy of the invoice so you have that on file. Include what the product was, any item number or expiration date, what the problem was, and what action was taken.

Purchasing

The goal of purchasing is to supply the restaurant with the best goods at the lowest possible cost. There are many ways to achieve this. The buyer must have favorable working relations with all suppliers and vendors. A large amount of time must be spent meeting with prospective sales representatives and companies. The buyer's responsibility is to evaluate and decide how to best make each of the purchases for the restaurant. Purchasing is a complex area that must be managed by someone who is completely familiar with all of the restaurant's needs. The kitchen director or manager would be the best choice to do the purchasing. It is preferable to have one or two people do all the purchasing for all areas of the restaurant. There are several advantages to this, such as greater buying power and better overall control.

Provided the buyer completes the necessary research and evaluates all of the possible purchasing options, she can easily recoup a large part of her salary from the savings made. The most critical element to grasp when purchasing is the overall picture. Price is not the top priority and is only one of the considerations in deciding how and where to place an order.

Cooperative Purchasing

Many restaurants have formed cooperative purchasing groups to increase their purchasing power. Many items are commonly used by all food service operators. By cooperatively joining together to place large orders, restaurants can usually get substantial price reductions. Some organizations even purchase their own trucks and warehouses and hire personnel to pick up deliveries. This can be quite advantageous for restaurants that are in the proximity of a major supplier or shipping center. Many items, such as produce, dairy products, seafood and meat, may be purchased this way. Chain-restaurant organizations have a centralized purchasing department and, often, large self-distribution centers.

RECEIVING

The goals of receiving are to make sure foods are fresh and safe when they enter your facility and to transfer them to proper storage as quickly as possible.

Most deliveries arrive during the day. They should only be received during the prescribed time periods, such as after breakfast or before and after the lunch. Some restaurants might have a receiving department that is responsible for receiving deliveries. Other restaurants, especially smaller operations, usually give this responsibility to the prep cooks. The buyer should also be present to ensure that each item is of the specification ordered.

Receiving and storing products is a very important job function. Mistakes in this area can be costly, so be sure to train your employees in this area thoroughly.

Listed below are some policies and procedures for receiving and storing all deliveries. A slight inaccuracy in an invoice or improper storing of a perishable item could cost the restaurant hundreds or thousands of dollars.

Watch for a common area of internal theft. A collusion could develop between the delivery person and the employee receiving the products. Items checked as being received and accounted for may not have been delivered at all. The driver simply keeps the items. (In an upcoming section we will discuss how to guard against internal theft.)

All products delivered to the restaurant must:

1. Be checked against the actual order sheet.

2. Be the exact specification ordered (weight, size, quantity).

3. Be checked against the invoice.

4. Be accompanied by an invoice containing current price, totals, date, company name and receiver's signature.

5. Have their individual weights verified on the pound scale.

6. Be dated, rotated and put in the proper storage area immediately.
    (For resources visit **www.dissolveaway.com** or call 1-800-847-0101.)

7. Be locked in their storage areas securely.

8. Credit slips must be issued or prices subtracted from the invoice when an error occurs. The delivery person must sign over the correction.

Keep an invoice box (a small mail box) in the kitchen to store all invoices and packing slips received during the day. Mount the box on the wall, away from work areas. Prior to leaving for the day, the receiver must bring the invoices to the manager's office and place them in a designated spot. Extreme care must be taken to ensure that all invoices are handled correctly. A missing invoice will throw off the bookkeeping and financial records and statements.

Rotation Procedures

1. New items go to the back and on the bottom.

2. Older items move to the front and to the left.

3. In any part of the restaurant: the first item used should always be the oldest.

4. Date and label everything. (For resources visit **www.dissolveaway.com** or call 1-800-847-0101.)

ISSUING

All raw materials from which portionable entrées are prepared, such as meat, seafood and poultry, must be issued on a daily basis. Whenever one of these bulk items is removed from a freezer or walk-in, it must be signed out. (An example of a **Sign-Out Sheet** may be found in the Appendix.) When a part of a case or box is removed, the weight of the portion removed must be recorded in the "Amount" column. The Sign-Out Sheet should be on a clipboard affixed to the walk-in or freezer. Once the item is signed out, the weight must be placed in the "Amount Used or Defrosted" column on the Preparation Form. (An example of a **Preparation Form** may be found in the Appendix.) This will show that the items signed out were actually used in the restaurant. From this information, the kitchen director can compute a daily yield on each item prepared. This yield will show that the portions were weighed out accurately and the bulk product that was used to prepare menu items. At any one of these steps pilferage can occur. The signing-out procedure will eliminate pilferage. Products such as dry goods or cleaning supplies may be issued in a similar manner. Dry goods and cleaning supplies are so numerous it is hard to keep track of to whom they are issued. If these or other items were being stolen, the cost of each would show up in the cost projections at the end of the month.

There are several important guidelines to keep in mind and tasks to complete as you get ready to receive food.

- Train employees in proper receiving procedures. This should include how to check quality in specific foods, how to identify food that has been refrozen, and signs of insect infestation. Ideally you will assign the receiving task to one or a only a few employees. This will help keep your receiving principles consistent.

- Make sure your receiving area is equipped with sanitary carts for transporting goods.

- Plan ahead for deliveries to ensure sufficient refrigerator and freezer space.

- Schedule deliveries for off-peak hours.

- If possible, only receive one delivery at a time. You should try to inspect and store each delivery before accepting another one to avoid any confusion and possible problems.

- Make sure the employee receiving items has a copy of an order sheet to check against the invoice to ensure all products that were ordered are delivered.

- Inspect deliveries immediately so you can deal with any problems or rejected items while the driver is still on the premises.

- Put items away as quickly as possible to prevent temperature abuses.

- Mark all items for storage with the date of arrival or the "use by" date.

- Keep the receiving area well lit and clean to discourage pests.

- Remove empty containers and packing materials immediately to a separate trash area.

- Keep all flooring clean of food particles and debris.

When the delivery truck arrives, make sure it looks and smells clean and is equipped with the proper food-storage equipment. Then inspect foods immediately.

- Check expiration dates of milk, eggs and other perishable goods.

- Make sure shelf life dates have not expired.

- Make sure frozen foods are in airtight, moisture-proof wrappings.

- Reject foods that have been thawed and refrozen. Look for signs of thawing and refreezing such as large crystals, solid areas of ice or excessive ice in containers.

- Reject cans that have any of the following: swollen sides or ends, flawed seals or seams, dents, or rust. Also reject any cans with foamy or bad-smelling contents.

- Check temperature of refrigerated and frozen foods, especially eggs and dairy products, fresh meat and fish, and poultry products.

- Look for content damage and insect infestations.

- Reject dairy, bakery and other foods that are delivered in dirty flats or crates.

- Food packages must be in good condition and protect the integrity of the contents so that the food is not exposed to potential contaminants.

- Ice for use as a food or cooling medium must be made from drinking water.

Checking Product Temperatures upon Delivery

Temperature control is a very important factor in keep foods safe. Restaurant owners, managers and employees should ensure that the food they receive is at the proper temperature. Deliveries should be inspected for temperature abuses upon receipt.

A food that is labeled frozen and shipped frozen should be received frozen.

Most potentially hazardous food, except milk and shellfish, should be kept at a temperature of 5°C (41°F) or below when received. Specific laws apply to the temperature of milk and shellfish.

Use the following guidelines when checking the temperatures of received foods:

- To check the temperature of meat, poultry and fish, insert the thermometer's probe into the thickest part of the product. You can also check the surface temperature if you desire.

- Check the temperature of vacuum-packed items by placing a thermometer between the packages.

- Check the temperature of liquids or packaged foods by opening a container and inserting the thermometer probe into the food to the proper depth to immerse the thermometer sensor.

- To check the thermometer of bulk foods, fold the bag around the thermometer.

- Check the temperature of live shellfish by inserting the thermometer probe into the middle of the case of shellfish and getting an ambient temperature reading.

- When checking eggs, be sure to check the ambient temperature of the delivery truck.

ACCEPTABLE RECEIVING TEMPERATURES FOR SEAFOOD, MEAT, POULTRY AND EGGS	
Fresh fish	41°F or lower
Fresh shellfish (clams, mussels, oysters, scallops)	Live: on ice at 45°F or lower Shucked: with an internal temperature of 45°F or lower
Fresh crustaceans (shrimp, lobster, crab)	Live: must be alive when shipped Processed: at an internal temperature of 41°F or lower
Fresh meat	At an internal temperature of 41°F or lower
Fresh poultry	At an internal temperature of 41°F or lower
Fresh eggs	At an air temperature of 45°F or lower

GUIDELINES FOR PURCHASING SPECIFIC FOODS

Raw and partially cooked seafood and meats. If a restaurant serves under-cooked whole-muscle, intact beef and does not inform the consumer, the restaurant management needs to obtain this meat from a food-processing plant. Upon request of the purchaser, the plant must package the steaks and label them, to indicate that the steaks meet the definition of whole-muscle, intact beef. The plant must also provide evidence that the meat is whole-muscle, intact beef, such as written buyer specifications or invoices.

Food in a hermetically sealed container. Food used in a restaurant that comes in a hermetically sealed container, such as a jar of pickles, must be obtained from a food-processing plant that is regulated by the food regulatory agency that has jurisdiction over the plant.

Milk products. Milk and milk products must be obtained from sources that comply with Grade A standards as specified by law.

Fish. Fish used in a restaurant must be commercially and legally caught or approved for sale or service.

Molluscan shellfish, such as shrimp, that are recreationally caught may not be received for sale or service. These must be obtained from sources according to law and the requirements specified in the U.S. Department of Health and Human Services, Public Health Service, Food and Drug Administration, and National Shellfish Sanitation Program Guide for the Control of Molluscan Shellfish.

Molluscan shellfish that are received in interstate commerce must be from sources that are listed in the Interstate Certified Shellfish Shippers List.

Wild mushrooms. Mushroom species that are picked in the wild must be obtained from sources where each mushroom is individually inspected and found to be safe by an approved mushroom identification expert.

There are some exceptions to this rule, however. Cultivated wild mushroom species that are grown, harvested and processed in an operation that is regulated by the food regulatory agency or wild mushroom species in packaged form and products of a processing plant that is regulated by the food regulatory agency do not have to be inspected.

Game animals. Game animals sold by a restaurant must be commercially raised for food. They also must be raised, slaughtered and processed under a voluntary inspection program that is conducted by the agency that has animal health jurisdiction or under a routine inspection program conducted by a regulatory agency other than the agency that has animal health jurisdiction. In addition, these animals must be raised, slaughtered and processed according to:

- Law governing meat and poultry.

- Requirements developed by the agency that has animal health jurisdiction and the agency that conducts the inspection program for factors such as the need for antemortem and postmortem examination by an approved veterinarian.

The USDA also has a voluntary inspection program for game animals such as exotic animals (reindeer, elk, deer, antelope, water buffalo or bison) that are inspected and approved in accordance with the Voluntary Exotic Animal Program or rabbits that are inspected and certified in accordance with the Rabbit Inspection Program.

Wild game animals that are live-caught must go through a routine inspection program conducted by a regulatory agency such as the agency that has animal health jurisdiction. They must be slaughtered and processed according to laws governing other meat and poultry as determined by the agency that has animal health jurisdiction and the agency that conducts the inspection program. In addition, the agency that has animal health jurisdiction and the agency that conducts the inspection program has the right to determine the need for antemortem and postmortem examination by an approved veterinarian.

If the wild game is field-dressed, the animal inspection agency ensures the animals receive a postmortem examination by an approved veterinarian and that they are field-dressed and transported according to requirements specified by the agency that has animal health jurisdiction and the agency that conducts the inspection program.

Keep in mind, a game animal may not be sold if it is a species that is listed on the Endangered and Threatened Wildlife and Plants list.

Additives. According to the Food Code, food cannot contain unapproved food additives or additives that exceed the amounts determined to be safe by the FDA (**http://vm.cfsan.fda.gov/~lrd/FCF17080.html**).

Guidelines for Receiving Specific Foods

All products should be inspected upon receipt to your establishment. Here are some specific guidelines for specific foods that will come in handy.

Eggs. Eggs should be purchased from approved, government-inspected suppliers. The USDA stamp on egg cartons indicates that the supplier has been inspected.

Make sure your supplier delivers your eggs in a refrigerated truck that's air temperature is 45°F or lower. Eggshells should be clean, dry and free of cracks, and the eggs should have no odor.

Liquid, frozen or dehydrated eggs must be pasteurized and bear the USDA inspection mark. When delivered they should be frozen or refrigerated. Be sure to make certain there is no indication of thawing and refreezing and the use-by dates have not expired.

Dairy products. Make sure to only purchase pasteurized dairy products. All milk products should also be labeled Grade A, indicating they meet the quality standards set by the USDA.

Frozen milk products, such as ice cream and cheeses, must be pasteurized as well, unless the cheese is cured. Cheese shall be obtained pasteurized unless alternative procedures to pasteurization are used for curing certain cheese varieties (**www.access.gpo.gov/nara/cfr/waisidx_03/21cfr133_03.html**). Always check cheese for proper temperatures and any signs of mold.

Milk and dairy products should be delivered at temperatures of 41°F or lower.

Any milk product that tastes or smells sour or bitter should be rejected. Make sure to check expiration dates on all dairy products.

When receiving butter, be sure the butter does not have any absorbed odors or has not turned rancid. Butter should have a uniform color and firm texture; check for signs of mold or foreign materials and be sure to check the packaging for cleanliness and wholeness.

Fish and shellfish. Fish and shellfish are very sensitive to temperature abuses and should be checked carefully when received.

Fresh fish should be packed in self-draining crushed ice. It should be received at 41°F or below. Fresh fish that is of good quality and in good condition will have the following characteristics:

- Firm flesh

- Clear eyes

- Pleasant smell

- Red, moist gills

- Bright skin

Fresh fish should not have a strong, fishy odor.

Frozen fish should be received frozen. Check for signs of thawing and refreezing. If fish has been refrozen it will often turn brown and have an off color and bad odor. Large amounts of ice or liquid at the bottom of the packaging may also indicate fish has been refrozen.

If the restaurant offers raw fish, such as for sushi, these products must be obtained from a supplier that freezes the fish on the premises. The fish should be frozen and stored at a temperature of -20°C (-4°F) or below for 168 hours (7 days) in a freezer or frozen at -35°C (-31°F) or below until solid and stored at -35°C (-31°F) for 15 hours. Tuna (Yellow Fin, Southern Blue Fin, Northern Blue Fin, and Big Eye), however, may be served or sold raw, raw-marinated or partially cooked without freezing according to the specifications above.

Shellfish includes clams, oysters and mussels. These can be shipped live, frozen, in the shell or shucked. Shellfish should only be obtained from suppliers on the list of the National Shellfish Sanitation Program Guide for the Control of Molluscan Shellfish or from those listed on the Interstate Certified Shellfish Shippers List (see the FDA's Web site at **http://vm.cfscan.fda.gov/seafood1.html**).

When received by a food service establishment, shell stock must be reasonably free of mud, dead shellfish, and shellfish with broken shells. Dead shellfish or shell stock with badly broken shells shall be discarded.

Raw shucked shellfish must be obtained in nonreturnable packages which carry a legible label that identifies:

- The name, address and certification number of the shucker-packer or repacker.

- The "sell by" date for packages of less than 1.87 L (one-half gallon) or the date shucked for packages with a capacity of 1.87 L or more.

A package of raw shucked shellfish that does not bear a label or has a label which does not contain all the information specified above will be subject to a hold order or seizure and destruction.

Live shellfish must be received on ice or at an ambient temperature of 45°F or less. When shipped live, shellfish must be delivered in nonreturnable containers and have shell stock identification tags.

The containers must bear legible source identification tags or labels that are affixed by the harvester and each dealer that depurates, ships or reships the shell stock.

The following information has to be on the harvester's tag or label in the following order:

1. The harvester's identification number that is assigned by the shellfish control authority.

2. The date of harvesting.

3. The most precise identification of the harvest location including the abbreviation of the name of the state or country in which the shellfish are harvested.

4. The type and quantity of shellfish.

5. The following statement in bold, capitalized type: "**THIS TAG IS REQUIRED TO BE ATTACHED UNTIL CONTAINER IS EMPTY OR RETAGGED AND THEREAFTER KEPT ON FILE FOR 90 DAYS**."

Each dealer's tag or label must contain the following information in the following order:

1. The dealer's name and address and the certification number assigned by the shellfish control authority.

2. The original shipper's certification number including the abbreviation of the name of the state or country in which the shellfish are harvested.

3. The same information as specified for a harvester's tag.

4. The following statement in bold, capitalized type: "**THIS TAG IS REQUIRED TO BE ATTACHED UNTIL CONTAINER IS EMPTY AND THEREAFTER KEPT ON FILE FOR 90 DAYS.**"

If a place is provided on the harvester's tag or label for a dealer's name, address and certification number, the dealer's information shall be listed first.

If the harvester's tag or label is designed to accommodate each dealer's identification, individual dealer tags or labels need not be provided.

Shell stock tags must remain attached to the container in which the shell stock are received until the container is empty. The identity of the source of shell stock must be maintained by retaining shell stock tags or labels for 90 calendar days from the date the container is emptied by:

1. Using a recordkeeping system that keeps the tags or labels in chronological order correlated to the date when, or dates during which, the shell stock are sold or served.

2. If shell stock are removed from their tagged or labeled container:

   a. Preserving source identification with a recordkeeping system.

   b. Ensuring that shell stock from one tagged or labeled container are not commingled with shell stock from another container before being ordered by the consumer.

Crustacea. Crustacea includes shrimp, lobster and crab. Fresh lobsters or crabs should show signs of movement, have a hard and heavy shell and react when their eyes are pinched. A good-quality fresh lobster will also curl its tail underneath when it is turned on its back.

Live lobsters and crabs should be received live. Dead ones should be discarded or returned to the vendor for credit.

All processed crustacean should have an internal temperature of 41°F.

Meats and poultry. Meat and poultry should be inspected by the USDA or a state inspection program. While grading meat, poultry and egg products is a voluntary service, inspection of these products is mandatory. You should see a USDA inspection stamp on these products. They will not be on every cut of meat, but should be on the packaging.

During the meat inspection process, inspectors check the carcass for any signs of illness and inspect processing plants for sanitation standards.

When receiving meat, look at the following:

- Beef should be bright red in color. Aged beef may be darker, but any meat that is brown or green should be rejected. Beef tends to spoil on the surface first, so if a cut is slimy or has an "off" odor, this should be rejected as well.

- Vacuum-packed, refrigerated meat has a purplish appearance. Reject the product if the seal has been broken or the package torn.

- Lamb should be light red in color. Do not accept a product that is brown or whitish on the surface.

- Pork should be light pink with firm, white fat. Do not accept any meat that has an excessively dark color, a sour odor or soft, rancid fat.

Poultry should be shipped on self-draining, crushed ice at a temperature of 41°F or lower.

Do not accept poultry that is purplish or green in color, has an "off" odor, has stickiness under the wing and around the joints, or has dark wing tips.

Fresh produce. Fresh produce has no specific shipping temperature mandates, except cut melons because cut melon is a potentially hazardous food. These should be shipped at 41°F or lower. To maintain quality in fresh-cut product, it is best shipped at temperatures between 33° and 41°F.

Fresh fruit and vegetables are very perishable, so they should be put into storage quickly when these items are received. In addition, do not wash produce, especially mushrooms and berries, before storing because this will cause it to spoil quicker.

Also be careful when handling produce; rough handling and bruising will cause produce to spoil faster as well. If produce is spoiled, you may see the following characteristics:

- Mold

- Blemishes

- Mushiness

- Wilting

- Discoloration

- Cuts

- Green on potato skins

- Unpleasant odor

When receiving produce, check it for signs of mishandling and check the cartons for signs of insects.

Frozen and refrigerated processed foods. Frozen and refrigerated processed foods include items such as precut meats, frozen or refrigerated entrées, and cut fruit and vegetables. All of these items help restaurant owners save time in the food preparation area and they can often save money in labor costs. While these foods are usually fully cooked or ready-to-eat, they can cause food-borne illness, and they must be handled properly.

- Make sure to check the packages of these items for rips, tears, holes, etc.

- These products should be delivered at temperatures of 41°F or lower.

- All frozen items should be delivered frozen (ice cream should be delivered at temperatures between 6° and 10°F).

- Check for signs of thawing and refreezing in frozen items.

Vacuum-packed, MAP and sous vide food. Vacuum-packed food is processed by removing air from the package the food product is in. Bacon, for example, is vacuum-packed. Foods that are packaged as MAP foods—Modified Atmosphere

Packaging—also have the air removed from the package, but the air is replaced with a gas such as carbon dioxide or nitrogen. These gases help extend a product's shelf life. Sous vide is French for "under vacuum." These foods are vacuum-packed in individual pouches, partially or fully cooked, and then chilled.

By reducing the oxygen in packages, processors help eliminate some of the chance of bacteria growing in the products, because one of the requirements for bacterial growth is oxygen. However, some bacteria can grow without oxygen, such a those that produce the botulism toxin. Because of this danger, the FDA does not let food establishments package by the MAP method on premises except under certain conditions. Operators must have a HACCP plan in place and limit the foods that are being packaged this way to those that cannot support the growth of Clostridium botulinum, the agent responsible for the botulism toxin.

When receiving goods that have been processed in this way make sure to:

- Ask the supplier if they have a HACCP plan in place.

- Ensure foods are delivered at 41°F or below.

- Frozen products are received frozen.

- Packages are whole without tears, rips or leaks.

- Products are not slimy and do not have bubbles.

- The color of the product does not look off.

- The products do not have expiration dates that have passed.

Dry and canned foods. Most dry and canned goods are fairly safe and have a long shelf life. However, canned products can provide an environment that allows for the growth of microorganisms that cause botulism, and dry goods can be susceptible to microorganisms that cause food-borne illness as well.

When receiving dry goods:

- Make sure dry goods are dry. Check products for dampness, moisture or signs of prior moisture such as a stained bag or container.

- Look for signs of insects in packaging including insect eggs, chewed packaging and insect droppings.

- Check for mold or other signs of spoilage.

When receiving canned goods:

- Check the can for swollen ends. This might indicate the presence of chemicals or the growth of bacteria. If one side of a can bugles when the other side is pressed on, get rid of it—the can has not been properly processed to eliminate food-borne microorganisms.

- Look for leaks and flawed seals.

- Check for rust. If a can is rusty, the contents might be too old. Furthermore, the rust might have eaten holes in the can which could lead to contamination.

- Check for dents. Dents may mean the can's seams are broken.

- Do not accept cans without labels.

- Spot check the contents of canned goods being received. If the contents have an off color or odor, reject them. In addition, reject cans that have contents that are foamy or milky colored.

- **Never taste the contents of a suspect can.** If the food is tainted with botulism, you can die simply by tasting and spitting out the tainted food.

Potentially hazardous hot food. Potentially hazardous foods that are cooked before delivery and delivered hot need to be received at a temperature of 60°C (140°F) or above. It should be delivered in containers that can maintain this temperature.

Juice. Pre-packaged juice shall be pasteurized or otherwise treated and obtained from a processor with a HACCP system.

STORING

While most food establishments use a variety of storage methods that require different safety guidelines, there are some general guidelines to follow for food storage.

Managers and employees must store food in a clean, dry location where it is not exposed to splashes, dust or other contamination. It must be stored at least 15 cm (6 in) above the floor as well.

However, food that is in packages and working containers may be stored less than 15 cm (6 in) above the floor on case lot handling equipment.

In addition, pressurized beverage containers, cased food in waterproof containers such as bottles or cans, and milk containers in plastic crates may be stored on a floor that is clean and not exposed to floor moisture.

Food may not be stored in the following locations:

- Locker rooms.

- Restrooms.

- Dressing rooms.

- Garbage rooms.

- Mechanical rooms.

- Under sewer lines that are not shielded to intercept potential drips.

- Under leaking water lines, including leaking automatic fire sprinkler heads or under lines on which water has condensed.

- Under open stairwells.

- Under other sources of contamination.

Potentially Hazardous Food in Vending Machines

If your establishment has vending machines, managers/owners must ensure that potentially hazardous food dispensed through a vending machine is in the package in which it was placed at the establishment or the food-processing plant at which it was prepared.

Label all food. All potentially hazardous food and ready-to-eat food must be labeled if they are going to be held for more than 24 hours. The label should contain the following information: date the food was prepared and date it should be consumed by or discarded. If you are preparing a lasagna, for example, and the ingredients are prepared in several steps on different days, the label must have the date the first ingredient was cooked rather than the date the entire item was assemble. If the ground beef was cooked on April 27 and the lasagna was fully assembled and stored on April 29, the label must carry April 27 as the date.

FIFO

All food items need to be rotated to ensure that the oldest items in inventory are used first. The "first in, first out" (FIFO) method of rotation is used to ensure that all food products are properly rotated in storage.

The FIFO method uses these principles:

1. New items go to the back and on the bottom.

2. Older items move to the front and to the left.

3. In any part of the restaurant, the first item used should always be the oldest.

4. Date and mark everything. (For resources visit **www.dissolveaway.com** or call 1-800-847-0101.)

Here are some addition storage guidelines:

Discard food past the expiration date. Don't let food lay around that has passed its expiration date. Potentially hazardous food that has been prepared in-house can be stored for a maximum of seven days at 41°F or lower.

Establish a purchasing schedule based on inventory counts. The first step in computing what item and how much of it to order is to determine the inventory level, or the amount needed on hand at all times. This is a simple procedure, and it requires that the order sheets are prepared as described in this chapter. To determine the amount you need to order, you must first know the amount you have in inventory. Walk through the storage areas and mark in the "On Hand" column the amounts that are there. To determine the "Build To" amount, you will need to know when regularly scheduled deliveries arrive for that item and the amount used in the period between deliveries. Add on about 25 percent to the average amount used; this will cover unexpected usage, a late delivery or a backorder at the vendor. The amount you need to order is the difference between the "Build To" amount and the amount "On Hand." Experience and food demand will reveal the amount an average order should contain. By purchasing too little, the restaurant may run out of supplies before the next delivery. Ordering too much will result in tying up money, putting a drain on the restaurant's cash flow. Buying items in large amounts can save money, but you must consider the cash-flow costs.

A buying schedule should be set up and adhered to. This would consist of a calendar showing:

- Which day's orders need to be placed.

- When deliveries will be arriving.

- When items will be arriving from which company.

- Phone numbers of sales representatives to contact for each company.

- The price the sales representative quoted.

Post the buying schedule on the office wall. When a delivery doesn't arrive as scheduled, the buyer should place a phone call to the salesperson or company immediately. Don't wait until the end of the day when offices are closed.

A **Want Sheet** may be placed on a clipboard in the kitchen. This sheet is made

available for employees to write in any items they may need to do their jobs more efficiently. This is a very effective form of communication; employees should be encouraged to use it. The buyer should consult this sheet every day. A request might be as simple as a commercial-grade carrot peeler. If, for example, the last one broke, and the preparation staff has been using the back of a knife instead, the small investment could save you from an increase in labor and food costs.

Transfer food between containers properly. When you take a food out of its original con-

---

tainer, make sure you store it in a clean and sanitized container with a lid. The new container should be labeled with the contents and its original use-by or expiration date. Make sure you never use empty chemical containers to store food.

Keep potentially hazardous food out of the temperature danger zone. Make sure you store foods as soon as they are inspected after they have been delivered. Also, take only as much food out as you need to prepare at one time. One tool you can use to help take out only as much food as you need is the Minimum Amount Needed Form.

The purpose of the **Minimum Amount Needed Form** is to guide the preparation cook in determining the amount of food that will need to be prepared for each day. (An example of the Minimum Amount Needed Form can be found in the Appendix.) The minimum amount needed must be large enough that the restaurant will not run out of any food during the next shift. However, too much prepared food will quickly lose its freshness and may spoil altogether.

To compute the minimum amount needed of each item for each particular day, consult the **Food Itemization Form** (see Appendix). This form will list the actual number of each menu item sold for every day of the past month. It will also indicate the percentage sold of that item in relation to the rest of the menu items for the month and for each day. Examine the last two months' product mixture figures. Based on this information, you should get a relatively accurate depiction of the amount of each item sold on each particular day of the week. Based on the average amount sold each day and the percentage sold in relation to the total menu, you will be able to project the minimum amount needed for the following months.

> **EXAMPLE:** According to the Food Itemization Form, last month the restaurant sold between 20 and 25 shrimp dinners each Saturday night. The restaurant served between 200 and 300 dinners for each of these nights, so about 10 percent of the menu selections sold were shrimp dinners. To project next month's minimum amount needed for an average Saturday evening, estimate the average number of dinners you expect to serve.
>
> Let's assume 250 dinners will be sold on an average Saturday evening. Multiply this figure (250) by the average percentage of the menu sold (10%, or .10); the answer (25) would be the approximate number of shrimp dinners you would sell on an average Saturday for the next month. This is, of course,

is only an educated guess; add 30 percent to the figure you projected to cover a busy night or an unusually high demand for that particular item. In the example, this extra 30 percent is 8 more dinners: 33 shrimp dinners are the minimum amount needed for Saturday night. Holidays and seasonal business changes need to be considered when setting minimum amounts.

The **Daily Yield Form** may also be helpful in determining amounts needed for a shift. Daily yields represent the actual usage of a product from its raw purchased form to the prepared menu item. The yield percentage is a measure of how efficiently this was accomplished, or how effectively a preparation cook eliminated waste. The higher the yield percentage, the more usable material was obtained from that product.

All meat, seafood and poultry products must have a yield percentage computed for each entrée every day. Yields are extremely important when determining menu prices. They are also a very useful tool in controlling food cost. Daily yields should be computed by the kitchen director.

The following table shows the temperature ranges for perishable items:

Temperature Ranges for Perishable Items	
All frozen items	-10°–0°F
Fresh meat and poultry	31°–35°F
Produce	33°–38°F
Fresh seafood	33°–38°F
Dairy products	33°–38°F
Beer	40°–60°F
Wine (Chablis, rosé)	45°–55°F
Wine (most reds)	55°–65°F

Check the temperatures of stored food and storage areas. Temperatures should be checked at the beginning of each shift.

Store food in designated storage areas. Do not store food in areas near chemicals or cleaning supplies, in restrooms, locker rooms, janitor closets, furnace rooms or under pipes.

KEEP STORAGE AREAS CLEAN AND DRY

A cabinet used to store food or cleaned and sanitized equipment, utensils, laundered linens, and single-service items cannot be located:

- In locker rooms.

- In restrooms.

- In garbage rooms.

- In mechanical rooms.

- Under sewer lines that are not shielded to intercept potential drips.

- Under leaking water lines including leaking automatic fire sprinkler heads or under lines on which water has condensed.

- Under open stairwells.

- Under other sources of contamination.

However, a cabinet used for linens or single-use items can be stored in a locker room. If an establishment does have a clothes washer or dryer, it must be located so that the washer or dryer is protected from contamination and only where there is no exposed food; clean equipment, utensils and linens; and unwrapped single-service items.

TYPES OF STORAGE

In general, there are four possible ways to store food:

1. In dry storage, for longer holding of less perishable items.

2. In refrigeration, for short-term storage of perishable items.

3. In specially designed deep-chilling units for short periods.

4. In a freezer, for longer-term storage of perishable foods.

Each type of storage has its own sanitation and safety requirements.

Dry Storage

There are many items that can be safely held in a sanitary storeroom. These include canned goods, baking supplies (such as salt and sugar), grain products (such as rice and cereals) and other dry items. In addition, some fruits (such as bananas, avocados and pears) ripen best at room temperature. Some vegetables, such as onions, potatoes and tomatoes, also store best in dry storage. A dry-storage room should be clean and orderly, with good ventilation to control temperature and humidity and retard the growth of bacteria and mold.

Keep in mind the following:

- For maximum shelf life, dry foods should be held at 50°F, but 60°–70°F is adequate for most products.

- Use a wall thermometer to check the temperature of your dry-storage facility regularly.

- To ensure freshness, store opened items in tightly covered containers. Use the FIFO rotation method, dating packages and placing incoming supplies in the back so that older supplies will be used first.

- To avoid pest infestation and cross-contamination, clean up all spills immediately and do not store trash or garbage cans in food storage areas.

- Do not place any items — including paper products — on the floor. Make sure the bottom shelf of the dry-storage room is at least 6 inches above the ground.

- To avoid chemical contamination, never use or store cleaning materials or other chemicals where they might contaminate foods. Store them, labeled, in their own section in the storeroom away from all food supplies.

Refrigerated Storage

Keep fresh meat, poultry, seafood, dairy products, most fresh fruit and vegetables and hot leftovers in the refrigerator at internal temperatures of below 40°F. Although no food can last forever, refrigeration increases the shelf life of most products. Most importantly, because refrigeration slows bacterial growth, the colder a food is, the safer it is.

Your refrigeration unit should contain open, slotted shelving to allow cold air to circulate around food. Do not line shelves with foil or paper. Also, do not overload the refrigerator, and be sure to leave space between items to further improve air circulation.

It is very important to store and label refrigerated foods properly. See www.dissolveaway.com for more details or the "HACCP Products" section at the back of this book.

- All refrigerated foods should be dated and properly sealed.

- Use clean, nonabsorbent, covered containers that are approved for food storage.

- Store dairy products separately from foods with strong odors such as onions, cabbage and seafood.

- To avoid cross-contamination, store raw or uncooked food away from and below prepared or ready-to-eat food.

- Never allow fluids from raw poultry, fish or meat to come into contact with other foods.

- Keeping perishable items at the proper temperature is a key factor in preventing food-borne illness. Check the temperature of your refrigeration unit regularly to make sure it stays below 40°F. Keep in mind that opening and closing the refrigerator door too often can affect temperature.

Many commercial refrigerators are equipped with externally mounted or built-in thermometers. These are convenient when they work, but it is important to have a backup. It's a good idea to have several thermometers in different parts of the refrigerator to ensure consistent temperature and accuracy of instruments. Record the temperature of each refrigerator on a chart, preferably once a day.

Deep Chilling

Deep or super chilling—that is, storing foods at temperatures between 26°F and 32°F—has been found to decrease bacterial growth. This method can be used to increase the shelf life of fresh foods, such as poultry, meat, seafood and other protein items, without compromising their quality by freezing. You can deep-chill foods in specially designed units or in a refrigerator set to deep-chilling temperature.

Frozen Storage

Frozen meats, poultry, seafood, fruits and vegetables, and some dairy products, such as ice cream, should be stored in a freezer at 0°F to keep them fresh and safe for an extended period of time.

As a rule, you should use your freezer primarily to store foods that are frozen when you receive them. Freezing refrigerated foods can damage the quality of perishable items. It's important to store frozen foods immediately. It's also important to remember that storing foods in the freezer for too long increases the likelihood of contamination and spoilage.

Like your refrigeration unit, the freezer should allow cold air to circulate around foods easily. Be sure to:

- Store frozen foods in moisture-proof material or containers to minimize loss of flavor, as well as discoloration, dehydration and odor absorption.

- Monitor temperature regularly, using several thermometers to ensure accuracy and consistent temperatures. Record the temperature of each freezer on a chart.

Remember that frequently opening and closing the freezer's door can raise the temperature, as can placing warm foods in the freezer. To minimize heat gain, open freezer doors only when necessary and remove as many items at one time as possible. You can also use a freezer "cold curtain" to help guard against heat gain.

Storing Specific Foods

Eggs. Raw shell eggs should be received and stored in refrigerated equipment that maintains an ambient air temperature of 7°C (45°F) or less.

You should also use the FIFO method of stock rotation. Plan to use all eggs within four to five weeks of the packing date.

Make sure shell eggs are kept in cold storage as long as possible; only take out as many eggs as you need at one time.

Do not combine cracked eggs in a bowl unless you plan to use them right away or hold them at 41°F or below.

Dried egg products can be stored in a cool, dry storeroom until they are reconstituted. At that point they should be stored in the refrigerator at 41°F or lower.

Dairy products. Dairy products should be stored at 41°F or lower. Frozen dairy products, like ice cream, should be stored between 6° and 10°F.

Also make sure to use the FIFO rotation method and to discard any product past the manufacturer's expiration date.

Fish and shellfish. Make sure you store fresh fish at 41°F or lower. Keep fillets in the original packaging. Whole fish can be stored over self-draining crushed ice, but you should change the ice and sanitize the container regularly.

Fish that is served raw, raw-marinated or partially cooked must be frozen at the processor. The fish should be frozen and stored at a temperature of -20°C (-4°F) or below for 168 hours (7 days) in a freezer or frozen at -35°C (-31°F) or below until solid and stored at -35°C (-31°F) for 15 hours. Tuna (Yellow Fin, Southern Blue Fin, Northern Blue Fin, and Big Eye), however, may be served or sold raw, raw-marinated or partially cooked without freezing according to the specifications above.

The manager/owner must record the freezing temperature and time and retain these records for 90 calendar days beyond the time of service or sale of the fish. (If the fish was frozen by a supplier, a written agreement or statement from the supplier stipulating that the fish supplied are frozen to a temperature and for the time specified may substitute for the establishment's records.)

In most cases, shellfish may not be removed from the container in which they are received other than immediately before sale or preparation for service.

For display purposes, however, shell stock can be removed from the container in which they are received, displayed on drained ice or held in a display container. A quantity specified by a customer can be removed from the display and provided to the customer if the source of the shell stock on display is correctly identified and recorded and the shell stock are protected from contamination.

Shucked shellfish may be removed from the container in which they were received and held in a display container for dispensing individual servings if the labeling information for the shellfish on display is retained and correlated to the date when, or dates during which, the shellfish are sold or served and the shellfish are protected from contamination.

Meat. Meat should be stored as soon as you have inspected it after delivery. It should be stored in its own compartment or in the coldest part of the refrigeration unit and held at 41°F or lower.

You should store frozen meat so that it stays frozen. Wrap all meats that are frozen airtight to prevent freezer burn.

Poultry. Raw poultry should be stored at an internal temperature of 41°F.
If it is removed from its original packaging be sure to place it an airtight wrap or container.

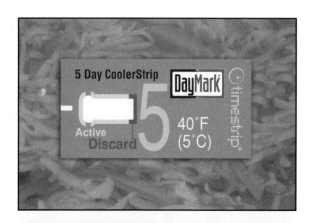

Pictured on cheese, salmon and steak, TimeStrip labels are specially designed to monitor food freshness. They are a disposable "visual alarm clock" where the color advances to show expiration. See www.dissolveaway .com for more details or the "HACCP Products" section at the back of this book.

You should store frozen poultry so that it stays frozen. Wrap all poultry that are frozen airtight to prevent freezer burn. Ice-packed poultry can be stored in the original container but the containers must be self-draining and the ice should be changed regularly.

Fresh produce. Many whole raw fruits should be stored at 41°F or lower, but not all will be able to withstand this temperature.

- Any produce—whole or cut—that is delivered packed in ice can be stored the way it arrives, but the containers must be self-draining and the ice should be changed regularly.

- Keep the relative humidity for stored fruits and vegetables at 85 to 95 percent.

- While most fruits do well in the refrigerator, the following should be allowed to ripen at room temperature:

  – Avocados

  – Bananas

  – Pears

  – Tomatoes

- Do not wash produce before storing because this could promote mold growth.

- Store citrus fruit and root vegetables in a cool dry storeroom at temperatures between 60° and 70°F.

Vacuum-packed, MAP and sous vide foods. These foods should always be stored at temperatures recommended by the manufacturer, usually this is below 41°F. If vacuum-packed, MAP or sous vide foods are frozen, they should be stored at temperatures that keep them frozen.

Canned goods and dry goods. Canned goods should be stored at temperatures between 50° and 70°F. Higher temperatures can shorten shelf life. Nonacidic foods last longer than acidic foods. In addition, acidic foods may develop pinholes in the metal over time.

Make sure to keep storerooms dry because moisture can cause rust on cans. Also, wipe cans with a sanitized towel before opening to help prevent dirt from falling into the can as you open it.

Grain products and flour and sugars should be stored in airtight containers. Before using the ingredients, be sure to check the containers for signs of insects or rodents.

Make sure to store dry goods in a nonhumid environment; humidity can make these items become moldy.

Preparing, holding, serving and reheating are the steps that pose the greatest threat of cross-contamination.

5

FOLLOWING THE FLOW OF FOOD: PREPARING, HOLDING, SERVING AND REHEATING

The next four steps in the flow of food all deal with preparation and cooked foods. These steps are crucial and pose the greatest threat of cross-contamination.

PREPARING

The next step in the flow of food is preparation. This step includes the cooking, cooling and reheating of food. Cross-contamination and temperature risks are the greatest at this step of the process.

Here are some general guidelines to follow when preparing foods:

- Use clean, sanitized surfaces, equipment and utensils.

- Be sure to properly wash your hands.

- Only take out as much product as you can use at one time.

- Never let surfaces, equipment or utensils that have been in contact with raw meat come into contact with raw vegetables unless the items have been cleaned and sanitized first.

- When preparing fruits and vegetables, be sure to wash them first so you do not introduce dirt from the skin into the part of the product that will be eaten.

Cross-Contamination

Food shall be protected from cross-contamination by:

1. Separating raw animal foods during storage, preparation, holding and display from raw ready-to-eat food including other raw animal food, fish for sushi, shellfish, vegetables and cooked ready-to-eat food.

2. Except when combined as ingredients, separate types of raw animal foods from each other such as beef, fish, lamb, pork and poultry during storage, preparation, holding and display by using separate equipment for each food type. Arrange each type of food in equipment so that cross-contamination is prevented and prepare each food type at different times or in separate areas.

3. Properly cleaning and sanitizing equipment and utensils (see next chapter for proper cleaning and sanitizing procedures).

4. Store food in packages, covered containers or wrappings. This does not apply to whole, uncut, raw fruits and vegetables; nuts in the shell; primal cuts or sides of raw meat; slab bacon that are hung on clean, sanitized hooks or placed on clean, sanitized racks; whole, uncut, processed meats such as country hams; smoked or cured sausages that are placed on clean, sanitized racks; food being cooled; and shell stock.

5. Cleaning hermetically sealed containers of visible soil before opening.

6. Protecting food containers that are received packaged together in a case or overwrap from cuts when the case or overwrap is opened.

7. Storing damaged, spoiled or recalled food.

8. Separating fruits and vegetables before they are washed.

Food Storage Containers

Working containers holding food ingredients that are removed from their original packages, such as cooking oils, flour, herbs, potato flakes, salt, spices and sugar, must be identified with the common name of the food. If the food can be readily and unmistakably recognized, such as dry pasta, the staff does not need to label these containers.

Pasteurized Eggs

Pasteurized eggs or egg products shall be substituted for raw shell eggs when preparing foods such as Caesar salad, hollandaise or Béarnaise sauce, mayonnaise, eggnog, ice cream and egg-fortified beverages that are not cooked.

Protection from Unapproved Additives

Food must be protected from contamination with unsafe or unapproved food or color additives and/or unsafe or unapproved levels of food or color additives.

In addition, an employee may not apply sulfating agents to fresh fruits and vegetables intended for raw consumption or to a food considered to be a good source of vitamin B1. Employees also cannot serve or sell food that is treated with sulfating agents before receipt by the restaurant, except grapes.

Washing Fruits and Vegetables

Raw fruits and vegetables must be thoroughly washed in water to remove soil and other contaminants before being cut, combined with other ingredients, cooked or served in ready-to-eat form. However, whole, raw fruits and vegetables that are intended for washing by the customer before consumption need not be washed before they are sold.

Ice As an Exterior Coolant

After being used to cool the exterior surfaces of food such as melons, fish or canned beverages, ice may not be used as food.

Storage or Display of Food in Contact with Water or Ice

Packaged foods should not be stored in direct contact with ice or water if the food is subject to the entry of water because of the nature of its packaging, wrapping or container or its positioning in the ice or water.

Unpackaged food, except the following, may not be stored in direct contact with undrained ice:

- Whole, raw fruits or vegetables.

- Cut, raw vegetables such as celery or carrot sticks or cut potatoes.

- Tofu.

- Raw chicken and raw fish that are received immersed in ice in shipping containers may remain in that condition while in storage awaiting preparation, display, service or sale.

PREVENTING CONTAMINATION FROM EQUIPMENT, UTENSILS AND LINENS

Food shall only contact surfaces of equipment and utensils that are cleaned and sanitized.

In-Use Utensils

During pauses in food preparation or dispensing, preparation and dispensing utensils shall be stored in one of the following manners:

- In food that is not potentially hazardous with their handles above the top of the food within containers or equipment that can be closed, such as bins of sugar, flour or cinnamon.

- On a clean portion of the food-preparation table or cooking equipment only if the in-use utensil and the food contact surface are cleaned and sanitized.

- In running water of sufficient velocity to flush particulates to the drain, if used with moist food such as ice cream or mashed potatoes.

- In a clean, protected location if the utensils, such as ice scoops, are used only with a food that is not potentially hazardous.

- In a container of water if the water is maintained at a temperature of at least 60°C (140°F) and the container is cleaned frequently.

Food Display

Except for nuts in the shell and raw whole fruits and vegetables, food on display must be protected from contamination by packaging; counter, service line or salad bar food guards; display cases; or other effective means.

Condiments

Condiments must be kept in dispensers that are designed to provide protection. Condiments at a vending machine location must be in individual packages or in dispensers that are filled at an approved location, such as the food establishment that provides food to the vending machine location, a food-processing plant that is regulated by the agency that has jurisdiction over the operation, or a properly equipped facility located on the site of the vending machine location.

Consumer Self-Service Operations

Raw, unpackaged animal food, such as beef, lamb, pork, poultry and fish, cannot be offered for self-service. However, it is appropriate to serve items for buffets or salad bars such as sushi or raw shellfish; ready-to-cook individual portions for immediate cooking and eating on the premises, such as items for a Mongolian barbecue; or raw, frozen, shell-on shrimp or lobster.

If you have a self-service operations, you must provide customers with suitable utensils or effective dispensing methods that protect the food from contamination.

Returned Food and Reservice of Food

Food that is unused or returned by the customer, such as bread slices or butter pats, may not be offered to other customers.

Items that are protected from contamination such as a narrow-neck bottle containing catsup, steak sauce, wine, packaged crackers, salt, or pepper in an unopened original package can be reused.

Do not reuse bread from a customer's bread basket.

Raw Animal Foods

Raw animal foods such as eggs, fish, meat and poultry must be cooked to heat all parts of the food to the appropriate, safe temperature and for a time that complies with one of the following methods:

63°C (145°F) or above for 15 seconds for:

- Raw shell eggs that are broken and prepared to order.

- Fish, meat and pork, as well as commercially raised game animals.

74°C (165°F) or above for 15 seconds for:

- Poultry, wild game, stuffed fish, stuffed meat, stuffed pasta, stuffed poultry or stuffing containing fish, meat or poultry.

- Whole beef roasts, corned beef roasts, pork roasts and cured pork roasts such as ham shall be cooked:

MINIMUM	
Temperature°C (°F)	Time
63°C (145°F)	3 minutes
66°C (150°F)	1 minute
70°C (158°F)	< 1 second (instantaneous)

For roasts, cooks should preheat the oven to the temperature specified for the roast's weight in the following chart and hold at that temperature:

Oven Type	Oven Temperature Based on Roast Weight	
	Less than 4.5 kg (10 lb)	4.5 kg (10 lb) or more
Still Dry	177°C (350°F) or more	121°C (250°F) or more
Still Dry	163°C (325°F) or more	121°C (250°F) or more
Still Dry	121°C (250°F) or less	121°C (250°F) or less
Relative humidity greater than 90% for at least 1 hour as measured in the cooking chamber or exit of the oven; or in a moisture-impermeable bag that provides 100% humidity.		

As specified in the following chart, heat all parts of the food to a temperature and for the holding time that corresponds to that temperature:

Temperature °C (°F)	Time in Minutes	Temperature °C (°F)	Time in Seconds[1]
54.4°C (130°F)	112	63.9°C (147°F)	134
55.0°C (131°F)	89	65.0°C (149°F)	85
56.1°C (133°F)	56	66.1°C (151°F)	54
57.2°C (135°F)	36	67.2°C (153°F)	34
57.8°C (136°F)	28	68.3°C (155°F)	22
58.9°C (138°F)	18	69.4°C (157°F)	14
60.0°C (140°F)	12	70.0°C (158°F)	0
61.1°C (142°F)	8		
62.2°C (144°F)	5		
62.8°C (145°F)	4		
[1]Holding time may include postoven heat rise.			

A raw or undercooked whole-muscle, intact beef steak may be served if:

1. The restaurant serves a population that is not a highly susceptible population.

2. The steak is labeled to indicate that it meets the definition of a whole-muscle, intact beef.

3. The steak is cooked on both the top and bottom to a surface temperature of 63°C (145°F) or above and a cooked color change is achieved on all external surfaces.

Raw animal foods such as raw eggs, raw fish, raw-marinated fish, raw molluscan shellfish, steak tartar or a partially cooked food such as lightly cooked fish, soft cooked eggs or rare meat (other than whole-muscle beef) may be served in a ready-to-eat form if:

1. The establishment serves a population that is not a highly susceptible population.

2. The customer is informed that to ensure safety, the food should be cooked to its proper, safe cooking temperature.

3. The regulatory authority grants a variance.

   - Documents scientific data or other information showing that a lesser time and temperature regimen results in a safe food.

   - Verifies that equipment and procedures for food preparation and training of employees at establishment meet the conditions of the variance.

Microwave Cooking

Raw animal foods cooked in a microwave must be:

- Rotated or stirred throughout or midway during cooking to compensate for uneven distribution of heat.

- Covered to retain surface moisture.

- Heated to a temperature of at least 74°C (165°F) in all parts of the food.

- Allowed to stand covered for 2 minutes after cooking to obtain temperature equilibrium.

Plant Food Cooking for Hot Holding

Fruits and vegetables that are cooked for hot holding must be cooked to a temperature of 60°C (140°F).

FREEZING

As previously stated, raw, raw-marinated, partially cooked or marinated partially cooked fish other than molluscan shellfish need to be frozen and stored at a temperature of -20°C (-4°F) or below for 168 hours (7 days) in a freezer or frozen at -35°C (-31°F) or below until solid and stored at -35° C (-31°F) for 15 hours.

The exceptions to this rule are if the fish are tuna of the species Thunnus alalunga, Thunnus albacares (Yellow Fin tuna), Thunnus atlanticus, Thunnus maccoyii (Blue Fin tuna, Southern), Thunnus obesus (Big Eye tuna) or Thunnus thynnus (Blue Fin tuna, Northern). These may be served or sold in a raw, raw-marinated or partially cooked ready-to-eat form without freezing as specified above.

If raw, raw-marinated, partially cooked, or marinated partially cooked fish are served or sold in ready-to-eat form, the person in charge must record the freezing temperature and time to which the fish are subjected and retain the records for 90 calendar days beyond the time of service or sale of the fish.

If the fish are frozen by a supplier, a written agreement or statement from the supplier stipulating that the fish supplied are frozen to a temperature and for a time specified above, this agreement may substitute for those records.

Reheating and Preparing for Immediate Service

Cooked and refrigerated food prepared for immediate service, such as a roast beef sandwich au jus, may be served at any temperature.

Reheating for Hot Holding

Potentially hazardous food that is cooked, cooled and reheated for hot holding shall be reheated so that all parts of the food reach a temperature of at least 74°C (165°F) for 15 seconds.

If a food is reheated in a microwave oven for hot holding, it needs to be reheated so that all parts of the food reach a temperature of at least 74°C (165°F) and the food is rotated or stirred, covered and allowed to stand covered for 2 minutes after reheating.

Ready-to-eat food that is taken from a commercially processed, hermetically sealed container must be heated to a temperature of at least 60°C (140°F) for hot holding. Reheating for hot holding shall be done rapidly, and the time the food is in the temperature danger zone may not exceed 2 hours.

THAWING AND MARINATING

Freezing food keeps most bacteria from multiplying, but it does not kill them. Bacteria that are present when food is removed from the freezer may multiply rapidly if thawed improperly at room temperature. Thus, it is critical to thaw foods out of the temperature danger zone. Never thaw foods on a counter or in any other nonrefrigerated area!

Some foods, such as frozen vegetables and pre-formed hamburger patties and chicken nuggets, can be cooked from the frozen state. It is important to note, however, that this method depends on the size of the item. For example, cooking from frozen is not recommended for large foods like a 20-pound turkey.

There are four acceptable methods for thawing foods:

1. In refrigeration at a temperature below 40°F.

2. Under clean, drinkable running water at a temperature of 70°F or less for no more than 2 hours, or just until the product is thawed.

3. In the microwave if the food is to be cooked immediately afterward.

4. As part of the cooking process.

Thawing in the Refrigerator

This is one of the better methods for thawing foods, but it does require planning. A large roast or whole turkey or chicken may take several days to fully thaw with this method.

Submerging Food Under Running Water

Make sure you have the water running high enough to wash any loose pieces into the drain, and be sure that the thawed item doesn't drip water onto other food or food-contact surfaces.

Microwave Thawing

If you have ever thawed a piece of chicken in the microwave, you know that microwave defrosting actually starts the cooking process. Therefore, it is important that if you thaw an item in the microwave, you plan to immediately cook it. This method is best for smaller items such as boneless chicken breast or pork medallions.

Thawing As Part of the Cooking Process

Some items can actually be cooked from the frozen state, such as hamburger patties. If you use this method, always make sure to check the internal cooking temperature before serving.

Marinating

Always marinate meat, fish and poultry in the refrigerator—never at room temperature.

Never save and reuse marinade. With all methods, be careful not to cross-contaminate!

PREPARING COLD FOODS

When you are preparing cold foods, you are at one of the most hazardous points in the food-preparation process. There are two key reasons for this: First, cold food preparation usually takes place at room temperature. Second, cold food is one of the most common points of contamination and cross-contamination.

Chicken salad, tuna salad, potato salad with eggs and other protein-rich salads are common sources of food-borne illness. Sandwiches prepared in advance and held unrefrigerated are also dangerous.

Because cold foods such as these receive no further cooking, it is essential that all ingredients used in them are properly cleaned, prepared and, where applicable, cooked. It is a good idea to chill meats and other ingredients and combine them while chilled.

Here are several other important precautions to keep in mind:

- Prepare foods no further in advance than necessary.

- Prepare foods in small batches and place in cold storage immediately. This will prevent holding food too long in the temperature danger zone.

- Always hold prepared cold foods below 40°F.

- Wash fresh fruits and vegetables with plain water to remove surface pesticide residues and other impurities such as soil particles.

- Use a brush to scrub thick-skinned produce, if desired.

- **Beware of cross-contamination!**

- Keep raw products separate from ready-to-serve foods.

- Sanitize cutting boards, knives and other food-contact surfaces after each contact with a potentially hazardous food.

- Discard any leftover batter, breading or marinade after it has been used.

Preparing Foods with Egg Products

Eggs can carry Salmonella Enteritidis. When preparing foods with eggs, be sure to follow these precautions:

- Use clean bowls and whisks.

- If you are preparing a dish with eggs that receive little to no cooking (such as Caesar salad dressing, mayonnaise or hollandaise sauce), be especially careful. Monitor temperatures closely with a thermometer.

- If you are pooling eggs, cracking a number into the same container for scrambled eggs, for example, exercise caution because if one egg is contaminated, it will spread to the other eggs in the container. If using pooled eggs, cook as soon as the eggs are combined or store at 41°F or lower.

- If you are cooking for a highly susceptible population, such as people in a hospital or nursing home, federal regulations require that only pasteurized shell eggs or egg products be used.

Because many homemade batters and breading are made with eggs and other dairy products, caution should be exercised with these products as well because they are susceptible to time and temperature abuses as well as cross-contamination.

If using batters or breading made from scratch, follow these guidelines:

- Use pasteurized eggs or egg products instead of raw shell eggs.

- Prepare batter in small batches and refrigerate portions of it, only bringing out what you need to work with at one time.

- Store batter and breading at 41°F or lower.

- Cook battered and breaded food thoroughly; the coating acts as an insulator.

- When frying battered or breaded food, don't overload the fryer, and make sure to bring the oil back up to temperature between cooking batches.

- Throw out leftover, unused batter and breading.

- Only use batter or breading for one product. Do not use a bath of breading to coat chicken breasts and then use the same breading for eggplant; this will help prevent cross-contamination.

Cooking

Even when potentially hazardous foods are properly thawed, bacteria and other contaminants may still be present. Cooking foods to the proper internal temperature will kill any existing bacteria and make food safe. It's important to remember, however, that conventional cooking procedures cannot destroy bacterial spores nor deactivate their toxins.

Following are the minimal internal cooking temperatures for foods:

Minimal Internal Cooking Temperatures	
Poultry stuffing or stuffed meats	165°F for 15 seconds
Ground meats	155°F for 15 seconds
Injected meats (such as brined ham)	155°F for 15 seconds
Pork, beef, lamb, veal	145°F for 15 seconds
Steaks/chops	145°F for 15 seconds
Roasts	145°F for 4 minutes
Fish	145°F for 15 seconds
Eggs	145°F for 15 seconds
Commercially processed ready-to-eat foods (cheese sticks, chicken wings, etc.)	135°F
Items cooked in microwave	165°F; let item sit for 2 minutes after cooking

Keep in mind the following safe cooking tips:

- Stir foods cooked in deep pots frequently to ensure thorough cooking.

- When deep-frying potentially hazardous foods, make sure fryers are not overloaded, and make sure the oil temperature returns to the required level before adding the next batch. Use a hot-oil thermometer designed for this special application.

- Regulate size and thickness of each portion to make cooking time predictable and uniform.

- Allow cooking equipment to heat up between batches.

- Never interrupt the cooking process. Partially cooking poultry or meat, for example, may produce conditions that encourage bacterial growth.

- Monitor the accuracy of heating equipment with each use by using thermometers. In addition, always use a thermometer to ensure food reaches the proper temperature during cooking. Use a sanitized metal-stemmed, numerically scaled thermometer (accurate to plus or minus 2°F) or a digital thermometer. Check food temperature in several places, especially in the thickest parts, to make sure the food is thoroughly cooked. To avoid getting a false reading, be careful not to touch the pan or bone with the thermometer.

- Always cook food to the proper internal temperature.

Serving and Holding

Food that has been cooked isn't necessarily safe. In fact, many outbreaks occur because improper procedures were used following cooking. Although it may be tempting to hold food at temperatures just hot enough to serve, it is essential to keep prepared foods out of the temperature danger zone. This means, specifically:

- Always keep hot foods in hot holding equipment above 140°F.

- Always keep cold foods in a refrigeration unit or surrounded by ice below 40°F.

For safer serving and holding:

- Use hot holding equipment, such as steam tables and hot-food carts, during service but never for reheating.

- Stir foods at reasonable intervals to ensure even heating.

- Check temperatures with a food thermometer every 30 minutes.

- Sanitize the thermometer before each use, or use a digital infrared thermometer that never touches the food.

- Cover hot holding equipment to retain heat and to guard against contamination.

- Monitor the temperature of hot holding equipment with each use.

- Discard any food held in the temperature danger zone for more than 4 hours.

- Hold hot food so that the internal temperature is 135°F. Cold food needs to be held at 41°F or lower.

- Do not store food directly on ice.

- Prepare food in small batches.

To avoid contamination, never add fresh food to a serving pan containing foods that have already been out for serving.

Some Key Points

- Always wash hands with soap and warm water for at least 20 seconds before serving food.

- Use cleaned and sanitized long-handled ladles and spoons so bare hands do not touch food.

- Never touch the parts of glasses, cups, plates or tableware that will come into contact with food.

- Never touch the parts of dishes that will come into contact with the customer's mouth.

- Wear gloves if serving food by hand.

- Cover cuts or infections with bandages, and if on hands, wear gloves.

- Discard gloves whenever they touch an unsanitary surface.

- Use tongs or wear gloves to dispense rolls and bread.

- Clean and sanitize equipment and utensils thoroughly after each use.

- Use lids and sneeze guards to protect prepared food from contamination.

To avoid contamination, always wash hands, utensils and other food-contact surfaces after contact with raw meat or poultry and before contact with cooked meat or poultry. For example, do not reuse a serving pan used to hold raw chicken to serve the same chicken after it's cooked, unless the pan has been thoroughly cleaned and sanitized.

Sanitary Self-Service

Like workers, customers can also act as a source of contamination. Unlike workers, customers — especially children — are, generally, not educated about food sanitation and may do the following unsanitary things:

- Use the same plate twice.

- Touch food with their hands.

- Touch the edges of serving dishes.

- Sneeze or cough into food.

- Pick up foods, such as rolls or carrot sticks, with their fingers.

- Eat in the food line.

- Dip their fingers into foods to taste them.

- Return food items to avoid waste.

- Put their heads under sneeze guards to reach items in the back.

Be sure to observe customer behavior and remove any foods that may have been contaminated. Also, as a precautionary measure, serve sealed packages of crackers, breadsticks and condiments, and prewrap, date and label sandwiches if possible.

Linens and Napkins

Linens and napkins may not be used in contact with food unless they are used to line a container for the service of food and the linens and napkins are replaced each time the container is refilled for a new customer.

Wiping Cloths

Cloths that are in use for wiping food spills cannot be used for any other purpose.

These cloths should be:

- Dry and used for wiping food spills from tableware and carry-out containers.

- Wet and stored in a chemical sanitizer at a specific concentration (see next chapter) and used for wiping spills from food contact and nonfood-contact surfaces of equipment.

- Dry or wet cloths that are used with raw animal foods shall be kept separate from cloths used for other purposes, and wet cloths used with raw animal foods shall be kept in a separate sanitizing solution.

- Wet wiping cloths used with a freshly made sanitizing solution and dry wiping cloths shall be free of food debris and visible soil.

Gloves

Single-use gloves shall be used for only one task such as working with ready-to-eat food or with raw animal food and discarded when damaged or soiled or when interruptions occur in the operation.

Slash-resistant gloves that are used to protect the hands during operations requiring cutting shall be used in direct contact only with food that is subsequently cooked. However, slash-resistant gloves may be used with ready-to-eat food that will not be subsequently cooked if the slash-resistant gloves have a smooth, durable and nonabsorbent outer surface or if the slash-resistant gloves are covered with another smooth, durable, nonabsorbent glove or a single-use glove.

Cloth gloves may not be used in direct contact with food unless the food is cooked after this contact.

Using Clean Tableware for Second Portions and Refills

Employees cannot use tableware already used by the customer to provide second portions or refills unless the employee is refilling a drinking cup. When refilling drinking cups, the employee must ensure there is no contact between the pouring utensil and the lip-contact area of the drinking cup or container.

Preventing Contamination from the Premises

Self-service customers cannot be allowed to use soiled tableware, including single-service items, when getting additional food (second helpings) from the display and serving equipment.

Drinking cups, however, may be reused by self-service customers if they are refilling the cup in a contamination-free manner.

Refilling Returnables

Food establishments cannot refill a take-home food container returned to them with a potentially hazardous food. However, personal take-out beverage containers, such as thermally insulated bottles, nonspill coffee cups and promotional beverage glasses, may be refilled by employees or the customer if they are refilling the cup in a contamination-free manner.

COOLING

Here, as at other critical points, every move you make can mean the difference between the safe and the unsafe.

It is often necessary to prepare foods in advance or use leftover foods. Unfortunately, this can easily lead to problems unless proper precautions are taken. In fact, problems at this stage are the number-one cause of food-borne illness. The two key precautions for preventing food-borne illness at this point in the process are rapid cooling and protection from contamination.

All potentially hazardous cooked leftovers should be chilled to an internal temperature of below 40°F. Quick-chill any leftovers larger than half a gallon or 2 pounds.

Chilling It Quickly

The FDA recommends a two-stage cooling process:

1. Cool cooked food from 135°F to 70°F within 2 hours.

2. Cool food from 70°F to 41°F in an additional 4 hours.

If the food does not reach 70°F within 2 hours, you need to reheat the food to 165°F for 15 seconds within 2 hours then properly cool it.

Some jurisdictions require a one-stage process that cools food to 41°F in 4 hours or less, so be sure to check with your health department on which cooling process is used in your area.

It's important to note that this time must be reduced if food has already spent time in the temperature danger zone at any other point in the preparation and serving process.

Here are some methods to use when cooling foods:

Cool food in small batches. If you are cooling a large stockpot of soup, for example, divide the soup into smaller containers. Reduce food mass. Smaller amounts of food will chill more quickly than larger amounts, so cut large items into pieces or divide food among several containers or shallow pans. Use shallow, prechilled pans (no more than 4 inches deep).

Use shallow pans for cooling. Try to use 2-inch-deep stainless steel pans to cool food. Shallower pans will help to cool items quickly. Use stainless-steel containers when possible; stainless steel transfers heat better and cools faster than plastic.

Stir frequently. Stirring accelerates cooling and helps to ensure that cold air reaches all parts of the food.

Ice-water baths. Ice-water baths help bring food temperature down quickly. Use a sink as a container for the ice-water bath, then place the containers with the food in that. Ideally, place food in an ice-water bath or quick-chill unit (26°–32°F). These options are best for two reasons:

- First, water is a much better heat conductor than air. As a result, foods can cool much more quickly in an ice bath than they can in a refrigerator.

- Second, refrigeration units are designed to keep cold foods cold rather than to chill hot foods. They can take too long to cool foods to safe temperatures.

Blast chillers. You can use these to cool your food down before placing it in the refrigerator. If the food is already cool when placed in the refrigerator, it helps to keep from bringing the ambient temperature of the refrigeration unit up and endangering other items stored. Stir food as it cools; this helps to bring the temperature down quicker. Another option is to prechill foods in a freezer for about 30 minutes before refrigerating.

Add cool water or ice as an ingredient. If you are making a recipe that requires water as an ingredient, such as a soup or stew, you can prepare the item with less water, then add ice or cool water in the cooling process to help bring the temperature down.

Do not cover pans. Let food that is cooling stay in the refrigerator uncovered until it is completely cooled. Also, position pans so air circulates around them.

Separate food items so air can flow freely around them. Do not stack shallow pans.

Tightly cover and label cooled foods. On labels, include preparation dates and times.

Never cool at room temperature.

To avoid contamination, be aware that although uncovered foods cool faster, they are at increased risk for cross-contamination. Be sure to store uncovered cooked and cooled foods on the upper shelves of the cooler, and cover them when they reach 45°F. Never store them beneath raw foods.

REHEATING

While assuming leftovers are safe might seem reasonable, it's not. In reheating and serving leftovers—just as in all phases of the food-preparation process—you must be careful to avoid contamination.

Food must be reheated to 165°F for 15 seconds within 2 hours. If it does not reach this temperature within 2 hours, it must be discarded.

If using the microwave to reheat foods, be sure to cover the product and rotate and stir it partway through the cooking process. Let it stand 2 minutes and be sure to check to make sure its internal temperature is 165°F.

Date Marking Ready-to-Eat, Potentially Hazardous Food

Except for individual meal portions served or repackaged items from a bulk container, ready-to-eat, potentially hazardous food prepared and held in an establishment for more than 24 hours

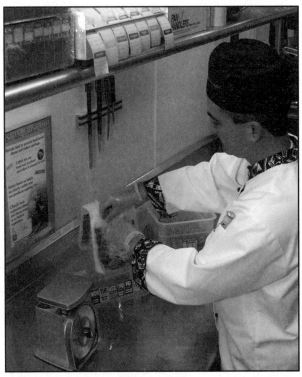

There are many labeling products available which are easy to use and can greatly reduce the risk of contamination. See www.dissolveaway.com for more details or the "HACCP Products" section at the back of this book.

must be clearly marked to indicate the date or day by which the food must be consumed on the premises, sold or discarded.

If the item is prepackaged (such as a one-pound can of tomatoes), once the original container is opened in a food establishment and if the food is held for more than 24 hours, the food item must be marked to indicate the date or day by which the food must be consumed, sold or discarded.

The day the original container is opened in the food establishment is counted as Day 1, and the day or date marked by the food establishment may not exceed a manufacturer's use-by date if the manufacturer determined the use-by date based on food safety.

A refrigerated, ready-to-eat, potentially hazardous food that is frequently rewrapped, such as lunchmeat or a roast, or for which date marking is impractical, such as a soft serve mix or milk in a dispensing machine, should also be day marked.

There are some exceptions to the USDA day-marking rules. The rules are as follows:

- Fermented sausages produced in a federally inspected food-processing plant that are not labeled "Keep Refrigerated" and which retain the original casing on the product.

- Shelf-stable, dry, fermented sausages.

- Shelf-stable salt-cured products such as prosciutto and Parma (ham) produced in a federally inspected food-processing plant that are not labeled "Keep Refrigerated."

A refrigerated, ready-to-eat, potentially hazardous food ingredient or a portion of a refrigerated, ready-to-eat, potentially hazardous food that is combined with additional ingredients must retain the date marking of the earliest-prepared or first-prepared ingredient.

Disposal of Ready-to-Eat, Potentially Hazardous Food

Food must be discarded if it:

1. Exceeds either of the temperature and time rules, except time that the product is frozen.

2. Is in a package that does not bear a date or day.

3. Is appropriately marked with a date or day that exceeds temperature and time rules.

Refrigerated, ready-to-eat, potentially hazardous food prepared in a restaurant or food establishment and dispensed through a vending machine with an automatic shutoff control must be discarded if it exceeds temperature and time rules for vending machine items.

Time As a Public Health Control

If time only, rather than time in conjunction with temperature, is used as the public health control, the following rules should be used:

1. Food must be marked to indicate the time that is 4 hours past when the food was removed from temperature control.

2. The food must be cooked and served or discarded within 4 hours of the point in time when the food is removed from temperature control.

3. Food in unmarked containers or packages or marked to exceed a 4-hour limit shall be discarded.

4. Written procedures are maintained and made available to the health department upon request.

In an establishment that serves a highly susceptible population, such as a nursing home or hospital, time by itself, rather than time and temperature, cannot be used as the public health control for raw eggs.

If a restaurant chooses to preserve food by another method, such as curing or smoking, the restaurant must receive a variance from the health department. Methods that require a variance include the following:

• Smoking food as a method of preservation.

• Curing food.

• Using food additives or adding components such as vinegar as a method of preservation.

- Packaging food using a reduced-oxygen packaging method except as a barrier for *Clostridium botulinum* when additional refrigeration also exists.

- Operating a molluscan shellfish life-support system display tank used to store and display shellfish.

- Custom processing animals that are for personal use as food that is not for sale or service in a food establishment.

- Preparing food by another method that is determined to require a variance by the health department.

Reduced-Oxygen Packaging

There are at least two barriers in place to control the growth and toxin formation of *C. botulinum*.

The restaurant must have a HACCP plan that:

- Identifies the food to be packaged.

- Limits the food packaged to food that does not support the growth of *Clostridium botulinum* because it complies with one of the following:

  – Has an aw (water activity) of 0.91 or less.

  – Has a pH of 4.6 or less.

  – Is a meat or poultry product cured at a food-processing plant regulated by the USDA.

  – Is a food with a high level of competing organisms such as raw meat or raw poultry.

The HACCP plan must also specify methods for maintaining food at 5°C (41°F) or below. The packages shall be prominently and conspicuously labeled (on the display panel) in bold contrasting type with instructions to maintain the food 5°C (41°F) or below, and for food held at refrigeration temperatures, discard the food within 14 calendar days of its packaging.

The plan must also limit the refrigerated shelf life to no more than 14 calendar days from packaging to consumption or the original manufacturer's "sell by" or "use by" date, whichever occurs first, and include operational procedures that:

- Prohibit contacting food with bare hands.

- Identify a designated area and the method to minimize cross-contamination, and access to the processing equipment is limited to responsible trained personnel familiar with the potential hazards of the operation.

The plan must delineate cleaning and sanitization procedures for food-contact surfaces and describe the training program that ensures that the individual responsible for the reduced-oxygen packaging operation understands the concepts required for a safe operation, equipment and facilities, and procedures and rules affecting this preservation. (Except for fish that is frozen before, during and after packaging, a restaurant may not package fish using a reduced-oxygen packaging method.)

Standards of Identity

Food that is served in a food establishment must be offered in a way that does not mislead or misinform the customer. Food or color additives, colored over-wraps or lights may not be used to misrepresent the true appearance, color or quality of a food.

Food Labels

Food that is packaged in the restaurant must be labeled as specified by law (**http://vm.cfsan.fda.gov/~lrd/FCF101.html** and **http://vm.cfsan.fda.gov/~lrd/9CF317.html**).

Label information shall include:

- The common name of the food or an adequately descriptive identity statement.

- If made from two or more ingredients, a list of ingredients in descending order of predominance by weight, including a declaration of artificial color or flavor and chemical preservatives.

- An accurate declaration of the quantity of contents.

- The name and place of business of the manufacturer, packer or distributor.

- Nutrition labeling where appropriate (**http://vm.cfsan.fda.gov/~lrd /FCF101.html** and **http://vm.cfsan.fda.gov/~lrd/9CF317.html**).

- For any salmonid fish containing canthaxanthin as a color additive, the labeling of the bulk fish container, including a list of ingredients, displayed on the retail container or by other written means, such as a counter card, that discloses the use of canthaxanthin.

Bulk food that is available for the customer to self-dispense must be prominently labeled with the following information in plain view of the customer:

- The manufacturer's or processor's label that was provided with the food.

- A card, sign or other method of notification that includes the information a label would usually contain.

Bulk, unpackaged foods such as bakery products and unpackaged foods that are portioned to customer specification need not be labeled if:

- A health, nutrient content or other claim is not made.

- There are no state or local laws requiring labeling.

- The food is manufactured or prepared on the premises of the food establishment or at another food establishment or a processing plant that is owned by the same person and is regulated by the food regulatory agency that has jurisdiction.

OTHER FORMS OF INFORMATION

If required by law, consumer warnings must be provided and the food establishment or manufacturers' dating information on foods may not be concealed or altered.

Consumer Advisory and Consumption of Raw or Undercooked Animal Foods

If an animal food such as beef, eggs, fish, lamb, milk, pork, poultry or shellfish that is raw, undercooked or not otherwise processed to eliminate pathogens is offered in a ready-to-eat form as a deli, menu, vended or other item, or as a raw ingredient in another ready-to-eat food, the owner must inform customers by brochures, deli case or menu advisories, label statements, table tents, placards or other effective written means of the significantly increased risk associated with certain especially vulnerable customers eating such food in raw or under-cooked form.

There are two components to satisfactory compliance: disclosure and reminder.

Disclosure is satisfied when:

- Items are described, such as:

    – Oysters on the half-shell (raw oysters).

    – Raw-egg Caesar salad.

    – Hamburgers (can be cooked to order).

- Items are asterisked to a footnote that states that the items:

    – Are served raw or undercooked.

    – Contain (or may contain) raw or undercooked ingredients.

Reminder is satisfied when the items requiring disclosure are asterisked to a foot-note that states:

- Regarding the safety of these items, written information is available upon request. (Essential criteria for such written information are available, with a downloadable model brochure, on the CFSAN Web page at **www .cfsan.fda.gov**. All brochures must meet these essential criteria.)

- Consuming raw or undercooked meats, poultry, seafood, shellfish or eggs may increase your risk of food-borne illness, especially if you have certain medical conditions.

Discarding or Reconditioning Unsafe, Adulterated or Contaminated Food

A food that is unsafe or not honestly presented must be reconditioned according to an approved procedure or discarded. Food that is not from an approved source shall be discarded. Ready-to-eat food that may have been contaminated by an employee shall be discarded. Food that is contaminated by employees, customers or other persons through contact with their hands, bodily discharges, such as nasal or oral discharges, or other means shall be discarded.

SPECIAL REQUIREMENTS FOR HIGHLY SUSCEPTIBLE POPULATIONS

Pasteurized Foods, Prohibited Reservice and Prohibited Food

The following criteria apply to juice:

- Prepackaged juice or a prepackaged beverage containing juice that bears a warning label (**http://vm.cfsan.fda.gov/~lrd/cf101-17.html**) may not be served or offered for sale.

- Unpackaged juice that is prepared on the premises for service or sale in a ready-to-eat form shall be processed under a HACCP plan.

Pasteurized shell eggs or pasteurized liquid, frozen, dry eggs or egg products shall be substituted for raw shell eggs in the preparation of:

- Foods such as Caesar salad, hollandaise or Béarnaise sauce, mayonnaise, eggnog, ice cream and egg-fortified beverages.

- Recipes in which more than one egg is broken and the eggs are combined (unless the raw eggs are combined immediately before cooking for one serving at a single meal; cooked and served immediately, such as an omelet, soufflé or scrambled eggs; or the raw eggs are combined as an ingredient immediately before baking and the eggs are thoroughly cooked to a ready-to-eat form, such as a cake, muffin or bread).

Food in an unopened original package may not be re-served. In addition, the following foods may not be served or offered for sale in a ready-to-eat form:

- Raw animal foods such as raw fish, raw-marinated fish, raw molluscan shellfish and steak tartare.

- A partially cooked animal food such as lightly cooked fish, rare meat, soft-cooked eggs that are made from raw shell eggs and meringue.

- Raw seed sprouts.

Exceptions to these rules for highly susceptible populations include the following. The preparation of the food is conducted under a HACCP plan that:

- Identifies the food to be prepared.

- Prohibits contacting ready-to-eat food with bare hands.

- Includes specifications and practices that ensure:

  – *Salmonella Enteritidis* growth is controlled before and after cooking.

  – *Salmonella Enteritidis* is destroyed by cooking the eggs according to the temperature and time rules.

- Contains procedures that control cross-contamination of ready-to-eat food with raw eggs, and delineates cleaning and sanitization procedures for food-contact surfaces and describes the training program that ensures that the employee responsible for the preparation of the food understands the procedures to be used.

The nation's 900,000 restaurants are expected to hit $476 billion in sales in 2005, according to the NRA's 2005 Restaurant Industry Forecast. It is very important to have a food safety system to protect the millions of people that will frequent these restaurants.

6

HACCP

New challenges to the U.S. food supply have prompted the FDA to consider adopting a HACCP-based food safety system on a wider basis. One of the most important challenges is the increasing number of new food pathogens. For example, between 1973 and 1988, bacteria not previously recognized as important causes of food-borne illness—such as Escherichia coli O157:H7 and Salmonella enteritidis—became more widespread.

There also is increasing public health concern about chemical contamination of food; for example, the effects of lead in food on the nervous system.

Another important factor is that the size of the food industry and the diversity of products and processes have grown tremendously—in the amount of domestic food manufactured and the number and kinds of foods imported. At the same time, the FDA and state and local agencies have the same limited levels of resources to ensure food safety.

One of the tools restaurants owners use to combat food-borne illness is HACCP—Hazard Analysis of Critical Control Points. Developed nearly 30 years ago for astronauts, the FDA intends to eventually use it for much of the U.S. food supply. The program for the astronauts focuses on preventing hazards that could cause food-borne illnesses by applying science-based controls, from raw material to finished products. The FDA's new system will do the same.

Traditionally, industry regulators have depended on spot-checks of manufacturing conditions and random sampling of final products to ensure safe food. This approach, however, tends to be reactive rather than preventive, and can be less efficient than the new system.

The HACCP system identifies biological, chemical and physical hazards at specific points in the flow of food and the ways these contaminates can be prevented from causing or spreading food-borne illnesses. Many of its principles already are in place in the FDA-regulated low-acid canned food industry. The FDA also established HACCP for the seafood industry in a final rule released December 18, 1995, and for the juice industry in a final rule released January 19, 2001. The final rule for the juice industry took effect on January 22, 2002, for large and medium businesses; January 21, 2003, for small businesses; and January 20, 2004, for very small businesses.

In 1998, the U.S. Department of Agriculture established HACCP for meat and poultry processing plants as well. Most of these establishments were required to start using HACCP by January 1999. Very small plants had until January 25, 2000. (USDA regulates meat and poultry; FDA all other foods.)

The FDA now is considering developing regulations that would establish HACCP as the food safety standard throughout other areas of the food industry, including both domestic and imported food products.

To help determine the degree to which such regulations would be feasible, the agency is conducting pilot HACCP programs with volunteer food companies. The programs have involved cheese, frozen dough, breakfast cereals, salad dressing, bread, flour and other products.

HACCP has been endorsed by the National Academy of Sciences, the Codex Alimentarius Commission (an international food standard-setting organization), and the National Advisory Committee on Microbiological Criteria for Foods.

A number of U.S. food companies already use the system in their manufacturing processes, and it is in use in other countries, including Canada.

HACCP is a common-sense technique to control food safety hazards. It is a preventive system of hazard control rather than a reactive one. Food establishments can use it to ensure safer food products for consumers. It is not a zero-risk system, but is designed to minimize the risk of food safety hazards. HACCP is not a stand-alone program, but is one part of a larger system of control procedures that must be in place in order for HACCP to function effectively.

The success of a HACCP program is dependent upon both people and facilities. Management and employees must be properly motivated and trained if a HACCP program is to successfully reduce the risk of food-borne illness. Education and training in the principles of food safety and management commitment to the implementation of a HACCP system are critical and must be continuously reinforced. Instilling food worker commitment and dealing with problems such as high employee turnover and communication barriers must be considered when designing a HACCP plan.

Successful implementation of a HACCP plan is also dependent upon the design and performance of facilities and equipment. The likelihood of the occurrence of a hazard in a finished product is definitely influenced by facility and equipment design, construction and installation, which play a key role in any preventive strategy.

> "Both parts of HACCP—the hazard analysis and the critical control points— are influenced by the design of equipment and structures in retail food establishments... Facility and process designs can help a HACCP system be more effective by preventing cross-contamination and meeting Standard Operating Procedures (SOPs); therefore allowing the hazard analysis to focus on significant hazards associated with the food itself."
>
> (Comments made by FDA HACCP Policy Strategic Manager, Dr. John Kvenberg, on June 24, 1996, to the Institute of Food Technologists' seminar on Legal Constraints in Facility/Process Design.)

HACCP's Seven Principles

HACCP focuses on how food flows through the process—from purchasing to serving. As we have said, at each step in the food-preparation process there are a variety of potential hazards. HACCP provides managers with a framework for implementing control procedures for each hazard. It does this through identifying critical control points (CCPs). These are points in the process where bacteria or other harmful organisms may grow or food may become contaminated.

HACCP involves seven principles:

1. **Analyze hazards.** Potential hazards associated with a food and measures to control those hazards are identified. The hazard could be biological, such as a microbe; chemical, such as a toxin; or physical, such as ground glass or metal fragments.

2. **Identify critical control points.** These are points in a food's production— from its raw state through processing and shipping to consumption by the consumer—at which the potential hazard can be controlled or eliminated.

Examples are cooking, cooling, packaging and metal detection.

3. **Establish preventive measures with critical limits for each control point.** For a cooked food, for example, this might include setting the minimum cooking temperature and time required to ensure the elimination of any harmful microbes.

4. **Establish procedures to monitor the critical control points.** Such procedures might include determining how and by whom cooking time and temperature should be monitored.

5. **Establish corrective actions** to be taken when monitoring shows that a critical limit has not been met. For example, reprocessing or disposing of food if the minimum cooking temperature is not met.

6. **Establish procedures to verify that the system is working properly.** For example, testing time- and temperature-recording devices to verify that a cooking unit is working properly.

7. **Establish effective recordkeeping** to document the HACCP system. This would include records of hazards and their control methods, the monitoring of safety requirements, and the action taken to correct potential problems. Each of these principles must be backed by sound scientific knowledge; for example, published microbiological studies on time and temperature factors for controlling food-borne pathogens.

Flow Diagram

A flow diagram that delineates the steps in the process from receipt to sale or service forms the foundation for applying the seven principles. The significant hazards associated with each step in the flow diagram should be listed along with preventative measures proposed to control the hazards. The flow diagram should be constructed by a HACCP team that has knowledge and expertise on the product, process and likely hazards. Each step in a process should be identified and observed to accurately construct the flow diagram. To follow are some examples of flow charts.

Flow Chart 1

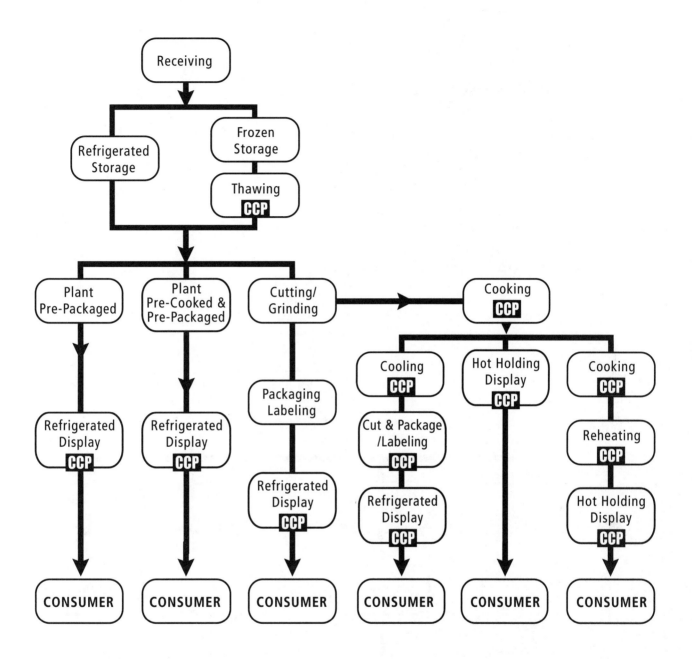

Flow Chart 2

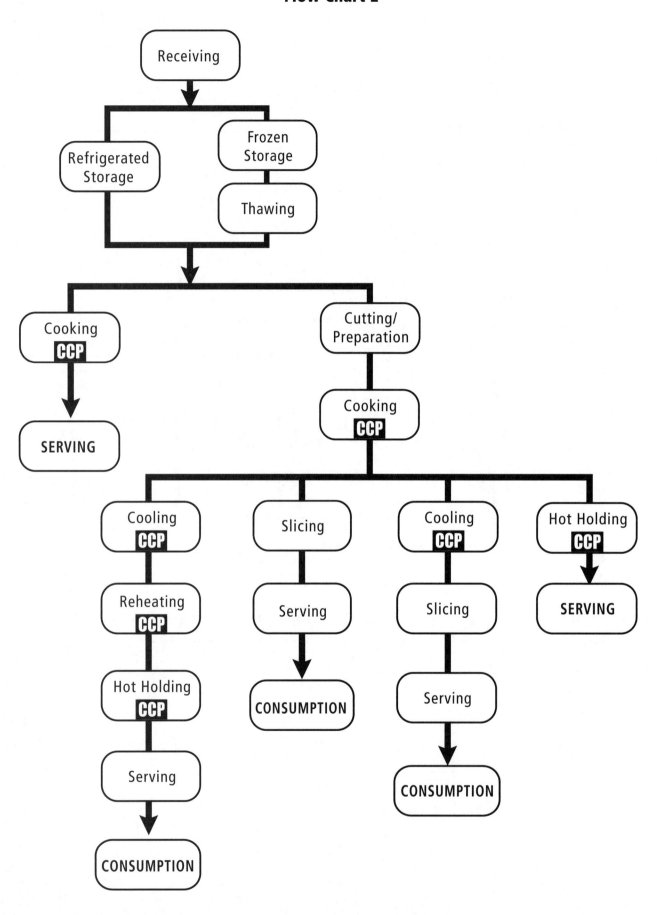

Contents of a HACCP Plan

The system should be a written plan based on the individual operation's menu, equipment, facility, customers and processes.

A HACCP plan must indicate:

- A list of the types of potentially hazardous foods on the menu such as soups and sauces; salads; bulk, solid foods such as meat roasts; or of other foods that are specified by the health department.

- A flow diagram by specific food or category type identifying critical control points and providing information on the ingredients, materials and equipment used in the preparation of that food, and recipes that include methods and procedural control measures that address the food safety concerns involved.

- Food employee and supervisory training plan that addresses food safety issues.

- A statement of standard operating procedures (SOPs) for the plan including clearly identifying each critical control point (CCP), the critical limits for each CCP, the method and frequency for monitoring and controlling each CCP, the method and frequency for manager/supervisor to routinely verify that the employee is following SOPs and monitoring CCPs, action to be taken by the person in charge if the critical limits for each CCP are not met, and records to be maintained by the person in charge to demonstrate that the HACCP plan is properly operated and managed. CCPs identify the points in the process that must be controlled to ensure the safety of the food. Critical limits are established that document the appropriate parameters that must be met at each CCP.

- Additional information, as required by the health department, supporting the determination that food safety is not compromised by the HACCP proposal.

A successful HACCP plan will contain the following elements:

- Good Manufacturing Practices (GMPs).

- SOPs.

- List of HACCP team members.

- List of individual products and their intended uses.

- A flow chart of the individual products through the system.

- Hazard analysis.

- CCPs.

- Critical limits (procedures) for each control point.

- CCP monitoring procedures.

- Corrective actions to be taken if a critical control point infraction occurs,

- Recordkeeping procedures.

- Verification procedures.

HACCP is a system that identifies and monitors specific food-borne hazards—biological, chemical or physical properties—that can adversely affect the safety of the food product. This hazard analysis serves as the basis for establishing CCPs. Monitoring and verification steps are included in the system, again, to ensure that potential hazards are controlled. Seven principles have been developed which provide guidance on the development of an effective HACCP plan.

HACCP represents an important food protection tool supported by SOPs, employee training and other programs that small independent businesses as well as national companies can implement to achieve managerial control of hazards associated with foods. Employee training is key to successful implementation. Employees must learn which control points are critical in an operation and what the critical limits are at these points, for each preparation step they perform. Establishment management must also follow through by routinely monitoring the food operation to verify that employees are keeping the process under control by complying with the critical limits.

The FDA has issued guidance to the industry in voluntarily applying HACCP principles in food establishments. The document entitled, *Managing Food Safety: A HACCP Principles Guide for Operators of Food Service, Retail Food Stores, and Other Food Establishments at the Retail Level* can be found at the Web site **http://vm.cfsan.fda.gov/~dms/hret-toc.html**. This guide recognizes that there are differences between using a HACCP plan in food manufacturing plants. By incorporating the seven principles of HACCP, a good set of SOPs, and using a process approach, this guide sets up a framework for the retail food industry to develop and implement a sound food safety management system. The FDA continues to evolve and improve this guide.

DEFINITIONS

Many terms are used in discussion of HACCP that must be clearly understood to effectively develop and implement a plan. The following definitions are provided for clarity:

- **Acceptable level** means the presence of a hazard which does not pose the likelihood of causing an unacceptable health risk.

- **Control point** means any point in a specific food system at which loss of control does not lead to an unacceptable health risk.

- **Critical control point**, as defined in the Food Code, means a point at which loss of control may result in an unacceptable health risk.

- **Critical limit**, as defined in the Food Code, means the maximum or minimum value to which a physical, biological or chemical parameter must be controlled at a critical control point to minimize the risk that the identified food safety hazard may occur.

- **Deviation** means failure to meet a required critical limit for a critical control point.

- **HACCP plan**, as defined in the Food Code, means a written document that delineates the formal procedures for following the HACCP principles developed by The National Advisory Committee on Microbiological Criteria for Foods.

- **Hazard**, as defined in the Food Code, means a biological, chemical or physical property that may cause an unacceptable consumer health risk.

- **Monitoring** means a planned sequence of observations or measurements of critical limits designed to produce an accurate record and intended to ensure that the critical limit maintains product safety. Continuous monitoring means an uninterrupted record of data.

- **Preventive measure** means an action to exclude, destroy, eliminate or reduce a hazard and prevent recontamination through effective means.

- **Risk** means an estimate of the likely occurrence of a hazard.

- **Sensitive ingredient** means any ingredient historically associated with a known microbiological hazard that causes or contributes to production of a potentially hazardous food as defined in the Food Code.

- **Verification** means methods, procedures and tests used to determine if the HACCP system in use is in compliance with the HACCP plan.

ADVANTAGES OF HACCP

The FDA is recommending the implementation of HACCP in food establishments because it is a system of preventive controls that is the most effective and efficient way to ensure that food products are safe. A HACCP system will emphasize the industry's role in continuous problem solving and prevention rather than relying solely on periodic facility inspections by regulatory agencies.

HACCP offers two additional benefits over conventional inspection techniques:

1. It clearly identifies the food establishment as the final party responsible for ensuring the safety of the food it produces. HACCP requires the food establishment to analyze its preparation methods in a rational, scientific manner in order to identify CCPs and to establish critical limits and monitoring procedures.

2. A HACCP system allows the regulatory agency to more comprehensively determine an establishment's level of compliance. A food establishment's use of HACCP requires the food service operation to develop a plan to prepare safe food. This plan is shared with the health department because it must have access to CCP monitoring records and other data necessary to verify that the HACCP plan is working.

Using conventional inspection techniques, an agency can only determine conditions during the time of inspection which provide a "snapshot" of conditions at the moment of the inspection. By adopting a HACCP approach, both current and past conditions can be determined. When health department officials review HACCP records, they have, in effect, a look back through time. Traditional inspection is relatively resource-intensive and inefficient and is reactive rather than preventive compared to the HACCP approach for ensuring food safety.

Examples of the successful implementation of HACCP by food establishments may be found throughout the food industry. During the past several years, the FDA and a number of state and local jurisdictions have worked with two national voluntary pilot projects for retail food stores and restaurants. These projects involved more than twenty food establishments and demonstrated that HACCP is a viable and practical option to improve food safety. The FDA believes that HACCP concepts have matured to the point at which they can be formally implemented for all food products on an industry-wide basis.

HACCP also offers the following advantages:

- Focuses on identifying and preventing hazards from contaminating food.

- Is based on sound science.

- Permits more efficient and effective government oversight, primarily because the recordkeeping allows investigators to see how well a firm is complying with food safety laws over a period rather than how well it is doing on any given day.

- Places responsibility for ensuring food safety appropriately on the food manufacturer or distributor.

- Helps food companies compete more effectively in the world market.

- Reduces barriers to international trade.

STANDARD OPERATING PROCEDURES (SOPS)

SOPs specify practices to address general hygiene and measures to prevent food from becoming contaminated due to various aspects of the food environment. When SOPs are in place, HACCP can be more effective because it can concentrate on the hazards associated with the food and its preparation and not on the food preparation facility.

There are three purposes for establishing SOPs:

1. Protect your products from contamination from bacterial, chemical and physical hazards.

2. Control bacterial growth that is a result of temperature abuse.

3. Ensure proper procedures are developed for maintaining equipment.

Using SOPs can help ensure that you are doing many things that decrease the likelihood of contamination in your restaurant. These procedures help ensure:

• You are buying products from approved suppliers/sources.

• Water used in food preparation and ice making is potable.

• Food-contact surfaces and utensils are cleaned and sanitized.

• Raw animal foods do not come into contact with and contaminate raw or cooked ready-to-eat food.

• Restroom facilities are maintained.

• Hand-washing facilities are available in food preparation and dishwashing areas, and restrooms.

• An effective pest-control system is in place.

• Toxic substances are properly labeled and stored and safely used.

• Toxic substances do not contact food, food-packaging material and food-contact surfaces.

• Food is not contaminated by physical hazards such as broken glass.

SOPs to Control Contamination of Food

Procedures must be in place to ensure that proper personnel health and hygienic practices are implemented including:

- Restricting or excluding workers with certain symptoms, such as vomiting or diarrhea.

- Practicing effective hand washing.

- Restricting eating, smoking and drinking in food preparation areas.

- Using hair restraints.

- Wearing clean clothing.

- Restricting the wearing of jewelry.

SOPs to control microbial growth ensure that all potentially hazardous food is received and stored at a refrigerated temperature of 41°F or below.

SOPs to maintain equipment ensure that:

- Temperature measuring devices (e.g., thermometers or temperature-recording devices) are calibrated regularly.

- Cooking and hot holding equipment (grills, ovens, steam tables, convey-or cookers, etc.) are routinely checked, calibrated if necessary, and are operating to ensure correct product temperature.

- Cooling equipment (refrigerators, rapid chill units, freezers, salad bars, etc.) are routinely checked, calibrated if necessary, and are operating to ensure correct product temperature.

- Ware-washing equipment is operating according to manufacturer's specifications.

SOPs are written so that the restaurant operator has a plan for dealing with hazards associated with food safety. Equipment and facility maintenance procedures, temperature controls and procedures to control hazards are all part of a facility's SOPs.

These procedures are tailored to address each step in the food flow:

- Purchasing

- Receiving

- Storing

- Preparing

- Serving

Some suggestions for SOPs in each step are listed below.

Purchasing

- Obtain food from approved sources.

- Inspect delivery trucks for cleanliness and proper temperature if they are refrigerated.

- Make ice from potable water or an approved source.

- Inspect food when it is delivered.

- When inspecting food, train employees to look for the following:

    - Foods shipped on ice and the ice has melted.

    - Frozen foods that have been thawed and refrozen.

    - Hazardous food (meat, poultry, fish, etc.) delivered at above 41°F.

    - Food with an "off" odor or appearance.

Receiving and Storing

- Immediately place food in walk-in coolers, freezers or appropriate dry storage areas.

- Store food 6 inches off the floor. Do not purchase more food than your establishment has adequate facilities to store.

- Do not store raw and unprocessed foods over ready-to-eat foods in coolers or refrigerators. (This is done to avoid cross-contamination from spills.)

- Label and date all food and use FIFO rotation procedures.

- All refrigeration units must have a working thermometer. Record air temperature at the beginning, middle and end of the workday. Refrigeration units must be able to maintain foods at 41°F or below. Freezers should be maintained at 0°F or below.

Food Preparation

- Follow all written recipes and HACCP procedures.

- Monitor minimum internal temperatures of food (see previous chapter for specific temperatures).

- Hot food must be held at 135°F. Make sure hot holding units are checked for a temperature of at least 135°F before allowing foods to be placed in them. Keep a temperature log for hot holding equipment and check periodically throughout the shift.

- Cold holding units should be kept at a temperature of 41°F or below before placing foods in them. Keep a temperature log and periodically check the equipment throughout the shift.

- Reheated foods must be heated to 165°F and can then be held at 140°F or above for serving. Do not use a crockpot or a warmer to reheat foods. These pieces of equipment reheat the food too slowly and invite bacterial growth.

- Do not mix fresh product into old product.

- Make sure to cool potentially hazardous foods from 140°F to 70°F degrees within 2 hours and then from 70°F degrees to 41°F or below within 4 more hours (within a total of 6 hours).

- Label foods stored in refrigerators or freezers with preparation dates and times.

- Cover stored food to avoid cross-contamination from spills.

- Stir foods that are being held for service regularly to maintain proper temperatures.

- Prevent cross-contamination by not letting raw meats, poultry and other potentially hazardous foods come into contact with other foods. Make sure to use separate, clean and sanitized equipment such as knives and cutting boards.

Facility/Equipment

- Clean and sanitize all food preparation areas, food-contact surfaces, dining facilities and equipment. Make sure you provide employees with written instructions on how to clean equipment and the facility.

- Make sure restrooms are checked regularly throughout the shift, and be sure they are stocked with soap, toilet paper and paper towels. If automatic hand dryers are used, make sure they are working properly.

- Make sure hand-washing facilities are easily accessible and supplied with soap and paper towels.

- Have a professional pest-control program in place.

- Store toxic chemicals away from food products and be sure they are properly labeled.

When considering your SOPs for cleaning equipment and facilities, consider making certain positions responsible for cleaning certain things. For example, make cleaning the slicer one of the tasks for which the prep cook is responsible. These responsibilities should be included as part of your employees' job descriptions, and you should provided verbal and written instructions on the proper methods to clean and sanitize equipment and the facility. You may want to post these instructions near the employee's workstation or beside the piece of equipment to help remind employees of the proper steps. You should also make a master cleaning list.

JOB DESCRIPTIONS AND JOB LISTS

While some of the training you will do is general and does not involve specific job responsibilities, most of the training you engage in will. Therefore, before you can actually begin designing your training plan, you must have written job descriptions and job lists for each position in your operation.

There are many books on writing job descriptions, such as *Writing Job Descriptions* by Alan Fowler and *A Guide to Writing Job Descriptions Under the Americans with Disabilities Act* by Robert L. Duston. Atlantic Publishing also offers food service job description software (**www.atlantic-publishing.com**). In addition, the National Restaurant Association has *Model Position Descriptions for the Restaurant Industry*. This book has over forty job descriptions and can be ordered by calling 1-800-482-9122.

When writing job descriptions, you need to include:

- Job title.

- Title of supervisor.

- Job summary—a general description of the position and its responsibilities.

- Essential functions or primary responsibilities—this section outlines the various tasks involved with the job. Always be sure one of these is "all other duties as assigned" so you have the flexibility to change responsibilities over time as the operation's needs change. This also provides employees an opportunity to grow within their positions.

- Qualifications and special skills.

The Appendix contains a job description template and some sample job descriptions.

Job Lists

Before you can teach someone a job, you must be able to break that job down into discrete steps. A job list is a list of all the duties a person in a particular position must perform. These lists can help managers in hiring, training and evaluating employees.

To develop these lists, you should break all jobs down into broad categories (such as customer service, opening duties, kitchen duties, etc.), and then group tasks associated with the job under these categories. Think about every single thing you can that is associated with a particular job function when developing these lists. Remember, for someone who has never preformed the job before, no task is

too small to mention. You might consider having an employee help you with these lists or you might want to trail an employee while creating the lists yourself.

You'll need to make a determination of how detailed you want these lists to be. "Taking an order" may be too general of a term to use for your training list, for example. You may need to break this task down into several stages (see the following server job list). How detailed your lists are partially depends on your establishment. If you have an extremely varied menu, your cook's job list may be very detailed and extensive, for example.

Also keep in mind that these lists are not static. Jobs will change over the course to time—make sure your job lists change as well!

For training purposes you can make these lists checklists, putting a blank before each task so you can check it off as the employee masters that particular skill. These duties should be listed as specifically as possible so there is no confusion about the actual duties you want employees to perform.

Some sample job checklists follow.

Server Job List

Name:_____

Reports to: _____ Hire Date:_____

Employee must be able to: (When employee has mastered each task, please place a check mark beside the task)

GENERAL
___Hospitable to guests

___Neat appearance

___Punctual and has a good attendance record

___Was trained in and follows correct procedures for finding subs

___Proper way to serve alcohol responsibly

___Tipping procedures and laws

___Company policies including scheduling, pay, break times and sexual harassment policy

___Personal hygiene

___Safe food handling

___Heimlich Maneuver

___Safe workplace procedures

SERVICE
___The sequence of service

___Greeting guests

___Filling drink orders

___Serving drinks

___Serving wine

___Suggestive selling

___Taking appetizer and entrée orders

___Serving appetizer and entrée orders

___Clearing table during meal service

___Suggest dessert

___Serving dessert

___Presenting check

___Properly busing table when service has concluded

___Resetting table

SIDE DUTIES
___Folding napkins

___Setting tables prior to service

___Stocking stations

___Making coffee/tea

___Refilling salt, pepper and condiments

___Refilling sugar

___Other_____

CLOSING DUTIES
___Cleaning side stations

___Restocking service areas

___Resetting tables for next shift

___Cleaning service trays

HANDLING GUEST CHECKS
___Knowledge of computerized cash register

___Opening a check

___Entering items on a check

___Procedure for voiding checks

___Deleting items from a check

___Proper customer payment procedures

___How to operate credit card machine

___Giving back change

___Running report at end of shift for open guest checks

MENU KNOWLEDGE
___Description (including taste) of all menu items

___Description of wines and how to pair wines with entrées

___Knowledge of preparation techniques

___Potential food allergies and customer diet concerns and alternatives

Bus Person Job List

Name:_____

Reports to: _____ Hire Date:_____

Employee must be able to: (When employee has mastered each task, please place a check mark beside the task)

GENERAL

____Hospitable to guests

____Neat appearance

____Punctual and has a good attendance record

____Was trained in and follows correct procedures for finding subs

____Company policies including scheduling, pay, break times and sexual harassment policy

____Personal hygiene

____Safe food handling

____Heimlich Maneuver

____Safe workplace procedures

SET-UP DUTIES

____Set up tables prior to service

____Rolling silverware

____Preparing water pitchers and water glasses

____Preparing bread baskets

____Cleaning bus pans and trays

____Checking restrooms for cleanliness

SERVICE DUTIES

____Clear dishes from table in a quiet and efficient manner

____Set up table place setting correctly

____Empty trash from dining room and kitchen

____Make and refill coffee and tea

____Seat guest

____Proper way to stack and carry dirty dishes from tables

____Delivering dishes to dishwasher

____Know how to work the dishwashing machine

____Proper way to deliver and stack clean dishes from dishwasher

____Know how to put away clean dishes and kitchenware

CLOSING DUTIES

____Cleaning back kitchen

____Cleaning bus pans and carts

____Resetting tables

____Sweeping

Cook Job List

Name:_____

Reports to: _____ Hire Date:_____

Employee must be able to: (When employee has mastered each task, please place a check mark beside the task)

GENERAL

___Hospitable to guests

___Neat appearance

___Punctual and has a good attendance record

___Was trained in and follows correct procedures for finding subs

___Company policies including scheduling, pay, break times and sexual harassment policy

___Personal hygiene

___Safe food handling

___Heimlich Maneuver

___Safe workplace procedures

PREP WORK

___Using scales and measuring devices for preparing foods

___Practice HACCP principles

___Filling out prep sheets

___Rotating food properly

OPENING DUTIES

___Reheating soups and other leftovers properly

___Turning on ovens, fryers, grills and steam tables correctly

___Stocking steam table and cold storage properly

SERVICE DUTIES

___Must be able to use ovens, fryers, grills, steam tables and refrigeration units safely

___Must be able to slice, dice and mince

___Must be able to use food scales properly and follow basic instructions for standardized recipes

___Timely preparation of hot foods

___Keeping foods out of the temperature danger zone

CLOSING DUTIES

___Turning off and cleaning grills, ovens, steam tables and fryers

___Properly labeling and storing foods

___Restocking for next shift

Bartender Job List

Name:_____

Reports to: _____ Hire Date:_____

Employee must be able to: (When employee has mastered each task, please place a check mark beside the task)

GENERAL

____Hospitable to guests

____Neat appearance

____Punctual and has a good attendance record

____Was trained in and follows correct procedures for finding subs

____Company policies including scheduling, pay, break times and sexual harassment policy

____Personal hygiene

____Safe food handling

____Heimlich Maneuver

____Safe workplace procedures

SET-UP DUTIES

____Inventorying and stocking bar

____Preparing drink garnishes

____Properly preparing dish water and sanitizer for dirty glasses

SERVICE DUTIES

____Prepare bar drinks such as Rusty Nails, Martinis, Manhattans and Gin and Tonics

____Be able to operate a cash register and make change

____Be astute as to the amount of alcohol a patron has consumed

____Be able to wash drink glasses and restock beverages

____Be able to select the appropriate drink glass for the appropriate beverage

CLOSING DUTIES

____Ringing up checks

____Inventorying and stocking bar

____Putting away drinkware and garnishes

JOB BREAKDOWNS

The next step is to prepare job breakdowns. These are more detailed than job lists, showing what needs to be performed, the materials needed to perform the tasks, and steps in performing the job. These breakdowns are great tools to use for individual training, such as when you have a new employee.

If you currently do not have job lists and job breakdowns, be sure to involve your employees in developing these. It is essential to get people actually doing the job to provide feedback on these tools.

Job breakdowns are useful for training in many ways. They can be used to plan training and as outlines for teaching. The job breakdowns give trainers a logical progression for their training sessions. Job breakdowns are also important in setting standards for evaluation.

The following is one example of a job breakdown.

Cook Job List—Clean-Up Duties	
What to Do	**How to Do It**
Turn off equipment	• Turn off fryers, grills, ovens, steam tables and plate warmers

Put food away into reach-in and/or walk-in refrigerator	• Put all food items in steam table and cold table into plastic receptacles.
	
	• Label items with day labels.
	
	• If some items are still warm, do not cover them until they are cool.
	
	• Make sure to follow FIFO principles when storing in the walk-in and reach-in — new items should go in the back and older items should be stored up front.
	
	• Before leaving, make sure all food is covered.
	
	• Make sure all food items are stored at proper temperatures:
	
	• All frozen items -10°–0°F
	
	• Fresh meat and poultry 31°–35°F
	
	• Produce 33°–38°F
	
	• Fresh seafood 33°–38°F
	
	• Dairy products 33°–38°F
	
	  – Use clean, nonabsorbent, covered containers that are approved for food storage.
	
	  – Store dairy products separately from foods with strong odors like onions, cabbage and seafood.
	
	  – To avoid cross-contamination, store raw or uncooked food away from and below prepared or ready-to-eat food.
	
	  – Never allow fluids from raw poultry, fish or meat to come into contact with other foods.
	
	• Keeping perishable items at the proper temperature is a key factor in preventing food-borne illness. Check the temperature of your refrigeration unit regularly to make sure it stays below 40°F. Keep in mind that opening and closing the refrigerator door too often can affect temperature.

Wipe down counters	• Using a damp cloth and sanitizer solution, wipe down counters and other surfaces (refrigerator fronts, steam table doors, prep areas, etc.).

Cook Job List—Clean-Up Duties

What to Do	How to Do It
Restock for next shift	• Make sure to restock all food items that will be needed for the next shift.
Clean grill	• Use grill cleaner to get large pieces of food off grill.
Clean fryer oil	• After oil has cooled, strain the oil each night to get rid of debris. • Fryer oil should be changed weekly. • To change oil carefully, lift the holder out of the fryer and dump the oil into the proper receptacle. Replace the holder, then fill with new oil. Take the old oil to the proper dumping facility.
Take dirty dishes to dishwasher and store clean dishes	• Take all dirty knives, pans and dishes to dishwasher before the end of the night. • Once the dishes are clean, retrieve them and put them in their proper storage areas. • Make sure you properly store knives.
Remove garbage	• Take all kitchen garbage to outside dumpster. • Put a new bag in the garbage cans.
Sweep and mop floor	• Sweep loose debris from the kitchen floor and back kitchen prep area. • Using detergent and hot water, mop up the kitchen and back area, making sure to use the "Caution—Wet Floor" sign.
Fill out paperwork	• Fill out clean-up sheet. • Fill out the daily cooks' form.

CLEAN-UP SHEET FOR EACH COOK

Place a check mark on all completed items.

___1. Turn off all equipment and pilots.

___2. Take all pots, pans and utensils to the dishwasher.

___3. Wrap, date and rotate all leftover food.

___4. Clean out the refrigerator units.

___5. Clean all shelves.

___6. Wipe down all walls.

___7. Spot clean the exhaust hoods.

___8. Clean and polish all stainless steel in your area.

___9. Clean out all sinks.

___10. Take out all trash. Break down boxes to conserve space in dumpster.

___11. Sweep the floor in your area.

___12. Replace all clean pots, pans and utensils.

___13. Check to see if your coworkers need assistance.

___14. Check out with the manager.

COOK _____ MANAGER _____

Time of leaving _____

Job lists can be used to develop training schedules. These lists will lay out the training objectives.

To follow is an example of a training schedule for new cooks developed from the sample job list on page 165.

NEW COOKS' TRAINING SCHEDULE	
Day	**Subject**
1	Orientation
1	Train head cook to gain knowledge of kitchen setup, stations and menu.
2	Train appetizer cook to gain knowledge of appetizer station.
2	Train entrée cook and sous chef to gain knowledge of their stations.
3	Work with prep cook preparing next day's prep—learn proper portion sizes, standardized recipes, how to fill out prep sheets, and proper food rotation.
3	Work with prep cook and manager on knife skills.
3	Go over safe food-handling procedures with manager.
4	Open with head cook to learn opening duties, including reheating soups and other leftovers properly; turning on ovens, fryers, grills and steam tables correctly; and stocking steam table and cold storage properly.
5	Close with head cook to learn proper closing duties, including turning off and cleaning grills, ovens, steam tables and fryers; properly labeling and storing foods; and restocking for next shift.
6	Work at station with head cook shadowing you.
6	Take quiz on menu—including portion sizes.

THE HACCP TEAM

The first thing you should do when developing and implementing a HACCP food safety system is to develop a HACCP team. This team should include the manager and the head cook or executive chef. You may want to consider including other employees as well, including sous chefs, line cooks, prep cooks, a representative from the servers, receiving and purchasing managers, and other key individuals in the flow of food. A written list of team members with names and job titles should be a component of the HACCP plan.

The team's first task will be to look at and develop a plan for the seven major principles in a HACCP system:

1. Assessing hazards.

2. Identifying critical control points.

3. Setting up control procedures and standards.

4. Monitoring critical control points.

5. Taking corrective action.

6. Developing a recordkeeping system.

7. Verification of the system.

PRINCIPLE #1: ANALYZING THE HAZARDS

The first step in the development of a HACCP plan for a food operation is identification of hazards associated with the product. A hazard may be a biological, chemical or physical property that can cause a food to be unsafe. The analysis of hazards requires the assessment of two factors with respect to any identified hazard; i.e., the likelihood that the hazard will occur and the severity if it does occur. Hazard analysis also involves establishment of preventive measures for control. Hazards that involve low risk and that are not likely to occur need not be considered for the purposes of HACCP.

The hazard analysis process accomplishes three things:

1. Hazards are identified.

2. A risk basis is determined for selecting likely hazards.

3. Identified hazards can be used to develop preventive measures for a process or product to ensure or improve food safety.

Numerous issues have to be considered during hazard analysis. These relate to factors such as ingredients, processing, distribution and the intended use of the product. These issues include whether a food contains ingredients that can create microbiological, chemical or physical hazards or whether sanitation practices that are used can introduce these hazards to the food that is being prepared or processed. Even factors beyond the immediate control of the food establishment, such as how the food will be treated if taken out by the consumer and how it will be consumed, must be considered because these factors could influence how food should be prepared or processed in the establishment.

HAZARDS FOR THE HACCP TEAM TO CONSIDER

Biological Hazards

Food-borne biological hazards include bacterial, viral and parasitic organisms. These organisms are commonly associated with humans and with raw products entering the food establishment. Many of these pathogens occur naturally in the environment where foods are grown. Most are killed or inactivated by adequate cooking and numbers are kept to a minimum by adequate cooling during distribution and storage.

Bacterial pathogens comprise the majority of reported food-borne disease outbreaks and cases. A certain level of the pathogens can be expected with some raw foods. Temperature abuse, such as improper hot or cold holding temperatures, can significantly magnify this number. Cooked food which has been subject to cross-contamination with pathogens often provides a fertile medium for their rapid and progressive growth.

Enteric viruses can be food-borne, water-borne or transmitted from a person or from animals. Unlike bacteria, a virus cannot multiply outside of a living cell. Hepatitis A and Norwalk viruses are examples of viral hazards associated with ready-to-eat foods.

Parasites are most often animal-host specific and can include humans in their life cycles. Parasitic infections are commonly associated with undercooking meat products or cross-contamination of ready-to-eat food. Fish-borne parasites in products that are intended to be eaten raw, marinated or partially cooked can be killed by effective freezing techniques.

The following are some of the biological hazards:

- *Clostridium botulinum*

- *Shigella dysenteries*

- *Trichinella spiralis*

- *Listeria monocytogenes*

- *Salmonella spp*

- *Shigella spp*

- *Enterovirulent Escherichia coli (EEC)*

- *Rotavirus*

- *Norwalk* virus group

- *Entamoeba histolytica*

- *Bacillus cereus*

- *Campylobacter jejuni*

- *Clostridium perfringens*

Chemical Hazards

Chemical hazards in foods should be considered during a hazard analysis. Chemical contaminants may be naturally occurring or may be added during the processing of food. Harmful chemicals at very high levels have been associated with acute cases of food-borne illnesses and can be responsible for chronic illness at lower levels.

The following list shows some examples of chemical hazards in food:

- Mycotoxins (e.g., aflatoxin) from mold.

- Scombrotoxin (histamine) from protein decomposition.

- Toxic mushroom species.

- Agricultural chemicals:
    - Pesticides, fungicides, fertilizers, insecticides.
    - Antibiotics and growth hormones.
    - Lead, zinc, arsenic, mercury and cyanide.

- Food additives:
    - Preservatives (nitrite and sulfiting agents).
    - Flavor enhancers (monosodium glutamate).
    - Chemicals used in establishments (e.g., lubricants, cleaners, sanitizers).

Food Allergens

Each year the FDA receives reports of consumers who experienced adverse reactions following exposure to an allergenic substance in foods. Frequently such reactions occur because the presence of the allergenic substances in the foods is not declared on the food label.

To combat this problem, the agency issued a letter titled "Notice to Manufacturers," dated June 10, 1996, which addressed labeling issues and Good Manufacturing Practices (GMPs). This letter is available on the FDA's Web site, **www.cfsan.fda.gov/~lrd/allerg7.html**.

The FDA believes there is scientific consensus that the following foods can cause serious allergic reactions in some individuals and account for more than 90 percent of all food allergies.

- Peanuts
- Fish
- Soybeans
- Crustacean
- Milk
- Tree nuts
- Eggs
- Wheat

Physical Hazards

Illness and injury can result from hard foreign objects in food. These physical hazards can result from contamination and/or poor procedures at many points in the food chain from harvest to consumer, including those within the food establishment.

Sources of physical hazards can include glass from jars, pieces of wood from wooden storage pallets, and metal fragments from equipment or cans.

Flow Charts and the HACCP Team

To assess the hazards present at each stage of the preparation process, track each HACCP food from purchasing and receiving through serving and reheating.

To begin, review your menus. Identify all potentially hazardous foods as well as those foods that may become contaminated during the process.

At this point, you may even want to reduce risks by removing highly hazardous food items from your menu. For example, you may want to avoid egg salad sandwiches if sandwiches must be transported and held before being served.

Once you have surveyed the foods on your menu, evaluate general preparation and cooking procedures to isolate any points where contamination might occur. Next, rank these hazards in terms of severity (how serious are the consequences) and probability (how likely are they to occur).

The HACCP team should begin with a list of the menu items prepared in the food service operation. For example, if the product is a whole chicken, the intended use should be included because this item may be cooked whole, used in soup, or cut into parts for single servings of grilled chicken sandwich. You also need to consider whether or not the product may need to be cooled and stored for later use. Therefore, the product's intended use, how it will be sold or used, and any special instructions should also be included.

A flow chart following the food product through the establishment should be created in order to help with assessment of hazards.

The team should review the process and identify the potential hazards at each step. When looking at this, make note of your current equipment and personnel situation and make sure that it makes sense to prepare this item at your establishment. If you have a small kitchen with limited cooking and storage space, you may want to consider not making certain items from scratch, for example.

Begin your HACCP plan by selecting a specific food or menu item to be assessed. To begin you will need to look at written standardized recipes for menu items.

Beginning with the most potentially hazardous foods served in the establishment, the team should look at each recipe.

The standardized recipe is an important tool for the food service manager. Use of a standardized recipe assures quality and consistency of menu items and it helps with cost control and menu pricing.

Some of the advantages to using standardized recipes are:

- Ensures product consistency.

- Improves cost control by controlling portion size.

- Lists item cost, which makes it easy to access and use this information for pricing.

- Helps make the kitchen run smoother and more efficiently.

- Helps create inventory and purchasing lists.

- Helps with employee training.

In developing your recipe file you will want to:

- Test all recipes in your kitchen—your kitchen's oven may cook muffins quicker than the oven used to create the recipe. If you don't test and find this out, your cooks will constantly burn the muffins because they are using the wrong cooking time.

- Have ingredients listed in the order they are used.

- Check for correct ingredient amounts.

- Make sure the sequence of work is clear.

- Make sure you have all the necessary equipment to prepare the recipe— if your staff is using various pans to cook something because you don't have the correct size, the item will not turn out the same each time, and you are forfeiting consistency.

- Give dry ingredients' measure by weight and liquid ingredients by volume, and be sure you have a scale to measure the weighed amounts.

- Make sure that you or a designated person records any changes to the recipe over time.

- Use it! Make sure you enforce the use of standardized recipes with your kitchen staff.

You may want to use index cards and an index cardholder, or you may want to use a three-ring binder with recipe sheets inserted into transparent envelopes that can be easily wiped clean.

Also be sure to organize your file in a meaningful way. You will probably want to group all the appetizers together, all the entrées together, all the soups, all the salads, and all the desserts.

The information you should include on your recipe form is listed below:

Name of item

Recipe number/identification within file system

Yield – What is the total quantity the recipe will prepare?

Portion size – This may be listed by weight or number of pieces. You may want to include what size of utensil to use for serving. For example, use the 6-oz ladle for a cup of soup.

Garnish – Be specific and make sure every plate goes out looking the same. This includes plate setup. You may want to draw a diagram or include a photograph to show your staff how the chicken should lean up against the polenta squares and the asparagus should sit at an angle on the other side of the chicken.

It is important to list portion size accurately.

Ingredients – List them in order. Make sure to list quantities of ingredients used, and keep the abbreviation used for quantities standard. If you use "oz" for ounce in one recipe, make sure you use it in all your recipes. Give the physical state of ingredients. Are the nuts whole or chopped? Is the flour sifted?

Preparation instructions – Be sure to include any preheating instructions. Use the correct terms for instructions. Do you want the eggs mixed into the batter or folded into it? Should the employee stir or mix with an electric mixer? Be sure to include any precautions or special instructions—if someone is preparing caramel, caution them that the sugar water is extremely hot and that they should take the mixture off the heat before adding the cream. This also should include pan sizes and preparation, cooking temperature, cooking time, how to test for doneness, and instructions for portioning.

Finishing – Describe any finish the product needs, such as brushing with oil or melted chocolate drizzled on top. Also include how to cool and at what temperature the product should be held. Can it sit at room temperature or does it need to be refrigerated?

You may also want to include a photo of the finished dish on your recipe card.

Cost – Not all restaurants include cost on the recipes. If you do, the recipe can be a resource in everyday ordering as well as menu design. Include every ingredient and every garnish for accuracy. You will need to look at product invoices to get unit prices, then determine the ingredient cost from this. Total the cost of each ingredient for your total recipe cost. This can then be divided by the number of portions and you will have a portion cost as well.

Sample Recipe

Recipe No. 126

Name: Blue Ridge Jambalaya

Portion size: 1.5 cups | Yields: 40 portions | Cost per Portion: $0.90

Ingredients	Weight/Measure	Cost
Chicken, boneless breast cut in 1-inch pieces	4 lbs	$8.00
Andouille sausage, sliced	2 lbs	$5.58
Celery, chopped	16 cups	$3.16
Red peppers, chopped	8 each	$6.00
Onions, chopped	4 each	$0.40
Garlic cloves, minced	8 each	$0.17
Short grain brown rice, dry	6 cups	$4.74
Beer	32 oz	$3.50
Chicken stock	60 oz	$1.72
Canned diced tomato	60 oz	$2.12
Tabasco sauce	4 tsp	$0.03
Parsley (garnish)		$0.04
Cornbread (side)		$0.58
TOTAL		$36.04

DIRECTIONS: Trim chicken and cut into 1-inch pieces. Heat vegetable oil in a large sauté pan. Add chicken and cook through. Add sausage and heat through.

In a large stockpot, sauté onion, garlic, celery and red pepper in oil. Add rice and coat rice with oil. Turn heat down to low, add beer and broth a little at a time, allowing the rice to absorb the liquid before adding more. When rice has simmered about 15 – 20 minutes, add tomato, chicken and sausage. Continue cooking until done and rice is tender (about 1 hour). Add Tabasco, salt and pepper.

Portion out the jambalaya into smaller containers to cool. Can refrigerate or use immediately for service.

SERVICE: Serve in a dinner bowl with a piece of cornbread on the side. Top with parsley.

Hazard Analysis Process

This point in hazard analysis consists of asking a series of questions which are appropriate to each step in the flow diagram. The hazard analysis should question the effect of a variety of factors upon the safety of the food.

Ingredients

- Does the food contain any sensitive ingredients that are likely to present microbiological hazards (e.g., Salmonella, Staphylococcus aureus), chemical hazards (e.g., aflatoxin, antibiotic or pesticide residues) or physical hazards (e.g., stones, glass, bone, metal)?

Intrinsic factors of food

Physical characteristics and composition (e.g., pH, type of acids, fermentable carbohydrate, water activity, preservatives) of the food during and after preparation can cause or prevent a hazard.

- Which intrinsic factors of the food must be controlled in order to ensure food safety?

- Does the food permit survival or multiplication of pathogens and/or toxin formation in the food before or during preparation?

- Will the food permit survival or multiplication of pathogens and/or toxin formation during subsequent steps of preparation, storage or consumer possession?

- Are there other similar products in the marketplace? What has been the safety record for these products?

Procedures used for preparation/processing

- Does the preparation procedure or process include a controllable step that destroys pathogens or their toxins? Consider both vegetative cells and spores.

- Is the product subject to recontamination between the preparation step (e.g., cooking) and packaging?

Microbial content of the food

- Is the food commercially sterile (e.g., low-acid canned food)?

- Is it likely that the food will contain viable spore-forming or nonspore-forming pathogens?

- What is the normal microbial content of the food stored under proper conditions?

- Does the microbial population change during the time the food is stored before consumption?

- Does the change in microbial population alter the safety of the food?

Facility design

- Does the layout of the facility provide an adequate separation of raw materials from ready-to-eat foods?

- Is positive air pressure maintained in product packaging areas? Is this essential for product safety?

- Is the traffic pattern for people and moving equipment a potentially significant source of contamination?

Equipment design

- Will the equipment provide the time/temperature control that is necessary for safe food?

- Is the equipment properly sized for the volume of food that will be prepared?

- Can the equipment be sufficiently controlled so that the variation in performance will be within the tolerances required to produce a safe food?

- Is the equipment reliable or is it prone to frequent breakdowns?

- Is the equipment designed so that it can be cleaned and sanitized?

- Is there a chance for product contamination with hazardous substances (e.g., glass)?

- What product safety devices, such as time/temperature integrators, are used to enhance consumer safety?

Packaging

- Does the method of packaging affect the multiplication of microbial pathogens and/or the formation of toxins?

- Is the packaging material resistant to damage, thereby preventing the entrance of microbial contamination?

- Is the package clearly labeled "Keep Refrigerated" if this is required for safety?

- Does the package include instructions for the safe handling and preparation of the food by the consumer?

- Are tamper-evident packaging features used?

- Is each package legibly and accurately coded to indicate production lot?

- Does each package contain the proper label?

Sanitation

- Can the sanitation practices that are employed impact upon the safety of the food that is being prepared?

- Can the facility be cleaned and sanitized to permit the safe handling of food?

- Is it possible to provide sanitary conditions consistently and adequately to ensure safe foods?

Employee health, hygiene and education

- Do the employees understand the food preparation process and the factors they must control to ensure safe foods?

- Will the employees inform management of a problem which could impact food safety?

Conditions of storage between packaging and the consumer

- What is the likelihood that the food will be improperly stored at the wrong temperature?

- Would storage at improper temperatures lead to a microbiologically unsafe food?

Intended use

- Will the food be heated by the consumer?

- Will there likely be leftovers?

Intended consumer

- Is the food intended for the general public (e.g., a population that does not have an increased risk of becoming ill)?

- Is the food intended for consumption by a population with increased susceptibility to illness (e.g., infants, the elderly, the infirm and immuno-compromised individuals)?

Developing preventive measures

The preventive measures procedure identifies the steps in the process at which hazards can be controlled.

After identifying the hazards the food establishment must then consider what preventive measures, if any, can be applied for each hazard. Preventive measures are physical, chemical or other factors that can be used to control an identified health hazard. More than one preventive measure may be required to control a specific hazard and more than one hazard may be controlled by a specified preventive measure.

For example, if a HACCP team were to conduct a hazard analysis for the preparation of hamburgers from frozen beef patties, enteric pathogens on the incoming raw meat would be identified as a potential hazard. Cooking is a preventive measure which can be used to eliminate this hazard. Thus, cooking, the preventive measure, would be listed along with the hazard (i.e., enteric pathogens) as follows:

Step	Identified Hazard	Preventive Measures
Cooking	Enteric pathogens	Cooking sufficiently to kill enteric pathogens

When working with flow charts, you need to do the following:

- **Identify potentially hazardous foods.** While any food item has the potential for contamination, meats, poultry, fish, eggs and dairy products are most likely to be implicated in a food-borne illness outbreak.

- **Identify ready-to-eat foods.** Ready-to-eat foods may become contaminated during storage or food handling, so you must identify what kind of contamination might occur with these foods.

- **Determine the severity or seriousness of the hazard.** How serious and how likely is it that the hazard will occur? Mishandling of raw meat and the risk of cross-contamination by raw meat is a distinct possibility and could be potentially very dangerous. The HACCP team should decide which hazards should be addressed in the HACCP plan.

PRINCIPLE #2: IDENTIFYING CRITICAL CONTROL POINTS

Critical control points are the points during receiving, storing, preparation and serving when potential hazards can be controlled or prevented. Examples of CCPs are thoroughly cooking items to proper minimum internal temperatures, cooling items properly, establishing and following time and temperature controls, prevention of cross-contamination, and certain aspects of employee and environmental hygiene. For example, cooking that must occur at a specific temperature and for a specified time in order to destroy microbiological pathogens is a CCP. Likewise, refrigeration or the adjustment of a food's pH to a level required to prevent hazardous microorganisms from multiplying or toxins from forming are also CCPs.

If we use our example, a grilled chicken sandwich, we know that chicken sandwiches are usually cooked to order and not held for extended periods. Therefore, hot holding and cooling are not typically issues. The CCPs occur during receiving, storing, preparation and cooking. Raw meats can contaminate ready-to-eat foods and food surfaces, so you must be careful to avoid cross-contamination. In addition, the meat must be properly cooked to kill any bacteria present.

To develop CCPs, you must develop procedures to prevent, reduce and eliminate hazards. The requirements you establish must be measurable and observable, and they must meet the state standards.

Many points in food preparation may be considered control points, but very few are actually critical control points. A control point is any point, step or procedure at which biological, physical or chemical factors can be controlled. Concerns that do not impact food safety may be addressed at control points; however, since these control points do not relate to food safety, they are not included in the HACCP plan.

Different facilities preparing the same food can differ in the risk of hazards and the points, steps or procedures which are CCPs. This can be due to differences in each facility such as layout, equipment, selection of ingredients or the process that is used. Generic HACCP plans can serve as useful guides; however, it is essential that the unique conditions within each facility be considered during the development of a HACCP plan.

CCPs must be carefully developed and documented. In addition, they must be used only for purposes of product safety.

The decision tree on the following page is helpful in verifying which of the food preparation steps should be designated as CCPs.

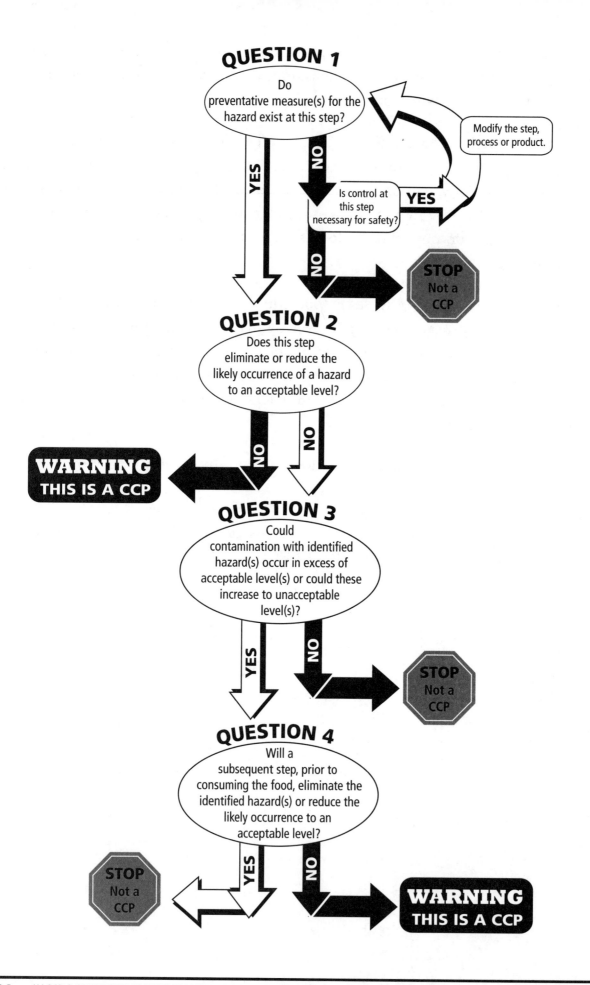

QUESTION 1

Do preventative measure(s) for the hazard exist at this step?

YES | **NO**

Is control at this step necessary for safety?

YES → Modify the step, process or product.

NO → **STOP** Not a CCP

QUESTION 2

Does this step eliminate or reduce the likely occurrence of a hazard to an acceptable level?

NO | **NO**

WARNING THIS IS A CCP

QUESTION 3

Could contamination with identified hazard(s) occur in excess of acceptable level(s) or could these increase to unacceptable level(s)?

YES | **NO**

NO → **STOP** Not a CCP

QUESTION 4

Will a subsequent step, prior to consuming the food, eliminate the identified hazard(s) or reduce the likely occurrence to an acceptable level?

YES | **NO**

STOP Not a CCP

WARNING THIS IS A CCP

PRINCIPLE #3: ESTABLISH CRITICAL LIMITS FOR PREVENTIVE MEASURES

In order to be sure a food passes safely through a CCP, you need to establish critical limits that must be met. These critical limits should be standards that are observable and measurable. They should include precise time, temperature and sensory requirements.

Specify exactly what should be done to meet each particular standard. For example, instead of saying that a "food must be thoroughly cooked," the standard might say, "Heat rapidly to an internal temperature of 165°F within 2 hours." In addition, make sure employees have calibrated, metal-stemmed or digital thermometers and that they use them routinely.

Make sure recipes state: 1) end-cooking, reheating and hot holding temperatures, and 2) specific times for thawing, cooking and cooling foods. Schedule sufficient staff in peak hours to prepare and serve foods safely.

The table below shows the most frequently used criteria for critical limits:

Criteria Most Frequently Used for Critical Limits
Time
Temperature
Humidity
aw
pH
Titratable acidity
Preservatives
Salt concentration
Available chlorine
Viscosity

According to the FDA, a critical limit is defined as a criterion that must be met for each preventive measure associated with a CCP. Each CCP will have one or more preventive measures that must be properly controlled to ensure prevention, elimination or reduction of hazards to acceptable levels.

Let's say we are cooking beef patties. The process should be designed to eliminate the most heat-resistant vegetative pathogen which could reasonably be expected to be in the product. Criteria may be required for factors such as temperature, time and meat patty thickness. The relationship between the CCP and its critical limits for the meat patty example is shown below:

Process Step	CCP	Critical Limits
Cooking	YES	Minimum internal temperature of patty: 68°C / 155°F Broiler temperature: _____ °C / _____ °F Time; rate of heating/cooling (e.g., conveyer belt speed in): cm/min: _____ ft/min _____ Patty thickness: _____ cm / _____ in Patty composition: e.g., % Fat, % Filler Oven humidity: _____ % RH

PRINCIPLE #4: MONITORING CRITICAL CONTROL POINTS

Once you have established CCPs, like the ones we have established in the diagram on page 186, you need to develop a system for monitoring these control points to make sure they are being followed. You need to observe and measure the requirements. This means, in part, keeping temperature logs and consistent observation and reinforcement by the manager.

Using your flowcharts or lists, follow potentially hazardous foods through every step in the process. Compare your operation's performance with the requirements you have set. Identify any areas of deficiency.

There are three main purposes for monitoring:

1. It tracks the system's operation so that we can see where control was lost and determine what corrective action must be taken.

2. It indicates when loss of control actually occurred.

3. It provides written documentation for use in verification of the HACCP plan.

Examples of Measurements for Monitoring
Visual observations
Temperature
Time
pH
aw

Continuous monitoring is always preferred when possible. For example, the temperature and time for an institutional cook-chill operation can be recorded continuously on temperature recording charts. If the temperature falls below the scheduled temperature or the time is insufficient, as recorded on the chart, the batch must be recorded as a process deviation and reprocessed or discarded.

Naturally, for these temperature logs to be meaningful, the thermometers must be properly calibrated, and records of calibrations must be maintained as a part of the HACCP plan documentation.

When it is not possible to monitor a critical limit on a continuous basis, you should establish a monitoring interval that will be reliable enough to indicate that the hazard is under control.

Most monitoring procedures for CCPs will need to be done rapidly because the time frame between food preparation and consumption does not allow for lengthy analytical testing. Microbiological testing is seldom effective for monitoring CCPs because of its time-consuming nature. Therefore, physical and chemical measurements are preferred because they may be done rapidly and can indicate whether microbiological control is occurring.

When assigning responsibility for monitoring CCPs, consider assigning the tasks to employees that are directly associated with the operation, such as the person in charge of the food establishment, chefs and departmental supervisors. This improves your likelihood of accurate monitoring and recording taking place.

Individuals monitoring CCPs must be trained in the monitoring technique. They must understand the purpose and importance of monitoring and be unbiased in monitoring and reporting so that monitoring is accurately recorded. These individuals must have access to the CCP being monitored and to the calibrated instrumentation designated in the HACCP plan.

The person responsible for monitoring must also record a food operation or product that does not meet critical limits and ensure that immediate corrective action can be taken. All records and documents associated with CCP monitoring must be signed or initialed by the person doing the monitoring.

Random checks may be useful in supplementing the monitoring of certain CCPs. They may be used to check incoming ingredients, serve as a check for compliance where ingredients are recertified as meeting certain standards, and assess factors such as equipment. Random checks are also advisable for monitoring environmental factors such as airborne contamination and cleaning and sanitizing gloves.

PRINCIPLE #5: TAKING CORRECTIVE ACTION

If you are monitoring CCPs and your procedures are not being followed, you need to develop specific corrective actions to take. The action that is taken should be reported to management and the action should be documented. In addition, you must ensure that the problem does not happen again.

Take corrective action as needed. Some examples are:

- If a product's temperatures are unacceptable when received, reject the shipment.

- If food is contaminated by hands or equipment, rewash or discard it.

- If food temperature is not high enough after cooking, continue cooking to the required temperature.

- If food temperature exceeds 55°F during cold prep or serving, discard it.

Although the HACCP system is intended to prevent deviations from occurring, perfection is rarely, if ever, achievable. Thus, there must be a corrective action plan in place to:

- Determine the disposition of any food that was produced when a deviation was occurring.

- Correct the cause of the deviation and ensure that the CCP is under control.

- Maintain records of corrective actions.

Because of the variations in CCPs for different food operations and the diversity of possible deviations, specific corrective action plans must be developed for each CCP. The actions must demonstrate that the CCP has been brought under control. Individuals who have a thorough understanding of the operation, product and HACCP plan must be assigned responsibility for taking corrective action. Corrective action procedures must be documented in the HACCP plan.

Food establishments covered by the Food Code will usually be concerned with food which has a limited shelf life and distribution. Primary focus for the application of this HACCP principle will be on the correction of the procedure or condition which led to the noncompliance. More frequent monitoring may be temporarily required to ensure that the deviation from the established critical limit is not continuing when the operation is resumed.

PRINCIPLE #6: SETTING UP A RECORDKEEPING SYSTEM

Develop a recordkeeping system to document the HACCP process and monitor your results. This may be any simple, quick system, such as a log, in which employees can record their compliance with standards at CCPs. These records are crucial and may provide proof that a food-borne illness did not originate at your establishment.

One conclusion of a study of HACCP performed by the U.S. Department of Commerce is that correcting problems without recordkeeping almost guarantees that problems will recur. The requirement to record events at CCPs on a regular basis ensures that preventive monitoring is occurring in a systematic way. Unusual occurrences that are discovered as CCPs are monitored or that otherwise come to light must be corrected and recorded immediately with notation of the corrective action taken.

The level of sophistication of the recordkeeping necessary for the food establishment is dependent on the complexity of the food preparation operation. A sous vide process or cook-chill operation for a large institution would require more recordkeeping than a limited menu cook-serve operation. The simplest effective recordkeeping system that lends itself well to integration within the existing operation is best.

A recordkeeping system should be easy to use or you probably won't continue to use it in the long term. Records documenting a HACCP plan should be kept until a self- inspection is conducted or deemed no longer relevant.

The approved HACCP plan and associated records must be on file at the food establishment. Here are some of the items you will want to keep as a part of your recordkeeping system:

- **Recipes.** Standardized recipes must be written.

- **Time/Temperature logs.** Logs must be kept for both heating and cooling equipment as well as product temperatures from delivery. Cooking, reheating and cooling logs also should be kept.

- **Employee training forms.** Employees must be adequately trained for a HACCP system to work. Be sure to keep all your training schedules and logs on file.

- **Cleaning schedules.** Cleaning schedules should be kept to document cleaning and sanitizing procedures.

- **Job descriptions.** Written job descriptions are important in clarifying duties and making sure all tasks get completed.

- **Listing of the HACCP team and assigned responsibilities.**

- **Description of the product and its intended use.**

- **Flow diagram of food preparation indicating CCPs.**

- **Hazards associated with each CCP and preventive measures.**

- **Critical limits.**

- **Monitoring system.**

- **Corrective action plans for deviations from critical limits.**

- **Recordkeeping procedures.**

- **Procedures for verification of HACCP system.**

In addition to listing the HACCP team, product description and uses and providing a flow diagram, other information in the HACCP plan can be tabulated as follows:

Process Step	CCP	Chemical Physical Biological Hazards	Critical Limit	Monitoring Procedures Frequency Person(s) Responsible	Corrective Action(s) Person(s) Responsible	HACCP Records	Verification Procedures/ Person(s) Responsible

The following chart is an example of a HACCP plan documentation for a product's cooling step in a retail level food establishment.

PROCESS STEP	COOLING
CCP	Critical Control Point #8
Criteria or Critical Limit	Cool Foods Rapidly in Small Quantities to 5°C (41°F)
Establish Monitoring	Department Personnel Break Down Food into Small Quantities and Monitor the Cooling Process
Corrective/Preventive Action	Modify Cooling Procedures/Discard
HACCP Records	Deli Cooking/Cooling Log
HACCP System Verification	Deli Safety Audit by Store Manager

PRINCIPLE #7: ESTABLISHING THAT THE HACCP SYSTEM IS WORKING

Verify that the HACCP process in your facility works. You can do this in a number of ways. For starters, be alert to how often you need to take corrective actions. If you need to take corrective actions frequently, this may indicate a need to change, or at least fine-tune, your system. In addition, think of tests you can do, like measuring the strength of your sanitizing solution. Also, examine your records and make sure employees are entering actual, valid data. An inspection by the health department can provide a good assessment of whether or not your process is working.

To establish your HACCP system is working, you must first verify that critical limits at CCPs are satisfactory. This can be complex and may require intensive involvement of highly skilled professionals from a variety of disciplines capable of doing focused studies and analyses. A review of the critical limits is necessary to verify that the limits are adequate to control the hazards that are likely to occur.

The second phase of verification ensures that the facility's HACCP plan is functioning effectively. A functioning HACCP system requires little end-product sampling, since appropriate safeguards are built in early in the food preparation. Therefore, rather than relying on end-product sampling, food establishments must rely on frequent reviews of their HACCP plan, verification that the HACCP plan is being correctly followed, review of CCP records, and determination that appropriate risk-management decisions and product dispositions are made when preparation deviations occur.

The third phase consists of documented periodic revalidations, independent of audits or other verification procedures, that must be performed to ensure the accuracy of the HACCP plan. Revalidations are performed by a HACCP team on a regular basis and/or whenever significant product, preparation or packaging changes require modification of the HACCP plan. The revalidation includes a documented on-site review and verification of all flow diagrams and CCPs in the HACCP plan. The HACCP team modifies the HACCP plan as necessary.

The fourth phase of verification deals with the health department's responsibility and actions to ensure that the establishment's HACCP system is functioning satisfactorily.

The following are some examples of HACCP plan verification activities which should be used as a part of a HACCP program:

- Establishment of appropriate verification inspection schedules.

- Review of the HACCP plan.

- Review of CCP records.

- Review of deviations and their resolution, including the disposition of food.

- Visual inspections of operations to observe if CCPs are under control.

- Random sample collection and analysis.

- Review of critical limits to verify that they are adequate to control hazards.

- Review of written records of verification inspections which certifies compliance with the HACCP plan or deviations from the plan and the corrective actions taken.

- Validation of HACCP plan, including on-site review and verification of flow diagrams and CCPs.

- Review of modifications of the HACCP plan.

Verification inspections should be conducted by the health department under the following circumstances:

- Routinely or on an unannounced basis, to ensure that selected CCPs are under control.

- When it is determined that intensive coverage of a specific food is needed because of new information concerning food safety.

- When foods prepared at the establishment have been implicated as a vehicle of food-borne disease.

- When requested on a consultative basis and resources allow accommodating the request.

- When established criteria have not been met.

- To verify that changes have been implemented correctly after a HACCP plan has been modified.

Training and Knowledge

Training and knowledge are very important in making HACCP successful in any food establishment. HACCP works best when it is integrated into each employee's normal duties rather than added as something extra.

The depth and breadth of training will depend on the particular employee's responsibilities within the establishment. Management or supervisory individuals will need a deeper understanding of the HACCP process because they are responsible for proper plan implementation and routine monitoring of CCPs such as product cooking temperatures and cooling times. The training plan should be specific to the establishment's operation rather than attempt to develop HACCP expertise for broad application.

The food employee's training should provide an overview of HACCP's prevention philosophy while focusing on the specifics of the employee's normal functions. The CCPs such as proper hand washing and use of utensils or gloves for working with ready-to-eat food should be stressed. The use of recipes or SOPs which include the critical limits of cooking times and temperatures, with a final cooking time and temperature measurement step, should be included.

For all employees, the fundamental training goal should be to make them proficient in the specific tasks which the HACCP plan requires them to perform. This includes the development of a level of competency in their decision making about the implementation of proper corrective actions when monitoring reveals violation of the critical limit. The training should also include the proper completion and maintenance of any records specified in the establishment's plan.

Training reinforcement is also needed for continued motivation of the food establishment employees. Some examples might include:

- A HACCP video training program such as the Pennsylvania Department of Environmental Regulation's "Food-Borne Illness: It's Your Business."

- Changing reminders about HACCP critical limits such as "HAND WASHING PAYS BIG DIVIDENDS" printed on employee's time cards or checks.

- Workstation reminders such as pictorials on how and when to take food temperatures.

Every time there is a change in a product or food operation within the establishment, the HACCP training needs should be evaluated. For example, when a food establishment substitutes a frozen seafood product for a fresh one, proper thawing critical limits should be taught and then monitored for implementation. The employees should be made sensitive to how the changes will affect food safety.

The HACCP plan should include a feedback loop for employees to suggest what additional training is needed. All employees should be made a part of the continuous food-safety improvement cycle because the old statement is very true: "The customer's health is in their hands." This helps maintain their active awareness and involvement in the importance of each job to the safety of the food provided by their establishment.

WHY USE HACCP IN YOUR FACILITY?

As a food service manager, you are responsible for protecting your customers by serving safe and wholesome food. To accomplish this, you have to educate your employees and motivate them to put into practice at every step what they've learned about food safety.

To do this, you need a systematic process for identifying potential hazards, for putting safety procedures in place, and for monitoring the success of your safety system on an ongoing basis. HACCP helps you do all of these things.

Using HACCP, you can identify potentially hazardous foods and places in the food-preparation process where bacterial contamination, survival and growth can occur. Then you can take action to minimize the danger.

HACCP is based on this principle: If the raw ingredients are safe, and the process is safe, then the finished product is safe.

A HACCP TRAINING GUIDE

Use of this guide is most effective when a team approach is used for designing and implementing a plan based on the HACCP principles. A team could be comprised of the owner and the chef or cook. Although managers are responsible for designing the system, implementation involves the efforts and commitment of every employee. Education and training of both management and employees are important in their respective roles of producing safe foods. You may consider working with outside consultants, university extension services and regulatory authorities to ensure your HACCP system is based on the best available science and will control identified hazards.

How to Use This Guide

This guide contains a model for assessing significant food safety hazards at each operational step in the flow of food. A short introduction to each step highlights important food safety concerns. For each operational step there is a worksheet and a worksheet summary page which discuss the CCPs and critical limits. These critical food safety limits are included in the Food Code. In addition, Annex 3 of the Food Code provides the public health reasons behind each control measure.

The guide addresses the significant food safety concerns for each operational step in the flow of food. For each step, a summary sheet and accompanying worksheet are provided to assist you in focusing on the controls that need to be in place in order to manage food safety hazards.

PROCEDURAL STEP 1

Group Menu Items

To get started, review how your menu items flow through your operation, note whether they undergo a cook step for same-day serving, receive additional cooling and reheating following a cook step, or have no cook step involved. (Refer to Chapter 2 for organizing your menu items by Process 1, 2 and 3.)

Looking at your menu, place each menu item or similar menu items (like "hot soups" or "cold salads") into the appropriate group. You may discover that more than one food process is conducted within your operation. You will also need to consult the Annexes to identify menu items that need very careful and special attention throughout the use of this guide. These menu items may pose special hazards that are not always readily apparent. If your operation serves any of the menu items listed in the Annexes, consult with your regulatory authority for additional information. To accomplish the first procedural step in developing your food safety management system, identify the food processes specific to your menu items.

List your menu items that belong to one of the three processes.

CHART 1: PROCESS-SPECIFIC LISTS		
PROCESS #1	**PROCESS #2**	**PROCESS #3**
List menu foods:	List menu foods:	List menu foods:
EXAMPLES:	EXAMPLES:	EXAMPLES:
salad greens	hamburgers	soups
fish for sushi	soup du jour	gravies
fresh vegetables	hot vegetables	sauces
oysters or clams served raw	entrées for "special of the day"	large roasts
tuna salad	cooked eggs	chili
Caesar salad dressing		taco filling
coleslaw		egg rolls
sliced sandwich meats		
sliced cheese		

Process 1: Food preparation with no cook step—ready-to-eat food that is stored, prepared and served.

Process 2: Food preparation for same-day service—food that is stored, prepared, cooked and served.

Process 3: Complex food preparation—food that is stored, prepared, cooked, cooled, reheated, hot held and served.

PROCEDURAL STEP 2

Conduct Hazard Analysis

In developing a food safety system, you need to identify the hazards that exist in the flow of foods in your operation from receiving to serving. Hazards include:

- Pathogens or toxins present in food when you receive them.

- Pathogens that may be introduced during preparation (example: using a raw animal food as one ingredient).

- Pathogen growth or toxin production during storage, preparation or holding.

- Pathogens or toxins that survive heating.

- Contaminants, (i.e., pathogens, chemicals, physical objects), that are introduced to food by food workers or equipment.

- Since you have grouped your menu items, including ingredients, into the three processes in Chart 1, you can identify hazards that are associated with each process. You will see that the more complex the process is, the greater the opportunities are for hazards to occur.

- In consultation with your regulatory authority, you need to identify the hazards associated with various foods and ingredients, such as:

  – Salmonella and Campylobacter jejuni in raw poultry.

  – E. coli O157:H7 in raw ground beef.

– Staphylococcus aureus toxin formation in cooked ham.

– Bacillus cereus spore survival and toxin formation in cooked rice.

– Clostridium perfringens spore survival and subsequent growth in cooked foods.

– Hazards specific to seafood.

This list is only a brief sample of hazards associated with specific foods. By identifying the hazards, you will be able to determine CCPs and critical limits on the worksheet. Another way of fulfilling the hazard analysis step is to understand the hazards associated with your specific menu items (Annex 3 of the Food Code is a resource for this purpose) and to adhere to the critical limits established in the Food Code. Those critical limits are based on the anticipated hazards.

Food Safety Management Worksheets and Summaries for Operational Steps

Worksheets and summaries are provided to enable you to:

- Identify those operational steps in the food flow that are specific to your operation.

- Write in your SOPs which are the general procedures that cross all flows and products.

- Reference the CCPs and critical limits pertaining to those process steps.

- Develop monitoring procedures and corrective actions which are customized to fit your operation.

- Consider the type of recordkeeping you need to document you are controlling significant food safety hazards.

- HACCP allows the flexibility for you to customize a food safety management system specific to your operations. The worksheets are provided to assist you in developing procedures to:

  – Monitor CCPs.

  – Take corrective actions when critical limits are not met.

  – Establish a verification procedure.

  – Establish a recordkeeping system.

Review the following worksheets and the summary page for each operational step. Determine the ones that are applicable to your operation and make copies of them so you can fill in your groupings of menu items (which you did preliminarily in Procedural Step 1). Then continue to use the forms and complete the information as you work through Procedural Steps 3 through 9.

Receiving

At receiving, your main concern is contamination from pathogens and the formation of harmful toxins. Obtaining food from approved sources and at proper temperatures are important purchase specifications for preventing growth and contamination during receiving. Approved sources are suppliers who are regulated and inspected by appropriate regulatory authorities.

Ready-to-eat, potentially hazardous food is a special concern at receiving. Because this food will not be cooked before service, microbial growth could be considered a significant hazard for receiving refrigerated, ready-to-eat foods. Having SOPs in place to control product temperature is generally adequate to control the hazards present at receiving of these products. Besides checking the product temperature, you will want to check the appearance, odor, color and condition of the packaging.

Federal regulations require that processors of seafood and seafood products for interstate distribution have a HACCP plan. These establishments are approved sources for seafood, and you may ask your interstate seafood supplier for documentation that the firm has a HACCP plan in place. Processors of seafood and seafood products that are sold or distributed only within a state may or may not be required to have a HACCP plan, depending on the state, local or tribal regulations.

Special consideration should be given to certain species of finfish and raw molluscan shellfish. Molluscan shellfish (oysters, clams, mussels and scallops) that are received raw in the shell or shucked must be purchased from suppliers who are listed on the FDA Interstate Certified Shellfish Shippers List (**www.cfsan.fda.gov/~ear/shellfis.html**) or on a list maintained by your state shellfish control authority. Shellfish received in the shell must bear a tag (or a label for shucked shellfish) which states the date and location of harvest, in addition to other specific information.

Finfish harvested from certain areas may naturally contain a certain toxin that is not readily apparent. This toxin is called ciguatera. Other finfish may develop toxins after harvest if strict temperature control is not maintained. This toxin is called scombrotoxin. Temperature control is important at receiving because this toxin cannot be eliminated by cooking.

OPERATIONAL STEP 1: RECEIVING

PROCESS 1: Examples: Salads, Sushi		CCP: ☐ Yes ☐ No
Hazard	**Monitoring**	**Corrective Actions**
* Microbial contamination * Bacterial growth * Parasites * Scombrotoxin * Ciguatera or other toxin contamination * Chemical contamination		
Critical Limits	**Verification**	**Records**
Receive at 41°F or below Approved source Seafood HACCP plan Proper chemical storage/use		

PROCESS 2: Examples: Hamburgers, Mahi-mahi		CCP: ☐ Yes ☐ No
Hazard	**Monitoring**	**Corrective Actions**
* Microbial contamination * Bacterial growth * Parasites * Scombrotoxin * Ciguatera or other toxin contamination * Chemical contamination		
Critical Limits	**Verification**	**Records**
Receive at 41°F or below Approved source Seafood HACCP plan Proper chemical storage/use		

PROCESS 3: Examples: Soups		CCP: ☐ Yes ☐ No	
Hazard		Monitoring	Corrective Actions
* Microbial contamination * Bacterial growth * Ciguatera or other toxin contamination * Scombrotoxin * Chemical contamination			
Critical Limits		Verification	Records
Receive at 41°F or below Approved source Seafood HACCP plan Proper chemical storage/use			
SOPS			
PROCESS #1: Food preparation with no cook step—ready-to-eat food that is stored, prepared and served. PROCESS #2: Food preparation for same day service—food that is stored, prepared, cooked and served. PROCESS #3: Complex food preparation—food that is stored, prepared, cooked, cooled, reheated, hot held and served.			

Storing

When food is in refrigerated storage, your management system should focus on preventing the growth of bacteria that may be present in the product. This is primarily achieved through temperature control. Special attention needs to be given to controlling and monitoring the temperatures of potentially hazardous ready-to-eat foods.

When determining the monitoring frequency of product storage temperature, it is important to make sure that the interval between temperature checks is established to ensure that the hazard is being controlled and time is allowed for an appropriate corrective action. For example, if you are storing potentially hazardous ready-to-eat foods under refrigeration, you may decide to set a critical limit for the refrigeration units to operate at 41°F or below. You may also want to set a target or operating limit, of 40°F for example, in order to provide a safety cushion that allows you the opportunity to see a trend toward exceeding 41°F and to intervene with appropriate corrective actions.

Monitoring procedures for ready-to-eat food ideally include internal product temperature checks. You need to assess whether it is realistic and practical for you to do this, depending on the volume of food you are storing.

You may choose to base your monitoring system on the air temperature of the refrigerated equipment as an SOP. How often you need to monitor the air temperature depends on:

- Whether the air temperature of the refrigerator accurately reflects the internal product temperature (remember, your food safety refrigeration temperature must be based on the internal product temperature of the food stored within a refrigeration unit, not the air temperature).

- The capacity and use of your refrigeration equipment.

- The volume and type of food products stored in your cold storage units.

- The SOPs that support monitoring this process.

- Shift changes and other operational considerations.

SOPs can be developed to control some hazards and assist in implementing a food safety system that minimizes the potential for bacterial growth and contamination. The control of cross-contamination can be done by separating raw foods from ready-to-eat products within your operation's refrigeration and storage facilities.

Special consideration should be given to the storage of scombroid fish due to the potential formation of histamine, a chemical hazard. To control histamine formation in scombroid toxin-forming fish, it is recommended that storage be a CCP with the critical limit not to exceed 41°F, as stated in the Food Code, unless you can show through scientific data that the food safety hazard will not result.

OPERATIONAL STEP 2: STORING

PROCESS 1: Examples: Salads, Sushi		CCP: ☐ Yes ☐ No
Hazard	Monitoring	Corrective Actions
* Bacterial growth * Cross-contamination * Parasites * Chemical contamination		
Critical Limits	Verification	Records
Store at 41°F or below Separate raw from ready-to-eat food Freeze fish to be consumed raw @ -4°F for 7 days or -31°F for 15 hours Proper chemical storage/use		

PROCESS 2: Examples: Hamburgers, Mahi-mahi		CCP: ☐ Yes ☐ No
Hazard	Monitoring	Corrective Actions
* Bacterial growth * Scombrotoxin * Cross-contamination * Chemical contamination		
Critical Limits	Verification	Records
Store at 41°F or below Separate raw from ready-to-eat food Proper chemical storage/use		

PROCESS 3: Examples: Soups		CCP: ☐ Yes ☐ No
Hazard	Monitoring	Corrective Actions
* Bacterial growth * Scombrotoxin * Cross-contamination * Chemical contamination		
Critical Limits	Verification	Records
Store at 41°F or below Separate raw from ready-to-eat food Proper chemical storage/use		

SOPS
PROCESS #1: Food preparation with no cook step—ready-to-eat food that is stored, prepared and served.
PROCESS #2: Food preparation for same-day service—food that is stored, prepared, cooked and served.
PROCESS #3: Complex food preparation—food that is stored, prepared, cooked, cooled, reheated, hot held and served.

Preparation

Of all the operational steps in food processes, preparation has the greatest variety of activities that must be controlled, monitored and, in some cases, documented. It is impossible to include in this model a summary guide that covers the diversity in menus, employee skills and facility design that impact the preparation of food. The preparation step may involve several processes, including thawing a frozen food, mixing together several ingredients, cutting, chopping, slicing or breading.

At the preparation step, SOPs can be developed to control some hazards and assist in implementation of a food safety system that minimizes the potential for bacterial growth and contamination from employees and equipment.

Front-line employees will most likely have the greatest need to work with the food. A well-designed personal hygiene program that has been communicated to all employees will minimize the potential for bacterial, parasitic and viral contamination. Your program must include instructions to your employees as to when and how to wash their hands. Procedures need to be in place that either eliminate employees' hand contact with ready-to-eat foods or implement an alternative personal hygiene program that provides an equivalent level of control of bacterial, parasitic and viral hazards. It is also very important to identify and restrict ill employees from working with food, especially if they have diarrhea.

Procedures must be in place to prevent cross-contamination from utensils and equipment. Designated areas or procedures that separate the preparation of raw foods from ready-to-eat foods minimize the potential for bacterial contamination. Proper cleaning and sanitizing of equipment and work surfaces are an integral SOP to this operational step.

Batch preparation is an important tool for controlling bacterial growth because limiting the amount of food prepared minimizes the time the food is kept at a temperature that allows growth. Planning your preparation ahead assists in minimizing the time food must be out of temperature at this operational step. Batch preparation also breaks the growth cycle of bacteria before they can reach dangerous levels.

When thawing frozen foods, maintaining proper product temperature and managing time are the primary controls for minimizing bacterial growth. Procedures need to be in place to minimize the potential for microbial, chemical and physical contamination during thawing.

Use of prechilled ingredients to prepare a cold product, such as tuna salad, will assist you in maintaining temperature control for this process.

Special consideration should be given to disallowing bare-hand contact in the preparation of ready-to-eat foods. You need to control the introduction of hazards during preparation. How will you accomplish controlling the hazard presented by hand contact with ready-to-eat food? You should review your operation to determine whether this operational step will be controlled as a CCP or an SOP.

Operational Step 3: PREPARATION

PROCESS 1: Examples: Salads, Sushi		CCP: ☐ Yes ☐ No
Hazard	Monitoring	Corrective Actions
* Bacterial growth * Cross-contamination * Contamination from employees * Chemical contamination		
Critical Limits	Verification	Records
Store at 41°F or below or use time to control growth Separate raw from ready-to-eat food Restrict ill employees; control bare-hand contact Proper chemical storage/use		

PROCESS 2: Examples: Hamburgers, Mahi-mahi		CCP: ☐ Yes ☐ No
Hazard	Monitoring	Corrective Actions
* Bacterial growth * Cross-contamination * Contamination from employees * Chemical contamination		
Critical Limits	Verification	Records
Store at 41°F or below or use time to control growth Separate raw from ready-to-eat food Restrict ill employees; control bare-hand contact Proper chemical storage/use		

PROCESS 3: Examples: Soups		CCP: ☐ Yes ☐ No
Hazard	Monitoring	Corrective Actions
* Bacterial growth * Cross-contamination * Contamination from employees * Chemical contamination		
Critical Limits	Verification	Records
Store at 41°F or below or use time to control growth Separate raw from ready-to-eat food Restrict ill employees; control bare-hand contact Proper chemical storage/use		
SOPs		
PROCESS #1: Food preparation with no cook step — ready-to-eat food that is stored, prepared and served. PROCESS #2: Food preparation for same day service—food that is stored, prepared, cooked and served. PROCESS #3: Complex food preparation—food that is stored, prepared, cooked, cooled, reheated, hot held and served.		

Cooking

This operational step only applies to those foods that you have listed in Processes #2 and #3. Cooking foods of animal origin is the most effective operational step in food processes for reducing and eliminating biological contamination. Hot temperatures will kill most harmful bacteria and with relatively few exceptions, such as cooking plant foods, this is a CCP. It is at this step that food will be made safe to eat. Therefore, product temperature and time measurements are very important. If the appropriate product temperature for the required amount of time is not achieved, bacteria, parasites or viruses may survive in the food.

Critical time and temperature limits vary according to the type of food. Employees should view ensuring proper cooking temperatures as an essential element in producing an acceptable product. A final cooking time and temperature chart for specific foods is included for your review. Simply reference the foods specific to your food establishment and incorporate the appropriate critical time and temperature limits into your management system.

You will need to determine the best system for you to use that will ensure that the proper cooking temperature and time are reached. Checking the internal product temperature is the most desirable monitoring method. However, when large volumes of food are cooked, a temperature check of each individual item may not be practical. For instance, a quick-service food operation may cook several hundred hamburgers during lunch. If checking the temperature of each hamburger is not reasonable for you to do, then you need to routinely verify that the specific process and cooking equipment are capable of attaining a final internal product temperature at all locations in or on the cooking equipment.

Once a specific process has been shown to work for you, the frequency of recordkeeping may be reduced. In these instances, a recordkeeping system should be established to provide scheduled product temperature checks to ensure that the process is working.

Special consideration should be given to time and temperature in the cooking of fish and other raw animal foods. To control the pathogens, it is recommended that cooking be a CCP, based upon the critical limits established by the Food Code, unless you can show through scientific data that the food safety hazard will not result.

Operational Step 4: COOKING

PROCESS 1: Examples: Salads, Sushi		CCP: ☐ Yes ☐ No
Hazard	Monitoring	Corrective Actions
Does not apply	Does not apply	Does not apply
Critical Limits	Verification	Records
Does not apply	Does not apply	Does not apply

PROCESS 2: Examples: Hamburgers, Mahi-mahi		CCP: ☐ Yes ☐ No
Hazard	Monitoring	Corrective Actions
* Bacterial, parasitic or viral survival or growth		
Critical Limits	Verification	Records
Cook to <u>Product</u> <u>Internal Temp</u> <u>Time</u> See Chart 2		

PROCESS 3: Examples: Soups		CCP: ☐ Yes ☐ No
Hazard	Monitoring	Corrective Actions
* Bacterial, parasitic or viral survival or growth		
Critical Limits	Verification	Records
Same as Process #2		
SOPs		
PROCESS #1: Food preparation with no cook step—ready-to-eat food that is stored, prepared and served. PROCESS #2: Food preparation for same-day service—food that is stored, prepared, cooked and served. PROCESS #3: Complex food preparation—food that is stored, prepared, cooked, cooled, reheated, hot held and served.		

CHART 2: FOOD CODE COOKING TEMPERATURES AND TIMES		
Product	**Final Internal Temperature**	**Time**
1a. Poultry Wild Game Animals Stuffed Fish Stuffed Meat Stuffed Pasta Stuffed Poultry Stuffed Ratites or Stuffing containing – Fish – Meat – Poultry – Ratites	1a. 165°F	1a. 15 seconds
1b. Animal foods cooked in a micro-wave oven	1b. 165°F; food rotated, stirred, covered	1b. Cover and allow to stand for 2 minutes
2a. Pork, ratites or injected meats	2a. 155°F	2a. 15 seconds
2b. Ground meat, fish, or game animals commercially raised for food	2b. 155°F	2b. 15 seconds
2c. Game animals under a voluntary inspection program	2c. 155°F	2c. 15 seconds
2d. Raw shell eggs that are NOT prepared for immediate service	2d. 155°F	2d. 15 seconds
3a. Raw shell eggs broken and prepared in response to consumer order and for immediate service	3a. 145°F	3a. 15 seconds
3b. Fish and meat including game animals except as specifically referenced on this chart	3b. 145°F	3b. 15 seconds
4a. Fruit and vegetables cooked for hot holding	4a. 140°F or above	4a. Instantaneous

CHART 2: FOOD CODE COOKING TEMPERATURES AND TIMES		
Product	**Final Internal Temperature**	**Time**
4b. Ready-to-eat food from a commercially sealed container for hot holding	4b. 140°F or above	4b. Instantaneous
4c. Ready-to-eat food from an intact package (from a food processing plant inspected by the regulatory authority with jurisdiction over the plant) for hot holding	4c. 140°F or above	4c. Instantaneous
5a. Beef roast/corned beef roasts (preheated oven temperatures)	5a. <u>LESS THAN 10 lbs.</u> • Still Dry: 350°F or more • Convection: 325°F or more (iii) High Humidity: 250°F or less <u>MORE THAN 10 lbs</u> • Still Dry: 250°F or more (ii) Convection: 250°F or more (iii) High Humidity: 250°F or less	
5b. Beef roast/corned beef roasts (internal food temperature for specified amount of time)	5b. <u>ACHIEVE ONE OF THE FOLLOWING:</u> • 130°F for 121 Minutes • 132°F for 77 Minutes • 134°F for 47 Minutes • 136°F for 32 Minutes • 138°F for 19 Minutes • 140°F for 12 Minutes • 142°F for 8 Minutes • 144°F for 5 Minutes • 145°F for 3 Minutes	

Cooling

This operational step is only used for those foods that you have listed in Process #3. One of the most labor-intensive operational steps is rapidly cooling hot foods to control microbial growth. Excessive time for the cooling of potentially hazardous foods has been consistently identified as one of the factors contributing to food-borne illness. Foods that have been cooked and held at improper temperatures provide an excellent environment for the growth of disease-causing microorganisms that may have survived the cooking process (spore-formers). Recontamination of a cooked food item by poor employee practices or cross-contamination from other food products, utensils and equipment is a concern at this operational step.

Special consideration should be given to large food items, such as roasts, turkeys, thick soups, stews, chili and large containers of rice or refried beans. These foods take a long time to cool because of their mass and volume. If the hot food container is tightly covered, the cooling rate will be further slowed down. By reducing the volume of the food in an individual container and leaving an opening for heat to escape by keeping the cover loose, the rate of cooling is dramatically increased.

Commercial refrigeration equipment is designed to hold cold food temperatures, not cool large masses of food. Some alternatives for cooling foods include:

- Using rapid-chill refrigeration equipment designed to cool the food to acceptable temperatures quickly by using increased compressor capacity and high rates of air circulation.

- Avoiding the need to cool large masses by preparing smaller batches closer to periods of service.

- Stirring hot food while the food container is within an ice water bath.

- Redesigning your recipe so that you prepare and cook a smaller or concentrated base and then add enough cold water or ice to make up the volume that you need. This may work for some water-based soups, for example.

Whatever the cooling method you choose, you need to verify that the process works. Once again, if a specific process has been shown to work for you, the frequency of recordkeeping may be reduced. A recordkeeping system should be established to provide scheduled product temperatures checks to ensure the process is working.

Operational Step 5: COOLING

PROCESS 1: Examples: Salads, Sushi		CCP: ☐ Yes ☐ No
Hazard	Monitoring	Corrective Actions
Does not apply	Does not apply	Does not apply
Critical Limits	Verification	Records
Does not apply	Does not apply	Does not apply

PROCESS 2: Examples: Hamburgers, Mahi-mahi		CCP: ☐ Yes ☐ No
Hazard	Monitoring	Corrective Actions
Does not apply	Does not apply	Does not apply
Critical Limits	Verification	Records
Does not apply	Does not apply	Does not apply

PROCESS 3: Examples: Soups		CCP: ☐ Yes ☐ No
Hazard	Monitoring	Corrective Actions
* Bacterial growth * Cross-contamination * Contamination from employees or equipment		
Critical Limits	Verification	Records
Cool food from 140°F to 70°F within 2 hours and from 70°F to 41°F within 4 hours Separate raw from ready-to-eat food Restrict ill employees; control bare-hand contact		
SOPs		
PROCESS #1: Food preparation with no cook step—ready-to-eat food that is stored, prepared and served. PROCESS #2: Food preparation for same-day service—food that is stored, prepared, cooked and served. PROCESS #3: Complex food preparation—food that is stored, prepared, cooked, cooled, reheated, hot held and served.		

Reheating

This operational step applies only to those foods that you listed in Process #3. If food is held at improper temperatures for enough time, pathogens have the opportunity to multiply to dangerous numbers. Proper reheating provides an important control for eliminating these organisms. It is especially effective in reducing contamination from bacterial spore-formers which survived the cooking process and may have multiplied because foods were held at improper temperatures.

Although proper reheating will kill most organisms of concern, it will not eliminate toxins, such as that produced by Staphylococcus aureus. If microbial controls and SOPs at previous operational steps have not been followed correctly and Staph toxin has been formed in the food, reheating will not make the food safe.

Incorporating a comprehensive personal hygiene program throughout the process will minimize the risk from Staph toxin. Along with personal hygiene, preventing cross-contamination through the use of cleaned and sanitized equipment and utensils is an important control measure.

Special consideration should be given to the time and temperature in the reheating of cooked foods. To control the pathogens, it is recommended that reheating be a CCP, based upon the critical limits established by the Food Code, unless you can show through scientific data that the food safety hazard will not result.

Operational Step 6: REHEATING

PROCESS 1: Examples: Salads, Sushi		CCP: ☐ Yes ☐ No
Hazard	Monitoring	Corrective Actions
Does not apply	Does not apply	Does not apply
Critical Limits	Verification	Records
Does not apply	Does not apply	Does not apply

PROCESS 2: Examples: Hamburgers, Mahi-mahi		CCP: ☐ Yes ☐ No
Hazard	Monitoring	Corrective Actions
Does not apply	Does not apply	Does not apply
Critical Limits	Verification	Records
Does not apply	Does not apply	Does not apply

PROCESS 3: Examples: Soups		CCP: ☐ Yes ☐ No
Hazard	Monitoring	Corrective Actions
* Bacterial, parasitic or viral survival or growth		
Critical Limits	Verification	Records
Reheat to 165°F within 2 hours		
SOPs		
PROCESS #1: Food preparation with no cook step—ready-to-eat food that is stored, prepared and served. PROCESS #2: Food preparation for same-day service—food that is stored, prepared, cooked and served. PROCESS #3: Complex food preparation—food that is stored, prepared, cooked, cooled, reheated, hot held and served.		

Holding

All three processes may involve holding. Proper temperature of the food while being held is essential in controlling the growth of harmful bacteria. Cold temperature holding may occur in Processes 1, 2 or 3. Hot temperature holding occurs primarily only in Processes 2 and 3. Where there is a cooking step as a CCP to eliminate pathogens, all but the spore-forming organisms should be killed or inactivated. If cooked food is not held at the proper temperature, the rapid growth of these spore-forming bacteria is a major food-safety concern.

When food is held, cooled and reheated in a food establishment, there is an increased risk from contamination caused by personnel, equipment, procedures or other factors. Harmful bacteria that are introduced into a product that is not held at proper temperature have the opportunity to multiply to large numbers in a short period of time. Once again, management of personal hygiene and the prevention of cross-contamination impact the safety of the food at this operational step.

Keeping food products at 140°F or above during hot holding and keeping food products at or below 41°F is effective in preventing microbial growth. As an alternative to temperature control, the Food Code details actions when time alone is used as a control, including a comprehensive monitoring and food-marking system to ensure food safety.

How often you monitor the temperature of foods during hot holding determines what type of corrective action you are able to take when 140°F is not met. If the critical limit is not met, your options for corrective action may include evaluating the time the food is out of temperature to determine the severity of the hazard and based on that information, reheating the food, if appropriate, or discarding it. Monitoring frequency may mean the difference between reheating the food to 165°F or discarding it.

When determining the monitoring frequency of cold product temperatures, it is important to make sure that the interval between temperature checks is established to ensure that the hazard is being controlled and time is allowed for an appropriate corrective action. For example, if you are holding potentially hazardous ready-to-eat foods under refrigeration, such as potato salad at a salad bar, you may decide to set a critical limit at 41°F or below. You may also want to set a target, or operating limit, of 40°F, for example, in order to provide a safety cushion that allows you the opportunity to see a trend toward exceeding 41°F and to intervene with appropriate corrective actions.

Special consideration should be given to the time and temperature in the hot or cold holding of potentially hazardous foods to control pathogens. It is recommended that hot or cold holding be a CCP, based upon the critical limits established by the Food Code, unless you can show through scientific data that the food safety hazard will not result.

Operational Step 7: HOLDING

PROCESS 1: Examples: Salads, Sushi		CCP: ☐ Yes ☐ No
Hazard	Monitoring	Corrective Actions
* Bacterial, parasitic or viral introduction, survival or growth		
Critical Limits	Verification	Records
41°F		

PROCESS 2: Examples: Hamburgers, Mahi-mahi		CCP: ☐ Yes ☐ No
Hazard	Monitoring	Corrective Actions
* Bacterial, parasitic or viral introduction, survival or growth		
Critical Limits	Verification	Records
140°F or 41°F		

PROCESS 3: Examples: Soups		CCP: ☐ Yes ☐ No
Hazard	Monitoring	Corrective Actions
* Bacterial, parasitic or viral introduction, survival or growth		
Critical Limits	Verification	Records
140°F or 41°F		
SOPs		
PROCESS #1: Food preparation with no cook step—ready-to-eat food that is stored, prepared and served. PROCESS #2: Food preparation for same-day service—food that is stored, prepared, cooked and served. PROCESS #3: Complex food preparation—food that is stored, prepared, cooked, cooled, reheated, hot held and served.		

Setup and Packing

Setup and packing is an operational step used by some retail food establishments including caterers (e.g., restaurant/caterer or interstate conveyance caterer), commissaries, grocery stores (for display cases), schools, nursing homes, hospitals or services such as delivery of meals to home-bound persons. Set up and packing can be controlled through an SOP and may involve wrapping food items, assembling these items onto trays, and packing them into a transportation carrier or placing them in a display case. An example would be an airline flight kitchen where food entrées are wrapped, assembled and placed into portable food carts which are taken to a final holding cooler. Hospital kitchens would be another example where patient trays are assembled and placed into carriers for transportation to nursing stations. Food may be placed into bulk containers for transportation to another site where it is served.

This operational step might not be considered a CCP, but it is a special consideration when setting up your program. This process can be controlled by strict adherence to SOPs to minimize the potential for bacterial contamination and growth, to eliminate bare-hand contact with ready-to-eat foods, to ensure proper hand washing, and to ensure food only comes into contact with cleaned and sanitized surfaces.

Following final assembly into either individual trays or into bulk containers, the food may be held for immediate service or for transportation to another site for service. This hot holding or cold holding operational step needs to be evaluated in the same manner as other holding operational steps on the worksheet.

Temperature control or using time as a control measure during transportation and holding and serving at a remote site must be evaluated and managed as part of your food safety system.

Special consideration should be given to time/temperature controls and the prevention of cross-contamination from equipment and utensils and contamination from employees' hands. This process may be adequately controlled through an SOP; however, holding and transportation should be considered CCPs.

Operational Step 8: SETUP AND PACKING

PROCESS 1: Examples: Salads, Sushi		CCP: ☐ Yes ☐ No
Hazard	Monitoring	Corrective Actions
* Bacterial Growth * Microbial contamination from employees	Does not apply	Does not apply
Critical Limits	Verification	Records
41°F No bare-hand contact or equivalent alternative	Does not apply	Does not apply

PROCESS 2: Examples: Hamburgers, Mahi-mahi		CCP: ☐ Yes ☐ No
Hazard	Monitoring	Corrective Actions
* Bacterial Growth * Microbial contamination from employees		
Critical Limits	Verification	Records
140°F or 41°F No bare-hand contact or equivalent alternative		

PROCESS 3: Examples: Soups		CCP: ☐ Yes ☐ No
Hazard	Monitoring	Corrective Actions
* Bacterial Growth * Microbial contamination from employees		
Critical Limits	Verification	Records
140°F or 41°F; No bare-hand contact or equivalent alternative		

Serving

This is the final operational step before the food reaches the customer. When employees work with food and food-contact surfaces, they can easily spread bacteria, parasites and viruses and contaminate these items. Managing employees' personal hygienic practices is important to controlling these hazards. A management program for employee personal hygiene includes proper hand washing, the appropriate use of gloves and dispensing utensils, and controlling bare-hand contact with ready-to-eat foods.

Minimizing the growth of bacteria is also a concern at hot and cold holding customer display areas. Maintaining food products at proper temperatures within these display units will control the growth of microorganisms. Refer to the HOLDING worksheet for additional information.

Special consideration needs to be given to minimizing contamination from the customer. Customer self-service displays, such as salad bars, require specific procedures to protect the food from contamination. Some suggestions for protecting food on display include:

- The use of packaging.

- Counter, service line or salad bar food guards.

- Display cases.

- Suitable utensils or effective dispensing methods.

- Not mixing an old product with fresh.

- Having employees monitor self-serve stations.

- Preventing cross-contamination from soiled utensils and equipment will minimize the potential for bacterial contamination of ready-to-eat foods.

Operational Step 9: SERVING

PROCESS 1: Examples: Salads, Sushi		CCP: ☐ Yes ☐ No
Hazard	Monitoring	Corrective Actions
* Bacterial, parasitic, viral or physical contamination		
Critical Limits	Verification	Records
Does not apply		

PROCESS 2: Examples: Hamburgers, Mahi-mahi		CCP: ☐ Yes ☐ No
Hazard	Monitoring	Corrective Actions
* Bacterial, parasitic, viral or physical contamination		
Critical Limits	Verification	Records
Cook to <u>Product</u> <u>Internal Temp</u> <u>Time</u> See Chart 2		

PROCESS 3: Examples: Soups		CCP: ☐ Yes ☐ No
Hazard	Monitoring	Corrective Actions
* Bacterial, parasitic, viral or physical contamination		
Critical Limits	Verification	Records
Same as Process #2		
SOPs		
PROCESS #1: Food preparation with no cook step—ready-to-eat food that is stored, prepared and served. PROCESS #2: Food preparation for same-day service—food that is stored, prepared, cooked and served. PROCESS #3: Complex food preparation—food that is stored, prepared, cooked, cooled, reheated, hot held and served.		

PROCEDURAL STEP 3

Identify CCPs and Critical Limits

The CCPs column identifies places in the flow of food where you can have a significant impact in controlling food safety hazards. A measurable critical limit has been identified for each of these CCPs. These critical limits provide the baseline for measuring the effectiveness of your food safety procedures.

For each of your operational steps, within your operation, review the CCPs and critical limits needed to minimize or eliminate significant food safety hazards. Does your operation currently have control measures in place that are at least equivalent to these critical limits?

On the worksheet, you will need to decide whether the operational step is a CCP or whether the hazard is controlled by your SOPs that address the prerequisite program elements.

In some operational step worksheets, such as the Cooking step, the guide recommends that the step be considered a CCP because there is no practical alternative to ensure control of the hazard. In other operational steps, you may have a choice as to how you will control the hazard. For example, in the Preparation step for ready-to-eat foods, you will identify contamination from employees' hands as a hazard. When controlling that hazard as a CCP, you must also identify the critical limits, establish monitoring and corrective actions, verification procedures and records. Alternatively, you may choose to control that hazard by instituting an SOP that disallows bare-hand contact with ready-to-eat food. You will need to decide the most effective method of controlling the hazard; that is, as a CCP or through use of an SOP.

PROCEDURAL STEP 4

Monitor CCPs

Use the worksheet to develop procedures, customized to your operation, for monitoring your CCPs. Consideration should be given to determining answers to the following questions.

- What critical limit at the CCP are you measuring?

- How is it monitored?

- When and how often will the CCP be monitored?

- Who will be responsible for monitoring it?

Monitoring is observing or measuring specific operational steps in the food process to determine if your critical limits are being met. This activity is essential in making sure your critical food processes are under control. It will identify where a loss of control occurs or if there is a trend toward a loss of control of a critical food process. Needed adjustments will then become obvious.

In your food safety management system, certain processes have been identified as CCPs. What you are going to monitor depends on the critical limits you have established at each CCP. Minimum critical limits for many CCPs have been established by the Food Code. For example, cooking hamburger (which is the CCP) to 155°F for 15 seconds (which is the critical limit) will kill most harmful bacteria. Therefore, final temperature and time measurements are very important, and you need to determine how you will effectively monitor the critical limits for each CCP.

Is monitoring equipment needed to measure a critical limit? The equipment you choose for monitoring must be accurate and routinely calibrated to ensure critical limits are met. For example, a thermocouple with a thin probe might be the most appropriate tool for measuring the final product temperature of hamburger patties.

When deciding how often you need to monitor, make sure that the monitoring interval will be reliable enough to ensure the hazard is being controlled. Your procedure for monitoring should be simple and easy to follow.

Individuals chosen to be responsible for a monitoring activity may be a manager, line-supervisor or a designated employee. Your monitoring system will only be effective if employees are given the knowledge, skills and responsibility for serving safe food. Train your employees to carefully follow your procedures, monitor CCPs and take corrective action if critical limits are not met.

PROCEDURAL STEP 5

Develop Corrective Actions

Decide what type of corrective action you need to take if a critical limit is not met.

- What measures do you expect employees to take to correct the problem?

- Is the corrective action understood by your employees?

- Can the corrective action be easily implemented?

- Are different options needed for the appropriate corrective actions, depending on the process and monitoring frequency?

- How will these corrective actions be documented and communicated to management so the system can be modified to prevent the problem from occurring again?

Whenever a critical limit is not met, a corrective action must be carried out immediately. Corrective actions may be simply continuing to heat food to the required temperature. Other corrective actions may be more complicated, such as rejecting a shipment of raw oysters that does not have the required tags or segregating and holding a product until an evaluation is done.

In the event that a corrective action is taken, you should reassess and modify, if necessary, your food safety system based upon the HACCP principles. Despite the best system, errors occur during food storage and preparation. A food safety system based upon the HACCP principles is designed to detect errors and correct them before a food safety hazard occurs. It is a benefit to the industry and regulators to be able to show that immediate action is taken to ensure that no food product that may be injurious to health is served to or purchased by a customer. It is important to document all corrective actions in written records.

PROCEDURAL STEP 6

Conduct Ongoing Verification

Because HACCP is a system to maintain continuous control of food safety practices, implementation of the plan needs to be audited or verified; verification is usually performed by someone other than the person who is responsible for performing the activities specified in the plan. That person might be a manager, supervisor, designated person or the regulatory authority.

There is ongoing verification which is conducted frequently, such as daily, weekly, monthly, etc., by designated employees of the establishment. It is important to note that routine monitoring should not be confused with audit or verification methods or procedures.

There is long-term verification, which is done less frequently. This will be discussed in Procedural Step 8.

Verification is an oversight auditing process to ensure that the HACCP plan and SOPs continue to:

- Be adequate to control the hazards identified as likely to occur.

- Be consistently followed (i.e., a comparison is made regarding observed, actual practices and procedures with what is written in the plan).

Ongoing verification activities include:

- Observing the person doing the monitoring: Is monitoring being done as planned?

- Reviewing the monitoring records: Are records completed accurately?

- Do records show that the predetermined frequency of the monitoring is followed?

- Was the planned corrective action taken when the person monitoring found and recorded that the critical limit was not met?

- Do records of the calibration of monitoring equipment indicate that the equipment was operating properly?

Verification Procedures

Procedures may include the following activities:

- Observe the person conducting the activities at the CCPs and recording information.

- Check monitoring records.

- Check corrective action records.

- Periodically review the total plan.

- Test product in process or finished product.

- Review equipment calibration records.

- Review recording thermometer accuracy (large operations and some processes such as large quantity cook and chill operations or smokers, etc.).

Verification Frequency

Verification should occur at a frequency that can ensure the HACCP plan is being followed continuously to:

- Avoid adulterated/unsafe product getting to the consumer.

- Be able to take corrective action without loss of product.

- Ensure prescribed personnel practices are consistently followed.

- Ensure personnel have the tools for proper personal hygiene and sanitary practices (e.g., hand-washing facilities, sanitizing equipment, cleaning supplies, temperature-measuring devices, sufficient gloves, etc.).

- Follow/comply with the control procedures established.

- Conduct calibrations as needed depending upon the type of equipment (some may be verified daily and others annually).

Verification Observations/Documentation—Examples

System Verification

Receiving: The manager reviews temperature logs of refrigerated products at various intervals, such as daily or weekly. An operation may want its HACCP plan to specify that the manager checks the monitoring records daily if receiving constitutes a high volume or products include particular items such as fresh tuna, mahi-mahi, mackerel (scombrotoxin-forming species), etc.

Chill step: Weekly, the production manager checks the "chilling log" that is maintained for foods that are either left over or planned for later service. Recorded on the log sheet are the time the food is placed into the cooler, its temperature, the type of container used (depth per SOP), and measurements of the time and temperature involved in cooling the food.

Hand-washing facilities and practices: Daily, the manager checks the log maintained at the hand-washing facilities and corrections made in areas where ready-to-eat food is prepared. Less frequent checks are made in other areas of the operation.

Process verification: The manager checks daily or weekly the time/temperature monitoring records at all CCPs (receiving, holding, preparation before cooking for scombrotoxin-forming seafood, cooking time/temp for hamburgers, etc.).

PROCEDURAL STEP 7

Keep Records

In order to develop the most effective recordkeeping system for your operation, determine what documented information will assist you in managing the control of food safety hazards. Some recorded information should already be part of your food safety system, like shellfish tags, and an additional records may not be needed. Your recordkeeping system can use existing paperwork, such as delivery invoices, for documenting product temperature. Another method could be maintaining a log to record the temperatures. A recordkeeping system can be simple and needs to be designed to meet the needs of the individual establishment. It can be accomplished many different ways that are customized to your operation as long as it provides a system to determine that activities are performed according to the HACCP plan.

Accurate recordkeeping is an essential part of a successful HACCP program. Records provide documentation that the critical limits at each CCP were met or that appropriate corrective actions were taken when the limits were not met. Records also show that the actions performed were verified.

Involve your employees in the development of your management system. Ask them how they are currently monitoring CCPs. Discuss with them the types of corrective actions they take when a critical limit is not met. Employees are an important source for developing simple and effective recordkeeping procedures. Managers are responsible for designing the system, but effective day-to-day implementation involves every employee.

The simplest recordkeeping system that lends itself to integration into existing operations is always best. A simple yet effective system is easier to use and communicate to your employees.

Recordkeeping systems designed to document a process rather than product information may be more adaptable within a retail food establishment, especially if you frequently change items on your menu. Accurately documenting processes like cooking, cooling and reheating, identified as CCPs, provides active managerial control of food safety hazards. Consistent process control by management reduces the risk of food-borne illness.

Simple logs for recording refrigeration equipment temperatures are perhaps the most common SOP records currently maintained. However, product temperature records are commonly CCP records.

Other records may include:

- Writing the product temperature on delivery invoices.

- Keeping a log of internal product temperatures of cooked foods.

- Holding shell stock tags for 90 days.

Some retail establishments have implemented comprehensive HACCP systems where records are maintained for each CCP. These records may be quality-control logs, but they can also constitute CCP records if they are designed to monitor activities that are, in fact, CCPs. The level of sophistication of recordkeeping is dependent upon the complexity of the food operation. For example, a cook-chill operation for a large institution would require more recordkeeping than a limited-menu, cook-serve operation.

Once a specific process has been shown to work for you, such as an ice bath method for cooling certain foods, the frequency of recordkeeping may be reduced. In these instances, a recordkeeping system provides a scheduled check (verification) of the process to ensure that it effectively controls the risk factor. This approach is extremely effective for labor-intensive processes related to:

- Cooking large volumes of food where a temperature check of each individual item is impractical.

- Implementing a verified process will allow employees to complete the procedure within the course of a scheduled work day.

- Cooling foods or leftovers at the end of the business day.

- Maintaining cold holding temperatures of ready-to-eat, potentially hazardous foods in walk-in refrigeration units.

PROCEDURAL STEP 8

Conduct Long-Term Verification

Once your food safety system is implemented, you will need to confirm that it is effective over time, an activity referred to in this document as long-term verification. You may benefit from both internal (quality control) verifications and external verifications that may involve assistance from the regulatory authority or consultants.

Long-term verification is conducted less frequently (e.g., yearly) than ongoing verification. It is a review or audit of the plan to determine if:

- Any new product/processes/menu items have been added to the menu.

- Suppliers, customers, equipment or facilities have changed.

- The SOPs are current and implemented.

- The worksheets are still current.

- The CCPs are still correct or if new CCPs are needed.

- The critical limits are set realistically and are adequate to control the hazard (e.g., the time needed to cook the food to meet the Food Code internal temperature requirement).

- Monitoring equipment has been calibrated as planned.

Long-term verification helps the operator:

- Ensure the food safety management system is implemented and the HACCP plan is being followed.

- Improve the system and HACCP plan by identifying weaknesses.

- Eliminate unnecessary or ineffective controls.

- Determine if the HACCP plan needs to be modified or updated.

Procedural Step 8: Long-Term Verification

Here is an example of a long-term verification form.

Long-Term Verification Form			
Name of person responsible for long-term verification: _____			
Title: _____			
Frequency at which the long-term verification is done: _____			
Reason, other than frequency, for doing a long-term verification: _____ _____			
Date of last long-term verification: _____			
The length of time this record is kept on file: _____			
1. (a) Has a new product, process or menu item been added since the last verification?	☐ No ☐ Yes	Does this change necessitate a change on the worksheet? ☐ No ☐ Yes	
(b) Has the supplier, customer, equipment or facility changed since the last verification?	☐ No ☐ Yes Go to Question #2		
2. Do the existing worksheets contain accurate and current information?	☐ No ☐ Yes Go to Question #3	Worksheet information updated:	Date: Name:
3. Are the existing CCPs correctly identified?	☐ No ☐ Yes Go to Question #4	CCPs updated:	Date: Name:
4. Are the existing critical limits appropriate to control each hazard?	☐ No ☐ Yes Go to Question #5	CLs updated:	Date: Name:
5. Do the existing monitoring procedures ensure that the critical limits are met?	☐ No ☐ Yes Go to Question #6	Monitoring procedures updated:	Date: Name:

6.	Do existing corrective actions ensure that no injurious food is served or purchased?	☐ No ☐ Yes Go to Question #7	Corrective actions updated:	Date:
				Name:
7.	Do the existing ongoing verification procedures ensure that the food safety system is adequate to control hazards and is consistently followed?	☐ No ☐ Yes Go to Question #8	Ongoing verification procedures updated:	Date:
				Name:
8.	Does the existing recordkeeping system provide adequate documentation that the critical limits are met and corrective actions are taken when needed?	☐ No ☐ Yes Go to Question #9	Recordkeeping procedures updated:	Date:
				Name:
9.	Are the existing SOPs current and implemented?	☐ No ☐ Yes	Does this necessitate a change in your plan? If so, start again with Question #1.	

The long-term verification procedure is now complete.

The next long-term verification is due _____.

The changes made to the food safety management system were conveyed to the line supervisor or front-line employees on _____.

Completed by:	Name: _____
	Title: _____
	Date: _____

HACCP CHECKLISTS

Here are some checklists you can use for your HACCP system.

MANAGER SELF-INSPECTION CHECKLIST	
DATE_____ OBSERVER_____	
Personal Dress and Hygiene	
☐ YES ☐ NO	Employees wear proper uniform including proper shoes. Corrective Action:
☐ YES ☐ NO	Hair restraint is worn. Corrective Action:
☐ YES ☐ NO	Fingernails are short, unpolished and clean. Corrective Action:
☐ YES ☐ NO	Jewelry is limited to watch, simple earrings and plain ring. Corrective Action:
☐ YES ☐ NO	Hands are washed or gloves are changed at critical points. Corrective Action:
☐ YES ☐ NO	Open sores, cuts, splints or bandages on hands are completely covered while handling food. Corrective Action:
☐ YES ☐ NO	Hands are washed thoroughly using proper hand-washing techniques at critical points. Corrective Action:

☐ YES ☐ NO	Smoking is observed only in designated areas away from preparation, service, storage and ware-washing areas. Corrective Action:
☐ YES ☐ NO	Eating, drinking and chewing gum are observed only in designated areas away from work areas. Corrective Action:
☐ YES ☐ NO	Employees take appropriate action when coughing or sneezing. Corrective Action:
☐ YES ☐ NO	Disposable tissues are used and disposed of when coughing/blowing nose. Corrective Action:
Large Equipment	
☐ YES ☐ NO	Food slicer is clean to sight and touch. Corrective Action:
☐ YES ☐ NO	Food slicer is sanitized between uses when used with potentially hazardous foods. Corrective Action:
☐ YES ☐ NO	All other pieces of equipment are clean to sight and touch (equipment on serving lines, storage shelves, cabinets, ovens, ranges, fryers and steam equipment). Corrective Action:
☐ YES ☐ NO	Exhaust hood and filters are clean. Corrective Action:

Refrigerator, Freezer and Milk Cooler

☐ YES ☐ NO	Thermometer is conspicuous and accurate. Corrective Action:
☐ YES ☐ NO	Temperature is accurate for piece of equipment. Corrective Action:
☐ YES ☐ NO	Food is stored 6 inches off floor in walk-ins. Corrective Action:
☐ YES ☐ NO	Unit is clean. Corrective Action:
☐ YES ☐ NO	Proper chilling procedures have been practiced. Corrective Action:
☐ YES ☐ NO	All food is properly wrapped, labeled and dated. Corrective Action:
☐ YES ☐ NO	FIFO (first in, first out) inventory is being practiced. Corrective Action:

Food Storage and Dry Storage

☐ YES ☐ NO	Temperature is between 50°F and 70°F. Corrective Action:

☐ YES ☐ NO	All food and paper supplies are stored 6 inches off the floor. Corrective Action:
☐ YES ☐ NO	All food is labeled with name and delivery date. Corrective Action:
☐ YES ☐ NO	FIFO (first in, first out) inventory is being practiced. Corrective Action:
☐ YES ☐ NO	There are no bulging or leaking canned goods in storage. Corrective Action:
☐ YES ☐ NO	Food is protected from contamination. Corrective Action:
☐ YES ☐ NO	All surfaces and floors are clean. Corrective Action:
☐ YES ☐ NO	Chemicals are stored away from food and other food-related supplies. Corrective Action:
Hot Holding	
☐ YES ☐ NO	Unit is clean. Corrective Action:
☐ YES ☐ NO	Food is heated to 165°F before placing in hot holding. Corrective Action:

☐ YES ☐ NO	Temperature of food being held is above 140°F. Corrective Action:
☐ YES ☐ NO	Food is protected from contamination. Corrective Action:

Food Handling	
☐ YES ☐ NO	Frozen food is thawed under refrigeration or under cold running water. Corrective Action:
☐ YES ☐ NO	Food is not allowed to be in the temperature danger zone for more than 4 hours. Corrective Action:
☐ YES ☐ NO	Food is tasted using proper method. Corrective Action:
☐ YES ☐ NO	Food is not allowed to become cross-contaminated. Corrective Action:
☐ YES ☐ NO	Food is handled with utensils, clean gloved hands or clean hands. Corrective Action:
☐ YES ☐ NO	Utensils are handled to avoid touching parts that will be in direct contact with food. Corrective Action:

Utensils and Equipment

☐ YES ☐ NO	Reusable towels are used only for sanitizing equipment surfaces and not for drying hands, utensils, floor, etc. Corrective Action:
☐ YES ☐ NO	All small equipment and utensils, including cutting boards, are sanitized between uses. Corrective Action:
☐ YES ☐ NO	Small equipment and utensils are air-dried. Corrective Action:
☐ YES ☐ NO	Work surfaces are clean to sight and touch. Corrective Action:
☐ YES ☐ NO	Work surfaces are sanitized between uses. Corrective Action:
☐ YES ☐ NO	Thermometers are washed and sanitized between each use. Corrective Action:
☐ YES ☐ NO	Can opener is clean to sight and touch. Corrective Action:
☐ YES ☐ NO	Drawers and racks are clean. Corrective Action:
☐ YES ☐ NO	Small equipment is inverted, covered or otherwise protected from dust and contamination when stored. Corrective Action:

Cleaning and Sanitizing

☐ YES ☐ NO	Three-compartment sink is used. Corrective Action:
☐ YES ☐ NO	Three-compartment sink is properly set up for ware-washing (wash, rinse, sanitize). Corrective Action:
☐ YES ☐ NO	Chlorine test kit or thermometer is used to check sanitizing process. Corrective Action:
☐ YES ☐ NO	The water temperatures are accurate. Corrective Action:
☐ YES ☐ NO	If heat sanitizing, the utensils are allowed to remain immersed in 170°F water for 30 seconds. Corrective Action:
☐ YES ☐ NO	If using chemical sanitizer, it is the proper dilution. Corrective Action:
☐ YES ☐ NO	The water is clean and free of grease and food particles. Corrective Action:
☐ YES ☐ NO	The utensils are allowed to air-dry. Corrective Action:
☐ YES ☐ NO	Wiping cloths are kept in sanitizing solution while in use. Corrective Action:

	Garbage Storage and Disposal
☐ YES ☐ NO	Kitchen garbage cans are clean. Corrective Action:
☐ YES ☐ NO	Garbage cans are emptied as necessary. Corrective Action:
☐ YES ☐ NO	Boxes and containers are removed from site. Corrective Action:
☐ YES ☐ NO	Loading dock and area around dumpster are clean. Corrective Action:
☐ YES ☐ NO	Dumpster is closed. Corrective Action:
	Pest Control
☐ YES ☐ NO	Screen on open windows and doors are in good repair. Corrective Action:
☐ YES ☐ NO	No evidence of pests is present. Corrective Action:

TEMPERATURE LOG

Month _____   ☐ **Freezer** ☐ **Refrigerator**

Date	Time	Temp	Initials	Date	Time	Temp	Initials

CRISIS MANAGEMENT PLAN

Even though you take all the precautions you can, food-borne illness or another crisis can hit your facility. Therefore, every restaurant operation should develop a crisis management plan. This written plan will identify resources and procedures to use in a crisis situation.

Here are the elements of a good crisis management plan:

- Develop a crisis management team.

- Identify potential crisis.

- Develop instructions for dealing with a crisis.

- Put together an emergency contact list.

- Develop a crisis communication plan.

- Assign a media spokesperson.

- Assemble a crisis kit.

- Test the plan with "fire drills."

Develop a crisis management team. Your crisis management team should consist of the owner, the manager, the chef, and possibly senior managers from finance, marketing and human resources. Take a look at the people in your organization and determine what positions seem like they could benefit a crisis management team.

Identify potential crisis. The main threat the team will focus on is food-borne illness, but don't forget other crisis situations such as fires, robbery, severe weather and trauma. You need to develop instructions for these common threats as well.

Develop instructions for dealing with a crisis. In the case of dealing with food-borne illness, put together an instruction sheet that includes the following steps: isolating the suspected food, obtaining samples of the food, preventing more sales of the food, removing suspect employees from handling food, and contacting your health department.

Put together an emergency contact list. Make sure you have a list by the phone of your crisis management team members and outside resources such as the police, fire department, poison control center and health department.

Develop a crisis communication plan. If a food-borne illness crisis occurs in your establishment, it is likely that the media will hit hard and fast. Make sure you have a communication plan in place to deal with this sudden onslaught. Be sure to include a list of media responses suggesting what managers should say to the media for each specific type of crisis. Also create sample press releases that can be quickly tailored to the specific event. Be sure to have protocols for communicating with employees as well. Be sure there is an employee phone list available.

Assign a media spokesperson. You should appoint a single spokesperson in the case of a crisis occurring. This person will deal with all media and health department inquires. By assigning one person to this task, you will be delivering a more consistent message to the public and controlling media access to your staff. These situations can be very stressful, so make sure your spokesperson has interviewing and crisis-management skills before assigning him or her to the task.

Assemble a crisis kit. Place this kit in an area that is easily accessible during the shift. It should include any written instructions you have prepared for crisis situations.

Test the plan with "fire drills." It's never a bad idea to conduct a drill in case a crisis happens. Set up a training situation in which employees role-play a food-borne illness outbreak or robbery. You may want to contact outside sources to help you with this training, such as the local office of the America Red Cross or your local fire department.

You may avoid a crisis situation altogether by responding quickly to customer complaints. If a customer calls in with a food-borne illness complaint, make sure you listen carefully, respond sincerely, and let the person know you will fully investigate the situation. Do not, however, admit any kind of liability or responsibility.

Make sure you fill out an incidence report. An incidence report should include the following information:

1. What the person ate at the establishment and when.

2. When the person became ill.

3. What the symptoms of the illness were.

4. How long did the symptoms last?

5. Did the person eat anything before or after dining at the facility?

6. Who ate the same food and did that person or persons become ill?

7. Did the customer seek medical attention?

8. What was the diagnosis and treatment?

Once gathering the information from the incidence report, bring your crisis management team together to assess the complaint. Have the team gather information and determine a plan of action. Be proactive and try to remain cool and collected. Do not act defensive, especially with the media.

If the health department determines that your establishment is the cause of the illness, accept the responsibility and express concern, and mean it. This will help you to not lose face (and customers).

Also, if you are at fault, be sure to get your information out through mediums other than the media such as newsletters, a Web site and advertising.

Finally, as you take steps in repairing the problem that allowed the crisis to occur in the first place, make sure you alert the media and your customers.

7

FACILITY PLAN

Many sanitation problems can occur because of facility or equipment issues.

In enforcing the provisions of the Food Code, the health department will assess existing facilities on the following considerations:

- Whether the facilities are in good repair and capable of being maintained in a sanitary condition.

- Whether food contact surfaces are in compliance with the Food Code.

- Whether the capacities of cooling, heating and holding equipment are sufficient.

- The existence of a documented agreement with the owner that the facilities will be replaced or upgraded or replaced as specified below.

A restaurant owner must submit plans and specifications for review and approval by the health department before:

- The construction of a food establishment.

- The conversion of an existing structure for use as a food establishment.

- The remodeling of a food establishment or a change of type of establishment or operation if the health department determines that plans and specifications are necessary to ensure compliance with the Food Code.

CONTENTS OF THE PLANS AND SPECIFICATIONS

The plans and specifications for a food establishment must include the type of food preparation and foods prepared as well as the following information to demonstrate conformance with Food Code provisions:

- Intended menu.

- Anticipated volume of food to be stored, prepared and sold or served.

- Proposed layout, mechanical schematics, construction materials and finish schedules.

- Proposed equipment, manufacturers, model numbers, locations, dimensions, performance capacities and installation specifications.

- Evidence that standard procedures that ensure compliance with the requirements of the Code are developed or are being developed.

- Other information the local or state health department might require.

When a HACCP plan is required, the establishment owner must submit the plan to the health department for approval before opening.

The health department will conduct one or more pre-operational inspections to verify that the food operation is constructed and equipped in accordance with the approved plan and approved modifications of those plans, has established standard operating procedures, and is in compliance with the law and the Food Code.

PERMIT TO OPERATE

A person cannot operate a food establishment without a valid permit issued by the health department.

An application for a permit must be submitted at least 30 calendar days before the date planned for opening a food establishment or the expiration date of the current permit for an existing facility. It must be a written application on a form provided by the health department.

To qualify for a permit, an applicant must:

- Be an owner of the food establishment or an officer of the legal ownership.

- Comply with the requirements of the Food Code.

- Agree to allow access to the food establishment and to provide required information.

• Pay the applicable permit fees at the time the application is submitted.

Contents of the Application

The application needs to include:

- The name, birth date, mailing address, telephone number and signature of the person applying for the permit, and the name, mailing address and location of the food establishment.

- Information specifying whether the establishment is owned by an association, corporation, individual, partnership or other legal entity.

- A statement specifying whether the food establishment is mobile or stationary and temporary or permanent, and whether or not the operation includes one or more of the following:

  – Prepares, offers for sale or serves potentially hazardous food only to order upon a customer's request or in advance in quantities based on projected customer demand and discards food that is not sold or served at an approved frequency.

  – Prepares potentially hazardous food in advance using a food preparation method that involves two or more steps which may include combining potentially hazardous ingredients, cooking, cooling, reheating, hot or cold holding, freezing or thawing.

  – Prepares food for delivery to and consumption at a location off the premises of the food establishment where it is prepared.

  – Prepares food that will be served to a highly susceptible population.

  – Prepares only food that is not potentially hazardous.

  – Does not prepare but offers for sale only prepackaged food that is not potentially hazardous.

- The name, title, address and telephone number of the person directly responsible for the food establishment.

- The name, title, address and telephone number of the person who functions as the immediate supervisor of the person directly responsible, such as the zone, district or regional supervisor.

- The names, titles and addresses of the people who have legal ownership of the facility and the local resident agent if one is required based on the type of legal ownership.

- A statement signed by the applicant that:

  – Attests to the accuracy of the information provided in the application.

  – Affirms that the applicant will comply with the Food Code and allow the health department access to the establishment.

For food operations that are required to submit HACCP plans, the health department will issue a permit to the applicant after:

- A properly completed application is submitted.

- The required fee is submitted.

- The required plans, specifications and information are reviewed and approved.

- A pre-operational inspection is completed.

The health department can renew a permit for an existing restaurant or it may issue a permit to a new owner of an existing establishment after a properly completed application is submitted, reviewed and approved, the fees are paid, and an inspection shows that the establishment is in compliance with the Food Code.

Denial of Application for Permit

If an application for a permit to operate is denied, the health department will provide the applicant with a notice that includes:

- The specific reasons and Code citations for the denial.

- The actions, if any, that the applicant must take to qualify for a permit.

- Advice on the applicant's right of appeal.

Responsibilities of the Health Department

At the time a permit is first issued, the health department will provide the permit holder with a copy of the Food Code so that the permit holder is notified of the compliance requirements and the conditions of retention that are applicable to the permit.

If the health department does not provide this information, however, it does not mean that they cannot take actions against the owner/permit holder for failing to comply with the regulations of the Food Code.

Responsibilities of the Permit Holder

Once the owner has the permit, he or she must do the following in order to retain the permit:

- Post the permit in a location on the premises that is conspicuous to customers.

- Comply with the provisions of the Food Code.

- Comply with any required HACCP plans.

- Immediately contact the health department to report an illness of an employee.

- Immediately discontinue operations and notify the health department if an imminent health hazard may exist.

- Allow representatives of the health department access to the food establishment.

- Replace existing facilities and equipment to comply with the Food Code if:

  - The health department directs the replacement because the facilities and equipment constitute a public health hazard or no longer comply with the criteria upon which the facilities and equipment were accepted.

  - The health department directs the replacement of the facilities and equipment because of a change of ownership.

– The facilities and equipment are replaced in the normal course of operation.

- Upgrade or replace refrigeration equipment to be in compliance with the Food Code.

- Comply with directives of the health department including time frames for corrective actions specified in inspection reports, notices, orders, warnings and other directives issued by the department with regard to the permit holder's establishment or in response to community emergencies.

- Accept notices issued and served by the health department according to the law.

- Be subject to the administrative, civil, injunctive and criminal remedies authorized in law for failure to comply with the Food Code or a directive of the health department, including time frames for corrective actions specified in inspection reports, notices, orders, warnings and other directives.

A permit is not transferable from one person to another, from one food establishment to another, or from one type of operation to another if the food operation changes from the type of operation specified in the application.

PHYSICAL FACILITIES

Safe and sanitary food service begins with a facility that is clean and in good repair. The entire facility — work areas as well as equipment — should be designed for easy cleaning and maintenance.

It's important to eliminate hard-to-clean work areas, as well as faulty or overloaded refrigerators or other equipment. Also get rid of dirty surroundings and any conditions that will attract pests. Remember, the easier the workplace is to clean, the more likely it will stay clean.

The physical facilities shall be maintained in good repair.

When remodeling or undertaking new construction, pay attention to the types of materials you are choosing. Materials for indoor floor, wall and ceiling surfaces must be:

- Smooth, durable and easily cleaned.

- Carpets must be closely woven and easily cleaned.

- Nonabsorbent for areas that are subject to moisture such as food preparation areas, walk-in refrigerators, dishwashing areas and restrooms.

Flooring

Floors, floor coverings, walls, wall coverings and ceilings must be designed, constructed and installed so they are smooth and easily cleaned. However, nonslip floor coverings or applications may be used for safety reasons.

One of the most important factors to look at when choosing flooring material is porosity. Porosity refers to the extent to which the floor absorbs liquids. If a flooring material is highly absorbent, it will encourage the growth of microorganisms. The Food Code recommends using nonabsorbent flooring material in food preparation areas, walk-in refrigerators, dishwashing areas and restrooms.

Resilient tile is a good choice for most areas in the restaurant. It is fairly inexpensive and easy to maintain. This type of flooring includes rubber tile, vinyl sheet tile and vinyl tile. Rubber tile is recommended for use in kitchens and restrooms. It is nonslip and less resistant to grease, but it is also less durable. Vinyl sheet tile is recommended for offices, kitchens and hallways. It is grease resistant and resilient. Vinyl tile is recommended for offices and restrooms. It is very resilient, but wears out quickly in high-traffic areas. It also requires a good deal of maintenance, including waxing.

Hard-surface flooring is another option. This type of flooring includes quarry tile, ceramic tile, brick, marble and hardwood. This type of material is nonporous but not resilient. These materials are also durable, but they may chip or crack if things are dropped on their surfaces. They do not absorb sound and can be more difficult to clean as well. In addition, these surfaces are more expensive to install. Ceramic tile is a good choice for restrooms, but make sure to use unglazed tiles so they are slip resistant.

If you are using resilient or hard-surface flooring, you must also install coving. Coving is a curved, sealed edge between the floor and the wall. It eliminates sharp corners and hiding places for insects and it helps prevent moisture.

Carpet is a popular choice for dining rooms because it absorbs sound. It can be maintained by vacuuming, but in areas with high traffic or that are prone to moisture, a more rigorous cleaning schedule will need to be applied.

A floor covering such as carpeting cannot be installed as a floor covering in food preparation areas, walk-in refrigerators, dishwashing areas, restrooms, garbage storage rooms, or other areas where the floor is subject to moisture, flushing or spray-cleaning methods.

If carpeting is installed as a floor covering in areas, it shall be:

- Securely attached to the floor with a durable mastic.

- Installed tightly against the wall under the coving or installed away from the wall with a space between the carpet and the wall and with the edges of the carpet secured by metal stripping or some other means.

If a temporary food establishment is graded to drain, a floor may be concrete, machine-laid asphalt or dirt or gravel if it is covered with mats, removable platforms, duckboards or other suitable and approved materials that are effectively treated to control dust and mud.

Mats and duckboards can also be used over hard surfaces. These can help in dish areas where there is standing water on the floor, and they can help provide relief from leg and back strain for your kitchen staff by allowing them to stand on a matted surface rather than a hard surface. These mats and duckboards must be designed to be removable and easily cleaned.

Walls and Ceilings

When selecting material for your interior walls and ceiling, remember that they must be easily cleanable. In food preparation areas choose light colors so that light is distributed in the room to make it easier to spot clean.

Make sure your walls and ceilings stay in good repair and are free of cracks and peeling paint and grout loss if you have ceramic wall tile.

Support structure for walls such as studs and joists should not be exposed in areas subject to moisture, and use oil-resistant, glossy paints that are easy to clean. Concrete, porous blocks or bricks used for indoor wall construction must be finished and sealed to provide a smooth, nonabsorbent and easily cleanable surface.

Utility service lines and pipes cannot be unnecessarily exposed. Exposed utility service lines and pipes must be installed so they do not obstruct or prevent cleaning of the floors, walls or ceilings. Furthermore, exposed horizontal utility service lines and pipes may not be installed on the floor.

Attachments to walls and ceilings, such as light fixtures, mechanical room ventilation system components, vent covers, wall-mounted fans and decorative items, also must be easy to clean. However, in a customer area, wall and ceiling surfaces and decorative items and attachments provided for ambiance do not need to meet this requirement if they are kept clean.

Light bulbs need to be shielded, coated or shatter resistant in areas where there is exposed food, clean equipment, utensils, linens and unwrapped single-service items. In areas used only for storing food in unopened packages, shielded, shatter-resistant bulbs do not need to be used if the integrity of the packages cannot be affected by broken glass falling onto them and they can be cleaned of debris from broken bulbs before they are opened.

An infrared or other heat lamp must be protected against breakage by a shield surrounding and extending beyond the bulb so that only the face of the bulb is exposed.

Lighting Intensity

Lighting levels are specified so that sufficient light is available to enable employees to perform certain functions such as reading labels; discerning the color of substances; identifying toxic materials; recognizing the condition of food, utensils and supplies; and safely conducting general food establishment operations and cleanup. Properly distributed light makes the need for cleaning apparent by making accumulations of soil conspicuous.

The light intensity should be:

- At least 110 lux (10 foot candles) at a distance of 75 cm (30 in) above the floor, in walk-in refrigeration units and dry food storage areas and in other areas and rooms during periods of cleaning.

- At least 220 lux (20 foot candles):

  - At a surface where food is provided for customer self-service such as buffets and salad bars or where fresh produce or packaged foods are sold or offered for consumption.

  - Inside equipment such as reach-in and under-counter refrigerators.

  - At a distance of 75 cm (30 in) above the floor in areas used for hand washing, dishwashing, equipment and utensil storage, and in restrooms.

- At least 540 lux (50 foot candles) at a surface where an employee is working with food, utensils or equipment, such as knives, slicers, grinders or saws where employee safety is a factor.

OUTDOOR AREAS

The outdoor walking and driving areas must be surfaced with concrete, asphalt, gravel or other materials that have been effectively treated to minimize dust, facilitate maintenance and prevent muddy conditions. Exterior walking and driving surfaces must be graded to drain. Outdoor garbage areas must be constructed in accordance with the law and they must be curbed and graded to drain to collect and dispose of liquid waste that results from the garbage and from cleaning the area and waste receptacles.

The outer openings of a food operation must be protected against insects and rodents by filling or closing holes and other gaps along floors, walls and ceilings; closed, tight-fitting windows; and solid, self-closing, tight-fitting doors. This does not apply, however, if the operation opens into a larger structure, such as a mall, airport or office building or into an attached structure, such as a porch, and the outer openings from the larger or attached structure are protected against the entry of insects and rodents.

Exterior doors used as exits need not be self-closing if they are:

- Solid and tight-fitting.

- Designated for use only when an emergency exists, by the fire protection authority.

- Are not used for entrance or exit from the building for purposes other than the designated emergency exit use.

If the windows or doors of a restaurant, or of a larger structure within which the establishment is located, are kept open for ventilation or other reasons, the openings need to be protected against the entry of insects and rodents by 16 mesh to 25.4 mm (16 mesh to 1 in) screens or properly designed and installed air curtains to control flying insects.

Perimeter walls and roofs of a food service operation must protect the establishment from the weather and the entry of insects, rodents and other animals. Servicing areas should have overhead protection except for areas that are used only for loading of water or the discharge of sewage and other liquid waste.

Dry Storage Areas

Like all areas of the facility, storerooms must be kept clean and litter-free. To accomplish this, be sure to sweep and scrub walls, ceilings, floors, shelves, light fixtures and racks on a routine basis. Check all storage areas frequently—this includes your refrigerator and freezer as well as your dry storage room. In checking storage areas:

- Look for damaged or spoiled foods, broken or torn packages and bulging or leaking cans.

- Remove any potentially spoiled foods immediately, and clean the area thoroughly.

- Make sure foods and other supplies are stored at least 6 inches from the walls and above the floor.

To avoid chemical contamination, store cleaning supplies and chemicals in a separate area away from food supply areas and other chemicals so they do not pose a hazard to food or people.

Dry storage areas should be made of easy-to-clean materials and these areas should have good airflow. Shelving should be made of corrosion-resistant metal or food-grade plastic. If there are windows in the storage area, they should be made of frosted glass or they should have shades because direct sunlight can raise the temperature of the room and affect the food. Hot-water heaters and steam pipes should not be located in storage areas for the same reason.

Storerooms should not have steam pipes or water lines running through them because these will promote moisture and condensation which will encourage bacterial growth.

To protect dry storage areas from insects, be sure to fill any cracks in the floor and walls. Also be sure outside doors and windows have screens with 16 mesh.

RESTROOMS AND HAND-WASHING AREAS

Your local health department can provide you with information on how many sinks, stalls, toilets and urinals your establishment must have to comply with local regulations. You should also try to provide separate restrooms for customers and employees. If this is not possible, be sure your customers don't have to come through kitchen or food prep areas to get to the restrooms; this will help ensure they do not contaminate food or food-contact surfaces.

Restrooms

Restrooms should be clean and sanitary and have a supply of toilet tissue as well as a covered trashcan (the trash receptacle lid should open with a foot pedal). A restroom must be completely enclosed and provided with a tight-fitting and self-closing door.

Scrub restrooms daily and keep the doors closed. You may also want to provide brushes to wash fingernails and sanitizing solution for soaking the brushes.

Hand-Washing Facilities

Hand-washing stations must be conveniently located in food prep areas so employees can wash their hands frequently. Hand-washing stations must be located in food preparation areas, service areas, dishwashing areas and restrooms and be equipped with the following:

- Hot and cold running water.

- A supply of hand-cleaning liquid, powder or bar soap.

- Individual, disposable towels.

- Continuous towel system that supplies the user with a clean towel or a heated-air hand-drying device.

- A receptacle for disposable towels.

- Signage that indicates employees must wash hands before returning to work.

A sink used for food preparation or washing utensils or a service sink or curbed cleaning facility used to dispose of mop water or similar wastes cannot be provided with the hand-washing aids and devices required for a hand-washing lavatory.

Dressing Areas and Employee Break Areas

Dressing rooms are not required by the FDA Food Code, but they should be designated if employees routinely change their clothes in the establishment.

These areas should not be in the same areas used for preparing food, washing dishes or food storage. Lockers or other suitable facilities also must be provided for the storage of employees' clothing and other possessions.

Areas designated for employees to eat, drink and use tobacco must be located so that food, equipment, linens and single-service items are protected from contamination.

Private Homes and Living or Sleeping Quarters

A private home, a room used as living or sleeping quarters, or an area directly opening into a room used as living or sleeping quarters may not be used for conducting food operations. Living or sleeping quarters that are located on the premises of a food establishment must be separated from rooms and areas used for food establishment operations by complete partitioning and solid self-closing doors.

Prohibiting Animals

In general, live animals are not allowed on the premises of a food establishment.

Live animals may be allowed in the following situations:

- Edible fish or decorative fish in aquariums, shellfish or crustacean on ice or under refrigeration, and shellfish and crustacean in display-tank systems.

- Patrol dogs accompanying police or security officers in offices and dining, sales and storage areas and sentry dogs running loose in outside fenced areas.

- In areas that are not used for food preparation and that are usually open for customers, such as dining and sales areas, service animals that are controlled by the disabled employee or person, if a health or safety hazard will not result from the presence or activities of the service animal.

- Pets in the common dining areas of institutional care facilities such as nursing homes, assisted living facilities, group homes or residential care facilities at times other than during meals if:

  - Effective partitioning and self-closing doors separate the common dining areas from food storage or food preparation areas.

  - Condiments, equipment and utensils are stored in enclosed cabinets or removed from the common dining areas when pets are present.

  - Dining areas including tables, countertops and similar surfaces are effectively cleaned before the next meal service.

- In areas that are not used for food preparation, storage, sales, display or dining in which there are caged animals or animals that are similarly confined, such as in a variety store that sells pets or a tourist park that displays animals.

- Live or dead fish bait may be stored if contamination of food, clean equipment, utensils and linens, and unwrapped single-service items cannot result.

CLEANING

The restaurant's physical facilities must be cleaned as often as necessary to keep them clean. Cleaning should be done during periods when the least amount of food is exposed, such as after closing. (This requirement does not apply to cleaning that is necessary due to a spill or other accident.)

Only dustless methods of cleaning should be used on floors, such as wet cleaning, vacuum cleaning, mopping with treated dust mops or sweeping using a broom and dust-arresting compounds. Spills or drippage on floors that occur between normal floor cleaning times should be cleaned:

- Without the use of dust-arresting compounds.

- In the case of liquid spills or drippage, with the use of a small amount of absorbent compound such as sawdust or diatomaceous earth applied immediately before spot cleaning.

Sawdust, wood shavings, granular salt, baked clay, diatomaceous earth or similar materials may not be used on floors.

Floors, walls and ceilings should be free of dirt, litter and moisture. Clean walls regularly by swabbing with a cleaning solution or by spraying with a pressure nozzle. Sweep floors, then clean them using a spray method or by mopping. Swab ceilings, instead of spraying them, to avoid soaking lights and ceiling fans. And don't forget corners and hard-to-reach places!

Food preparation sinks, restrooms and dishwashing equipment may not be used for the cleaning of maintenance tools, the preparation or holding of maintenance materials, or the disposal of mop water and similar liquid wastes.

After use, mops must be placed in a position that allows them to air-dry without soiling walls, equipment or supplies.

Ventilation

Good ventilation is a critical factor in maintaining a clean food service environment. Ventilation removes steam, smoke, grease and heat from food preparation areas and equipment. This helps maintain indoor air quality and reduces the possibility of fires from accumulated grease. In addition, good ventilation eliminates condensation and other airborne contaminants. It also:

- Reduces the accumulation of dirt in the food preparation area.

- Reduces odors, gases and fumes.

- Reduces mold growth by reducing humidity.

To ensure good ventilation, be sure to:

- Use exhaust fans to remove odors and smoke.

- Use hoods over cooking areas and dishwashing equipment.

- Check exhaust fans and hoods regularly to make sure they are clean and operating properly.

- Clean hood filters routinely according to the instructions provided by the hood manufacturer.

Intake and exhaust air ducts should be cleaned and filters changed so they are not a source of contamination by dust, dirt and other materials.

If vented to the outside, ventilation systems cannot create a public health hazard, nuisance or unlawful discharge.

Exhaust Hood Cleaning Service

Contact a company that specializes in the cleaning of exhaust hoods and ventilation systems. They should appraise and inspect the whole ventilation system prior to opening. Depending upon the amount and type of cooking performed, they will recommend a service that will keep the system free from grease and carbon buildup. Usually twice-a-year cleaning is required. Without this service, the exhaust hoods and vents will become saturated with grease, causing a dangerous fire hazard. All that would be necessary to ignite a fire would be a hot spark landing on the grease-saturated hood. Most of these companies also offer grease and fat (deep fryer oil) removal.

JANITORIAL AND MAINTENANCE SERVICE

Depending upon the size and operating hours of the restaurant, you may wish to use the services of a professional cleaning company. This would be highly recommended. Restaurant cleanliness is such an important area, it shouldn't be left to chance by having an amateur responsible for it.

The cleaning service usually arrives during the night after closing time. They will clean and maintain the areas previously agreed upon in the service contract. Their work is guaranteed. Never will a customer enter the restaurant and see a dirty fork left on the floor from the night before.

Cleanliness also has an important effect upon the employees. A spotless restaurant will create the environment for positive employee work habits. They will become more organized, neater and cleaner in their jobs and the areas they affect. The maintenance service company selected must have impeccable references. The company should be insured against liability and employee pilferage. Employees should be bonded. You will probably need to give the owner of the company his or her own keys to the entrance, maintenance closets, security system and possibly the office for cleaning. It must be made very clear that food and liquor are completely off limits to their employees.

Some important factors to consider when choosing a maintenance company:

- Can they assist with cleaning prior to opening?

- Request bids for the job; they vary widely. Look at the contracts and proposals closely.

- What hours they will be in the restaurant.

- Who is to purchase cleaning supplies and equipment such as soaps, chemicals, vacuums, brooms, etc.

- Have a trial period written into the contract.

- Have your lawyer examine the contract before signing.

- How will you communicate to discuss problems?

- Request references from other restaurants.

- Make them aware that toxic chemicals are not allowed in the kitchen.

- Inexperienced companies can cause damage to items cleaned incorrectly. Use a company with a proven track record.

- All doors should be locked once the employees are inside. The perimeter alarm system should also be on.

- Garbage emptied from the offices should be kept in dated plastic garbage bags and saved for one week. They may contain important information or papers accidentally thrown away.

To follow are some basic maintenance functions any service contract should contain. This is just a basic outline; the actual contract must contain specific items such as what must be cleaned and when. Both you and the maintenance company supervisor should have a check-off list of everything that must be completed each night. The morning following the service, walk through the restaurant spot checking from the check-off sheet that all items have been completed as prescribed. Notify the supervisor immediately of any unsatisfactory work. At first it may take a great deal of communication to get the desired results. Once operating a few months, however, it will run smoothly.

Items to be cleaned daily:

- All floors washed and treated.

- Vacuum entire restaurant.

- Dust windowsills, woodwork, pictures, chairs, tables, etc.

- Outside area: sweep and clean, patrol parking lot for trash.

- Public bathrooms: clean, sanitize and deodorize; replace supplies (toilet paper, soap, napkins, tampons, etc.).

- Trash containers: empty and sterilize.

- All sinks and floor drains cleaned.

- Maintenance room: clean and organize.

Weekly services:

- All windows cleaned inside and out.

- Polish all chairs and woodwork.

- Strip, wax and polish decorative floors.

Annually:

- Steam clean all carpets.

As previously indicated, these examples describe a generalized outline of some of the major points a service contract should contain. All of these areas plus the ones that pertain to your restaurant need to be expanded to detail precisely how, when and what needs to be done.

Some manufacturers include in their equipment detailed instructions for the cleaning of their product. Special cleaners must be used on some equipment.

Improperly cleaning a piece of equipment can ruin it forever. Keep all of this information in a loose-leaf binder in the office. The cleaning supervisor should have access to this manual and must be thoroughly familiar with its contents.

Kitchen Cleanliness

Kitchen cleanliness must always be of constant concern to both management and employees. A maintenance company should do little cleaning in the kitchen. They have not been trained in the cleaning procedures that must be used in the kitchen to maintain food safety requirements. A maintenance company should only be used, perhaps, for cleaning and washing the kitchen floor. The rest of the kitchen cleaning and maintenance is the responsibility of the staff.

All employees must be made aware that their daily cleanups are as critical as any of their other responsibilities—perhaps more so. Every employee must be completely familiar with their cleanup duties.

The most effective cleanup policy to institute is to make each employee responsible for his or her own area. Every workstation must have its own cleaning check-off sheet for the end of each shift. (See the example on following page.) These sheets should be sealed in plastic so that a grease pencil can be used to check off each completed item. Every employee must have his or her cleanup checked by a manager. You must inspect employee cleanup carefully and thoroughly. Once a precedent is set for each cleanup it must be maintained. At the end of a long shift, some employees may need a little prodding to get the desired results.

CLEANUP SHEET FOR EACH COOK
Place a check mark on all completed items.

___1.	Turn off all equipment and pilots.
___2.	Take all pots, pans and utensils to the dishwasher.
___3.	Wrap, date and rotate all leftover food.
___4.	Clean out the refrigerator units.
___5.	Clean all shelves.
___6.	Wipe down all walls.
___7.	Spot clean the exhaust hoods.
___8.	Clean and polish all stainless steel in your area.
___9.	Clean out all sinks.
___10.	Take out all trash. Break down boxes to conserve space in dumpster.
___11.	Sweep the floor in your area.
___12.	Replace all clean pots, pans and utensils.
___13.	Check to see if your coworkers need assistance.
___14.	Check out with the manager.

COOK _____

MANAGER _____

TIME OF LEAVING _____

EQUIPMENT

Materials and equipment that come into contact with food must be:

- Safe.

- Durable, corrosion resistant and nonabsorbent.

- Sufficient in weight and thickness to withstand repeated washing.

- Finished to have a smooth, easily cleanable surface.

- Resistant to pitting, chipping, crazing, scratching, scoring, distortion and decomposition.

Only commercial equipment should be used in food service operations; equipment made for household use will not be able to hold up to the wear and tear. Equipment must be maintained in a state of proper repair and condition.

Components such as doors, seals, hinges, fasteners and kick plates must be kept intact, tight and adjusted in accordance with the manufacturer's specifications, and cutting or piercing parts of can openers must be kept sharp to minimize the creation of metal fragments that can contaminate food when the container is opened.

Installing Equipment

When purchasing and installing major equipment and designing your kitchen and food prep areas, be sure to establish a workflow that will minimize the amount of time foods spend in the temperature danger zone. Locate storage near receiving areas to prevent storage delays and locate prep tables near refrigeration units. Also be sure to consider cross-contamination issues when installing equipment. Don't place dirty equipment next to areas with clean equipment or food. Finally, makes sure all equipment is accessible to your employees. Not only will this make your employees' tasks easier, it will also help to keep equipment cleaner. With this in mind, stationary equipment should be affixed at least 6 inches off the floor and tabletop equipment should be mounted on legs that give at least a 4-inch clearance. If tabletop equipment doesn't have legs, it should be tiltable or sealed to the countertop with a nontoxic, food-grade sealant. If equipment is sealed to the floor or a counter or wall, any seam that is greater than $1/32$ inch must be filled with a nontoxic sealant to prevent food buildup and pests.

TYPES OF EQUIPMENT

Dishwashing Machine

There are a variety of dishwashing machines available for restaurant use, but there are two main categories: High-temperature machines sanitize dishes with extremely high temperatures as their name suggests, and chemical sanitizing machines that use chemicals to sanitize. A dishwashing machine is a big investment and not easily replaceable, so be sure to consider all factors when buying a dishwashing machine. Think about your current needs and any plans you have expanding your operation.

Here is a list of the most common types of dishwashing machines:

Common Types of Dishwashing Machines	
Single-tank stationary-rack	Holds a stationary rack of dishes. Dishes are washed by soap and water from below. Wash cycle followed by a hot water or chemical sanitizer.
Conveyor	A conveyor moves the rack of dishes through the wash, rinse and sanitize cycles. These machines may be single- or multiple-tank.
Circular conveyor	Dishes are moved through the machine on a peg-type conveyor or in racks. This is a multi-tank machine.
Flight-type	This machine has a peg conveyor and multiple tanks. It may also have a built-in dryer.
Batch-type	A stationary rack machine that combines wash and rinse cycles in a single tank. Wash and rinse water are drained after each cycle. Machine automatically dispenses detergent and hot water or chemical sanitizer.
Recirculating door-type	A stationary rack machine. It does not completely drain water between cycles. Wash water is diluted with fresh and reused for each cycle.

Here are some features the FDA requires you to have for any type of dishwashing machine you purchase:

- A dishwashing machine must have an easily accessible and readable data plate affixed to the machine by the manufacturer that indicates the machine's design and operating specifications including:

  – Temperatures required for washing, rinsing and sanitizing.

  – Pressure required for the fresh-water sanitizing rinse unless the machine is designed to use only a pumped sanitizing rinse.

  – Conveyor speed for conveyor machines or cycle time for stationary rack machines.

- The dishwashing machine wash and rinse tanks must be equipped with baffles, curtains or other means to minimize internal cross-contamination of the solutions in wash and rinse tanks.

- A dishwashing machine must be equipped with a thermometer that indicates the temperature of the water in each wash and rinse tank and as the water enters the hot-water sanitizing final rinse.

- If hot water is used for sanitization in manual dishwashing, the sanitizing compartment of the sink must be designed with an integral heating device that is capable of maintaining water at a temperature not less than 77°C (171°F) and have a rack or basket to allow complete immersion of equipment and utensils into the hot water.

- A dishwashing machine that is installed after adoption of the Food Code by the local health department must be designed and equipped to:

  – Automatically dispense detergents and sanitizers.

  – Incorporate a visual means to verify that detergents and sanitizers are delivered or a visual or audible alarm to signal if the detergents and sanitizers are not delivered to the respective washing and sanitizing cycles.

- Dishwashing machines that provide a fresh hot-water sanitizing rinse must be equipped with a pressure gauge or similar device such as a transducer that measures and displays the water pressure in the supply line immediately before entering the dishwashing machine. If the flow pressure-measuring device is upstream of the fresh hot-water sanitizing rinse control valve, the device shall be mounted in a 6.4 millimeter, or ¼ inch, Iron Pipe Size (IPS) valve.

- Sinks and drain boards of dishwashing sinks and machines must be self-draining.

- The machine must be at least 6 inches off the floor to permit easy cleaning.

- Pressure-measuring devices that display the pressures in the water supply line for the fresh hot-water sanitizing rinse must have increments of 7 kilopascals (1 pound per square inch) or smaller and be accurate to 14 kilopascals (2 pounds per square inch) in the 100–170 kilopascals (15–25 pounds per square inch).

- A test kit or other device that accurately measures the concentration of sanitizing solutions must be provided.

You should also keep these guidelines in mind when installing your dishwashing machine:

- Install your machine so the water pipes are short to prevent heat loss to the water entering the machine.

- The items you put into a dishwashing machine must be able to withstand the wear and tear.

- Post information near the machine that includes proper water temperature, conveyor speed and chemical concentration.

- Make sure the thermometer is placed in a readable spot.

- Make sure you train your dishwashing staff on using the machine. To follow is a job breakdown for the dishwasher position that you may find useful for training purposes.

- A dishwashing machine and the compartments of sinks, basins or other receptacles used for washing and rinsing equipment, utensils or raw food and drain boards must be cleaned before use, throughout the day at a frequency necessary to prevent recontamination, and, if used, at least every 24 hours.

- A dishwashing machine must be operated in accordance with the machine's data plate and other manufacturers' instructions. Its conveyor speed or automatic cycle times also must be maintained accurately and timed in accordance with manufacturer's specifications.

Dishwasher Job Breakdown – Operating the Dish Machine	
What to Do	How to Do It
Prepare dishes for putting into dish machine.	• Scrape items. • Separate dishes, glasses, silverware, etc. • Rack items with like items, avoiding stacking. • Place cups, bowls and glasses upside down. • Pre-rinse all items.
Taking items out of dish machine.	• Remove items from dish machine without touching food-contact surfaces. • Check for cleanliness. • When dry, store clean items in a clean area until they are put in their proper storage places.

Maintaining the dish machine.	• Check temperature gauges throughout shift. Temperatures should be as follows:
	
	  – Prewash: 80°–110°F
	
	  – Wash: 140°–160°F
	
	  – Rinse: 170°–180°F
	
	  – Final rinse: 180°F
	
	• Check water tanks throughout the shift.

Manual Dishwashing

If you use a manual dishwashing system, you must provide a sink with at least three compartments for manually washing, rinsing and sanitizing equipment and utensils. When used for dishwashing, the wash compartment of a sink or mechanical dishwasher must contain a wash solution of soap, detergent, acid cleaner, alkaline cleaner, degreaser, abrasive cleaner or other cleaning agent according to the cleaning agent manufacturer's label instructions.

The wash, rinse and sanitize solutions must be kept clean.

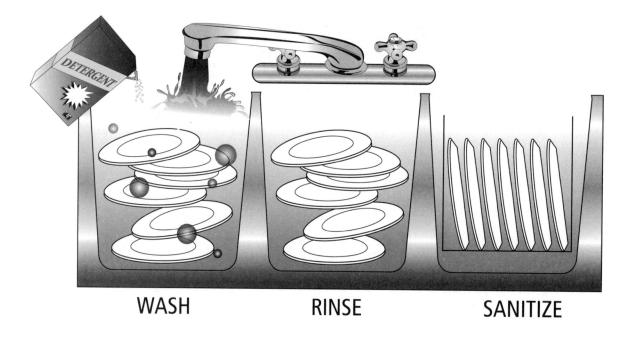

WASH   RINSE   SANITIZE

The temperature of the wash solution in manual dishwashing equipment must be maintained at not less than 43°C (110°F) or the temperature specified on the cleaning agent manufacturer's label instructions.

The temperature of the wash solution in spray-type dishwashers that use hot water to sanitize may not be less than:

- For a stationary rack, single-temperature machine, 74°C (165°F).

- For a stationary rack, dual-temperature machine, 66°C (150°F).

- For a single-tank, conveyor, dual-temperature machine, 71°C (160°F).

- For a multi-tank, conveyor, multi-temperature machine, 66°C (150°F).

The temperature of the wash solution in spray-type dishwashers that use chemicals to sanitize may not be less than 49°C (120°F).

If immersion in hot water is used for sanitizing in a manual operation, the temperature of the water shall be maintained at 77°C (171°F) or above.

In a mechanical operation, the temperature of the fresh hot-water sanitizing rinse as it enters the manifold may not be more than 90°C (194°F) or less than:

- For a stationary rack, single-temperature machine, 74°C (165°F).

- For all other machines, 82°C (180°F).

(The maximum temperature does not apply to the high-pressure and temperature systems with wand-type, hand-held spraying devices used for the in-place cleaning and sanitizing of equipment such as meat saws.)

The flow pressure of the fresh hot-water sanitizing rinse in a ware-washing machine may not be less than 100 kilopascals (15 pounds per square inch) or more than 170 kilopascals (25 pounds per square inch) as measured in the water line immediately downstream or upstream from the fresh hot-water sanitizing rinse control valve.

Sanitizing solutions shall be used in accordance with the EPA-approved manufacturer's label use instructions and shall be used as follows:

- A chlorine solution shall have a minimum temperature based on the concentration and pH of the solution as listed in the following chart.

- An iodine solution shall have:

  – A minimum temperature of 24°C (75°F).

  – A pH of 5.0 or less or a pH no higher than the level for which the manufacturer specifies the solution is effective.

  – A concentration between 12.5 mg/L and 25 mg/L.

Minimum Concentration	Minimum Temperature	
mg/L	pH 10 or less	pH 8 or less
25	49°C (120°F)	49°C (120°F)
50	38°C (100°F)	24°C (75°F)
100	13°C (55°F)	13°C (55°F)

- A quaternary ammonium compound solution shall:

  – Have a minimum temperature of 24°C (75°F).

  – Have a concentration as indicated by the manufacturer's use directions included in the labeling.

  – Be used only in water with 500 mg/L hardness or less or in water having a hardness no greater than specified by the manufacturer's label.

If another chemical solution is used by an establishment, the owner must demonstrate that the solution achieves sanitization. If a chemical sanitizer other than chlorine, iodine or a quaternary ammonium compound is used, it must be applied in accordance with the manufacturer's use directions included in the labeling.

If a detergent-sanitizer is used in a cleaning and sanitizing procedure where there is no distinct water rinse between the washing and sanitizing steps, the agent applied in the sanitizing step must be the same detergent-sanitizer that is used in the washing step.

The concentration of the sanitizing solution shall be accurately determined by using a test kit or other device.

The sink compartments for manual dishwashing must be large enough to immerse the largest equipment and utensils. If equipment or utensils are too large for the sink, a dishwashing machine or alternative equipment must be used.

Alternative manual dishwashing equipment may include:

- High-pressure detergent sprayers.

- Low- or line-pressure spray detergent foamers.

- Other task-specific cleaning equipment.

- Brushes or other implements.

- If a two-compartment sink is approved and the establishment owner limits the number of items cleaned and sanitized in the sink and limits dishwashing to batch operations for cleaning kitchenware such as between cutting one type of raw meat and another or cleanup at the end of a shift. The cleaning and sanitizing solutions must be made immediately before use and drain them immediately after use, and use a detergent-sanitizer to sanitize and apply the detergent-sanitizer in accordance with the manufacturer's label instructions or uses a hot-water sanitization immersion step.

A two-compartment sink may not be used for dishwashing when cleaning and sanitizing solutions are used for a continuous or intermittent flow of dishware or kitchenware in an ongoing dishwashing process.

Drain boards, utensil racks or tables large enough to accommodate all soiled and cleaned items that accumulate during hours of operation must be provided before cleaning and after sanitizing.

Finally, when dishes are washed by hand, a thermometer must be provided and readily accessible for frequently measuring the washing and sanitizing temperatures.

A sink used for dishwashing may not be used for hand washing. If it is used to wash wiping cloths, wash produce or thaw food, the sink must be cleaned before use, throughout the day at a frequency necessary to prevent recontamination, and, if used, at least every 24 hours. Sinks used to wash or thaw food shall be sanitized before and after use.

Clean-in-Place (CIP) Equipment

Some of your equipment is designed to be cleaned right where it is rather than ran through a dishwasher. For this type of equipment, you run a detergent, hot-water rinse and sanitizing solution right through the equipment. Frozen yogurt makers are one example of this type of equipment. CIP equipment must be designed and constructed so that:

- Cleaning and sanitizing solutions circulate throughout and contact all interior food-contact surfaces.

- The system is self-draining or capable of being completely drained of cleaning and sanitizing solutions.

CIP equipment that is not designed to be disassembled for cleaning must be designed to ensure that all interior food-contact surfaces can be cleaned.

Refrigerators and Freezers

Most food service operations have both walk-in and reach-in refrigerators and freezers. These should be constructed of stainless steel or a combination of stainless steel and aluminum. The doors need to be constructed in order to meet heavy-use requirements and they should close easily and snugly. A drain must be provided for condensation and to defrost the units. A forced-air circulating fan is also necessary for the units to maintain their proper temperatures.

When purchasing a refrigerator or freezer, look for the NSF International mark or UL EPH product mark. NSF International develops and publishes standards for sanitary equipment design. If your unit has this marking, it has been tested, evaluated and certified by NSF International and meets international commercial food equipment standards. The organization Underwriter Laboratories (UL) provides sanitation classification listings for equipment in compliance with NSF standards.

Other criteria to take into consideration when purchasing a refrigerator or freezer include:

- Choose a unit with enough storage space. You want to make sure you don't overcrowd a refrigerator or freezer, because this can lead to the unit not being able to hold its temperature. Uncrowded units are also easier to clean.

- Be sure walk-in units can be sealed to the floor. This will eliminate the possibility of pests or rodents.

- When purchasing reach-in units, choose one with legs; this will make cleaning under them easier.

- Make sure the unit has a built-in thermometer.

Molluscan Shellfish Tanks

Molluscan shellfish life-support system display tanks cannot be used to display shellfish that will be consumed and must be conspicuously marked so that it is obvious to the customer that the shellfish are for display only.

Tanks used to store and display shellfish that are for human consumption must be operated and maintained in accordance with a variance granted by the regulatory authority, and the establishment must have a HACCP plan that is submitted by the establishment owner and approved by the regulatory authority.

The owner also must ensure that water used with fish other than molluscan shellfish does not flow into the molluscan tank, the safety and quality of the shellfish are not compromised by the use of the tank, and the identity of the source of the shellstock is retained as specified under the Food Code.

Vending Machines

The dispensing compartment of a vending machine, including a machine that is designed to dispense prepackaged snack food that is not potentially hazardous such as chips, party mixes and pretzels, must be equipped with a self-closing door or cover if the machine is:

- Located in an outside area that does not have protection from an enclosure against the rain, windblown debris, insects, rodents and other contaminants that are present in the environment.

- Available for self-service during hours when it is not under the full-time supervision of an employee.

Can openers on vending machines must be protected from manual contact, dust, insects, rodents and other contamination.

A machine that vends potentially hazardous foods such as sandwiches or dairy products must have an automatic control that prevents the machine from vending food if there is a power failure, mechanical failure or other condition that results in an internal machine temperature that cannot maintain proper food temperatures. The machine will need to be serviced and restocked with food that has been maintained at proper temperatures.

When the automatic shutoff within a machine is activated in a refrigerated vending machine, the ambient temperature may not exceed any time/temperature combination for more than 30 minutes immediately after the machine is filled, serviced or restocked.

When the automatic shutoff within a machine is activated in a hot holding vending machine, the ambient temperature may not be less than 60°C (140°F) for more than 120 minutes immediately after the machine is filled, serviced or restocked.

Vending machines that hold beverages packed in containers made from paper products must have diversion devices and retention pans or drains for container leakage.

Vending machines that dispense beverages in bulk, such as a coffee machine, must have an internally mounted waste receptacle to collect drips, spillage and overflow, and they must be equipped with an automatic shutoff device that will turn off the machine before the waste receptacle overflows.

Vending machine doors, access openings and container storage spaces must be tight-fitting so that the space along the entire interface between the doors or covers, if the doors or covers are in a closed position, is no greater than 1.5 millimeters. This can be accomplished by:

- Being covered with louvers, screens or materials that provide an equivalent opening of not greater than 1.5 millimeters or ¹/₁₆ inch. Screening of 12 or more mesh to 2.5 centimeters (12 mesh to 1 inch) meets this requirement.

- Being effectively gasketed.

- Having interface surfaces that are at least 13 mm or ½-inch wide.

- Jambs or surfaces used to form an L-shaped entry path to the interface.

Service connection openings through an exterior wall of a machine must be closed by sealants, clamps or grommets so that the openings are no larger than 1.5 mm or ¹/₁₆ inch.

Case Lot Handling Equipment

Equipment used to store and transport large quantities of packaged foods received from a supplier, such as dollies, pallets, racks and skids, must be designed to be moved by hand or by conveniently available equipment such as hand trucks and forklifts.

Cooling, Heating and Holding Capacities

Equipment for cooling and heating food and holding cold and hot food shall be sufficient in number and capacity to provide proper food temperatures as discussed previously.

Linens

If work clothes or linens are laundered on the premises, a mechanical clothes washer and dryer must be used. If, however, laundering is limited to wiping cloths intended to be used moist or if wiping cloths are air-dried, a mechanical washer and dryer need not be provided.

Linen Service

In choosing a linen service, you must carefully look at your restaurant's available capital and sales volume. These factors will determine which option is the most economical for the establishment.

The linen service will provide the restaurant with tablecloths, napkins, uniforms and bar towels. They will pick up dirty linen and leave clean, ready-to-use items, ensuring they have left enough linen to carry you through until the next delivery. Generally there are two fees for this service. The restaurant will be charged for the use of the linen and for cleaning and pressing. You may also be charged for linen that is torn or soiled from misuse. Many medium to large restaurants purchase their own linen from their food service supplier. The linen company would then be used to service the used linen. If you have the capital to spend on purchasing your own linen, this way is usually advantageous. During the course of a year, new linen will be needed to replace torn and soiled items. Remember to allocate funds for this and to compute this figure into the total cost when examining the options.

Many large-volume restaurants install their own in-house laundry systems. Hotels have been doing this for years. Restaurants can, under the right circumstances, save a great deal of money. There are many different machines and systems available. Some are very good and have built solid reputations, while many others have just entered this growing market and do not seem to have all the mechanical bugs quite worked out.

Examine all machines that are available. In making a choice about which laundry system and machines to use, get as many references as possible. Call other restaurants and hotels; find out what machines they are using. They will tell you quite honestly if they are satisfied with the results. Service warranties and the machine's load capacity are two important considerations. Machines use a great deal of electricity or gas and a lot of hot water. Compute these additional costs into the total projection. Detergents and soaps must also be considered in these costs. A complete detergent system may be set up by the dishwashing chemical supplier. You will also need to hire a person to do the laundry every day. This employee must be trained precisely in the operation and maintenance of the equipment.

A complete in-house laundry system costs several thousand dollars to set up and operate; a thorough examination of all costs and available capital is required to see if the investment can be made. Over a number of years, the system will easily recoup the initial investment many times over in savings.

Microwave Ovens

Microwave ovens must meet the FDA's safety standards (**www.accessdata.fda .gov/scripts/cdrh/cfdocs/cfCFR/CFRSearch.cfm?FR=1030.10**).

Cutting Boards

Some health departments allow food service operations to use wooden or synthetic cutting boards. Check with your local health department to find out the specific rules you need to follow.

Synthetic boards are easier to clean, so many food service operators prefer these anyway. If you can and do use wooden boards, be sure they are made from non-absorbent hardwood such as maple or oak. They also must be nontoxic and free of seams or cracks.

Whichever type of cutting board you use, be sure to use separate boards for raw and ready-to-eat foods to prevent cross-contamination. Also, wash, rise and sanitized cutting boards between uses.

LIMITATION OF USE FOR SEVERAL TYPES OF EQUIPMENT

Several types of equipment have limited use in a food service operation according to the FDA Food Code. The following section provides guidelines on these limitations.

Cast Iron

Cast iron may not be used as a utensil or come into contact with food unless the cast iron is used as a surface for cooking or utensils for serving food if the utensils are used only as part of an uninterrupted process from cooking through service.

Lead in Ceramic, China and Crystal Utensils

Ceramic, china, crystal utensils and decorative utensils such as hand-painted ceramic or china that are used in contact with food must be lead-free or contain levels of lead not exceeding the limits of the following categories:

Utensil Category	Description	Maximum Lead mg/L
Hot Beverage Mugs	Coffee Mugs	0.5
Large Hollowware	Bowls 1.1 L (1.16 QT)	1
Small Hollowware	Bowls < 1.1 L (1.16 QT)	2.0
Flat Utensils	Plates, Saucers	3.0

Copper

Copper and copper alloys such as brass may not be used in contact with food that has a pH below 6, such as vinegar, fruit juice or wine or for a fitting or tubing installed between a backflow-prevention device and a carbonator, except for the copper and copper alloys used in contact with beer brewing ingredients that have a pH below 6 in the prefermentation and fermentation steps of a beer brewing operation such as a brewpub or microbrewery.

Galvanized Metal

Galvanized metal may not be used for a utensil or as a food-contact surface with acidic food.

Sponges

Sponges may not be used in contact with cleaned and sanitized or in-use food-contact surfaces.

Lead in Pewter Alloys

Pewter alloys containing lead in excess of 0.05 percent may not be used as a food-contact surface.

Lead in Solder and Flux

Solder and flux containing lead in excess of 0.2 percent may not be used as a food-contact surface.

Wood

Wood and wood wicker may not be used as a food-contact surface unless the wood is:

- Hard maple or an equivalently hard, close-grained wood which may be used for:

  - Cutting boards, cutting blocks, bakers' tables and utensils such as rolling pins, doughnut dowels, salad bowls and chopsticks.

  - Wooden paddles used in confectionery operations for pressure-scraping kettles when manually preparing confections at a temperature of 110°C (230°F) or above.

- Whole, uncut, raw fruits and vegetables and nuts in the shell may be kept in the wood shipping containers in which they were received until the fruits, vegetables or nuts are used.

- If the nature of the food requires removal of rinds, peels, husks or shells before consumption, the whole, uncut, raw food may be kept in:

  - Untreated wood containers.

  - Treated wood containers if the containers are treated with a preservative.

Nonstick Coatings

Multi-use kitchenware such as frying pans, griddles, sauce pans, cookie sheets and waffle bakers that have a perfluorocarbon resin coating must be used with nonscoring or nonscratching utensils and cleaning aids.

Nonfood-Contact Surfaces

Nonfood-contact surfaces of equipment that are exposed to splash, spillage or other food soiling or that require frequent cleaning must be constructed of a corrosion-resistant, nonabsorbent and smooth material.

Single-Service and Single-Use

Materials that are used to make single-service and single-use articles cannot let harmful elements or colors, odors or tastes into the single-serving packages, and they must be clean and safe.

Thermometers

Thermometers may not have sensors or stems constructed of glass unless they are encased in a shatterproof coating, such as candy thermometers.

CLEANABILITY OF EQUIPMENT AND FOOD-CONTACT SURFACES

The following are guidelines provided in the Food Code on cleanability of various types of equipment and food-contact surfaces.

Food-Contact Surfaces

Food-contact surfaces that are used for different kinds of foods must be smooth; free of breaks, open seams, cracks, chips, inclusions, pits and similar imperfections; free of sharp internal angles, corners and crevices; finished to have smooth welds and joints; and accessible for cleaning and inspection without being taken apart or easily taken apart with handheld tools.

"V" Threads

Except for hot oil cooking or filtering equipment, "V" type threads may not be used on food-contact surfaces.

Hot Oil Filtering Equipment

Hot oil filtering equipment must have easily accessible filters for filter replacement and cleaning.

Can Openers

The cutting or piercing parts of can openers must be removable for cleaning and replacement.

Nonfood-Contact Surfaces

Nonfood-contact surfaces must not have unnecessary ledges, projections or crevices, and they must be designed and constructed to allow for easy cleaning and maintenance.

Removable Kick Plates

Kick plates must be designed so that the areas behind them are accessible for inspection and cleaning by being removable or capable of being rotated open.

Ventilation Hood Systems and Filters

An establishment must have sufficient ventilation hood systems and devices to prevent grease or condensation from collecting on walls and ceilings.

Filters or other grease-extracting equipment must be designed to be removable for cleaning and replacement if not designed to be cleaned in place.

Exhaust ventilation hood systems in food preparation and dishwashing areas, such as hoods, fans, guards and ducting, must prevent grease or condensation from draining or dripping onto food, equipment, utensils, linens and single-service items.

Equipment Openings, Closures and Deflectors

A cover or lid for equipment must overlap the opening and be sloped to drain.

An opening located within the top of a unit that has a cover or lid must be flanged upward at least 5 millimeters.

Fixed piping, thermometers, rotary shafts and other parts extending into equipment must have a watertight joint at the point where the item enters the equipment. If a watertight joint is not provided, the parts extending through the openings must be equipped with an apron designed to deflect condensation, drips and dust from openings into the food, and the opening must be flanged.

Dispensing Equipment, Protecting Equipment and Food

In equipment that dispenses or vends liquids or ice in unpackaged form, the delivery tube, chute, opening and splash surfaces directly above the container receiving the item must have barriers, baffles or drip aprons so that drips from condensation and splashes are diverted from the opening of the container receiving the food or drink item.

The delivery tube, chute and opening also must be protected from manual contact by being recessed and protected from dust, insects, rodents and other contamination by a self-closing door if the equipment is:

- Located in an outside area that does not afford the protection of an enclosure against the rain, windblown debris, insects, rodents and other contaminants that are present in the environment.

- Available for self-service during hours when it is not under the full-time supervision of an employee.

The lever used for self-service beverage dispensing equipment must be designed to prevent contact with the lip-contact surface of glasses or cups that are refilled.

Leakproof Bearings and Gear Boxes

Equipment that contains bearings and gears requiring lubricants must be constructed so that the lubricant cannot leak, drip or be forced into food or onto food-contact surfaces.

Beverage Tubing

Beverage tubing and cold-plate beverage cooling devices cannot be installed where they will come into contact with stored ice. (This does not apply to cold plates that are constructed integrally with an ice storage bin.)

Ice Units

Liquid waste drain lines cannot pass through an ice machine or ice storage bin.

Condenser Unit

If a condenser unit is an integral component of a piece of equipment, the condenser unit must be separated from food and the food storage space by a dustproof barrier.

Single-Service and Single-Use Articles

A food establishment without facilities for cleaning and sanitizing kitchenware and tableware must only provide single-use kitchenware items, such as plastic utensils and paper plates. Single-service items may not be reused.

Shells

Mollusk and crustacean shells may not be used more than once as serving containers.

CLEANING AND SANITIZING EQUIPMENT

Equipment

Equipment, food-contact surfaces and utensils must be kept clean to sight and touch. The food-contact surfaces of cooking equipment and pans shall be kept free of encrusted grease deposits and other soil accumulations. Nonfood-contact surfaces must be kept free of an accumulation of dust, dirt, food residue and other debris.

Heat or chemicals can be used to reduce the number of bacteria to acceptable levels. They can also be used for certain other harmful microorganisms.

Heat sanitizing involves exposing equipment to high heat for an adequate length of time. This may be done manually by immersing equipment in water maintained at a temperature of 170°–195°F for at least 30 seconds or in a dishwashing machine that washes at 150°F and rinses at 180°F.

For either method, it is important to check water temperature frequently. Thermometers and heat-sensitive tapes and labels are available for determining whether adequate sanitation temperatures have been achieved.

Chemical sanitizing can be accomplished by immersing an object in, or wiping it down with, bleach or sanitizing solution. For bleaching, use ½ ounce or 1 tablespoon of 5 percent bleach per gallon of water. For using commercial products, follow the manufacturers' instructions.

Chemical sanitizers are regulated by the EPA, and manufacturers must follow strict labeling requirements regarding what concentrations to use, data on minimum effectiveness, and warnings of possible health hazards. Chemical test strips are available for testing the strength of the sanitizing solution. Because sanitizing agents become less effective as they kill bacteria and are exposed to air, it is important to test the sanitizing solution frequently.

Equipment, food-contact surfaces and utensils must be cleaned:

- Before each use with a different type of raw animal food such as beef, fish, lamb, pork or poultry.

- Each time there is a change from working with raw foods to working with ready-to-eat foods.

- Between uses with raw fruits and vegetables and with potentially hazardous food.

- Before using a food thermometer.

- At any time during the operation when contamination may have occurred.

(The above rule does not apply if the food-contact surface or utensil is in contact with a succession of different raw animal foods each requiring a higher cooking temperature than the previous food, such as preparing raw fish followed by cutting raw poultry on the same cutting board.)

If used with potentially hazardous food, equipment, contact surfaces and utensils must be cleaned throughout the day at least every 4 hours.

Surfaces, utensils and equipment contacting potentially hazardous food may be cleaned less frequently than every 4 hours if:

- In storage, containers of potentially hazardous food and their contents are

---

maintained at proper temperatures and the containers are cleaned when they are empty.

- Utensils and equipment are used to prepare food in a refrigerated room or area that is maintained at one of the temperatures in the following chart and they are cleaned at the frequency in the following chart that corresponds to the temperature:

Cleaning Temperature Frequency	
5.0°C (41°F) or less	24 hours
>5.0°C–7.2°C (>41°F–45°F)	20 hours
>7.2°C–10.0°C (>45°F–50°F)	16 hours
>10.0°C–12.8°C (>50°F–55°F)	10 hours

The cleaning frequency based on the ambient temperature of the refrigerated room or area must be documented in the restaurant.

Containers in serving situations such as salad bars, delis and cafeteria lines that hold ready-to-eat, potentially hazardous foods that are intermittently combined with additional supplies of the same food must have the containers cleaned at least every 24 hours.

Equipment used for storage of packaged or unpackaged food, such as a reach-in refrigerator, must be cleaned at a frequency necessary to eliminate the accumulation of soil residues. The cleaning schedule will be based on the following:

- The type of food involved.

- The amount of food residue accumulation.

- The temperature at which the food is maintained during the operation and the potential for the rapid and progressive multiplication of pathogenic or toxigenic microorganisms that are capable of causing food-borne disease.

In-use utensils can be stored in a container of water maintained at 60°C (140°F) or more and the utensils and container are cleaned at least every 24 hours or at a frequency necessary to get rid of accumulated soil residues.

Utensils and equipment which come into contact with food that is not potentially hazardous must be cleaned as follows:

- At any time when contamination may have occurred.

- At least every 24 hours for iced tea dispensers and self-service utensils such as tongs, scoops or ladles.

- Before restocking self-service equipment and utensils such as condiment dispensers and display containers.

Equipment such as ice bins and beverage dispensing machines must be cleaned at a frequency specified by the manufacturer. If there are no specifications, the items should be cleaned at a frequency necessary to avoid the accumulation of soil or mold.

Sanitizing Portable Equipment

To properly clean and sanitize portable equipment you must have a sink with three separate compartments for cleaning, rinsing and sanitizing. There should be a separate area for scraping and rinsing food and debris into a garbage container or disposer before washing, and separate drain boards for clean and soiled items. To sanitize a piece of equipment, use the following procedure:

1. Clean and sanitize sinks and work surfaces.

2. Scrape and rinse food into garbage or disposal. Presoak items, such as silverware, as necessary.

3. In the first sink, immerse the equipment in a clean detergent solution at about 120°F. Use a brush or a cloth to loosen and remove any remaining visible soil.

4. Rinse in the second sink using clear, clean water between 120°F and 140°F to remove all traces of food, debris and detergent.

5. Sanitize in the third sink by immersing items in hot water at 170°F for 30 seconds or in a chemical sanitizing solution for 1 minute. Be sure to cover all surfaces of the equipment with hot water or the sanitizing solution and keep them in contact with it for the appropriate amount of time.

6. If soapsuds disappear in the first compartment or remain in the second, if the water temperature cools, or if water in any compartment becomes dirty and cloudy, empty the compartment and refill it.

7. Air-dry. Wiping can recontaminate equipment and can remove the sanitizing solution from the surfaces before it has finished working.

8. Make certain all equipment is dry before putting it into storage; moisture can foster bacterial growth.

Sanitizing In-Place Equipment

Larger and immobile equipment should also be washed, rinsed and sanitized. Use the following procedure:

1. Unplug electrically powered equipment, such as meat slicers.

2. Remove fallen food particles and scraps.

3. Wash, rinse and sanitize any removable parts using the manual immersion method described in steps 3 through 5 above.

4. Wash the remaining food-contact surfaces, and rinse with clean water. Wipe down with a chemical sanitizing solution mixed according to the manufacturer's directions.

5. Wipe down all nonfood-contact surfaces with a sanitized cloth, and allow all parts to air-dry before reassembling. Sanitize cloth before and during sanitizing by rinsing it in sanitizing solution.

6. Resanitize the external food-contact surfaces of the parts that were handled during reassembling.

7. Scrub wooden surfaces, such as cutting boards, with a detergent solution and a stiff-bristled nylon brush; rinse in clear, clean water; then wipe down with a sanitizing solution after every use.

Cooking and Baking Equipment

The food-contact surfaces of cooking and baking equipment must be cleaned at least every 24 hours.

The cavities and door seals of microwave ovens must be cleaned at least every 24 hours by using the manufacturer's recommended cleaning procedure.

Nonfood-Contact Surfaces

Nonfood-contact surfaces must be cleaned at a frequency necessary to avoid the accumulation of soil residues.

Dry Cleaning

If used, dry-cleaning methods such as brushing, scraping and vacuuming must only come into contact with surfaces that are soiled with dry food residues that are not potentially hazardous.

Cleaning equipment used in dry cleaning food-contact surfaces may not be used for any other purpose.

Pre-Cleaning

Food debris on equipment and utensils must be scraped over a waste disposal unit or garbage can or removed in a dishwashing machine with a pre-wash cycle.

If necessary, utensils and equipment should be preflushed, presoaked or scrubbed with abrasive pads and/or cleaners.

Loading of Soiled Items into Dishwashing Machines

Soiled items to be cleaned in a dishwashing machine must be loaded into racks, trays, baskets or onto conveyors in a position that exposes the items to the unobstructed spray from all cycles and allows the items to drain.

Wet Cleaning

Equipment, food-contact surfaces and utensils must be effectively washed to remove or loosen soils manually or mechanically. The washing procedures that are used will be determined based on the type and purpose of the equipment or utensil and on the type of soil to be removed.

Washing Procedures for Alternative Manual Dishwashing Equipment

If washing in sink compartments or a dishwashing machine is impractical, such as when the equipment is fixed or the utensils are too large, washing can be done by using alternative manual dishwashing equipment if the following procedures are used:

- Equipment must be disassembled as necessary to allow access of the detergent solution to all parts.

- Equipment components and utensils are scraped or rough cleaned to remove food particles.

- Equipment and utensils are washed according to the guidelines given previously.

Rinsing Procedures

Washed utensils and equipment need to be rinsed so that abrasives and cleaning chemicals are removed or diluted using water or a detergent-sanitizer solution by using one of the following procedures:

- You should use a distinct, separate water rinse after washing and before sanitizing if using:

  – A three-compartment sink.

  – Alternative manual dishwashing equipment equivalent to a three-compartment sink.

  – A three-step washing, rinsing and sanitizing procedure in a dishwashing system for CIP equipment.

- You should use a detergent-sanitizer if using:

  – Alternative dishwashing equipment that is approved for use with a detergent-sanitizer.

  – A dishwashing system for CIP equipment.

- You should use a water rinse that is integrated in the hot-water sanitation immersion step of a two-compartment sink operation.

- If using a dishwashing machine that does not recycle the sanitizing solution or alternative manual dishwashing equipment such as sprayers, use a water rinse that is:

– Integrated in the application of the sanitizing solution.

– Drained immediately after each application.

- If using a dishwashing machine that recycles the sanitizing solution for use in the next wash cycle, you must use a water rinse that is integrated in the application of the sanitizing solution.

Returnables

A container for beverages may be refilled if:

- Only a beverage that is not a potentially hazardous food is used.

- The design of the container and rinsing equipment and the nature of the beverage allow effective cleaning at home or in the restaurant.

- Facilities for rinsing before refilling returned containers with fresh, hot water are provided as part of the dispensing system.

- The customer-owned container returned to the food establishment for refilling is refilled for sale or service only to the same customer.

Sanitizing Food-Contact Surfaces and Utensils

Equipment, food-contact surfaces and utensils must be sanitized before use and after cleaning.

After being cleaned, equipment, food-contact surfaces and utensils should be sanitized in:

- Hot-water manual operations by immersion for at least 30 seconds.

- Hot-water mechanical operations by being cycled through equipment that reaches a surface temperature of 71°C (160°F) as measured by an irreversible registering temperature indicator.

- Chemical manual or mechanical operations, including the application of sanitizing chemicals by immersion, manual swabbing, brushing or pressure-spraying methods.

The exposure times for these chemical solutions are:

- At least 10 seconds for a chlorine solution.

- At least 7 seconds for a chlorine solution of 50 mg/L that has a pH of 10 or less and a temperature of at least 38°C (100°F).

- At least 7 seconds for a chlorine solution 50 mL or a pH of 8 or less and a temperature of at least 24°C (75°F).

- At least 30 seconds for other chemical sanitizing solutions.

Clean Linens

Clean linens must be free from food residues and other soiling matter.

Linens that do not come in direct contact with food need to be laundered between operations if they become wet, sticky or visibly soiled. Cloth gloves should be laundered before being used with a different type of raw animal food such as beef, lamb, pork and fish. Linens and napkins should be laundered between each use. Wet wiping cloths shall be laundered daily, and dry wiping cloths should be laundered as necessary to prevent contamination.

Storage of Soiled Linens

Soiled linens must be kept in clean, nonabsorbent receptacles or clean, washable laundry bags and stored and transported to prevent contamination of food, clean equipment, clean utensils and single-service items.

Linens should be cleaned in a washer and dryer rather than by hand.

Use of Laundry Facilities

Laundry facilities on the premises of a food operation should be used only for washing and drying items used in the operation. Separate laundry facilities located on the premises for general laundering such as for institutions providing boarding and lodging may also be used for laundering food establishment items.

Air-Drying Equipment and Utensils

After cleaning and sanitizing equipment and utensils, they should be air-dried and drained before use. They may not be cloth-dried, but utensils that have been air-dried may be polished with cloths that are maintained clean and dry.

Wiping cloths laundered in an operation that does not have a mechanical clothes dryer should be air-dried in a location and in a manner that prevents contamination.

Lubricating and Reassembling Food-Contact Surfaces

Lubricants should be applied to food-contact surfaces that require lubrication in a manner that does not contaminate the surfaces.

Equipment should be reassembled so that food-contact surfaces are not contaminated.

Storing Equipment, Utensils, Linens, and Single-Service and Single-Use Articles

Cleaned equipment, utensils, laundered linens and single-service items must be stored in a clean, dry location. Additionally, they should not be exposed to splashes, dust or other contamination, and they should be stored a least 15 cm (6 in) above the floor. However, items that are kept in closed packages may be stored less than 15 cm (6 in) above the floor on dollies, pallets, racks and skids.

Clean equipment and utensils must be stored in a self-draining position that allows air-drying, and they should be covered or inverted.

Single-service items must be stored in the original protective package or stored by using other means that afford protection from contamination until used.

Cleaned and sanitized equipment, utensils, linens and single-service items may not be stored:

- In locker rooms.

- In restrooms.

- In garbage rooms.

- In mechanical rooms.

- Under sewer lines that are not shielded to intercept potential drips.

- Under leaking water lines including leaking automatic fire sprinkler heads or under lines on which water has condensed.

- Under open stairwells.

- Under other sources of contamination.

However, laundered linens and single-service items that are packaged or in a facility such as a cabinet may be stored in a locker room.

Handling Kitchenware and Tableware

Single-service items and utensils must be handled, displayed and dispensed so that contamination of food- and lip-contact surfaces is prevented.

Knives, forks and spoons that are not prewrapped must be presented so that only the handles are touched by employees and by customers if self-service is provided.

Single-service items intended for food or lip contact must be furnished for customers with the original individual wrapper intact or from an approved dispenser.

Soiled and Clean Tableware

Soiled tableware should be removed from public eating and drinking areas and handled so that clean tableware is not contaminated.

Preset Tableware

If tableware is preset:

- It must be protected from contamination by being wrapped, covered or inverted.

- Exposed, unused settings must be removed when a customer is seated.

- Exposed, unused settings must be cleaned and sanitized before further use if the settings are not removed when a customer is seated.

WATER AND PLUMBING

Improper plumbing can have serious ramifications in the restaurant industry. Plumbing that has not been installed properly and plumbing that has not been maintained can cause potable and nonpotable water to mix. This can cause outbreaks of hepatitis A, Norovirous and many other illnesses.

Since plumbing regulations vary with locale, it is highly recommended that you work with a licensed plumber.

Water

A food service operation's water source and system must be of sufficient capacity to meet the peak water demands of the establishment, and hot-water generation and distribution systems must be sufficient to meet the peak hot-water demands throughout the operation.

Water under pressure must be provided to all fixtures and equipment that are required to use water except for water supplied to a temporary food establishment or in response to a temporary interruption of a water supply.

Water shall be received from the source through:

- An approved public water main.

- One or more of the following that shall be constructed, maintained and operated according to law:

  - Nonpublic water main, water pumps, pipes, hoses, connections and other appurtenances.

  - Water transport vehicles.

  - Water containers.

Water must be available for a mobile facility, a temporary food establishment, (such as a booth at a fair) and for a food establishment with a temporary interruption of its water supply through:

- A supply of containers of commercially bottled drinking water.

- One or more closed portable water containers.

- An enclosed vehicular water tank.

- An on-premise water storage tank.

- Piping, tubing or hoses connected to an adjacent approved source.

Drinking Water

In food establishments, drinking water must be obtained from a public water system or a nonpublic water system that is constructed, maintained and operated according to the law.

A restaurant's drinking water system must be flushed and disinfected before being placed in service after construction, repair or modification and after an emergency situation, such as a flood, that may introduce contaminants to the system.

Water from a public water system must meet National Primary Drinking Water Regulations and state drinking water quality standards. Water from a nonpublic water system also must meet state drinking water quality standards. Water from a nonpublic water system needs to be sampled and tested at least annually and as required by state water quality regulations. The most recent sample report for the nonpublic water system must be retained on file in the operation or the report shall be maintained as specified by state water quality regulations.

Bottled drinking water used or sold in a food service operation must be obtained from approved sources. For more information, go to **www.access.gpo.gov/nara /cfr/waisidx_03/21cfr129_03.html**.

Nondrinking Water

A nondrinking water supply can be used only if its use is approved. Non-drinking water should be used only for nonculinary purposes such as air conditioning, fire protection and irrigation.

Plumbing

A plumbing system in a food service operation must be designed, constructed and installed according to law. The system and hoses conveying water shall be constructed and repaired with approved materials according to law, and a water filter shall be made of safe materials.

One of the biggest challenges in plumbing for a food service operation is cross-connections, the links through which contaminants from drains and other waste water sources can enter the potable water source. Cross-connections can cause the contaminants to backflow into the clean water source whenever the pressure of the clean water source drops below that of the contaminated source.

There are two ways to help prevent backflow:

1. **Vacuum breaker.** This device should be installed on threaded faucets to prevent backflow. A backflow-prevention device must be located so that it may be serviced and maintained.

2. **Air gap.** An air gap is the space used to separate a water supply outlet from a contaminated source. Sinks usually have two air gaps: one between the faucet head and the flood rim of the sink and one between the drain pipe and floor drain. An air gap is the only completely reliable method for preventing backflow. An air gap between the water supply inlet and the flood level rim of the plumbing fixture or equipment must be at least twice the diameter of the water supply inlet and may not be less than 25 mm (1 in). A backflow- or back siphonage-prevention device installed on a water supply system must meet American Society of Sanitary Engineering (A.S.S.E.) standards for construction, installation, maintenance, inspection and testing for that specific application and type of device.

A device such as a water treatment device or backflow preventer must be scheduled for inspection and service, in accordance with manufacturer's instructions and as necessary to prevent device failure based on local water conditions, and records demonstrating inspection and service shall be maintained by the owner and/or management.

If not provided with an air gap, a double-check valve with an intermediate vent preceded by a screen of not less than 100 mesh to 25.4 mm (100 mesh to 1 in) should be installed upstream from a carbonating device and downstream from any copper in the water supply line. A single- or double-check valve attached to the carbonator need not be of the vented type if an air gap or vented backflow-prevention device has been otherwise provided.

Water Reservoir of Fogging Devices

A reservoir that is used to supply water to a device such as a produce fogger shall be maintained and cleaned in accordance with manufacturer's specifications.

Cleaning procedures shall include at least the following steps and shall be conducted at least once a week:

1. Draining and complete disassembly of the water and aerosol contact parts.

2. Brush-cleaning the reservoir, aerosol tubing and discharge nozzles with a suitable detergent solution.

3. Flushing the complete system with water to remove the detergent solution and particulate accumulation.

4. Rinsing by immersing, spraying or swabbing the reservoir, aerosol tubing and discharge nozzles with at least 50 mg/L hypochlorite solution.

Hand-Washing Facility

A plumbing fixture such as a hand-washing facility, toilet or urinal must be easily cleanable.

A hand-washing lavatory must be equipped to provide water at a temperature of at least 38°C (100°F). A steam mixing valve may not be used in a hand-washing lavatory. A self-closing, slow-closing or metering faucet should provide a flow of water for at least 15 seconds without the need to reactivate the faucet. An automatic hand-washing facility should be installed in accordance with the manufacturer's instructions.

At least one hand-washing lavatory, a number of hand-washing lavatories necessary for the convenient use by employees, shall be provided. If approved and capable of removing the types of soils encountered in the food operation, automatic hand-washing facilities may be substituted for hand-washing lavatories in an establishment that has at least one hand-washing lavatory.

When food exposure is limited and hand-washing lavatories are not conveniently available, such as in some mobile or temporary food establishments or at some vending machine locations, employees may use chemically treated towelettes for hand washing.

A hand-washing facility must be located for convenient use by employees who do food preparation, food dispensing and dishwashing and in, or immediately adjacent to, restrooms.

The FDA Food Code also requires at least one toilet and not fewer than the toilets required by law shall be provided. At least one service sink or one curbed cleaning facility equipped with a floor drain must be provided and conveniently located for the cleaning of mops or similar wet floor cleaning tools and for the disposal of mop water and similar liquid waste.

Mobile Water Tanks

A mobile food operation's water tank inlet shall be:

- 19.1 mm (¾ in) in inner diameter or less.

- Provided with a hose connection of a size or type that will prevent its use for any other service.

A water tank, pump and hoses must be flushed and sanitized before being placed in service after construction, repair, modification and periods of nonuse.

If not in use, a water tank and hose inlet and outlet fitting needs to be protected using a cover or other protective device. A water tank, pump and hoses used for drinking water must be used for no other purpose. However, water tanks, pumps and hoses approved for liquid foods may be used for conveying drinking water if they are cleaned and sanitized before they are used to convey water.

Materials that are used in the construction of a mobile water tank must be safe, durable, corrosion resistant, nonabsorbent and have a smooth, easy-to-clean surface.

A mobile water tank must be enclosed from the filling inlet to the discharge outlet and sloped to an outlet that allows complete drainage of the tank.

If a water tank is designed with an access port for inspection and cleaning, the opening needs to be in the top of the tank, flanged upward at least 13 mm (½ in). The port cover assembly should have a gasket and a device for securing the cover in place, and should be flanged to overlap the opening and sloped to drain.

A fitting with "V"-type threads on a water tank inlet or outlet is allowed only when a hose is permanently attached. If provided, a water tank vent needs to end in a downward direction and be covered with 16 mesh to 25.4 mm (16 mesh to 1 in) screen or equivalent when the vent is in a protected area or a protective filter when the vent is in an area that is not protected from windblown dirt and debris.

A water tank and its inlet and outlet shall be sloped to drain. It also needs to be positioned so that it is protected from contaminants such as waste discharge, road dust, oil or grease.

A hose used for conveying drinking water from a water tank must be:

- Safe.

- Durable, corrosion resistant and nonabsorbent.

- Resistant to pitting, chipping, crazing, scratching, scoring, distortion and decomposition.

- Finished with a smooth interior surface.

- Clearly and durably identified as to its use if not permanently attached.

Sewage

Sewage can be full of contaminants, and it is critical to prevent any food contamination by sewage or wastewater.

If there is a sewage backup on the floor, you should immediately close the facility and correct the problem by a thorough cleaning.

Make sure you have sufficient drainage to handle your establishment's needs and that you have a drainage system designed to keep floors from being flooded.

A direct connection may not exist between the sewage system and a drain originating from equipment in which food, portable equipment or utensils are placed. If allowed by law, a dishwashing machine may have a direct connection between its waste outlet and a floor drain when the machine is located within 1.5 m (5 ft) of a trapped floor drain and the machine outlet is connected to the inlet side of a properly vented floor drain trap. Additionally, if allowed by law, a dishwashing or food prep sink may have a direct connection.

Sewage must be conveyed to the point of disposal through an approved sanitary sewage system, including the use of sewage transport vehicles, waste retention tanks, pumps, pipes, hoses and connections that are constructed, maintained and operated according to the law.

Sewage must be disposed through a public sewage treatment plant or an individual sewage disposal system that is sized, constructed, maintained and operated according to the law.

GARBAGE AND RECYCLABLES

The Environmental Protection Agency recommends three approaches for managing waste:

1. Reduce the amount of waste produced.

2. Re-use whenever possible.

3. Recycle.

Refuse, recyclables and returnables should be stored in receptacles or waste-handling units so that they are inaccessible to insects and rodents. Storage areas, enclosures and receptacles for refuse, recyclables and returnables must be maintained in good repair.

An area designated for refuse, recyclables, returnables and a redeeming machine for recyclables or returnables must be located so that it is separate from food, equipment, utensils, linens and single-service items and a public health hazard or nuisance is not created.

A redeeming machine may be located in the packaged food storage area or customer area if food, equipment, utensils, linens and single-service items are not subject to contamination from the machines and a public health hazard is not created. The location of receptacles and waste-handling units may not create a public health hazard or interfere with the cleaning of adjacent space.

Outdoor Storage

An outdoor storage area used for refuse, recyclables and returnables must be constructed of nonabsorbent material such as concrete or asphalt, and it should be smooth, durable and sloped to drain. If used, an outdoor enclosure must be constructed of durable and cleanable materials.

Receptacles for refuse, recyclables and returnables used with materials containing food residue and used outside must be designed and constructed to have tight-fitting lids, doors or covers.

Receptacles for refuse and recyclables, such as an on-site compactor, must be installed so that debris and insect and rodent attraction are minimized. The area around and under the machine should be kept clean to avoid infestations.

Refuse receptacles not meeting the requirements of the Food Code, such as receptacles that are not rodent resistant, unprotected plastic bags and paper bags or baled units that contain materials with food residue, may not be stored outside.

Cardboard or other packaging material that does not contain food residues and that is awaiting regularly scheduled delivery to a recycling or disposal site may be stored outside without being in a covered receptacle if it is stored so that it does not create a rodent harborage problem.

Receptacles in Vending Machines

A refuse receptacle may not be located within a vending machine, except for a receptacle for beverage bottle crown tops.

Storage Areas, Rooms and Receptacles

Indoor and outdoor storage rooms and areas and enclosures and receptacles must be of sufficient capacity to hold refuse, recyclables and returnables that accumulate.

A receptacle shall be provided in each area of the operation where refuse is generated or commonly discarded or where recyclables or returnables are placed.

Receptacles and waste-handling units for refuse, recyclables and returnables and for use with materials containing food residue must be durable, cleanable, insect- and rodent resistant, leakproof and nonabsorbent. Plastic bags and wet strength paper bags may be used to line receptacles for storage inside the establishment or within outside closed receptacles.

Receptacles and waste-handling units shall be kept covered if the receptacles and units contain food residue and are not in continuous use or after they are filled.

If disposable towels are used at hand-washing lavatories, a waste receptacle should be located at each lavatory or group of adjacent lavatories.

A restroom used by females shall be provided with a covered receptacle for sanitary napkins.

Suitable cleaning implements and supplies such as high-pressure pumps, hot water, steam and detergent must be provided for effective cleaning of receptacles and waste-handling units.

Waste Removal

Receptacles and waste-handling units for refuse, recyclables and returnables must be thoroughly cleaned in a way that does not contaminate food, equipment, utensils, linens or single-service items.

Soiled receptacles and waste-handling units must be cleaned as frequently as necessary to prevent them from developing a buildup of soil or becoming attractants for insects and rodents. They should be removed from the premises at a frequency that will minimize the development of objectionable odors and other conditions that attract or harbor insects and rodents.

Refuse, recyclables and returnables must be removed from the premises by portable receptacles that are constructed and maintained according to the law or a transport vehicle that is constructed, maintained and operated according to the law.

Solid waste not disposed of through the sewage system, such as through grinders and pulpers, should be recycled or disposed of in an approved public or private community recycling or refuse facility. A pulper is a machine that grinds food and sometimes paper waste into small parts that are flushed with water. The water is removed so the solid waste weighs less and can be compacted. Alternately, solid waste can be disposed of in an individual refuse facility such as a landfill or incinerator, which is sized, constructed, maintained and operated according to the law.

PEST MANAGEMENT

Bug and insect infestation in a restaurant is the result of poor sanitation practices. Aside from being a nuisance, they are a threat to food safety. Flies, cockroaches and other insects all carry bacteria, and many, because of where they get their food, carry disease. Bugs, insects and animals require the same three basic necessities of life as bacteria: food, water and warmth. When healthful, thriving bugs and insects are visible, this is an indicator that proper sanitation procedures have not been carried out.

Eliminate the environment that these pests need to live, and you will be eliminating their existence. Combining proper sanitation practices with periodic extermination spraying will stop any problems before they start.

The presence of insects, rodents and other pests must be controlled to minimize their presence on the premises by:

- Routinely inspecting incoming shipments of food and supplies.

- Routinely inspecting the premise for evidence of pests.

- Using methods, if pests are found, such as trapping devices or other means of pest control.

- Eliminating harborage conditions.

The best way to control insects and rodents is to not let them into your facility in the first place. Once they come in and start to multiply, they can be very difficult to get rid of. Food service facilities should implement an integrated pest-management program to deal with this issue. An integrated pest-management program uses prevention measures to keep insects and rodents from entering the establishment and control measures to eliminate pests once they do enter.

The three basic principles of an integrated pest-management program are:

1. Deny pests access to the facility.

2. Deny pests food, water and nesting places.

3. Work with a licensed pest-control operator to eliminate pests when they do enter.

Choosing a Pest-Control Operator

The greatest protection against cockroaches is your exterminator. Of course, the exterminator will be of little value if you do not already have good sanitary practices in place.

Hiring a pest-control operator is like hiring any supplier or contractor. Make sure to do some research before entering into a relationship. Here are some guidelines that will help you with this process:

- Talk to other food service managers to find out who they use and if they are satisfied with the work of their pest-control operator.

- When talking to pest-control operators, get references and check them.

- Make sure the pest-control operator has experience working in food service establishments and knows the specific challenges in these establishments.

- Make sure the pest-control operator is licensed in your state.

- Get proof of insurance from the pest-control operator.

Once you have chosen a pest-control operator, you will enter into a written service contract. This contract will state what is expected of you and the pest-control operator. The contract should include:

- A description of services provided (initial visit, follow-up inspections, emergency service).

- A warranty for the work done.

- Price.

- The period of service.

- Legal liability of the pest-control operator.

- Your duties, including preventative measures.

- Records to be kept by the pest-control operator (pests sighted, chemicals used, building and maintenance problems noted, schedule for checking and cleaning traps, written summary reports).

In addition, the food service operation should keep copies of the written summary reports.

Access to the Food Service Operation

Pests get into food service establishments by being brought in with deliveries or through openings in the building. To prevent pests from entering with deliveries, make sure your receiving person is checking all deliveries for signs of insects or rodents, such as egg casings or chewed cardboard. Also be sure to use reputable suppliers.

To stop pests from entering through openings in your building, be sure to check the following possible entryways:

Doors, Windows and Vents

- Screen all windows and vents with mesh that is at least 16 mesh per inch screening.

- Install self-closing door devices.

- Install door sweeps.

- Install air curtains.

- Keep drive-through windows closed when not being used.

Floors and Walls

- Seal all cracks with permanent sealant.

- Seal cracks where equipment is affixed to the floor.

- All doorjambs and building cracks, even the thinnest ones, must be sealed.

Pipes

- Fills holes around pipe openings with concrete or cover with sheet metal.

- Put screens over ventilation pipes and ducts on roof.

- Cover floor drains with hinged grates.

Here are some additional guidelines for discouraging pests from entering your facility:

- Clean up spills, including crumbs and scraps, immediately.

- Clean the facility thoroughly and regularly. This can eliminate the food supply, destroy eggs, and reduce the number of possible hiding places.

- Store recyclables in clean, pest-proof containers as far from the building as allowable.

- Dispose of garbage quickly.

- Keep garbage containers in good shape—keep them clean and tightly covered.

- Be cautious when receiving deliveries. Bugs may be in the boxes or crates.

- Keep food away from walls and at east 6 inches off the floor.

- Keep humidity at 50 percent or lower (low humidity helps keep roach eggs from hatching).

- Refrigerate food like cocoa and nuts after opening.

- Rotate products so pests don't have time to breed.

- Store wet mops on hooks—roaches frequently hide in them.

- Empty cleaning water buckets.

- In outdoor areas, remove dirty dishes and food as quickly as possible.

Identifying Pests

Even if you take all the preventive measures possible, you may get pests in your establishment. If you do, you should know what these pests look like and the signs of infestation.

Roaches. Roaches reproduce quickly and can adapt to some pesticides, so they can be difficult to control. There are several different types of roaches, but in general, they live and breed in dark, moist, hard-to-clean places. Typical hiding places include areas behind refrigerators, freezers and stoves; in sinks and floor drains; spaces around hot-water pipes; under shelf liner and wallpaper; under rubber mats; in delivery boxes; and inside equipment. Roaches feed in the dark, so if you see one in the daylight, you may have a major infestation.

If you think you have roaches, check for the following signs: a strong oily odor, droppings (they look like grains of black pepper). Egg cases are brown, dark red or black and look smooth or shiny.

You and your pest-control operator can use glue traps to find out what kind of roaches you have. The type of roach will determine the type of treatment your pest-control operator uses.

Flies. Flies feed on garbage and animal wastes, and they carry the germs from these on their feet, hair and mouth. Flies are a well-known transmitter of food-borne illness, and measures should be taken to control them. Houseflies prefer to sit on the rim of objects, such as garbage cans. They are drawn to decay, garbage and animal waste to lay their eggs and find food.

To prevent the spread of flies in your establishment, keep all doors, windows and screens closed at all times. Ensure that garbage is sealed in airtight containers and is picked up regularly. All trash must be cleaned off the ground; flies can deposit their eggs on the thinnest scrap of food. Dumpsters must be periodically steam cleaned and deodorized. They should never contain any decaying food scraps.

Other insects you and your pest-control operator may need to control include:

- Beetles

- Moths

- Ants

- Spiders

- Bees

- Mosquitoes

- Gnats

Rodents also pose a serious health risk. As rodents move about, they urinate and defecate, and their waste products can fall into food and contaminate surfaces. Rats and mice hide during the day and look for food at night. Rats and mice, like flies, are attracted to exposed garbage. They do not travel far from their nests—rats generally travel 100 to 150 feet and mice travel 10 to 30 feet. A rat can get through an opening the size of a quarter and a mouse can fit through a dime-sized opening.

Rodents are prolific breeders, producing as many as 50 offspring in a lifespan of one year. They tend to hide during the day, but they can be discovered by their telltale signs.

Ensure that your building's foundation is airtight. Keep all food products at least 6 inches off the floor; this enables the exterminator to get under the shelving to spray. Rat bait, a poisoning capsule resembling food, is particularly effective when spread around the building and dumpsters. As with any poison or chemical you use, make certain that it is labeled clearly and stored away from food storage areas.

Looks for these signs of rodent infestation:

- **Gnawing.** Both rats and mice gnaw to get to food.

- **Droppings.** Fresh droppings are black and shiny. Older ones will look gray.

- **Tracks.** Shine a light at a low angle across dusty surfaces to check for rodent tracks.

- **Nesting materials.** Mice will use any soft material for nesting such as scraps of paper or tissue, hair and cloth. Rats nest in burrows, so look for signs of holes.

Animal pests, such as rats and mice, may be very serious problems for the restaurant operator. These rodents can eat through a cement wall to gain access to your building. They are filthy animals that will eat any sort of garbage or decaying food available.

Rats are infested with bacteria and, often, disease. They have been known to bite people, as have their fleas, which also spread their bacteria and disease. Rats and mice have evolved into creatures highly developed for survival. Once they have become settled in an area, they are very difficult to get rid of.

CONTROL MEASURES

Pest-control operators use a variety of control methods that are safe for the food establishment.

Insects

Repellents. These are liquids, powders or mists that keep insects away from an area. These are usually used in hard-to-reach places.

Sprays. Chemical pesticide sprays are used to control insects. There are residual sprays and contact sprays. Residual sprays leave a film on the insecticide that insects absorb as they crawl across the surface. This is often used for cracks and crevices. Contact sprays kill insects on contact, as the name suggests. Chemicals sprayed in a restaurant must be of the nonresidual type. These are safe and approved for use in food service establishments.

Baits. Sometimes chemical bait is used for roaches or ants. When the insect eats the bait, the bait kills the insect. Kitchen areas do not need to be prepared for this control measure.

Traps. There are several types of traps: light-only, electronic, and units that use both light and sound. The light-only units attract insects to crawl inside where they find it difficult to escape. The electronic eliminator use an electrically charged grid to kill the insects, and the other units that use both light and sound attract the insects onto a glueboard.

Insect-control devices that are used to electrocute or stun flying insects must be designed to retain the insect within the device. These devices should be installed so that they are not located over a food preparation area and dead insects and insect fragments are prevented from falling on exposed food, clean equipment, utensils, linens and unwrapped single-service items.

A tracking powder pesticide may not be used in a food establishment. If a nontoxic tracking powder such as talcum or flour is used, it cannot contaminate food, equipment, utensils, linens or single-service items.

Rodents

Traps. Traps are a good tool to use for mice and rats, but if you have a large infestation, this may take awhile. Make sure to check traps often and remove the rodents carefully. If it is still alive, call your pest-control operator to remove it.

Glueboards. Glueboards kills mice, but they are not effective for rats because rats are usually strong enough to escape. The mice stick to the board and die in several hours due to exhaustion or lack of water or air.

Bait. Chemical baits should only be administered by your pest-control operator in areas that will not contaminate food or food-contact surfaces. Your pest-control operator may have to change the bait and location frequently; rats can easily detect chemical bait and they often avoid it. Rodent bait must be contained in a covered, tamper-resistant bait station.

Removing Dead or Trapped Birds, Insects, Rodents and Other Pests

Dead or trapped birds, insects, rodents and other pests should be removed from control devices and the premises in order to prevent their accumulation, decomposition or the attraction of other pests.

Storing Pesticides

While you may think it makes more sense to buy and store pesticides yourself, there are a number of reasons you should leave this to your pest-control operator:

- Pesticides are dangerous to you, your staff and customers.

- If pesticides are not applied properly, they won't be effective.

- Pests can develop immunity to certain pesticides, and your pest-control operator will know which ones are effective.

- Some pesticides are not approved for use in food service establishments; your pest-control operator will be aware of which ones can be used.

To help eliminate some of the hazards of using pesticides, make sure your pest-control operator only applies them during hours the facility is closed and employees are not on-site. Also, be sure to cover all equipment and food-contact surfaces that can't be moved out of the area while the pesticide is being applied. After the pesticide has been applied, clean and sanitize all the surfaces you covered.

If you do decide to store pesticides on-site, be sure to do the following:

- Have the corresponding Material Safety Data Sheet (MSDS).

- Keep pesticides in original containers.

- Store pesticides in locked cabinets away from food storage areas.

- Store pressurized spray cans in a cool place; temperatures over 120°F could cause them to explode.

- Check local regulations on disposal.

TOXIC MATERIALS

Containers of poisonous or toxic materials must bear a legible manufacturer's label. In addition, containers that are used to store poisonous or toxic materials such as cleaners and sanitizers taken from bulk supplies must be clearly and individually identified with the common name of the material.

Poisonous or toxic materials must be stored so they cannot contaminate other poisonous or toxic materials by:

- Separating the poisonous or toxic materials by spacing or partitioning.

- Locating the materials in an area that is not above poisonous or toxic materials. (Equipment and utensil cleaners and sanitizers that are stored in dishwashing areas do not have to meet this requirement.)

Only those poisonous or toxic materials that are required for the operation and maintenance of a food establishment, such as material for the cleaning and sanitizing equipment and the control of insects and rodents, are allowed in a food establishment.

Poisonous or toxic materials must be used according to:

- The law and the FDA Food Code.

- Manufacturer's use directions included in labeling or a pesticide manufacturer's label instructions that state that use is allowed in a food establishment.

- The conditions of certification, if certification is required, for use of the pest-control materials.

- Additional conditions that may be established by the health department.

Poisonous or toxic materials must be applied so that a hazard to employees or other persons is not constituted and contamination including toxic residues due to drip, drain, fog, splash or spray on food, equipment, utensils, linens and single-service items is prevented.

A restricted-use pesticide can only be applied by an applicator that is certified. For a restricted-use pesticide, this is achieved by removing the items, covering the items with impermeable covers, or taking other appropriate preventive actions, and then cleaning and sanitizing equipment and utensils after the application.

A container previously used to store poisonous or toxic materials may not be used to store, transport or dispense food.

Chemicals

Chemical sanitizers and other chemical antimicrobials applied to food-contact surfaces shall meet the requirements specified in 21 CFR 178.1010 of the Code of Federal Regulations.

Chemicals used to wash or peel raw whole fruits and vegetables shall meet the specified requirements (**http://vm.cfsan.fda.gov/~lrd/FCF173.html**).

Boiler Water Additives

Chemicals used as boiler water additives must meet specific requirements (**www.access.gpo.gov/nara/cfr/waisidx_00/21cfr173_00.html**).

Drying Agents

Drying agents used in conjunction with sanitization must:

- Contain only components that are listed as one of the following:

– Generally recognized as safe for use in food as specified in 21 CFR 182 (**http://vm.cfsan.fda.gov/~lrd/FCF182.html**) or 21 CFR 184 (**http://vm.cfsan.fda.gov/~lrd/FCF184.html**).

– Generally recognized as safe for the intended use as specified in 21 CFR 186 (**http://vm.cfsan.fda.gov/~lrd/FCF186.html**).

– Approved for use as a drying agent under a prior sanction specified in 21 CFR 181 (**http://vm.cfsan.fda.gov/~lrd/FCF181.html**).

– Specifically regulated as an indirect food additive for use as a drying agent as approved for use as a drying agent under the threshold of regulation process established by 21 CFR 170.39 (**http://vm.cfsan.fda.gov/~dms/opa-gg2.html**).

Lubricants

Lubricants must meet the requirements specified in 21 CFR 178.3570 if they are used on food-contact surfaces, on bearings and gears located on or within food-contact surfaces, or on bearings and gears that are located so that lubricants may leak, drip or be forced into food or onto food-contact surfaces.

First-Aid Supplies

Only those medicines that are necessary for the health of employees are allowed in a food operation.

Medicines that are in an operation for the employees' use must be labeled and located to prevent the contamination of food, equipment, utensils, linens and single-service items.

Medicines belonging to employees that require refrigeration must be:

- Stored in a package or container and kept inside a covered, leakproof container that is identified as a container for the storage of medicines.

- Located so they are inaccessible to children.

TRAINING YOUR STAFF

Every restaurant employee is responsible for preparing and serving quality and safe food products. Each employee must be thoroughly familiar with basic food safety and sanitation practices. This section will describe the fundamental methods and procedures that must be practiced in order to control food contamination, the spread of infectious diseases, and personal safety practices.

Management must provide employees with the training, knowledge and tools that will enable them to establish and practice proper food-handling and sanitation procedures. Through the use of this section, and under the guidance of your local department of health, you and your staff can obtain training and knowledge. First, however, the restaurant must be equipped with the proper tools, training and working conditions. Employees will never establish good sanitation procedures if they do not first have the proper environment in which to practice them.

Every member of your staff should be trained in food safety. Causing a foodborne illness can have a major impact on your sales. Not only do you have the chance of being sued, but many health departments and newspapers publicize food-borne illness incidents, and this is not the kind of advertisement that will bring in customers! In addition, food-borne illness can be potentially life threatening. Older customers, children and those with chronic diseases are particularly vulnerable to serious consequences from food-borne illness.

There are many ways to train servers about food safety. While in-house training will go a long way in getting your employees off to a good start, you should consider enrolling them in the National Restaurant Association's ServSafe program or other similar programs at area colleges. This way your employees can become certified by the state.

Getting employees to do things right means taking the time to train them properly from the start so that they understand what needs to be done, how to do it, and why it should be done that way. Effective training, however, involves more than simply providing information. Training is not a problem, and it cannot be "solved" and then forgotten. Managers and supervisors at every level must soon realize that training is a continual process; as is learning, it must never stop.

The most effective training technique is interactivity. Get people to stand up and do things. Show them how to set a table, look for lipstick on a glass, wash their hands properly, use a thermometer, wash a dish, make a martini, garnish a plate. Let the employees participate.

Most managers and supervisors think of training as teaching new employees skills, such as dishwashing or bartending. Training needs to be far more than that; management must look beyond its own interests. As mentioned before, we must start to consider the employee's interests, goals, needs and desires if we are to become successful.

The employee must know not only her job and how to perform it, but how her performance affects others in their jobs in other parts of the restaurant. She must visualize her position as an integral part of an efficient machine, not as a separate, meaningless function. For example, take the plight of the dishwasher in most restaurants. Dishwashers are vitality important to the success of any restaurant, yet few managers, and virtually no other employees, are consciously aware of their importance. Rather than being treated with dignity and respect, they are considered, in most establishments, insignificant menial laborers. They are often paid minimum wage with little—usually no—benefits, expected to do all the dirty work, cleaning up after others, and working in poor conditions, while all the other employees shout orders and instructions. The only time they are really communicated with is when they do something wrong or when someone needs something done or a mess needs to be cleaned up. Is there really any wonder why an entirely new crew will have to be trained in two weeks? Many managers themselves don't fully realize the importance of this function or that it is far harder to find a good dishwasher than it is a good waitperson. I have always mandated that every new hire perform at least one shift in this position to fully understand its importance. Try giving the dishwashing staff an hour-long break one night and see the resulting chaos.

Telling an employee that his position and performance is crucial to the restaurant's success and showing him the reasons why are two entirely different things. The importance of performing his job in the manner in which he was trained must by physically demonstrated to the employee, as well as the ramifications of varying from these procedures. Using the example of the frustrated dishwasher, let's apply this philosophy with some practical, hands-on management.

Start the training program by having all of the dishwashers come into the restaurant for dinner, lunch or a pre-shift meal with you. While the waitperson is performing her service, point out the importance of having clean, grease-free dishes, and explain why silverware and wine glasses must be checked for spots.

Show them why the waitstaff needs their stock rapidly and what happens if they don't get it.

Type out a list describing the cost of each plate, glass and so forth in the restaurant. This is the most effective way to show why they must be so concerned and careful about breakage. List the cost of the other articles that pertain to their job, such as the dishwashing machine, chemicals, soaps, pots, pans and knives.

Show them that you are concerned with them and their performance. Pay more than the other restaurants in the area so that you will attract the best people. Set up some small benefits such as a free meal and free soda per shift. A financial incentive is the most effective type of motivating force. Establish bonuses for the dishwashers, such as giving them 3–5 cents extra for each cover served that night. The small cost of these little extras will be substantiated with lower turnover rates and higher production.

Apply this principle of demonstrating rather than lecturing to illustrate your points with all of your employees, and you will have the basis for a good training program and good employee relations.

Safe Food-Handling Primer

Food-borne illnesses. Most of us are familiar with salmonella and E. coli, but there are many other food-borne illnesses with a range of similar symptoms. For more information on these illnesses, log on to the Center for Disease Control's Web site at **www.cdc.gov/health/default.htm#F** and look under the topic "food-borne illness." To train your servers on the various illnesses, use flash cards. Have the illness on one side and what causes it on the other. Then, create a game and see who can get the most flash cards right in a three-minute period. Award the winner a movie gift certificate!

Cross-contamination. Food-borne illnesses are often caused by cross-contamination. This means that the bacteria from one food source crosses to another. While most cross-contamination cases occur in the back-of-the-house, servers can cause this situation as well. An example of this is using the same cutting board to cut salad tomatoes and to slice raw chicken. Keep separate cutting boards for the salad and server areas. There are colored acrylic cutting boards on the market that can serve as a reminder for the board's use (see **www.atlantic -pub.com**). Hang a sign over the area the cutting boards are stored, telling servers the green ones are for salad ingredients.

AVOID BACTERIAL CROSS-CONTAMINATION

One of the most common causes of food-borne illness is cross-contamination: the transfer of bacteria from food to food, hand to food, or equipment to food.

Food to food. Raw, contaminated ingredients may be added to foods, or fluids from raw foods may drip into foods that receive no further cooking. A common mistake is to leave thawing meat on a top shelf in the refrigerator where it can drip down onto prepared foods stored below.

Hand to food. Bacteria are found throughout the body: in the hair; on the skin; in clothing; in the mouth, nose and throat; in the intestinal tract; and on scabs or scars from skin wounds. These bacteria often end up on the hands where they can easily spread to food. People can also pick up bacteria by touching raw food and then transfer it to cooked or ready-to-eat food.

Equipment to food. Bacteria may pass from equipment to food when equipment that has touched contaminated food is then used to prepare other food without proper cleaning and sanitizing. For example, cross-contamination can occur when surfaces used for cutting raw poultry are then used to cut foods that will be eaten raw, such as fresh vegetables.

Coverings, such as plastic wrap and holding and serving containers, can also harbor bacteria that can spread to food. A can opener, a plastic-wrap box or a food slicer can also become a source of cross-contamination if not properly sanitized between uses.

Unsanitary practices. Unsanitary practices your servers should avoid include chewing gum, eating food in food preparation areas, and tasting food using their fingers. Also, make sure that servers cover any cuts and use gloves when handling food. In addition, encourage your workers to stay home if they are ill. Someone with a cold or the flu should not be handling food. Restaurant workers are notorious for coming to work sick in order to avoid losing money. Encourage your employees to practice food safety by putting policies in place that will encourage them to stay home when ill. Consider providing your employees with sick time. Perhaps you could add it as a benefit after an employee has been with you for a certain length of time. By adding this benefit, you can keep your food supply safer and lower your turnover rate.

Danger zone. Keep foods out of the temperature danger zone (45°–140°F). Make sure to keep hot foods hot and cold foods cold.

Thawing foods. Thaw foods in the refrigerator or microwave or under cold running water. If using the running water method, do not leave foods out for more than 2 hours, and cook immediately upon thawing.

Reheating food. Do not use a steam table to reheat foods. Also, be sure that when reheating, you bring the food's temperature up to 165°F.

Cooling food. When cooling soups or stews, put it in several shallow pans so it will cool quickly. Use an ice bath to expedite the cooling process.

Using thermometers. If using an instant-read thermometer, be sure to place the stem into the food item so the dimple is covered. Also be sure thermometers are properly calibrated.

FIFO. Be sure to stress the importance of the "first in, first out" method of storage. This will ensure foods don't become outdated. Be sure to label, date and cover all food items and keep cleaning supplies in a separate storage area.

Information resources. There are many food safety information resources on the Web. Log on to the following sites for more information:

- Food Safety Training and Education Alliance at **www.fstea.org** offers training materials including videos and brochures.

- The USDA has training materials available on their Web site, as well as HACCP materials at **www.nal.usda.gov/fnic/foodborne/haccp/index. shtml**.

- The Food Safety and Inspection Service of the United States Department of Agriculture at **www.fsis.usda.gov/OA/consedu.htm** has information and training resources.

- The American Food Safety's Web site is **www.americanfoodsafety.com**. This site offers courses in food safety and Food Protection Manager Certification.

- The National Restaurant Association's Educational Foundation at **www .nraef.org** offers ServSafe® certification.

- Food Safety First offers videos you can use for training at **www.foodsafety first.com**.

- Resources on **www.restaurantbeast.com** provide many downloads pertaining to food safety, including a food-borne illness complaint form checklist for documentation, a food safety brochure with food handling facts and recommendations, a food safety quiz, FDA guidelines for HACCP programs, and a hand-washing sign.

Other sites include:

- Gateway to U.S. Government Food Safety Information: **www.foodsafety .gov**

- Bad Bug Book: **http://vm.cfsan.fda.gov/~mow/intro.html**

- Safety Alerts: **www.safetyalerts.com**

- E. Coli Food Safety News: MedNews.Net®: **www.MedNews.Net/bacteria**

- Safe Food Consumer: **www.safefood.org**

- Food Safe Program: **http://foodsafe.ucdavis.edu/homepage**

- International Food Safety Council: **www.nraef.org/ifsc/ifsc_about .asp?level1_id=2&level2_id=1**

Bacteria Primer

Bacteria are everywhere: in the air, in all areas of the restaurant and all over one's body. Most bacteria are microscopic and of no harm to people. Many forms of bacteria are actually beneficial, aiding in the production of such things as cheese, bread, butter, alcoholic beverages, etc. Only a small percentage of bacteria will cause food to spoil and can generate a form of food poisoning when consumed.

Bacteria need food, water and warmth in order to survive. Their growth rate depends upon how favorable these conditions are. Bacteria prefer to ingest moisture-saturated foods, such as meats, dairy products and produce. They will not grow as readily on dry foods such as cereals, sugar or flour.

Bacteria will grow most rapidly when the temperature is between 85°–100°F. In most cases, the growth rate will slow down drastically if the temperature is hotter or colder than this. It is vitally important that perishable food items are refrigerated before bacteria have a chance to establish themselves and multiply. Certain bacteria can survive in extreme hot and cold temperature ranges. By placing these bacteria in severe temperatures, you will be slowing down their growth rate, but not necessarily killing them.

Bacteria prefer to ingest moisture-saturated foods, such as meats, dairy products and produce. They will not grow as readily on dry foods such as cereals, sugar or flour.

The greatest problem in controlling bacteria is their rapid reproduction cycle. Approximately every 15 minutes the bacteria count will double under optimal living conditions. The more bacteria present, the greater the chance of bacterial infection. This is why food products that must be subjected to conditions favorable to bacteria are done so for the shortest period possible.

An important consideration when handling food products is that bacteria need several hours to adjust to a new environment before they are able to begin rapidly multiplying. If you had removed a food product from the walk-in refrigerator and had inadvertently introduced bacteria to it, advanced growth would not begin for several hours. If you had immediately placed the item back into the walk-in, the temperature would have killed the bacteria before it became established.

Bacterial forms do not have a means of transportation; they must be introduced to an area by some other vehicle. People are primarily responsible for transporting bacteria to new areas. The body temperature of 98.6°F is perfect for bacterial existence and proliferation. A person coughing, sneezing or wiping their hands on a counter can introduce bacteria to an area. Bacteria may be transmitted also by insects, air, water and articles onto which they have attached themselves, such as boxes, blades, knives and cutting boards.

TABLEWARE-HANDING TECHNIQUES

Some tableware-handling techniques you may want to address in training include the following:

- Use plastic gloves if directly handling food (remember, just because you have a glove on does not mean you can't cross-contaminate).

- Use plastic scoops in the ice machine.

- Avoid touching food-contact surfaces. For instance, servers should not carry glasses by the rim, and they should carry plates by the bottom or edge, keeping their hands away from eating surfaces. Employees should also pick up silverware by the handles.

Servers should always keep their hands away from eating surfaces.

AIDS

AIDS is not an airborne, waterborne or food-borne disease; it cannot be transmitted through air, water or food. The only medically documented manner in which HIV, the virus which causes AIDS, can be contracted is by sexual contact, by shared needles (usually associated with drug addiction), by infusion of contaminated blood, or through the placenta from mother to fetus.

You cannot contract AIDS by casual, social contact; touching people; sharing bathroom facilities; breathing air in which people have sneezed or coughed; or sharing food, beverages or eating utensils. This means that, with regard to AIDS, food service operations are safe places to work and dine.

SAFETY

A big part of any food service operation's overall food safety plan should also include general safety.

By its nature, the food service environment is full of potential hazards to employees' safety. Knives, slicers, grinders, glass, hot surfaces and wet or greasy floors are only a few of the hazards food service workers face every day. Fortunately, most accidents also involve human error and, therefore, can be prevented.

Workplace accidents happen. How you respond to them can make all the difference between life and death. The first thing to do is to have a safety plan in place, and train your servers to know and understand the elements of this plan so that they can respond calmly and quickly.

You may also want to have an outside agency such as the American Red Cross or your local fire department come in for safety training.

Red Cross. The Red Cross can make sure all of your servers know universal precautions, first aid, the abdominal thrust maneuver and CPR. You can contact the Red Cross at **www.redcross.org**.

Fire department. Your local fire department will give your employees free training on how to use fire extinguishers. More fires occur in food service than in any other type of operation. Fire extinguishers should be available in all areas where fires are likely, especially in the kitchen near grills and deep fryers. But be careful: Don't keep extinguishers so close to the equipment that they will be inaccessible in the event of a fire. All employees should be trained in avoiding fires as well as in the use of fire extinguishers and in evacuation procedures. Remember, always call the fire department first, before using a fire extinguisher!

OSHA can also provide you with safety training information. OSHA is the federal agency that oversees safety in the workplace; make sure you are in compliance with all their regulations. To find out more about their requirements for food service establishments and to explore training materials they offer, visit them online at **www.osha.gov**.

Training Employees on Fire Safety

General Objective: To teach employees safe actions to take during times of fire emergency.

Time Required: 2 hours

Materials Needed: Fire extinguishers, fire excavation route map.

Content	Process	Who	Comments
1. Fire safety policy	Presentation	Entire group	Go over the company's fire safety plan and the fire evacuation route. Tell employees where the route is posted (may want to use a PowerPoint presentation or overhead when going over the evacuation route). If you live in an area that experiences tornado activity, include what to do in the event. All plans should include fire diagrams. You should also have a posted fire egress route, fire extinguishers and first-aid kits on the premises.
2. Causes of fires	Discussion	Entire group	Ask group to name different causes of fire and list them on a flip chart or blackboard.
3. Fire extinguishers	Demonstration from fire safety professional/practice.	Entire group	Have someone from the fire department come in and show employees proper way to use fire extinguishers and let them practice.
4. Drill	Exercise	Entire group	Put your employees through fire and tornado drills. If an incident occurs, it will be up to your employees to help your customers out, so make sure they know what to do. You can also engage in first-aid drills during training meetings. Have one employee fake an illness or injury and see how appropriately and quickly other employees respond.
5. Reinforcement	Display certificates of trained employees in a prominent area for both employees and customers to see.		

SAMPLE FIRE EVACUATION PLAN

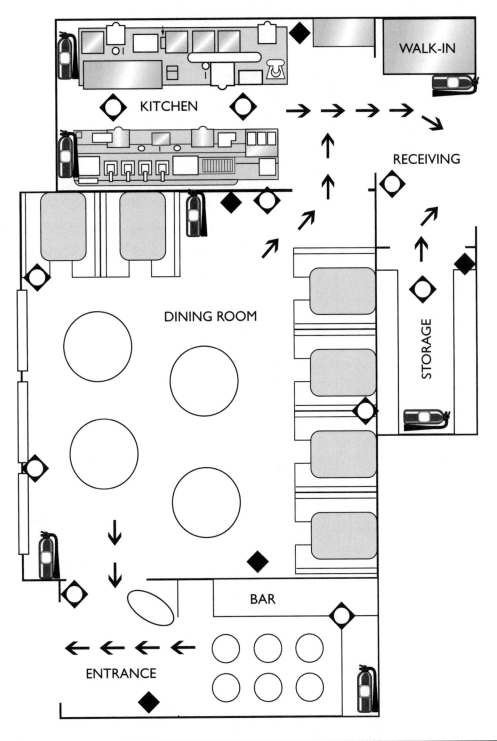

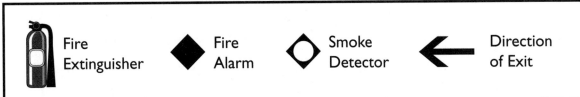

	Fire Extinguisher		Fire Alarm		Smoke Detector		Direction of Exit

First Aid and Safety

There are many potential hazards in a restaurant, so make sure your employees are trained on what to do in case of a first-aid safety emergency.

Training Employees on First Aid and CPR			
General Objective: To teach employees safe actions to take during times of emergency.			
Time Required: 3–4 hours			
Materials Needed: CPR dummies, first-aid kits, fire extinguishers.			
Content	Process	Who	Comments
1. First aid	Lecture/Practice	Entire group for lecture, then break into pairs.	Have a representative from the American Red Cross come in and lecture on and demonstrate proper first-aid measures, then let employees practice techniques they have learned on each other. Use other visual aids as well (see choking handout).
2. Heimlich Maneuver	Demonstration/ Practice	Entire group in pairs.	If you are using a Red Cross representative for first-aid training, they will go over this technique. Be sure to get signs and illustrations to hang in your back kitchen and break areas to remind employees about the correct procedure.
3. CPR	Lecture/Practice	Entire group for lecture, then break into pairs.	Have a representative from the American Red Cross come in an lecture on and demonstrate proper CPR methods, and then let employees practice techniques they have learned on the CPR dummies. Be sure to get signs and illustrations to hang in your back kitchen and break areas to remind employees about the correct procedure.
4. Preventing accidents	Discussion	Entire group	Ask group to list all the accidents that could happen in the facility (see visual aid).
5. Hazardous chemicals	Presentation/ Discussion	Entire group	Use MSD sheets to demonstrate how to read these. Ask employees to name hazardous chemicals used in your facility and discuss how to handle these specific substances and what your facility's emergency procedure is.

Training Employees on First Aid and CPR			
General Objective:	To teach employees safe actions to take during times of emergency.		
Time Required:	3–4 hours		
Materials Needed:	CPR dummies, first-aid kits, fire extinguishers.		
Content	**Process**	**Who**	**Comments**
6. Reinforcement	Display certificates of trained employees in a prominent area for both employees and customers to see.		

PREVENTING ACCIDENTS

Accidents are both dangerous and costly. Most accidents are avoidable and are the results of such careless acts as:

- Failure to immediately clean up foods spilled on the floor to prevent anyone from slipping.

- Failure to set trays and dishes back from the edges of the side tables or counters so that they will not be knocked off in passing.

- Loading trays in such a way that the dishes will slide off.

- Piling dishes in tall stacks that may be upset easily.

- Failure to nest cups by turning the handles in opposite directions to make them fit together securely.

- Stacking piles of dishes unevenly so that the stack is likely to upset.

- Carrying several water glasses in the fingers so that the rims touch; they frequently are cracked or nicked by this method of handling.

- Failure to keep long handles on containers turned away from the edges of the hot plates or counters.

- Leaving cupboard doors ajar so that a person may hit the corner and be injured.

- Failure to enter the serving pantry and kitchen by the entrance door ("In") and to leave by the exit door ("Out"). If there is only one door, open it carefully to avoid hitting someone who may be entering from the other side.

- Not watching the movement of other employees in the vicinity, and moving immediately into their paths without warning them.

- Not warning the guests when plates, containers or handles are very hot.

- Failure to hold hot plates and handles with the side towel to avoid burns.

CHOKING

As kids, we probably all heard our parents say: "Don't eat so fast! Chew your food properly!" They may have added, "Don't talk while you're eating," and "Drink your milk carefully!"

It's good advice for children — and for adults. Anyone can choke on food if he or she is not careful. That's why an important part of food service safety is being alert to your customers.

Approximately 4,000 people die from accidental choking in the Unied States annually.

Here's what to look for and what to do:

- If a person has both hands to the throat and cannot speak or cough, it is likely he or she is choking.

- If this person can talk, cough or breathe, do not pat him or her on the back or interfere in any way.

- If this person cannot talk, cough or breathe, you will need to take action. Use the Heimlich Maneuver, and call for help immediately.

You can also get a choke aid to demonstrate to employees.

The Choke Aid Kit is an FDA-approved choke-relieving device. It has a patented design with reach-extending handles and energy flex system, making it possible to save a choking victim safely and effectively. The device comes with a complete training kit, which includes a wall mount, booklet, poster and video that describes in detail how to save a choking victim with or without the device. Your establishment needs at least one of these kits in every workstation. Order online at **www.atlantic-pub.com**.

HACCP

While your entire staff needs to be trained on food safety principles, your kitchen staff should receive additional training in the HACCP principles. Until recently, HACCP was almost exclusively used in food production plants, but restaurants are beginning to adopt this approach to food safety. Having a HACCP system in place could save you a fortune in liability costs. If a situation arises, you may be able to prove you were using reasonable care, and this can go a long way in a liability suit.

Training Kitchen Employees on HACCP Principles

General Objective: Teach kitchen employees HACCP principles so your restaurant is serving safe food.

Time Required: 3 hours

Materials Needed: Video and handouts, PowerPoint if you have a presentation.

Content	Process	Who	Comments
Introduction to importance of food safety: What is HACCP?	Presentation	Entire group	
7 HACCP principles	Presentation	Entire group	See presentation notes.
Video	Video	Entire group	Developed from a chef's perspective, this training program is designed as an introductory program for new employees and as a refresher course. Contains detailed instructions on hand washing, cross-contamination, heating and cooling of foods, temperature danger zones, thawing, storage, and cleaning procedures. Includes on-screen questions and a companion test and study guide. Thirty-five minutes. English and Spanish versions available (**www.atlantic-pub.com**).
Bacteria primer	Presentation	Entire group	See notes and handout that follow.
Quiz		Entire group	

Below is training material to use when training kitchen staff on kitchen and knife safety.

Training Employees on Kitchen Safety			
General Objective: Train kitchen employees on proper safety techniques to avoid injury. Time Required: Materials Needed:			
Content	**Process**	**Who**	**Comments**
Introduction	Presentation	Entire group	Go over general safety information.
Heat and burns	Presentation	Entire group	Use videos or handouts. Check with OSHA or local Red Cross chapter for safety training materials.
Cuts	Presentation	Entire group	Check with OSHA or local Red Cross chapter for safety training materials.
Electrical shock	Presentation	Entire group	Check with OSHA or local Red Cross chapter for safety training materials.
Strains	Presentation/ Demonstration	Entire group	Demonstrate proper way to lift. Also show employees various safety belts available for them to wear at work to protect their backs. Check with OSHA or local Red Cross chapter for safety training materials.
Slips and falls	Presentation	Entire group	Check with OSHA or local Red Cross chapter for safety training materials.
Reinforcement	Display certificates of trained employees in a prominent area for both employees and customers to see		

HEAT AND BURNS

There are many ways employees can get burned in a food service environment unless they're very careful. Burns can result from contact with hot surfaces such as grills, ovens, burners, fryers and other heating equipment. Burns can also be caused by escaping steam or by hot food or drinks that are splattered, splashed or spilled.

To prevent burns:

- Use thick, dry potholders or mitts, and stir food with long-handled spoons or paddles.

- Turn on hot-water faucets cautiously.

- Wear insulated rubber gloves for rinse water that is 170°F.

- Follow instructions for the use of cooking equipment—particularly steam equipment.

- Be sure all steam is expelled from steamers before opening the doors.

- Lift cooking lids and similar equipment away from yourself to avoid burns from steam.

- To avoid splattering and splashing, don't fill kettles too full. Also, don't allow food to boil over.

- Remember that oil and water don't mix, so be sure food is dry before you place it in a fryer.

- Point pan handles away from foot traffic, but also within reach, to avoid knocking over other pans.

- Do not crowd cooking surfaces with hot pans.

- Remove cooked foods from cooking surfaces immediately.

- Allow oil to cool, and use extreme caution when cleaning fryers.

- Use caution when removing hot pans from the oven. Wear insulated gloves or mitts, and be certain no one is in the removal path.

- Do not wear clothing that may drape onto a hot spot and catch on fire.

ELECTRICAL SHOCK

Because of the variety of electrical equipment used in food service, electrical shock is a common concern.

To prevent electrical shock:

- Properly ground all electrical equipment.

- Ensure that employees can reach switches without touching or leaning against metal tables or counters.

- Replace all worn or frayed electrical cords.

- Use electrical equipment only when hands are dry.

- Unplug equipment before cleaning.

- Locate electrical switches and breakers to permit rapid shutdown in the event of an emergency.

STRAINS

Carrying equipment or food items that are too heavy can result in strains to the arms, legs or back.

To prevent strains:

- Store heavy items on lower shelves.

- Use dollies or carts when moving objects that are too heavy to carry.

- To move objects from one area to another, use carts with firm shelves and properly operating wheels or casters.

- Don't carry too many objects at one time; instead, use a cart.

- Don't try to lift large or heavy objects by yourself.

- Use proper lifting techniques. Remember to bend from your knees, not your back.

SLIPPING AND FALLING

To prevent slips and falls:

- Clean up wet spots and spills immediately.

- Let people know when floors are wet. Use signs that signal caution, and prominently display them. Wear shoes that have nonslip soles.

- Do not stack boxes or other objects too high; they can fall and cause people to trip.

- Keep items such as boxes, ladders, step stools and carts out of the paths of foot traffic.

EXPOSURE TO HAZARDOUS CHEMICALS

Improper exposure to cleaning agents, chemical pesticides and chemical sanitizers may cause injury to the skin or poisoning. To protect workers from exposure to hazardous materials, special precautions need to be taken, including certain steps that are required by law.

For example, OSHA requires food service establishments to keep a current inventory of all hazardous materials.

Manufacturers are required to make sure hazardous chemicals are properly labeled and must supply a Material Safety Data Sheet (MSDS) to be kept on file at the food service facility. The MSDS provides the chemical name of the product and physical hazards, health hazards and emergency procedures in case of exposure.

Information about each chemical—including its common name, when it is used, who is authorized to use it, and information from the MSDS—must also be provided to workers.

To prevent improper exposure to hazardous materials, make sure:

- Only properly trained workers handle hazardous chemicals.

- Employees have safety equipment to use when working with hazardous chemicals.

- Employees wear nonporous gloves and eye goggles when working with sanitizing agents and other cleaners.

Improper handling of food products or neglecting sanitation and safety procedures will certainly lead to health problems and/or personal injury. A successful restaurant must develop a reputation for serving quality food in a safe environment. Should there ever be a question in your customers' minds as to the wholesomeness or quality of a product, the restaurant will quickly lose its hard-earned reputation. The sanitation and safety procedures described in this section are very simple to initiate, but management must follow up and enforce them.

How to Read the MSDS
There are six sections of the MSDS that provide you with safe handling instructions: 1. Product name. 2. Whether the product is a fire hazard. 3. What health hazards occur if exposure or overexposure occurs. 4. Steps to follow in case of a spill. 5. Special protection needed when using the substance (gloves, goggles, etc.). 6. Special precautions to take when handling and storing.

A sample MSDS sheet can be found on the following page.

<table>
<tr><td colspan="3">MATERIAL SAFETY DATA SHEET</td></tr>
<tr><td>CARBON KLEEN</td><td>Aerosol</td><td>#1016</td></tr>
</table>

Manufacturer's Name: Takeo Enterprises Corp. dba Diablo Products Phone # 1-800-548-1385
Address: P.O. Box 756, Fort Dodge, IA 50501

Section 1 - PRODUCT IDENTIFICATION

This Material Safety Data Sheet contains environmental, health, and toxicology information. It also contains information to help you meet community right to know emergency response reporting requirements under SARA TITLE III and many other laws.

D.O.T. PROPER SHIPPING NAME: ORM-D **CONSUMER COMMODITY**
NFPA CODES: HEALTH – 2 FLAMMABILITY – 3 REACTIVITY – 0 SPECIAL - 0
Trade name: Carbon Kleen, Aerosol Product Type: Carbon Stripper

Section 2 - Components

Chemical Name/Common Name	CASE NO.	PERCENT(Optional)	TLV(Source)
Dichloromethane	75-09-02	60-80	25ppm
Methanol	67-56-1	1-5	200ppm
2-butoxyethanol, glycol ether	111-76-2	1-5	25ppm
Toluene	108-88-3	1-5	200ppm
Propane	74-98-6	8	1000ppm
Butane	106-97-8	7	800ppm

No toxic chemicals subject to the reporting requirements of section313 of Title III and 40 CFR 372 are present.
This product may contain chemicals known to the State of California to cause cancer, birth defects or reproductive harm.

Section 3 – Physical Data

Boiling Point: (F) 104 deg Freezing Point: <0 deg (F) Specific Gravity: (H_2O = 1.0) 1.01 pH: N/A
Vapor Pressure: (mmHg) 25 @ 20deg (C) Vapor Density: 2.9
Solubility in water: Slight
Evaporation Rate (vs ether): 1
Appearance and Odor: Aerosol product

Section 4 – Fire and Explosion Hazard Data

Flash Point (T.C.C.): Level 2 Aerosol

Extinguishing Media: Foam, alcohol foam, CO2, dry chemical, water fog

Special Fire Fighting Procedures: Water may be ineffective. Water may be used to cool containers to prevent pressure build-up and explosion when exposed to extreme heat. If water used fog nozzles preferred. Wear goggles and SCBA

Unusual Fire and Explosion Hazards: Closed containers may explode from internal pressure build-up when exposed to extreme heat and discharge contents. Vapor accumulation can flash or explode if ignited. Over exposure to decomposition products may cause a health hazard. Symptoms may not be readily apparent. Obtain medical attention.

Section 5 – Reactive Data

Stability: Stable Incompatibility: Strong oxidizing agents
Hazardous Decomposition Products: Phosgene & Muratic Acid when in contact with open flame.

Section 6 – Health Hazards

Threshold Limit Value – Product (see section 2 for ingredient TLV): 200ppm
Primary Routes of Exposure: Eyes – Yes Skin – Yes Inhalation – Yes Ingestion – Yes
Signs and Symptoms of Over-exposure (Acute): Irritation to the eyes and skin. Fatigue, numbness, weakness, tingling of the limbs, nausea.
Carcinogen or Suspect Carcinogen Ingredients:

Section 7 – Emergency and First Aid procedures

Eyes: Flush with water for at least 15 minutes, get medical attention.
Skin: Thoroughly wash exposed area with soap and cold water.
Ingestion: DO NOT INDUCE VOMITING. Get medical attention. If vomiting occurs spontaneously, prevent vomitus from entering the lungs by keeping victims head below hips.
Inhalation: Remove victim to fresh air. If breathing is difficult, administer oxygen. Get medical attention.

Section 8 – Special Protection Information

Respiratory Protection: none under normal use Ventilation Requirements: well ventilated area
Protective Gloves: Rubber. Eye Protection: Safety glasses

Section 9 – Spill or Leak Procedures.

Steps to be taken if Released or Spilled: Wear protective equipment including self contained breathing apparatus for large spills. Keep spilled material out of sewers, storm drains and soils.
Waste Disposal Methods: Consult state and local agencies to ascertain proper disposal procedures

Section 10 – Storage and Handling Information

Precautions to be taken in Handling and Storage: Store in a cool, dry, well ventilated area away from incompatible materials.

Section 11 – Disclaimer

The information contained herein is based on data considered accurate. However, no warranty is expressed r implied regarding the accuracy of the data or the results to be obtained from the use thereof. Because the information contained herein may be applied under conditions beyond our control, we assume no responsibility for its use.

Emergency Number:	**1-800-255-3924**

CUTS

Food service workers need to take precautions to prevent cuts. And it's not just knives that can cause trouble: workers can hurt themselves—or their coworkers—with the sharp edges of equipment and supplies or with broken glass. Nails and staples used in food packaging can also be dangerous.

To prevent cuts, take the following precautions:

- Use appropriate tools (not bare hands) to pick up and dispose of broken glass. Immediately place broken glass into a separate, clearly marked garbage container.

- Take care when cutting rolls of kitchen wrap with the cutter.

- Be careful with can openers and the edges of open cans. Never use a knife to open cans or to pry items loose.

- Use a pusher to feed food into a grinder.

- Turn off and unplug slicers and grinders when removing food and cleaning.

- Use guards on grinders and slicers.

- Replace equipment blades as soon as they are cleaned.

- Be aware that left-handed people need to take extra care when working with slicers and similar equipment. This is because the safety features on this equipment are usually designed for right-handed people.

- Keep knives sharp. Dull blades are harder to work with and cause more cuts than sharp ones.

- Never leave knives or equipment blades in the bottom of a sink.

- Carry knives by the handle with the tip pointed away from you. Never try to catch a falling knife.

- Cut away from yourself on a cutting board.

- Slice, do not hack.

When you're storing or cleaning equipment, be sure to:

- Store knives and other sharp tools in special places when not in use.

- Wash dishes and glasses separately to help prevent them from being crushed by heavier objects and breaking in the dishwasher or sink.

- Do not stack glasses or cups inside one another.

- Watch out for nails, staples and protruding sharp edges while unpacking boxes and crates.

Training Cooks on Knife Use and Safety

Knife safety is very important in the kitchen, and you want to be sure your employees know how to handle knives properly.

Training Cooks on Knife Use and Safety			
General Objective: To teach employees correct and safe way to handle knives.			
Time Required: 1–2 hours			
Materials Needed: Set of kitchen knives, sharpening steel, various vegetables and meats to practice cuts.			
Content	Process	Who	Comments
1. Knife safety: Show employees how to handle knives.	Demonstration	Entire group	See teaching aids.
2. Show employees proper way to sharpen and clean knives.	Demonstration	Entire group	See teaching aids.

Training Cooks on Knife Use and Safety, cont.			
3. Show employees different types of knives and their uses.	Demonstration	Entire group	See teaching aids.
4. Show employees proper cuts and go over cutting terms.	Demonstration	Entire group	See teaching aids.
5. Have employees demonstrate their skills.	Practice	Individuals	Go around the room coaching and offering constructive criticism on knife techniques.

Knife Safety Handout

Knife Safety Tips
• Always use the right knife for the job.
• Keep knives sharp—a dull knife requires more pressure to cut, so you are more likely to cut yourself.
• Cut away from your body.
• Don't use knives improperly (to open cans, bottles, etc.).
• Always use a cutting board.
• Put a damp cloth under cutting boards to keep them from sliding.
• When carrying a knife, keep it to your side with the point down and cutting edge back and away from you.
• Don't try to catch a knife if it falls.
• Do not put dirty knives into a sink full of soapy water. Lay them to the side so the person washing dishes does not accidentally get cut.
• Don't leave knives near the edges of tables.
• Always store knives properly — put them in a rack or case so the blade is protected.

Types of Knives		
Type	**Description**	**Use**
Chef's Knife	Blade is usually 8–14-inches long	All-purpose knife used most frequently in the kitchen. Used for chopping, slicing and mincing.
Paring Knife	Blade is usually 2–4-inches long	Used to trim and peel vegetables.
Utility Knife	Blade is 5–7-inches long	Used in cold food prep for cutting fruits, vegetables, etc.
Slicer	Has a long blade with a rounded end. Usually has a fluted edge.	Used to carve and slice cooked meats.
Boning Knife	Blade is thinner and shorter than a Chef's knife. Blade is usually 6-inches long.	Used to bone raw meats.

GLOSSARY

Approved Source – Acceptable to the regulatory authority based on a determination of conformity with principles, practices and generally recognized standards that protect public health.

Bacteria – Living single-cell organisms. Bacteria can be carried by water, wind, insects, plants, animals and people and survive well on skin and clothes and in human hair. They also thrive in scabs, scars, the mouth, nose, throat, intestines and room-temperature foods.

CCP – Critical control point.

Contamination – The unintended presence of potentially harmful substances, including microorganisms, chemicals, and physical objects in food.

Cross-Contamination – The transfer of harmful substances or disease-causing microorganisms to food by hands, food-contact surfaces, sponges, cloth towels and utensils that touch raw food, are not cleaned, and then touch ready-to-eat foods. Cross-contamination can also occur when raw food touches or drips onto cooked or ready-to-eat foods.

Corrective Action – An activity that is taken by a person whenever a critical limit is not met.

Critical Control Point (CCP) – An operational step or procedure in a process, production method or recipe at which control can be applied to prevent, reduce or eliminate a food safety hazard.

Critical Limit – A measurable limit at a CCP that can be monitored to control the identified hazard to a safe level in the food.

Fish – a) Means fresh or saltwater finfish, crustaceans and other forms of aquatic life (including alligator, frog, aquatic turtle, jellyfish, sea cucumber, and sea urchin and the roe of such animals) other than birds or mammals, and all mollusks, if such life is intended for human consumption. b) Includes an edible human food product derived in whole or in part from fish, including fish that have been processed in any manner.

Food – Raw, cooked or processed edible substance, ice, beverage, chewing gum or ingredient used or intended for use or for sale in whole or in part for human consumption.

Food Establishment – An operation at the retail level; i.e., that serves or offers food directly to the consumer and that, in some cases, includes a production, storage or distributing operation that supplies the direct-to-consumer operation.

Food-Borne Illness – Sickness resulting from acquiring a disease that is carried or transmitted to humans by food containing harmful substances.

Food-Borne Outbreak – The occurrence of two or more people experiencing the same illness after eating the same food.

HACCP – Hazard Analysis of Critical Control Points.

HACCP Plan – A written document which is based on the principles of HACCP and which describes the procedures to be followed to ensure the control of a specific process or procedure.

HACCP System – The result of implementing the HACCP principles in an operation that has a foundational, comprehensive, prerequisite program in place. A HACCP system includes the HACCP plan and all SOPs.

Hazard – A biological, physical, or chemical property that may cause a food to be unsafe for human consumption.

Internal Temperature – The temperature of the internal portion of a food product.

Meat – The flesh of animals used as food including the dressed flesh of cattle, swine, sheep or goats and other edible animals, except fish, poultry, and wild game animals.

Microorganism – A form of life that can be seen only with a microscope; including bacteria, viruses, yeast and single-celled animals.

Molluscan Shellfish – Any edible species of raw fresh or frozen oysters, clams, mussels and scallops or edible portions thereof, except when the scallop product consists only of the shucked adductor muscle.

Monitoring – The act of observing and making measurements to help determine if critical limits are being met and maintained.

National Shellfish Sanitation Program (NSSP) – The voluntary system by which regulatory authorities for shellfish harvesting waters and shellfish processing and transportation and the shellfish industry implement specified controls to ensure that raw and frozen shellfish are safe for human consumption.

Operational Step – An activity in a food establishment, such as receiving, storage, preparation, cooking, etc.

Parasite – An organism that grows, feeds and is sheltered on or in a different organism and contributes to its host.

Pathogen – A microorganism (bacteria, parasites, viruses or fungi) that is infectious and causes disease.

Personal Hygiene – Individual cleanliness and habits.

Potentially Hazardous Food – A food that is natural or synthetic that requires temperature control because it is capable of supporting:

a. The rapid and progressive growth of infectious or toxigenic microorganisms.

b. The growth and toxin production of Clostridium botulinum.

c. In raw shell eggs, the growth of Salmonella Enteritidis.

Potentially hazardous food includes foods of animal origin that are raw or heat-treated; foods of plant origin that are heat-treated or consists of raw seed sprouts; cut melons; and garlic and oil mixtures that are not acidified or otherwise modified at a processing plant in a way that results in mixtures that do not support growth of pathogenic microorganisms as described above.

Procedural Step – An individual activity in applying this guide to a food establishment's operations.

Process Approach – A method of categorizing food operations into one of three modes:

1. Food preparation with no cook step wherein ready-to-eat food is stored, prepared and served.

2. Food preparation for same-day service wherein food is stored, prepared, cooked and served.

3. Complex food preparation wherein food is stored, prepared, cooked, cooled, reheated, hot held and served.

Ready-to-Eat Food – A food that is in a form that is edible without washing, cooking or additional preparation by the food establishment or consumer and that is reasonably expected to be consumed in that form.

Ready-to-eat food includes potentially hazardous food that has been cooked; raw, washed, cut fruits and vegetables; whole, raw, fruits and vegetables that are presented for consumption without the need for further washing, such as at a buffet; and other food presented for consumption for which further washing or cooking is not required and from which rinds, peels, husks, or shells have been removed.

Record – A documentation of monitoring observation and verification activities.

Regulatory Authority – A federal, state, local or tribal enforcement body or authorized representative having jurisdiction over the food establishment.

Risk – An estimate of the likely occurrence of a hazard.

Shellfish – Bi-valve molluscan shellfish.

Standard Operating Procedure (SOP) – A written method of controlling a practice in accordance with predetermined specifications to obtain a desired outcome.

Temperature Measuring Device –
A thermometer, thermocouple, thermistor or other device for measuring the temperature of food, air or water.

Toxin – A poisonous substance that may be found in food.

Verification – The use of methods, procedures or tests by supervisors, designated personnel or regulators to determine if the food safety system based on the HACCP principles is working to control identified hazards or if modifications need to be made.

Virus – A protein-wrapped genetic material which is the smallest and simplest life-form known, such as hepatitis A.

APPENDIX

This section contains all forms referenced throughout the previous chapters as well as additional forms, charts, posters and worksheets to implement an effective HACCP program. Following is the list of the contents:

Sign-Out Sheet			
Item	Date	Amount/Wt.	Employee

Preparation Form					
Item	Minimum Amount	Amount Def./Ord.	Beginning Amount	Amount Prepped	Starting Total

Minimum Amount Needed Form							
Item	MON	TUES	WED	THURS	FRI	SAT	SUN

Item	Starting Weight (oz)	# of Portions	Total Portion Weight (oz)	Yield %	Prep. Cook

Want Sheet				
Item	Employee	Approved	Ordered On	Received

Standardized Recipe

Menu Item:

INGREDIENTS:

RECIPE YIELD: _____

PORTION SIZE: _____

PORTION COST: _____

PREPARATION:

NOTES:

Standardized Recipe II

MENU ITEM:

INGREDIENTS	PORTION	UNIT COST

RECIPE PROCEDURE:

_____

_____

_____

_____

Total Recipe Cost	$ _____
Per-Serving Cost	$ _____
Menu Price	$ _____
Food Cost %	_____
Gross Profit	$ _____

_____

_____

_____

_____

_____

_____

_____

Standardized Recipe III

Menu Item: _____

TOOLS NEEDED:

☐ _____

☐ _____

☐ _____

☐ _____

☐ _____

☐ _____

☐ _____

☐ _____

☐ _____

photo of finished dish

INGREDIENTS	QUANTITY	PROCEDURE

Standardized Recipe Cost Sheet

MENU ITEM:

RECIPE YIELD: _____

PORTION SIZE: _____

PORTION COST: _____

Total Recipe Cost: _____   Total Portions: _____

Portion Cost: _____   Date Costed: _____

Previous Portion Cost: _____   Previous Date Costed: _____

INGREDIENTS		INGREDIENTS COST	
Item	Amount	Unit Cost	Total Cost

Storage Life of Meat Products

Maximum storage time recommendations for fresh, cooked and processed meat. For best quality, fresh meats should be used within 2 or 3 days; ground meat should be used within 24 hours.

ITEM	REFRIGERATOR (36° to 40°F)	FREEZER (0°F or lower)
Ground beef, veal & lamb	1 to 2 days	3 to 4 months
Beef (fresh)	2 to 4 days	6 to 12 months
Corned beef	7 days	2 weeks
Veal (fresh)	2 to 4 days	6 to 9 months
Lamb (fresh)	2 to 4 days	6 to 9 months
Ground pork	1 to 2 days	1 to 3 months
Pork (fresh)	2 to 4 days	3 to 6 months
Sausage, fresh pork	7 days	2 months
Sausage, smoked	3 to 7 days	should not freeze
Sausage, dry & semi-dry	2 to 3 weeks	should not freeze
Variety meats	1 to 2 days	3 to 4 months
Bacon	5 to 7 days	1 month
Smoked ham, whole	7 days	2 months
Ham slices	3 to 4 days	2 months
Leftover cooked meat	4 to 5 days	2 to 3 months
Luncheon meats	7 days	should not freeze
Hot dogs/frankfurters	4 to 5 days	1 month
Meat pies (cooked)	-----	3 months
Swiss steak (cooked)	-----	3 months
Stews (cooked)	-----	3 months
Prepared meat dinner	-----	2 to 6 months

Cooking Temperature Guide

Meat Thermometer Readings	
BEEF	
Rare (cold, red center)	140°F
Medium Rare	150°F (warm, red center)
Medium	160°F (warm, pink center)
Medium Well	165°F (hot, pink center)
Well-Done	170°F (brown center, no pink)
VEAL	170°F
LAMB	
Rare	140°F
Medium	160°F
Well-Done	170°-180°F
FRESH PORK	170°F
SMOKED PORK	
Fully cooked	140°F
Cooked before eating	160°F
Oven Temperature Guide	
Very slow oven	250°-275°F
Slow oven	300°-325°F
Moderate oven	350°-375°F
Hot oven	400°-475°F
Extremely hot oven	500°-525°F
Candy & Frosting Syrup Temperatures	
Thread	230°-234°F
Soft Ball	234°-240°F
Firm Ball	244°-248°F
Hard Ball	250°-266°F
Soft Crack	270°-290°F
Hard Crack	300°-310°F

Thaw Pull Chart

All thaw items should be pulled far enough in advance so they are THAWED COMPLETELY at the time of use. All thaw items must be labeled, dated and rotated.

Item	Thaw Time	Shelf Life	On Hand	Pull

Be sure to thaw food correctly in one of the following ways:

UNDER COLD RUNNING WATER

IN THE REFRIGERATOR

DURING THE COOKING PROCESS

IN THE MICROWAVE

Detailed Layout of Kitchen Equipment

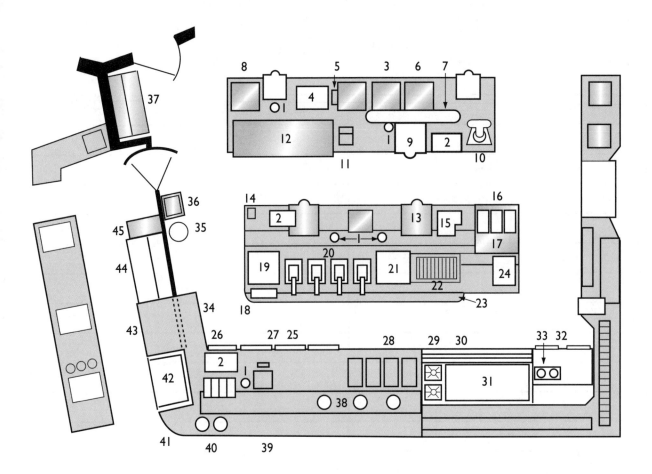

1. Knife wells (five)
2. Composition cutting boards (three)
3. Stainless-steel combination pot and pan washing table with three-compartment sink and meat and vegetable drawers (two)
4. Disposal (3 h.p. hammermill type)
5. Recirculating centrifugal pump
6. Flexible spray rinse arm
7. Overhead pot rack
8. Single-compartment sink
9. Stainless-steel salad preparation work table with undershelf
10. 12-quart mixer on mobile stand
11. Portion scale
12. Reach-in refrigerator
13. Stainless-steel meat and vegetable preparation worktable with angle-compartment sink, drawers (two), overshelf and undershelf

14. Can opener
15. Slicer
16. Closed-top range
17. Exhaust canopy
18. Wooden cutting board
19. Microwave oven
20. Deep fat fryers (four)
21. Griddle
22. Open-top broiler
23. Base cabinet refrigerator with overshelf
24. Steamer
25. Base cabinet refrigerator
26. Cold food wells (eight)
27. Sandwich grill
28. Hot food wells (four) and undercounter dish storage
29. Open-top burners (two)

30. Wooden cutting board
31. Griddle
32. Base cabinet refrigerator
33. Waffle grill
34. Pass-through window
35. Trash can
36. Wash basin
37. Ice machine
38. Heat lamps (two)
39. Waitstaff pickup counter
40. Soup wells (two)
41. Soup bowl lowerators
42. Reach-in refrigerator, sliding-door type
43. Customer takeout back counter
44. Fountain
45. Milkshake machine

Emergency Contacts

Our address is:

_____

_____

AMBULANCE: _____

FIRE-RESCUE: _____

HOSPITAL:_____

PHYSICIAN:_____

POLICE:_____

POISON CONTROL: _____

LOCAL OSHA OFFICE: _____

Incident Log

Prepared By: _____ Manager on Duty: _____

Day: _____ Date: _____ Shift: _____

TIME INCIDENT OCCURRED:

Describe Incident: _____

_____

_____

_____

_____

_____

Patron's Name: _____ Phone Number: _____

Address: _____

_____

City, State & Zip: _____

Employee(s) Involved: _____

Witness Name: _____

Address: _____

_____

City, State & Zip: _____

Phone Number(s): _____

Witness Name: _____

Address: _____

_____

City, State & Zip: _____

Phone Number(s): _____

WARNING

All employees — Please be aware that the premises will be fumigated on:

DATE TO SPRAY: _____

TIME TO SPRAY: _____

Opening employees due in at:

Kitchen: _____
Dining Room: _____
Bar: _____

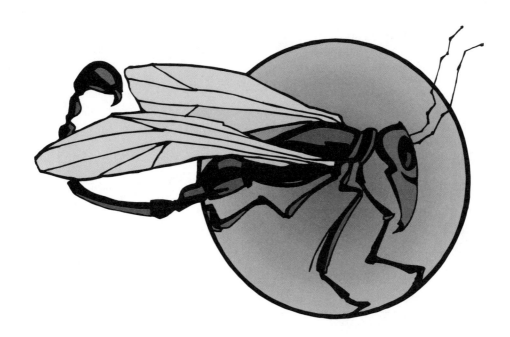

Kitchen Safety Inspection Form

Date Completed: _____ Shift: _____

Prepared By: _____ Manager on Duty: _____

EQUIPMENT

Is all kitchen equipment clean, well-maintained and in proper working order? ❑ Yes ❑ No

Are grease traps cleaned regularly? ❑ Yes ❑ No

Are the fryers in a separate location, away from grills, griddles and open flames? ❑ Yes ❑ No

Is all refrigeration equipment free from dust and grease? ❑ Yes ❑ No

Comments or Corrective Actions Needed: _____

_____

_____

_____

_____

FIRE PREVENTION

Is there a fire-prevention system installed and in good, working order? ❑ Yes ❑ No

Has the system been inspection by a professional and been
marked with a valid inspection tag? ❑ Yes ❑ No

Are all cooking areas adequately covered by the fire-suppression system? ❑ Yes ❑ No

Are the fire-prevention nozzles aimed correctly? ❑ Yes ❑ No

Are fire extinguishers easily accessible? ❑ Yes ❑ No

Are fire extinguishers charged and inspected yearly? ❑ Yes ❑ No

Has the automatic sprinkler system been inspected yearly and tagged? ❑ Yes ❑ No

Is the sprinkler system valve open and in good condition? ❑ Yes ❑ No

Comments or Corrective Actions Needed: _____

_____

_____

_____

_____

VENTILATION SYSTEMS

Are exhaust vents and fans clean and inspected on a regular basis?   ❏ Yes   ❏ No

Does the exhaust hood adequately cover all cooking areas?   ❏ Yes   ❏ No

Are all the exhaust hood filters clean, well-maintained and free of grease?   ❏ Yes   ❏ No

Comments or Corrective Actions Needed: _____

_____

_____

_____

_____

ELECTRICAL

Is the electrical room also used for storage?   ❏ Yes   ❏ No

Is the fuse box or fuse panel easily accessible?   ❏ Yes   ❏ No

In the fuse box, are all the breakers labeled clearly?   ❏ Yes   ❏ No

Are any of the breaker switches covered with tape?   ❏ Yes   ❏ No

Are all electrical switches covered?   ❏ Yes   ❏ No

Are all electrical outlets covered?   ❏ Yes   ❏ No

Are all electrical junction boxes and fittings covered?   ❏ Yes   ❏ No

Are there any extension cords in use?   ❏ Yes   ❏ No

Are all exposed electrical cords untangled, properly insulated and in good condition?   ❏ Yes   ❏ No

Comments or Corrective Actions Needed: _____

_____

_____

_____

_____

Notes: _____

_____

_____

_____

_____

Dining Room Safety Inspection Form

Date Completed: _____	Shift: _____
Prepared By: _____	Manager on Duty: _____

FLOORING, STAIRWAYS & EXITS

Are floor mats in use, especially near wet or greasy areas? ❑ Yes ❑ No

For high-traffic areas, are rugs and runners utilized? ❑ Yes ❑ No

Is there adequate lighting in areas with steps or staircases? ❑ Yes ❑ No

Are steps equipped with handrails and slip guards? ❑ Yes ❑ No

Do all exits have properly lit exit signs? ❑ Yes ❑ No

Are all exits free from obstructions? ❑ Yes ❑ No

Do all exit doors have panic bars? ❑ Yes ❑ No

Do all exit doors open easily? ❑ Yes ❑ No

Comments or Corrective Actions Needed: _____

_____

_____

_____

_____

EMERGENCY PROCEDURES

Is there a functional emergency lighting system? ❑ Yes ❑ No

Are all employees instructed in emergency procedures? ❑ Yes ❑ No

Are the emergency numbers clearly posted for fire, police, hospital and ambulance? ❑ Yes ❑ No

Are any employees trained in first-aid procedures such as CPR or Heimlich Maneuver? ❑ Yes ❑ No

Comments or Corrective Actions Needed: _____

_____

_____

_____

_____

ELECTRICAL

Are all electrical switches covered?   ❑ Yes ❑ No

Are all electrical outlets covered?   ❑ Yes ❑ No

Are there any extension cords in use?   ❑ Yes ❑ No

Are all exposed electrical cords untangled, properly insulated and in good condition?   ❑ Yes ❑ No

Comments or Corrective Actions Needed: _____

_____

_____

_____

_____

EQUIPMENT

Is all equipment clean, well-maintained and in good working order?   ❑ Yes ❑ No

Do hot beverage machines, such as coffee urns, have scald warnings posted?   ❑ Yes ❑ No

Before using any piece of equipment, are all employees properly trained?   ❑ Yes ❑ No

Comments or Corrective Actions Needed: _____

_____

_____

_____

_____

Notes: _____

_____

_____

_____

_____

_____

_____

_____

General Kitchen Sanitation Compliance Checklist

FOOD PRODUCTION AREA

☐ Equipment, appliances, walls and screens are clean in food service area.

☐ Food-preparation equipment is cleaned and sanitized after every use. This would include choppers, mixers and can openers.

☐ Frozen food is thawed using the proper thawing procedures.

☐ Cutting boards are sanitized properly after each use and when alternating between raw and cooked foods.

☐ Prior to preparation, fruits and vegetables are thoroughly washed.

☐ Foods are cooked properly and internal temperatures checked.

☐ Foods that are potentially hazardous are held at the correct temperature. Hot foods at 140°F or above; cold foods at 41°F or below. Frozen food must be at or below 0°F at all times.

☐ Steam tables or food warmers are used properly and not used to reheat or prepare food.

☐ Food service employees do not touch cooked food with bare hands.

☐ The food preparation area is not used by employees for smoking or eating. All beverage containers and cups are covered and contain some type of drinking straw.

☐ Employees who are ill are sent home or restricted to activities where they do not come into contact with food.

☐ Employees are wearing hair restraints.

☐ Employees wash their hands thoroughly after using the bathroom, after coughing or sneezing, after handling garbage, or after any activity that could cause food contamination.

☐ The kitchen has an easily accessible, clean sink specifically for hand washing with soap and disposable towels. A sign with proper hand washing procedures is posted near the sink.

☐ Lighting has covers or bulbs that will not shatter.

☐ In holding areas, food temperatures are checked regularly with a clean, sanitized thermometer.

☐ Uncovered glassware and dishes of food items are not stacked.

DISHWASHING AREA

☐ A high-temperature dishwashing machine is used, with wash-cycle water temperatures over 140°F, and rinse-cycle water temperatures over 160°F.

☐ A low-temperature dishwashing machine is used with a chemical agent. Manufacturer's specifications are adhered to for proper temperature and chemical concentration.

☐ For manual washing, a three-compartment sink is used. The sink has a bleach sanitizing solution or iodine, and chemical strips are used to verify the sanitizing solution's strength.

☐ Glassware and dishes are not stacked while wet.

☐ Glassware or dishes that are cracked or chipped are immediately discarded.

☐ Clean dishes, glassware, utensils and pots and pans do not have any food residue.

CHEMICAL & NON-FOOD STORAGE

☐ Dirty water is discarded after use. All mops, brooms and cleaning equipment are cleaned and put away.

☐ The storage area is easily accessible and clean with no refuse or food residue.

☐ Toxic materials are in the proper container and clearly labeled.

REFRIGERATORS & FREEZERS

☐ Shallow containers are used for cooked foods in the refrigerator.

☐ Air can circulate freely throughout the freezer or refrigerator. Food should not be stored too closely.

☐ Freezers and refrigerators are clean and free from debris.

☐ Freezers are at a temperature of 0°F or lower. Refrigerators are at a temperature of 41°F or lower.

☐ Any frozen food with freezer burn or spoilage is immediately discarded.

☐ Frozen foods are stored in their original container or are properly packaged, labeled and dated using the "first in, first out" method.

☐ Proper storage order is observed with prepared foods on the top shelves.

☐ Raw items, meat and eggs are stored below thawed or cooked foods.

☐ Refrigerated foods are well wrapped, labeled and dated using the "first in, first out" method.

☐ Seven days is the maximum holding time for refrigerated leftovers. At 45°F, food can only be held for four days.

TRASH & REFUSE AREA

☐ Trash receptacles do not leak and are clean and in good condition.

☐ Exterior dumpsters and all trash receptacles are securely covered.

FOOD TRANSPORTATION

☐ Service trays are used once and then thoroughly washed and sanitized.

☐ Carts used to transport food are clean and well-maintained.

☐ Dairy items or eggs are transported in a cart at 41°F or lower. If coolers are used, they are packed with ice.

DRY FOOD STORAGE

☐ Storage and food-handling areas are clean with no insects or rodent droppings.

☐ Food packages are tightly sealed.

☐ Labeled, clean containers are used for dry bulk food items.

☐ Unprotected or exposed water or sewer lines are not in or near food storage areas.

☐ Food is stored on shelves at least 4 inches from the floor for proper cleaning.

☐ The food storage shelves are clean and well-organized without debris or empty boxes.

☐ Foods are properly dated and shelved, using the "first in, first out" method.

☐ Dented cans are discarded.

☐ All shelving units are at least 6 inches from walls, so rodents, bugs and other pests cannot nest between walls and shelves.

☐ Food items have a separate storage area from cleaning agents, pesticides and other toxic substances.

Notes: _____

_____

_____

_____

_____

_____

_____

_____

_____

_____

General Food Safety & Sanitation Checklist

Check each item when completed.

EMPLOYEES

○ Employees have a designated area for storing all personal items, which is separate from food preparation areas.

○ An area is designated for non-food items such as for recipes and non-food tools.

○ Employees practice proper hand washing between tasks, at a designated hand washing sink, with soap and single-use paper towels.

○ Employees preparing food wear clean uniforms or aprons.

○ Hair restraints are worn and no jewelry is allowed (except a wedding band). No false nails or nail polish is allowed.

○ Employees do not eat, drink, smoke or chew gum in the food preparation areas.

○ Employees with any illness are sent home. Any cuts, wounds or abrasions are bandaged, and gloves are worn over the bandage.

RECEIVING FOOD

○ Receiving trucks meet standards of cleanliness and food safety storage.

○ Food is received by designated employee and checked for acceptable condition, date and temperature.

○ Once food is received, it is noted on invoice and put away immediately.

○ Any damaged or open item will not be accepted, including dented or rusted cans.

○ Food is covered, labeled and stored, using the "first in, first out" system.

○ Cross-contamination is avoided by storing raw meats and un-rinsed vegetables away from ready-to-eat food.

FOOD

○ Food is thawed properly in the refrigerator or under running water.

○ Bulk food receptacles are clean and clearly labeled. Scoops with handles are used and stored separately.

○ Ice scoops are not stored in ice.

○ Cross-contamination is not possible between foods and food-contact surfaces or staff and chemicals.

○ If possible, pasteurized eggs are used rather than raw eggs.

○ Food is cooked or reheated to the proper temperature (above 165°F).

○ Food is cooled in quick-chill manner such as in a shallow pan in ice or on the top shelf of the walk-in freezer.

○ Potentially hazardous foods are prepared according to safety standards.

EQUIPMENT

○ Freezer and refrigerators: Record area/temperature readings

Freezer 1 _____ / _____

Freezer 2 _____ / _____

Refer 1 _____ / _____

Refer 2 _____ / _____

Refer 3 _____ / _____

O Equipment is cleaned and maintained according to a set schedule per manufacturer's specifications.

O Hand sinks are easily accessible, clean and in good condition.

O Towels that are in use for wiping are replaced every 4 hours. They are stored in sanitizer solution (200ppm) in labeled buckets.

O Refrigerators are stocked to allow adequate air circulation. Water should not be pooled on bottom shelf, and condensers should be clear and visible.

O Thermometers are available for all cold-holding equipment. Every thermometer is accessible, in good repair and calibrated regularly (ice water 32°F; boiling water 212°F).

O The gaskets are clean and in excellent condition.

O Preparation equipment is clean and well-maintained including range, deep fat fryer, oven, grill and broiler. Equipment with small parts are in good condition without cracks or leaks.

O The ice machine is sanitized, clean and free from rust, mildew, scale and deposits. The water filters are properly tagged.

O Beverage machines are cleaned and sanitized daily, including soda gun and holster, and soft drink nozzles are cleaned inside.

O Glass mats are cleaned/sanitized daily.

O Equipment not in use and spare parts are stored in separate area and cannot contaminate food or harbor pests.

DISHWASHING

O Employees wash their hands at hand-wash sinks, regularly using proper hand washing techniques.

O A three-compartment sink is used with separate compartments for pre-scrape, wash and rinse.

O The three-compartment sink uses the correct temperature water and sanitizer @ _____ (200ppm).

O Clean utensils are stored properly (upside down) and away from contamination and dirty utensils.

FACILITY

O The plumbing is in good condition with no leaking pipes, slow drains or leaking faucets. Pipes are 2 inches above drains.

O All fixtures, walls, ceilings and ventilation are clean and in good repair.

O Floors are clean and in good condition, and floor mats are pressure-cleaned regularly.

O Lighting is adequate and shatterproof.

O Break areas and wash stations are clean and free from clutter.

O Maintenance is done regularly and repairs made in a timely manner.

RESTROOMS

O Sinks are clean and stocked with soap and single-use paper towels. Hot water is at or above 110°F.

O Hand-washing signs are posted.

○ The facilities have adequate supplies and are disinfected, clean and in good repair.

CHEMICAL STORAGE

○ Chemicals are labeled, stored in designated areas (away from food), with material safety data sheets (MSDS).

FIRE & SAFETY

○ Fire extinguishers are available, charged, tagged and mounted, and employees have been instructed how to use them properly.

○ Extension cords are not used.

○ CO_2 tanks are stored upright and secured.

○ Bulletin boards with tacks or pins are not used in food preparation, washing or storage areas.

PEST CONTROL

○ There is no evidence of insects, rodents or birds (such as droppings).

○ The building is pest-proof, with sealed doors, working fly fans and no exterior holes or cracks.

○ Traps are tamper-proof and secured.

○ The pest-control operator manual has pesticide lists, map of traps and emergency-contact list.

GARBAGE & REFUSE

○ The dumpsters are clean and the lids are closed.

○ The outside premises are clean, free from trash and debris.

○ The grease bin and surrounding area is maintained and clean.

○ The recycle bins and surrounding area is maintained and clean.

○ When washing or degreasing trash cans, food bins or other equipment, wastewater does not run into storm drains.

○ Garbage and waste food cans have plastic liners and are pressure-cleaned and disinfected.

GENERAL

○ Employees have been properly trained in food protection and hazcom procedures. All training is documented.

○ Health permits are current and prominently posted.

○ A food-safety-certified manager is on the premises at all times.

○ Water quality is checked annually and reports are on file.

○ Cleaning tools such as mops and brooms are stored separately from food, dishes and utensils.

○ The mop sink is easily accessible and clean, with hot and cold water. Mop heads are air-dried upside down and clean.

Comprehensive Food Facility Compliance Checklist

Circle Yes or No for every applicable item.

RECEIVING

Y N 1. Food is received only from previously approved vendors.

Y N 2. Food deliveries are inspected immediately for proper condition and temperature, with potentially hazardous foods delivered at a temperature of 41°F.

Y N 3. Frozen foods are delivered in frozen state with no evidence of thawing or refreezing.

Y N 4. Raw or frozen clams, mussels, scallops and oysters have a temperature below 45°F and are properly labeled, with labels maintained on-site for at least 90 days.

Y N 5. Deliveries are rejected if the food is not at the proper temperature or in unacceptable condition.

Y N 6. Food is promptly placed in proper storage locations, with refrigerated and frozen foods stored immediately.

STORAGE

Y N 1 All food is stored away from chemicals, vermin, insects, etc., and cannot be contami-nated.

Y N 2. All food is properly labeled using the "first in, first out" system, including prepackaged and bulk foods.

Y N 3. Shelving for food storage is at least 6 inches from floor and walls.

Y N 4. Items to be returned and damaged goods are stored separately.

Y N 5. Proper layering is used in refrigerated storage, with raw meat and fish stored below and away from ready-to-eat foods (produce, vegetables, beverages).

Y N 6. All food in storage is properly covered and sealed.

Y N 7. Contaminated food is promptly discarded.

PREPARATION

Y N 1. Frozen foods thawed properly using an acceptable method:

In a refrigerator.

In a microwave.

Under cold running water.

As part of the cooking process.

Y N   2. Hot foods (which can be potentially hazardous) are cooled quickly by the following methods before placement in a refrigerator or freezer:

With a rapid, cool stirring device.

Stirring while in an ice bath.

In a blast chiller.

Adding ice to the food.

In shallow, iced pans.

Separating food into smaller portions.

Y N   3. Separate sinks are available and used only for food preparation activities—not hand washing or janitorial use.

Y N   4. Potentially hazardous foods do not have sulfite added.

Y N   5. Potentially hazardous foods are cooked thoroughly with proper internal temperatures:

Poultry–165°F (comminuted poultry, game birds, stuffed meats, stuffed pasta and reheated foods).

Beef–155°F (ground beef, other comminuted meats and foods containing comminuted meat).

Pork–155°F.

Eggs–145°F (food containing raw eggs and other cooked, potentially hazardous food).

 SERVING

Y N   1. All prepackaged foods are labeled properly with name, list of ingredients, net weight and name and address of manufacturer.

Y N   2. Any food returned from customers uneaten is discarded (not reused or reserved).

Y N   3. Food and utensils in self-service areas, such as salad bars, buffets, snack counters and beverage dispensers, are protected from contamination by customers (e.g., sneezing, coughing and handling).

Y N   4. Bare hands are not used for food service, and serving utensils, such as spoons, tongs and ladles, are provided.

TEMPERATURES

Y N 1. Hot, potentially hazardous foods kept at or above 140°F.

Y N 2. Cold, potentially hazardous foods kept at or below 41°F.

Y N 3. The danger zone for potentially hazardous foods is 42°–140°F. When cooling or reheating foods, the time spent in this temperature range is kept to a minimum.

Y N 4. Properly calibrated thermometers are visible in the warmest part of each refrigeration and freezer unit.

Y N 5. If serving potentially hazardous food, a metal probe-type thermometer is used to check temperature prior to service.

Y N 6. Thermometers are sanitized before and after each use.

Y N 7. Thermometers are calibrated regularly.

Y N 8. While in use, tongs, scoops, spoons, ladles or other serving utensils for potentially hazardous foods are kept at or below 41°F or above 140°F, or in a dipper well that has clean water continually provided.

DISHWASHING

Y N 1. Plates, glasses and silverware are sanitized by mechanical dishwasher according to manufacturer specifications. If manually washed, they are sanitized by one of the following methods: 100ppm chlorine for 30 seconds; 25ppm iodine for 60 seconds; 200ppm quaternary ammonium for 60 seconds; or 180°F water for 30 seconds.

Y N 2. All mechanical dishwashers are provided with dual-integral drain boards.

Y N 3. During operation of dish machines, the correct temperature is maintained as well as proper amounts of sanitizer and chemicals.

Y N 4. When sanitizing utensils, a test strip or thermometer is used to check effectiveness.

Y N 5. A three-compartment (preferred) or two-compartment sink is available for utensil washing.

Y N 6. All compartments can fully submerge the largest utensil in use.

Y N 7. Utensils are maintained and clean.

Y N 8. Utensils used in the kitchen or for serving are regularly cleaned and sanitized.

Y N 9. Only commercial-grade utensils that are certified by an American National Standards Institute (ANSI)-accredited program are used.

Y   N   10. Utensils are stored away from any possible contamination including dirt, rodents, insects and chemicals.

Y   N   11. Single-use customer utensils are used only once and disposed.

 RESTROOMS

Y   N   1 Restroom facilities are provided for employees.

Y   N   2. Restroom facilities are provided for customers.

Y   N   3. Toilet stalls have self-closing, locking doors.

Y   N   4. Restroom facilities are not used for storage of food, utensils, equipment or supplies.

Y   N   5. Restroom facilities have adequate supplies such as toilet paper, single-use sanitary towels (or air dryer) and sanitizing hand cleanser.

Y   N   6. A hand washing sink has pressurized hot and cold water.

Y   N   7. Restroom facilities have adequate ventilation.

 HANDWASHING

Y   N   1. A separate hand-washing sink is located in, or adjacent to, restrooms and kitchens.

Y   N   2. The hand-washing sink has adequate supplies including single-service sanitary towels (or air dryers) and sanitizing hand cleanser.

Y   N   3. The hand-washing sink has pressurized hot and cold water.

Y   N   4. The hand-washing sink is easily accessible at all times.

Y   N   5. A separate hand-washing sink is used exclusively for hand washing in food prep areas and is conveniently located.

CHEMICALS & CLEANING

Y   N   1.   Chemicals are labeled properly.

Y   N   2.   Chemicals are not stored in food preparation area.

Y   N   3.   The only pesticides used have been specifically approved for food facility usage.

Y   N   4.   All chemicals, pesticides and hazardous materials are used properly. Employees have access to MSDS information on all chemicals.

Y   N   5.   Cleaning supplies and equipment are stored in a separate area away from food-preparation, food storage, dishwashing and utensil storage areas.

Y   N   6.   A separate janitorial sink has hot and cold water with a back-flow prevention device.

Y   N   7.   All mops, buckets, brooms and other cleaning equipment is kept away from food and utensils.

 LIGHTING

Y   N   1.   In food preparation and utensil cleaning areas, lighting has a minimum intensity of 20 footcandles (fc).

Y   N   2.   In dining and other areas, lighting has a minimum intensity of 10 fc, but intensity of at least 20 fc available during cleaning operations.

Y   N   3.   Food preparation, food storage and utensil cleaning areas have shatterproof light covers installed and are in good repair.

 PEST INFESTATION

Y   N   1.   Rodents, insects and other vermin are not in the building.

Y   N   2.   Building does not have cracks or openings where rodents and insects can enter, and any droppings and dead insects are cleaned up.

Y   N   3.   All building entrances have air curtains or tight-fitting, self-closing doors. All windows are protected by screens.

Y   N   4.   Any fumigation or pest control is done by a licensed pest-control operator.

GARBAGE

Y N 1. Garbage is removed frequently and proper facilities are provided for disposal and storage.

Y N 2. Garbage containers have tight-fitting lids, do not leak and are rodent-proof.

Y N 3. Before being placed in the dumpster, all garbage is in securely fastened plastic bags.

 EMPLOYEES

Y N 1. Employees wear clean uniforms or approved clothing.

Y N 2. Employees only use tobacco products in designated areas, away from food preparation, storage and service.

Y N 3. Employees wash hands thoroughly and frequently. Hands are washed after engaging in any activity that may cause contamination including working between raw food and ready-to-eat foods, after coughing or sneezing, after touching soiled equipment or utensils and after using restrooms.

Y N 4. Ill employees are sent home or do not come to work.

Y N 5. Employees practice safe food-handling procedures and have been trained in food safety.

Y N 6. Employees check temperatures of potentially hazardous foods during storage, preparation and serving. Employees also check utensil-cleaning chemical levels, water temperatures and water pressures.

Y N 7. A separate employee changing area is provided, apart from toilets, food storage, food preparation, utensil cleaning and utensil storage areas.

 PLUMBING

Y N 1. Water supply has been tested and comes from an approved source.

Y N 2. Adequate amounts of hot and cold water are available.

Y N 3. Sewage and wastewater is disposed properly into a sewer or septic system.

Y N 4. All equipment that discharges waste, such as prep sinks, steam tables, salad bars, ice machines, ice storage bins, beverage machines, display cases or refrigeration/freezer units,

---

have a floor sink or funnel drain provided for indirect waste drainage.

Y N   5. Receptacles for indirect waste are accessible and cleaned regularly.

Y N   6. Plumbing is clean, in good repair and operating properly.

Y N   7. A licensed company cleans out grease interceptors and septic tanks regularly.

 SIGNAGE

Y N   1. Restrooms have hand washing signs posted and clearly visible.

Y N   2. Hand-washing sinks have signage with proper hand-washing procedures posted and clearly visible.

Y N   3. "No smoking" signs are clearly visible throughout the facility, especially in food preparation, food-storage, utensil cleaning and utensil storage areas.

Y N   4. A choking first-aid poster is visible and readily accessible to employees (in facilities with sit-down dining).

 FACILITY

Y N   1. Facility is fully enclosed, clean and well maintained.

Y N   2. The building meets all applicable building and fire codes.

Y N   3. Exterior premises is clean and well maintained.

Y N   4. All equipment is clean, well maintained and meets applicable ANSI-accredited certification program standards.

Y N   5. No unused, out-dated or broken equipment is on the premises.

Y N   6. Cooking equipment and high-temperature dish machines have ventilation and exhaust systems installed over areas of operation.

Y N   7. In food preparation and storage areas, flooring is level, non-skid, durable, non-absorbent and easily cleaned.

Y N   8. In janitorial facilities, restrooms and employee changing areas flooring is smooth, non-skid, durable, non-absorbent and easily cleaned.

Y N   9. In food preparation and food storage areas, janitorial facilities, restrooms and employee changing areas, walls and ceilings are smooth, durable, non-absorbent and easily cleaned.

Y N   10. The health department has approved all construction, remodeling and new equipment installation prior to work.

Y   N   11. All soiled linens are held in a clean container, and a linen storage area is provided.

Y   N   12. Tobacco permit is valid, up to date and posted in a prominent location (if applicable).

Y   N   13. Health permit is valid, up to date and posted in a prominent location.

Notes: _____

_____

_____

_____

_____

_____

_____

_____

_____

_____

_____

_____

_____

_____

_____

_____

_____

_____

_____

_____

_____

_____

_____

Comprehensive Sanitation Compliance Checklist

DATE: _____ TIME: _____

EMPLOYEE(S): _____

JANITORIAL ROOM

Is it clean and neat?	Yes No
Are buckets empty and stored upside down?	Yes No
Are there rodent or insect droppings visible?	Yes No
Are all toxic materials (including pesticides) in their original containers and clearly labeled?	Yes No

DISHWASHING AREA

	MAIN KITCHEN	AUX KITCHEN
Wash cycle temperature	_____ °F	_____ °F
Rinse cycle temperature	_____ °F	_____ °F
Are there any obstructions or contaminants in the jets and nozzles (such as food particles)?	Yes No	Yes No
Is the dishwashing equipment cleaned daily to remove food particles, chemicals and debris?	Yes No	Yes No
Is the proper amount or level of detergent and/or sanitizer being used consistently in the wash cycle?	Yes No	Yes No
Do separate employees remove and store clean tableware?	Yes No	Yes No
Do dishwashing employees practice proper hand washing between handling soiled tableware and sanitized ware?	Yes No	Yes No
Do employees pre-scrape and flush dishes and utensils prior to washing?	Yes No	Yes No
Once dishes and utensils are cleaned and sanitized, are they stored in a clean, dry location (off the floor)?	Yes No	Yes No
Are utensils and tableware toweled properly?	Yes No	Yes No

SERVICE AREA

	MAIN KITCHEN	AUX KITCHEN
Are floors, tables and chairs clean and dry in the dining area?	Yes No	Yes No
Is the floor being swept or cleaned while food is being served or when customers are eating?	Yes No	Yes No
Is the temperature correct in the dining area for customer comfort?	Yes No	Yes No
Does the dining area have any unpleasant odors?	Yes No	Yes No
Are the dishes and silverware clean, sanitized and stored correctly to prevent contamination?	Yes No	Yes No
Are condiment containers clean and in good repair?	Yes No	Yes No
Are menus clean and in good repair, without food marks or stains?	Yes No	Yes No
Are food warmers or steam tables used to re-heat prepared foods?	Yes No	Yes No
Is food being held in the hot-holding equipment at or above 140°F?	Yes No	Yes No
Is cold food being held at 41°F or lower?	Yes No	Yes No
Are cold- and hot-holding cabinets equipped with thermometers?	Yes No	Yes No
Are tongs or other serving utensils available and used to pick up rolls, bread, butter pats, ice or other food to be served?	Yes No	Yes No
Are tableware towels clean, dry and only used for wiping food spills?	Yes No	Yes No
Are servers wearing proper uniforms that are clean and in good condition?	Yes No	Yes No
Do servers show any signs of illness, such as coughing or wiping their noses?	Yes No	Yes No
Do servers handle drinking glasses and silverware properly, without touching glass tops or silverware blades?	Yes No	Yes No

PERSONAL SANITATION

	MAIN KITCHEN	AUX KITCHEN
Are all employees involved with food handling properly dressed in clean uniforms or attire?	Yes No	Yes No
Are employees wearing jewelry other than a wedding band?	Yes No	Yes No
Are employees wearing hair restraints?	Yes No	Yes No
Do employees have a noticeable odor, such as strong perfume or body odor?	Yes No	Yes No
Do employees have properly groomed hands, without fingernail polish and with short, clean fingernails?	Yes No	Yes No
If employees have any wounds, are they properly covered and free of infection?	Yes No	Yes No
Do employees show any signs of illness, such as sneezing or coughing?	Yes No	Yes No
Do employees scratch their head, face or body?	Yes No	Yes No
Are employees seen eating in food preparation or serving areas?	Yes No	Yes No

GENERAL SANITATION

	MAIN KITCHEN	AUX KITCHEN
Are cleaning supplies and chemicals stored separately from the food preparation and service areas?	Yes No	Yes No
Is prepared food held correctly at the correct temperature and in the proper containers?	Yes No	Yes No
Are clean, sanitary towels available?	Yes No	Yes No
Are frozen foods thawed correctly, either in the refrigerator, under cold, running water or thawed during the cooking process?	Yes No	Yes No
Is a separate sink available for food preparation that is not used for hand washing or cleaning?	Yes No	Yes No

GENERAL SANITATION (continued)

	MAIN KITCHEN	AUX KITCHEN
Is preparation equipment cleaned and sanitized between and after each use or at the end of the day?	Yes No	Yes No
Are equipment and utensils not in use clean?	Yes No	Yes No
Are all dishes, pots, pans and other utensils stored correctly to prevent contamination?	Yes No	Yes No
Is food stored in coolers and freezers covered and spaced correctly to allow air circulation?	Yes No	Yes No
Are cutting boards in good condition and used only for specific types of food preparation to avoid cross-contamination?	Yes No	Yes No
Are cutting boards cleaned and sanitized after each use?	Yes No	Yes No

DRY STORAGE

	MAIN KITCHEN	AUX KITCHEN
Is the food storage area enclosed, dry and free from dampness?	Yes No	Yes No
Are food supplies labeled, dated and stored to ensure "first in, first out" use?	Yes No	Yes No
Is food stored separately from non-food supplies?	Yes No	Yes No
Is there any evidence of insects or rodent droppings in the storage areas?	Yes No	Yes No
Is the food storage area clean and free of dust, empty food cartons and other debris (including shelves and floor)?	Yes No	Yes No
Are shelves at least 6 inches away from walls and floors?	Yes No	Yes No
Is the area underneath the shelves easily accessible for cleaning?	Yes No	Yes No

WALK-IN FREEZERS

	MAIN KITCHEN	AUX KITCHEN
Temperature	_____ °F	_____ °F
Are shelves and floor clean and free of empty cartons or debris?	Yes No	Yes No
Are all foods properly stored and covered?	Yes No	Yes No
Are food supplies labeled, dated and stored to ensure "first in, first out" use?	Yes No	Yes No
Can air circulate freely around stored food?	Yes No	Yes No
Does freezer need defrosting?	Yes No	Yes No

WALK-IN REFRIGERATORS

	MEAT	DAIRY	VEGE	AUX KITCHEN
Temperature	_____ °F	_____ °F	_____ °F	_____ °F
Are refrigerators clean, with no mold or offensive odors?	Yes No	Yes No	Yes No	Yes No
Can air circulate freely around stored food?	Yes No	Yes No	Yes No	Yes No
Is food stored on the floor of the refrigerators?	Yes No	Yes No	Yes No	Yes No
Are foods labeled, dated and stored to ensure "first in, first out" use?	Yes No	Yes No	Yes No	Yes No
Are large-quantity containers used for storing cooked foods (ground meat, dressing or gravy)?	Yes No	Yes No	Yes No	Yes No
Are all containers clearly labeled with date and food item?	Yes No	Yes No	Yes No	Yes No
Is spoiled or outdated food promptly discarded?	Yes No	Yes No	Yes No	Yes No
Are proper storage techniques used, with cooked food on the top and raw meats or poultry on the bottom shelves?	Yes No	Yes No	Yes No	Yes No
Are shelves at least 6 inches from the floor to allow cleaning underneath?	Yes No	Yes No	Yes No	Yes No
Are cooked foods stored in clean, sanitized, covered containers (not their original cartons)?	Yes No	Yes No	Yes No	Yes No

Cold Food Production

Date: **Employee:**

❑ YES   ❑ NO   1.   Before food preparation, are all equipment and utensils cleaned and sanitized (including work surfaces)?

❑ YES   ❑ NO   2.   Are all utensils and containers cleaned and sanitized prior to use?

❑ YES   ❑ NO   3.   Are potentially hazardous ingredients (including tuna fish and mayonnaise) refrigerated at least 24 hours before use?

❑ YES   ❑ NO   4.   Are all fruits and vegetables properly washed prior to use?

❑ YES   ❑ NO   5.   Before handling food, do employees wash hands properly with soap and water?

❑ YES   ❑ NO   6.   Is prepared food properly covered, labeled and refrigerated, and taken directly to the serving line?

❑ YES   ❑ NO   7.   Do all workstations have ready access to sanitizer solution?

❑ YES   ❑ NO   8.   After each use, are work areas cleaned and sanitized?

❑ YES   ❑ NO   9.   While preparing food, are employees wearing disposable gloves?

❑ YES   ❑ NO   10.   Are all sinks in the food preparation area sanitized after each use?

❑ YES   ❑ NO   11.   Are hand-washing sinks easily accessible and stocked with handsoap from a proper dispenser and single-use paper towels?

❑ YES   ❑ NO   12.   At the end of each day, is all food production equipment cleaned and sanitized?

Action Plan: **Completed By:**   **Comments:**

                            Supervisor:

Vending Locations

Date: **Employee:**

❏ YES   ❏ NO   1.   Is the vending area clean and uncluttered, with no trash or other debris?

❏ YES   ❏ NO   2.   Is the vending machine area clean, in good condition and protected from overhead water, waste or sewer piping leakage and condensation?

❏ YES   ❏ NO   3.   Does the vending area have adequate lighting and proper ventilation?

❏ YES   ❏ NO   4.   Is the vending area free of insects and rodents?

❏ YES   ❏ NO   5.   Are cold, potentially hazardous foods held at the proper temperatures (41°F or less) at all times?

❏ YES   ❏ NO   6.   Are hot, potentially hazardous foods held at the proper temperatures (140°F or higher) at all times?

❏ YES   ❏ NO   7.   Do the vending machines have thermometers that are checked daily to ensure machines are maintaining safe, accurate temperatures?

❏ YES   ❏ NO   8.   Is food sold in the vending machines properly packaged and protected from contamination?

❏ YES   ❏ NO   9.   Are all vending machines cleaned on a regular basis?

❏ YES   ❏ NO   10.   Is a trash receptacle located near vending machines to properly dispose of food cartons and other debris?

Action Plan: **Completed By:**   **Comments:**

Supervisor:

Vending/Catering Food Transport Vehicles

Date: **Employee:**

❑ YES   ❑ NO   1.   During transport, are cold, potentially hazardous foods held at the proper temperatures (41°F or less) at all times?

❑ YES   ❑ NO   2.   During transport, are hot, potentially hazardous foods held at the proper temperatures (140°F or higher) at all times?

❑ YES   ❑ NO   3.   Are insulated containers used for food transport?

❑ YES   ❑ NO   4.   If warming cabinets are used, is the temperature 140°F or higher when handling or transporting hot foods?

❑ YES   ❑ NO   5.   Are foods and beverages protected from contaminations such as dirt, dust and insects?

❑ YES   ❑ NO   6.   Are vehicles cleaned and sanitized after each use?

Action Plan:	Completed By:	Comments:
	Supervisor:	

Hot Food Production

Date: _____ **Employee:** _____

❏ YES ❏ NO 1. Before and after food preparation, are all equipment and utensils cleaned and sanitized (including work surfaces)?

❏ YES ❏ NO 2. Are frozen foods thawed correctly, either in the refrigerator, under cold, running water or thawed during the cooking process?

❏ YES ❏ NO 3. Are potentially hazardous foods cooked thoroughly with proper internal temperatures: poultry, 165°F; beef, 155°F; pork, 155°F; and eggs, 145°F?

❏ YES ❏ NO 4. Are hot, potentially hazardous foods cooled quickly by one of the following methods: with a rapid, cool stirring device, stirring while in an ice bath, in a blast chiller, by adding ice to the food, in shallow, iced pans or by separating food into smaller portions?

❏ YES ❏ NO 5. Are leftovers heated to 165°F?

❏ YES ❏ NO 6. Are sinks used for food preparation cleaned and sanitized between each use?

❏ YES ❏ NO 7. Are hand-washing sinks accessible and properly stocked with single-use towels and soap dispensers so employees can wash hands before food preparation?

❏ YES ❏ NO 8. Are spills wiped up immediately?

❏ YES ❏ NO 9. Are floors kept clean with regular sweeping and mopping?

❏ YES ❏ NO 10. Does every workstation have easy access to sanitizing solution?

Action Plan: **Completed By:**   **Comments:**

Supervisor:

Line Serving Areas

Date: **Employee:**

❏ YES   ❏ NO   1. Do all refrigerators have properly calibrated thermometers and maintain a temperature of 41°F or below?

❏ YES   ❏ NO   2. Are all deli or line items refrigerated until placement on the deli bar?

❏ YES   ❏ NO   3. Are all items held at 45°F while on the deli bar?

❏ YES   ❏ NO   4. Are properly calibrated thermometers used regularly to check product temperatures?

❏ YES   ❏ NO   5. Are floors kept clean with regular sweeping and mopping?

❏ YES   ❏ NO   6. At the end of each day, is all the deli bar equipment cleaned and sanitized?

❏ YES   ❏ NO   7. Does every workstation have easy access to sanitizing solution?

Action Plan: **Completed By:**   **Comments:**

Supervisor:

Line Service/Hot Foods

Date: **Employee:**

☐ YES   ☐ NO   1.   Do all refrigerators have properly calibrated thermometers and maintain a temperature of 41°F or below?

☐ YES   ☐ NO   2.   Are refrigerated items stored properly, with cooked or ready-to-eat items above raw products?

☐ YES   ☐ NO   3.   Are all refrigerated products stored in properly covered containers and labeled?

☐ YES   ☐ NO   4.   Is raw meat refrigerated prior to cooking?

☐ YES   ☐ NO   5.   Is the grill clean, in good working order and properly maintained?

☐ YES   ☐ NO   6.   Is the steam table clean and in good working condition?

☐ YES   ☐ NO   7.   Are all hot, cooked foods held at 140°F or higher?

☐ YES   ☐ NO   8.   Do soup kettles have a temperature of 140°F or higher?

☐ YES   ☐ NO   9.   Are properly calibrated thermometers used to take frequent temperature checks?

☐ YES   ☐ NO   10. Are spills wiped up immediately?

☐ YES   ☐ NO   11. Are floors mopped and swept on a regular basis?

Action Plan: **Completed By:**   **Comments:**

Supervisor:

Restrooms

❏ YES   ❏ NO   1.   Are restrooms clean and odor-free?

❏ YES   ❏ NO   2.   Are restrooms well ventilated?

❏ YES   ❏ NO   3.   Do toilet stalls have self-closing, locking doors?

❏ YES   ❏ NO   4.   Are soap and towel dispensers well stocked and working properly?

❏ YES   ❏ NO   5.   Does the sink(s) and have faucets with pressurized hot and cold water?

❏ YES   ❏ NO   6.   Are the trash containers cleaned and emptied on a regular basis?

❏ YES   ❏ NO   7.   Is the restroom used for storage of food, utensils, equipment or supplies?

Action Plan:	Completed By:	Comments:
	Supervisor:	

Dry Storage

Date: _____   **Employee:** _____

❏ YES   ❏ NO   1.   Are all food goods stacked neatly, labeled and in proper containers?

❏ YES   ❏ NO   2.   Are all storage shelves or racks at least 6 inches off the floor?

❏ YES   ❏ NO   3.   Are shelves and storage area clean, free of dust, empty cartons and other debris?

❏ YES   ❏ NO   4.   Is storage area swept daily?

❏ YES   ❏ NO   5.   Are food items rotated properly using the "first in, first out" system?

❏ YES   ❏ NO   6.   Is temperature of the dry storage area regulated (between 60°F and 70°F) and ventilated to avoid dampness?

❏ YES   ❏ NO   7.   Is the storage area large enough for ease of use?

❏ YES   ❏ NO   8.   Is the storage area inspected for evidence of rodents and insects on a regular basis?

❏ YES   ❏ NO   9.   Are food supplies stored separately from chemicals, cleaners and pesticides?

❏ YES   ❏ NO   10.   Are water or sewer lines located in a separate area away from food storage?

❏ YES   ❏ NO   11.   Is contaminated or spoiled food promptly discarded?

❏ YES   ❏ NO   12.   Is the storage area well lit?

Action Plan: **Completed By:**   **Comments:**

Supervisor:

Dishroom/Pot & Pan Areas

Date: **Employee:**

- ❑ YES   ❑ NO   1. Are the dishroom floors cleaned and sanitized on a regular basis?

- ❑ YES   ❑ NO   2. Are sinks cleaned and sanitized before use?

- ❑ YES   ❑ NO   3. Are sanitizing chemicals used according to specifications and at the proper strength?

- ❑ YES   ❑ NO   4. Is a three-compartment sink utilized for dishwashing?

- ❑ YES   ❑ NO   5. Before washing, all are dishware, utensils, pots and pans scraped and flushed?

- ❑ YES   ❑ NO   6. Are dishes and utensils immersed for at least 30 seconds in hot water that is at or above 170°F?

- ❑ YES   ❑ NO   7. Are sanitizer concentrations checked using test strips?

- ❑ YES   ❑ NO   8. Is a sanitation log book kept of test results?

- ❑ YES   ❑ NO   9. Are all dishware, pots and pans air-dried?

- ❑ YES   ❑ NO   10. Are all dishware, pots and pans stored in the proper manner, free from splashes and contamination?

- ❑ YES   ❑ NO   11. If used, is the dish machine in good working order?

- ❑ YES   ❑ NO   12. Is the final rinse temperature of the dish machine at or greater than 180°F?

- ❑ YES   ❑ NO   13. Is the dish machine cleaned daily at the end of its use?

- ❑ YES   ❑ NO   14. Are the detergent levels of the dish machine checked regularly?

Action Plan: **Completed By:**   **Comments:**

Supervisor:

Refrigerator & Freezer Storage

Date: **Employee:**

❑ YES   ❑ NO   1.   Is the interior temperature of the refrigerators 41°F or lower?

❑ YES   ❑ NO   2.   Are all refrigerators and freezers equipped with interior and exterior thermometers?

❑ YES   ❑ NO   3.   Are the interior and exterior thermometers of the refrigerators and freezers calibrated regularly?

❑ YES   ❑ NO   4.   Are refrigerators cleaned on a regular basis (including coils, grills and compressor area) and free of mold and odors?

❑ YES   ❑ NO   5.   Is shelving at least 6 inches from the floor and free from dust or other debris?

❑ YES   ❑ NO   6.   Are foods and products covered, dated and properly spaced to provide adequate air circulation?

❑ YES   ❑ NO   7.   Are foods stored to allow "first in, first out" usage?

❑ YES   ❑ NO   8.   Are raw meats stored on the bottom shelves, away from cooked or prepared food?

❑ YES   ❑ NO   9.   Are all spills cleaned up immediately?

❑ YES   ❑ NO   10. Are cooked foods labeled and stored in clean, sanitized, covered containers?

❑ YES   ❑ NO   11. Is the temperature of freezer units 0°F or lower?

❑ YES   ❑ NO   12. Are products in the freezer stored above floor level?

❑ YES   ❑ NO   13. Are all frozen foods wrapped and covered to avoid freezer burn?

❑ YES   ❑ NO   14. Are freezers clean, in good working condition and defrosted on a regular basis?

Action Plan: **Completed By:**   **Comments:**

Supervisor:

Garbage/Refuse Storage & Disposal Areas

Date: _____ **Employee:** _____

☐ YES ☐ NO 1. Is the garbage area clean and well maintained with no spilled liquids, food materials or debris?

☐ YES ☐ NO 2. Are garbage and refuse containers durable and easily cleaned?

☐ YES ☐ NO 3. Is garbage area cleaned regularly and are containers washed?

☐ YES ☐ NO 4. Are garbage and refuse containers insect- and rodent-proof with tight-fitting lids?

☐ YES ☐ NO 5. Are garbage and refuse materials disposed of on a regular basis so there is no overflow or odors?

☐ YES ☐ NO 6. Are there any visible rodents or rodent droppings?

☐ YES ☐ NO 7. Is there any evidence of insect infestation?

☐ YES ☐ NO 8. Are dumpsters maintained and in good working condition?

☐ YES ☐ NO 9. Are hot water and detergents available to properly wash garbage containers?

☐ YES ☐ NO 10. Are refrigerated garbage rooms or boxes clean and in proper condition?

Action Plan: **Completed By:** **Comments:**

Supervisor:

Cold Beverage Areas

Date: **Employee:**

❑ YES   ❑ NO   1.   Are reach-in refrigerators used for storing cold beverages at a temperature of 41°F or lower?

❑ YES   ❑ NO   2.   Are all beverage hoses and nozzles maintained in a sanitary manner and cleaned regularly?

❑ YES   ❑ NO   3.   Are beverage dispensers maintained in a sanitary manner and cleaned regularly?

❑ YES   ❑ NO   4.   Are drinking cups, lids and straws easily accessible and stored in an orderly and sanitary manner?

❑ YES   ❑ NO   5.   Are ice machines cleaned and sanitized regularly?

❑ YES   ❑ NO   6.   Is the top of the ice machine free of obstructions and not being used as a storage area?

❑ YES   ❑ NO   7.   Are ice scoops being used in a sanitary manner and placed on a clean surface when not in use?

❑ YES   ❑ NO   8.   Are the storage cabinets under cold beverage dispensers clean, organized and inspected regularly?

Action Plan: **Completed By:**   **Comments:**

Supervisor:

Salad Bar

Date: _____ **Employee:** _____

❑ YES ❑ NO 1. Are salad bar utensils and dishes properly cleaned, sanitized and stored?

❑ YES ❑ NO 2. Is the area underneath the counter clean?

❑ YES ❑ NO 3. Are all salad bar crockery or containers in good condition, without chips or cracks?

❑ YES ❑ NO 4. Is the salad bar area cleaned and sanitized daily?

❑ YES ❑ NO 5. Are all spills cleaned up immediately?

❑ YES ❑ NO 6. Are all salad bar items kept at a temperature of 41°F?

❑ YES ❑ NO 7. Is the floor around the salad bar regularly swept and mopped?

❑ YES ❑ NO 8. Are ingredients on the salad bar refrigerated for at least 24 hours before use?

❑ YES ❑ NO 9. If ingredients need to be refilled, are the refill items from refrigerated materials?

❑ YES ❑ NO 10. Are all vegetables and fruits properly washed before placement on the salad bar?

❑ YES ❑ NO 11. Is the temperature of salad bar items maintained and checked on a regular basis?

❑ YES ❑ NO 12. Do all food-handling employees wear gloves during salad preparation?

Action Plan:	Completed By:	Comments:
	Supervisor:	

Employee Personal Hygiene

Date: **Employee:**

❑ YES   ❑ NO   1.   Are employees wearing clean uniforms or approved garments?

❑ YES   ❑ NO   2.   Is all jewelry removed (except plain wedding band) during working hours?

❑ YES   ❑ NO   3.   Are employees' fingernails clean and short, with no false fingernails or nail polish?

❑ YES   ❑ NO   4.   Do employees refrain from touching hair or scratching head and face while on duty?

❑ YES   ❑ NO   5.   Do employees practice proper hand-washing techniques using soap or sanitizer?

❑ YES   ❑ NO   6.   Do employees wash hands after any activity that may cause contamination including when working between raw food and ready-to-eat foods, after coughing or sneezing, after touching soiled equipment or utensils and after using restrooms?

❑ YES   ❑ NO   7.   Do employees wear hats or hair coverings in the food preparation and serving areas?

❑ YES   ❑ NO   8.   Do employees refrain from eating, smoking, chewing gum and using toothpicks while on duty?

❑ YES   ❑ NO   9.   Do employees use tobacco products only in designated areas, away from food preparation, storage and service areas?

❑ YES   ❑ NO   10.   Do employees show any sign of illness such as coughing or sneezing?

❑ YES   ❑ NO   11.   Have employees been trained in safe food-handling procedures and food safety?

Action Plan: **Completed By:**   **Comments:**

Supervisor:

Receiving

Date:	Employee:

❏ YES ❏ NO   1. Is the receiving area clean, uncluttered and easily accessible?

❏ YES ❏ NO   2. Is food accepted only from previously approved vendors?

❏ YES ❏ NO   3. Does a designated employee inspect all incoming food shipments for any infestations, spoilage and/or unacceptable conditions, such as food not at the proper temperature, dented cans or open products?

❏ YES ❏ NO   4. Does a designated employee inspect non-food supplies for infestations and foreign materials?

❏ YES ❏ NO   5. Upon arrival, are all food and non-food supplies properly labeled and dated?

❏ YES ❏ NO   6. Are potentially hazardous foods delivered at a temperature of 41°F?

❏ YES ❏ NO   7. Are frozen foods delivered frozen, with no evidence of thawing or refreezing?

❏ YES ❏ NO   8. Are deliveries rejected if the food is not at the proper temperature or in unacceptable condition?

❏ YES ❏ NO   9. Is food placed in proper storage locations promptly, with refrigerated and frozen foods stored immediately.

❏ YES ❏ NO   10. Are all empty shipping and packing materials promptly and properly discarded?

Action Plan:	Completed By:	Comments:
	Supervisor:	

Food Safety Temperatures

212°F — **Boiling Point**
Most, but not all, bacteria are killed at this temperature.

165°F — Minimum Reheating Temperature

140°F — Minimum Hot Holding Temperature

DANGER ZONE
Rapid bacterial growth occurs
between 42°F and 140°F.

41°F
32°F Cold Storage Temperature Range
FREEZING

0°F

Frozen Food Storage

-10°F

Timed HACCP Checklist

DATE:	9:00 a.m. EMPLOYEE:
	3:00 p.m. EMPLOYEE:
	10:00 p.m. EMPLOYEE:

Receiving & Storage — Cold Storage	9:00 a.m.	3:00 p.m.	10:00 p.m.
Walk-in refrigerator temperature	_____ °F	_____ °F	_____ °F
Walk-in freezer temperature	_____ °F	_____ °F	_____ °F
Other storage temperature (list area) _____	_____ °F	_____ °F	_____ °F
Raw meats stored in separate location or below any fruits, vegetables or cooked/prepared foods	❏ Y ❏ N	❏ Y ❏ N	❏ Y ❏ N

Back-of-House Preparation Area	9:00 a.m.	3:00 p.m.	10:00 p.m.
Temperature of concentrate(s), list:			
_____	_____ °F	_____ °F	_____ °F
_____	_____ °F	_____ °F	_____ °F
_____	_____ °F	_____ °F	_____ °F
Temperature of soup(s), list:			
_____	_____ °F	_____ °F	_____ °F
_____	_____ °F	_____ °F	_____ °F
_____	_____ °F	_____ °F	_____ °F
_____	_____ °F	_____ °F	_____ °F
Temperature of water in steam table	_____ °F	_____ °F	_____ °F
Effective sanitizing solution available	❏ Y ❏ N	❏ Y ❏ N	❏ Y ❏ N
Hand-washing sink stocked with soap and disposable, single-use towels	❏ Y ❏ N	❏ Y ❏ N	❏ Y ❏ N

Grill Area	9:00 a.m.	3:00 p.m.	10:00 p.m.
Temperature inside service refrigerator	_____ °F	_____ °F	_____ °F
Sandwich boards and cutting boards cleaned and sanitized	❏ Y ❏ N	❏ Y ❏ N	❏ Y ❏ N
Forks and spatulas on hot grill	❏ Y ❏ N	❏ Y ❏ N	❏ Y ❏ N

Sandwich Preparation Area	9:00 a.m.	3:00 p.m.	10:00 p.m.
Temperature inside service refrigerator	_____ °F	_____ °F	_____ °F
Temperature of mayonnaise or dressings	_____ °F	_____ °F	_____ °F
Temperature inside reach-in freezer	_____ °F	_____ °F	_____ °F
Cold table above refrigerator covered	❏ Y ❏ N	❏ Y ❏ N	❏ Y ❏ N
Cutting boards clean and sanitized	❏ Y ❏ N	❏ Y ❏ N	❏ Y ❏ N
Microwaved products cooking times clearly marked	❏ Y ❏ N	❏ Y ❏ N	❏ Y ❏ N

Cold Food Preparation Area	9:00 a.m.	3:00 p.m.	10:00 p.m.
Temperature inside pie/salad refrigerator	_____ °F	_____ °F	_____ °F
Temperature inside service refrigerator	_____ °F	_____ °F	_____ °F
Temperature of mayonnaise or dressings	_____ °F	_____ °F	_____ °F
Temperature of side items, list:	_____ °F	_____ °F	_____ °F
_____	_____ °F	_____ °F	_____ °F
_____	_____ °F	_____ °F	_____ °F
_____	_____ °F	_____ °F	_____ °F
Microwaved products cooking times clearly marked	❏ Y ❏ N	❏ Y ❏ N	❏ Y ❏ N
Sanitizing solutions available and accessible	❏ Y ❏ N	❏ Y ❏ N	❏ Y ❏ N

NOTES:

_____

_____

_____

_____

_____

_____

_____

_____

_____

_____

Receiving Checklist

SUPPLIER: **TIME OF DELIVERY:**   a.m./p.m.

❑ Y ❑ N   Frozen products arrive frozen solid   ❑ Y ❑ N   Refrigerated products put away within 30 minutes of delivery

❑ Y ❑ N   Refrigerated products arrive at a temperature below 41°F   ❑ Y ❑ N   Refrigerated and frozen products dated and stored for FIFO usage

❑ Y ❑ N   Frozen products put away within 15 minutes of delivery   ❑ Y ❑ N   Damaged products rejected

EMPLOYEE CHECKING IN PRODUCTS: **DATE:**

SUPPLIER: **TIME OF DELIVERY:**   a.m./p.m.

❑ Y ❑ N   Frozen products arrive frozen solid   ❑ Y ❑ N   Refrigerated products put away within 30 minutes of delivery

❑ Y ❑ N   Refrigerated products arrive at a temperature below 41°F   ❑ Y ❑ N   Refrigerated and frozen products dated and stored for FIFO usage

❑ Y ❑ N   Frozen products put away within 15 minutes of delivery   ❑ Y ❑ N   Damaged products rejected

EMPLOYEE CHECKING IN PRODUCTS: **DATE:**

SUPPLIER: **TIME OF DELIVERY:**   a.m./p.m.

❑ Y ❑ N   Frozen products arrive frozen solid   ❑ Y ❑ N   Refrigerated products put away within 30 minutes of delivery

❑ Y ❑ N   Refrigerated products arrive at a temperature below 41°F   ❑ Y ❑ N   Refrigerated and frozen products dated and stored for FIFO usage

❑ Y ❑ N   Frozen products put away within 15 minutes of delivery   ❑ Y ❑ N   Damaged products rejected

EMPLOYEE CHECKING IN PRODUCTS: **DATE:**

NOTES/CONCERNS:

Kitchen Sanitation Schedule Daily Tasks

BATHROOM MIRRORS

WHEN: Once per shift

HOW: As needed

CLEANSER: Glass cleaner

PERSON RESPONSIBLE: _____

INITIAL UPON COMPLETION: _____

BATHROOM SUPPLIES

WHEN: Once per shift

HOW: Hand soap, paper towels, toilet paper

PERSON RESPONSIBLE: _____

INITIAL UPON COMPLETION: _____

BATHROOM FIXTURES AND SURFACES

(other than floor, tiles and mirror)

WHEN: Daily

HOW: Spray, rinse and wipe with disposable towel

CLEANSER: Bathroom cleaner

PERSON RESPONSIBLE: _____

INITIAL UPON COMPLETION: _____

CONDIMENT CONTAINERS

WHEN: Daily

HOW: Wash, rinse, sanitize

CLEANSER: Dish machine

PERSON RESPONSIBLE: _____

INITIAL UPON COMPLETION: _____

COOLING RACKS

WHEN: Daily

HOW: Wipe clean of food debris with in-use wiping cloth

CLEANSER: Water and sanitizer 200ppm

PERSON RESPONSIBLE: _____

INITIAL UPON COMPLETION: _____

COUNTERS/SHELVES (FRONT)

WHEN: End of shift

HOW: Wash, rinse, sanitize

CLEANSER: Cleanser, fresh water and sanitizer 200ppm

PERSON RESPONSIBLE: _____

INITIAL UPON COMPLETION: _____

COUNTERS/SHELVES (COOLER)

WHEN: End of shift

HOW: Wash, rinse, sanitize

CLEANSER: Cleanser, fresh water and sanitizer 200ppm

PERSON RESPONSIBLE: _____

INITIAL UPON COMPLETION: _____

COUNTERS (DELIVERY)

WHEN: End of shift

HOW: Wash, rinse, sanitize

CLEANSER: Cleanser, fresh water and sanitizer 200ppm

PERSON RESPONSIBLE: _____

INITIAL UPON COMPLETION: _____

COUNTERS (PREP)

WHEN: Between uses/every 4 hours

HOW: Wash, rinse, sanitize

CLEANSER: Cleanser, fresh water and sanitizer 200ppm

PERSON RESPONSIBLE: _____

INITIAL UPON COMPLETION: _____

DISH RACKS

WHEN: Daily

HOW: Wash, rinse, sanitize

CLEANSER: Cleanser, fresh water and sanitizer 200ppm

PERSON RESPONSIBLE: _____

INITIAL UPON COMPLETION: _____

DOORS (FRONT ENTRY)

WHEN: As needed

HOW: Spot clean glass; wipe clean other surfaces

CLEANSER: Glass cleaner

PERSON RESPONSIBLE: _____

INITIAL UPON COMPLETION: _____

DRAIN COVERS

WHEN: Daily

HOW: Clear debris; wash, rinse, sanitize

CLEANSER: Dish machine

PERSON RESPONSIBLE: _____

INITIAL UPON COMPLETION: _____

DRY STORAGE AREAS

WHEN: Daily

HOW: Sweep/mop

CLEANSER: Approved sanitizer

PERSON RESPONSIBLE: _____

INITIAL UPON COMPLETION: _____

FLOORS

WHEN: Daily/as needed

HOW: Sweep/mop

CLEANSER: Approved sanitizer

PERSON RESPONSIBLE: _____

INITIAL UPON COMPLETION: _____

FREEZERS

WHEN: Daily

HOW: Sweep/mop if walk-in; wipe exterior

CLEANSER: Approved sanitizer

PERSON RESPONSIBLE: _____

INITIAL UPON COMPLETION: _____

HAND-WASHING SINK

WHEN: Every 4 hours

HOW: Wash, rinse, sanitize

CLEANSER: Cleanser, fresh water and sanitizer 200ppm

PERSON RESPONSIBLE: _____

INITIAL UPON COMPLETION: _____

HOOD FILTERS

WHEN: Every other p.m., end of shift

HOW: Soak in degreaser; spray clean with fresh water; air-dry

CLEANSER: Non-caustic degreaser

PERSON RESPONSIBLE: _____

INITIAL UPON COMPLETION: _____

HOOD GREASE PANS

WHEN: Bi-weekly

HOW: Empty into grease bin; run through dish-washer; replace

CLEANSER: Dish machine

PERSON RESPONSIBLE: _____

INITIAL UPON COMPLETION: _____

ICE CARRIERS

WHEN: Every 4 hours

HOW: Wash, rinse, sanitize; run through dishwasher; replace

CLEANSER: Dish machine

PERSON RESPONSIBLE: _____

INITIAL UPON COMPLETION: _____

ICE CREAM DIPPER WELL

WHEN: Daily

HOW: Wash, rinse, sanitize

CLEANSER: Cleanser, fresh water and sanitizer 200ppm

PERSON RESPONSIBLE: _____

INITIAL UPON COMPLETION: _____

KNIFE HOLDERS

WHEN: Every 4 hours

HOW: Wash, rinse, sanitize

CLEANSER: Cleanser, fresh water and sanitizer 200ppm

PERSON RESPONSIBLE: _____

INITIAL UPON COMPLETION: _____

MIXER BASE/EXTERIOR

WHEN: Daily

HOW: Wash, rinse, sanitize

CLEANSER: Cleanser, fresh water and sanitizer 200ppm

PERSON RESPONSIBLE: _____

INITIAL UPON COMPLETION: _____

MOPS/BRUSHES

WHEN: Daily

HOW: Wash, rinse and sanitize in mop sink; hang upside down to drip dry over sink

CLEANSER: Cleanser, fresh water and sanitizer 200ppm

PERSON RESPONSIBLE: _____

INITIAL UPON COMPLETION: _____

PIZZA OVEN

WHEN: Throughout shift

HOW: Wipe interior with clean, moist towel

CLEANSER: Water only

PERSON RESPONSIBLE: _____

INITIAL UPON COMPLETION: _____

PREMISES EXTERIOR

WHEN: Daily

HOW: Sweep entire areas of debris/trash

CLEANSER: Water spray if needed

PERSON RESPONSIBLE: _____

INITIAL UPON COMPLETION: _____

PREPARATION AREAS

WHEN: Each use

HOW: Wash, rinse, sanitize

CLEANSER: Cleanser, fresh water and sanitizer 200ppm

PERSON RESPONSIBLE: _____

INITIAL UPON COMPLETION: _____

REACH-IN HANDLES

WHEN: Daily

HOW: Wipe exterior with moist cloth

CLEANSER: Sanitizer bucket at 200ppm

PERSON RESPONSIBLE: _____

INITIAL UPON COMPLETION: _____

REACH-INS AND WELLS

WHEN: Daily

HOW: Wash, rinse, sanitize; moist cloth

CLEANSER: Cleanser, fresh water and sanitizer 200ppm

ROTISSERIE SKEWERS/TINES

WHEN: End of use and end of day

HOW: Degrease and sanitize

CLEANSER: Non-caustic degreaser

PERSON RESPONSIBLE: _____

INITIAL UPON COMPLETION: _____

ROTISSERIE: HOLDING DRAWERS, EXTERIOR

WHEN: Daily

HOW: Wash, rinse, sanitize; buff exterior

CLEANSER: Cleanser, fresh water and sanitizer 200ppm

PERSON RESPONSIBLE: _____

INITIAL UPON COMPLETION: _____

SCALES

WHEN: Between each use, and every 4 hours

HOW: Wash, rinse, sanitize

CLEANSER: Cleanser, fresh water and sanitizer 200ppm

PERSON RESPONSIBLE: _____

INITIAL UPON COMPLETION: _____

SLICERS AND STAND

WHEN: Between each use (Stand: Daily)

HOW: Wash, rinse, sanitize

CLEANSER: Cleanser, fresh water and sanitizer 200ppm

PERSON RESPONSIBLE: _____

INITIAL UPON COMPLETION: _____

STORAGE BINS

WHEN: Daily

HOW: Wipe exterior with moist cloth

CLEANSER: Sanitizer 200ppm

PERSON RESPONSIBLE: _____

INITIAL UPON COMPLETION: _____

THREE-COMPARTMENT SINK

WHEN: Daily or between use

HOW: Wash, rinse, sanitize

CLEANSER: Cleanser, fresh water and sanitizer 200ppm

PERSON RESPONSIBLE: _____

INITIAL UPON COMPLETION: _____

TRASH RECEPTACLES

WHEN: Daily

HOW: Wipe exterior with disposable cloth

CLEANSER: Water and sanitizer 200ppm

PERSON RESPONSIBLE: _____

INITIAL UPON COMPLETION: _____

UTENSILS (IN-USE)

WHEN: Every 4 hours or between products

HOW: Wash, rinse, sanitize

CLEANSER: Dish machine

PERSON RESPONSIBLE: _____

INITIAL UPON COMPLETION: _____

WALK-IN

WHEN: Daily

HOW: Sweep and clean floor

CLEANSER: Tile cleaner

PERSON RESPONSIBLE: _____

INITIAL UPON COMPLETION: _____

WIPING CLOTHS (IN-USE)

WHEN: Every 4 hours

HOW: Put in designated container to launder

PERSON RESPONSIBLE: _____

INITIAL UPON COMPLETION: _____

NOTES:

Hazard Analysis of Critical Control Points (HACCP) Chart

EMPLOYEE: _____ **DATE:** _____

WALK-IN COOLERS

A.M.	MIDDAY	P.M.	CORRECTIVE ACTION TAKEN:

COLD HOLDING STANDARDS: Foods should be held at a temperature of 41°F or below.

CORRECTIVE ACTION: Discard or if food has not been at the correct temperature for less than 4 hours, rapidly cool to 41°F or less.

COOKLINE COOLERS

A.M.	MIDDAY	P.M.	CORRECTIVE ACTION TAKEN:

COOKING

A.M.	MIDDAY	P.M.	CORRECTIVE ACTION TAKEN:

COOKING STANDARDS:
  Poultry products: 165°F/15 seconds
  Ground beef: 155°F/15 seconds
  Eggs, fish, pork, beef: 145°F/15 seconds
  All other foods: 145°F/15 seconds

CORRECTIVE ACTION: Continue cooking.

REHEATING

A.M.	MIDDAY	P.M.	CORRECTIVE ACTION TAKEN:

REHEATING STANDARDS: Reheat foods to 165°F within 2 hours.

CORRECTIVE ACTION: Discard if not reheated within 2 hours.

HOT HOLDING

A.M.	MIDDAY	P.M.	CORRECTIVE ACTION TAKEN:

HOT HOLDING STANDARDS: All foods should be held at 140°F or above.

CORRECTIVE ACTION: Discard or if food has been out of temperature for less than 4 hours, rapidly reheat to 165°F or hotter.

COOLING

2 Hours	6 Hours	CORRECTIVE ACTION TAKEN:

COOLING STANDARDS: Cool cooked foods from 140°F to 70°F in 2 hours. Continue to cool from 70°F to 41°F in 4 hours. Food made from room-temperature ingredients cooled to 41°F in 4 hours.

CORRECTIVE ACTION: Discard or reheat to 165°F, cool properly and serve.

RECEIVING

TEMPERATURE AT RECEIPT	CORRECTIVE ACTION TAKEN:

RECEIVING STANDARDS: All potentially hazardous foods must be at 41°F or less.

CORRECTIVE ACTION: Reject and discard food if not at proper temperature.

Weekly Thermometer Calibration Chart

ICE WATER METHOD

Thermometers should be calibrated at least once a week. New thermometers should be calibrated before initial use. To calibrate a thermometer, fill a small container with ice and add water to form slush. Insert the stem of the thermometer into the slush. Temperature should read 32ºF. If necessary, use a wrench to hold the nut at the base of the thermometer in place while turning the dial of the thermometer while it is still immersed until it reads the correct temperature. Boiling water (212ºF) may also be used in the same manner.

BOILING WATER METHOD

WEEK 1   DATE: _____

CALIBRATED BY: _____   INITIALS: _____

WEEK 2   DATE: _____

CALIBRATED BY: _____   INITIALS: _____

WEEK 3   DATE: _____

CALIBRATED BY: _____   INITIALS: _____

WEEK 4   DATE: _____

CALIBRATED BY: _____   INITIALS: ____

WEEK 5   DATE: _____

CALIBRATED BY: _____   INITIALS: ____

WEEK 6   DATE: _____

CALIBRATED BY: _____   INITIALS: _____

WEEK 7   DATE: _____

CALIBRATED BY: _____   INITIALS: _____

WEEK 8   DATE: _____

CALIBRATED BY: _____   INITIALS: _____

WEEK 9   DATE: _____

CALIBRATED BY: _____   INITIALS: ____

WEEK 10   DATE: _____

CALIBRATED BY: _____   INITIALS: ____

Hot/Cold Holding Chart

STANDARDS/CRITICAL LIMITS
Hot holding 140°F or above.
Cold holding 41°F or below.

CORRECTIVE ACTION
Rapidly reheat to 165°F or rapidly chill to 41°F and place back in the hot or cold holding unit. Discard if out of temperature more than 4 hours.

AREA	TIME & TEMPERATURE					
	a.m./p.m.	a.m./p.m.	a.m./p.m.	a.m./p.m.	a.m./p.m.	a.m./p.m.
STEAM TABLE						
FOOD ITEMS						
COOKLINE COOLER						
WALK-IN						
FREEZER						
CORRECTIVE ACTION TAKEN:						

CCP Decision Tree

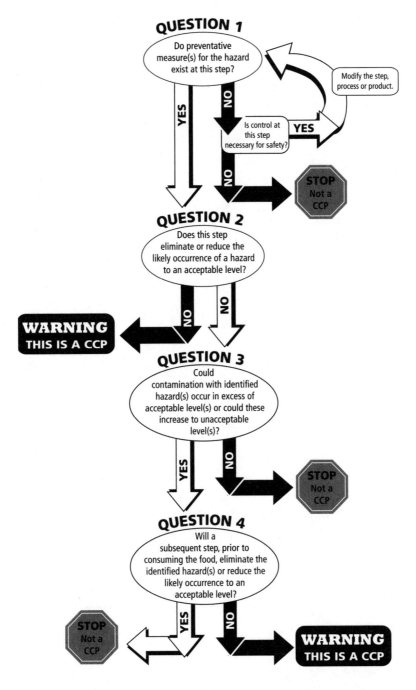

QUESTION 1
Do preventative measure(s) for the hazard exist at this step?

Modify the step, process or product.

Is control at this step necessary for safety?

YES **NO**

YES

NO

STOP
Not a CCP

QUESTION 2
Does this step eliminate or reduce the likely occurrence of a hazard to an acceptable level?

NO **NO**

WARNING
THIS IS A CCP

QUESTION 3
Could contamination with identified hazard(s) occur in excess of acceptable level(s) or could these increase to unacceptable level(s)?

YES **NO**

STOP
Not a CCP

QUESTION 4
Will a subsequent step, prior to consuming the food, eliminate the identified hazard(s) or reduce the likely occurrence to an acceptable level?

YES **NO**

STOP
Not a CCP

WARNING
THIS IS A CCP

CONSIDERATIONS WHEN USING THE DECISION TREE:

- After hazard analysis, use the decision tree.

- At a the step where a significant hazard has been identified, the decision tree is used.

- A subsequent step in the process may be more effective for controlling a hazard and may be the preferred CCP.

- To control a hazard, more than one step in the process may be involved.

- A specific control measure may take care of more than one hazard.

Hazard Analysis — CCP Decision Tree Form

DATE:	PRODUCT:

Process Step	Potential hazard introduced, controlled or enhanced at this step. B = Biological C = Chemical P = Physical	Should the hazard be addressed in the HACCP plan?	Justification for decision.	What control measures can be applied to prevent the significant hazards?

CCP Decision Tree Table

PRODUCT: DATE:

A critical control point is defined as a point, step or procedure at which control can be applied and a food-safety hazard can be prevented, eliminated or reduced. Steps presenting a significant potential food-safety risk (Q1, Hazard Analysis) are listed.

Process Step	Hazard B = Biological C = Chemical P = Physical	Q1. Do preventative measure(s) for the hazard exist at this step?	Q2. Does this step eliminate or reduce the likely occurrence of a hazard to an acceptable level?	If Q2 is NO Q3. Could contamination with identified hazard(s) occur in excess of acceptable level(s) or could these increase to unacceptable level(s)?	Q4. Will a subsequent step, prior to consuming the food, eliminate the identified hazard(s) or reduce the likely occurrence to an acceptable level?	CCP#

Establishing Critical Limits, Monitoring & Corrective Actions

PRODUCT:		DATE:	

Process Step/CCP	Critical Limits	Monitoring Procedures (Who/What/When/How)	Corrective Actions
		Who: What: When: How:	1. 2. 3. 4.
		Who: What: When: How:	1. 2. 3. 4.
		Who: What: When: How:	1. 2. 3. 4.
		Who: What: When: How:	1. 2. 3. 4.

Recordkeeping & Verification

PRODUCT:		DATE:

Process Step/CCP	Records	Verification Procedures
		1. 2. 3. 4.
		1. 2. 3. 4.
		1. 2. 3. 4.
		1. 2. 3. 4.

HACCP Plan Summary

PRODUCT:		DATE:

Process Step	
Hazard Description	
CCP Description	
Monitoring Procedures/ Frequency/ Person Responsible	Who: What: When: How:
Corrective Actions	
HACCP Records	
Verification Procedures/ Person Responsible	

HACCP Monitoring — Equipment Inspection Form

Equipment Inspected: _____

Inspected By: _____ Inspection Date: _____

Condition: _____

Improvements Needed: _____

Equipment Inspected: _____

Inspected By: _____ Inspection Date: _____

Condition: _____

Improvements Needed: _____

Equipment Inspected: _____

Inspected By: _____ Inspection Date: _____

Condition: _____

Improvements Needed: _____

Equipment Inspected: _____

Inspected By: _____ Inspection Date: _____

Condition: _____

Improvements Needed: _____

Equipment Inspected: _____

Inspected By: _____ Inspection Date: _____

Condition: _____

Improvements Needed: _____

Equipment Inspected: _____

Inspected By: _____ Inspection Date: _____

Condition: _____

Improvements Needed: _____

HACCP Monitoring — Temperature/Food Safety Chart

FOOD ITEM: **DATE:**

RECEIVING/STORING

CONTROL CRITERIA
- ☐ Approved source
- ☐ Item(s) inspected
- ☐ Shellfish tags
- ☐ Raw/cooked/separated in storage
- ☐ Refrigerated at 45°F or less
- ☐ Product condition (dents, open products, torn bags)

MONITORING
- ☐ Shellfish tags available and complete
- ☐ Food temperature checked
- ☐ Raw foods stored below cooked or ready-to-eat foods

ACTION
- ☐ Discard food
- ☐ Return food
- ☐ Separate raw and cooked food
- ☐ Discard cooked food contaminated by raw food
- ☐ Discard if food temperature is more than 45°F for 2 hours or if more than 70°F

NOTES

COOKING

CONTROL CRITERIA
- ☐ Temperature to kill pathogens: Food temperature at thickest part at least _____°F

MONITORING
- ☐ Measure food temperature at thickest part

ACTION
- ☐ Continue cooking until food temperature at thickest part is at least _____°F

NOTES

THAWING

CONTROL CRITERIA
- ☐ Refrigeration
- ☐ Under running water less than 70°F
- ☐ Microwave
- ☐ Cooked in frozen state (less than 3 lbs only)

MONITORING
- ☐ Select thawing method, check food temperature

ACTION
- ☐ Discard if food temperature is more than 45°F for 2 hours or if more than 70°F

NOTES

HOT HOLDING

CONTROL CRITERIA

☐ Food temperature at thickest part at least _____°F

MONITORING

☐ Measure food temperature at thickest part during hot holding every _____ minutes

ACTION

☐ Food Temperature: 140°–120°F
More than or equal to 2 hours, discard; less than 2 hours, reheat to 165°F and hold at 140°F

☐ Food Temperature: 120°–45°F
More than or equal to 2 hours, discard; less than 2 hours, reheat to 165°F and hold at 140°F

NOTES

PRE-COOKING

CONTROL CRITERIA

☐ Food temperature no more than 45°F

MONITORING

☐ Observe quantity of food at room temperature
☐ Observe time food held at room temperature

ACTION

☐ Discard if food temperature is more than 45°F for 2 hours or if more than 70°F

NOTES

REHEATING

CONTROL CRITERIA

☐ Food temperature at thickest part more than or equal to 165°F

MONITORING

☐ Measure food temperature at thickest part during reheating

ACTION

☐ Food temperature at thickest part less than 165°F, continue reheating

NOTES

CONTROL CRITERIA

Prevent contamination by:

- ☐ Employees' hands not touching ready-to-eat food
- ☐ Employees wash hands correctly and frequently
- ☐ No ill employees
- ☐ All utensils clean and sanitized
- ☐ Cold, potentially hazardous food at a temperature less than or equal to 45°F
- ☐ Hot, potentially hazardous food at a temperature more than or equal to 140°F

MONITORING

- ☐ Use of gloves and utensils
- ☐ Hand-washing techniques and frequency
- ☐ Observe employees' health
- ☐ Use prechilled ingredients for cold foods
- ☐ Minimize quantity of food at room temperature

ACTION

Discard food if any of the following is observed:

- ☐ Cold, potentially hazardous food: More than 45°F more than or equal to 2 hours, discard; more than 70°F, discard

- ☐ Hot, potentially hazardous food:
  140°–120°F
  More than or equal to 2 hours, discard; less than 2 hours, reheat to 154°F and hold at 140°F
  120°–45°F
  More than or equal to 2 hours, discard; less than 2 hours, reheat to 154°F and hold at 140°F
- ☐ If raw food has contaminated other food or equipment/utensils, discard food in question or reheat to 165°F
- ☐ Ill worker handling food

NOTES

CONTROL CRITERIA

- ☐ Hot Food: Temperature at thickest part at least 140°F
- ☐ Cold Food: Temperature at thickest part at least 45°F

MONITORING

- ☐ Measure food temperature at thickest part during hot holding every _____ minutes

ACTION

- ☐ Cold holding, potentially hazardous food: More than 45°F more than or equal to 2 hours, discard; more than 70°F, discard

- ☐ Hot holding, potentially hazardous food:
  140°–120°F
  More or equal to 2 hours, discard; less than 2 hours, reheat to 154°F and hold at 140°F

  120°–45°F
  More or equal to 2 hours, discard; less than 2 hours, reheat to 165°F and hold at 140°F

NOTES

COOLING

CONTROL CRITERIA

- ☐ Food 120°F to 70°F in 2 hours;
  70°F to 45°F in 4 additional hours by the following methods:
- ☐ Product depth 4 inches or less
- ☐ Ice water bath, stirring
- ☐ Rapid-chill refrigeration
- ☐ Do not cover until cold

MONITORING

- ☐ Measure food temperature every _____ minutes
- ☐ Food depth
- ☐ Food iced
- ☐ Food stirred
- ☐ Food size
- ☐ Food placed in rapid-chill refrigeration unit
- ☐ Food uncovered

ACTION

- ☐ Food Temperature:
  120°–70°F
  More than 2 hours, discard food

  70°–45°F
  More than 4 hours, discard food

  45°F or less
  But cooled too slowly, discard food

NOTES

NOTES

HACCP Monitoring — Cooking/Cooling Log

EMPLOYEE:		DATE:	

PRODUCT	FINAL COOKING		INITIAL TEMP		2 HOURS		4 MORE HOURS		INITIALS
	TIME	TEMP	TIME	TEMP	TIME	TEMP	TIME	TEMP	

1. **Time & Temperature** – Always record the time when the temperature is taken.

2. **Final Cooking** – The foods' internal temperature must reach a minimum of 170°F.

3. **Initial Cooling** – Initial cooling begins at 140°F. Meet all cooling requirements:
   - Cool foods from 140°F to 70°F within 2 hours; and from 70°F to below 41°F within 4 hours, for a total of 6 hours. If food item goes directly into hot holding after cooking, cooling is not required.

4. **2-Hour Requirement** – Internal temperature must reach 70°F within 2 hours of initial temperature.

5. **4-Hour Requirement** – Internal temperature must reach below 41°F within 4 hours from the time the food is 70°F.

6. **Total Cooling Time 6 Hours** – The final column should be initialed by the employee to certify the food has been cooled properly and checked at each increment.

7. **Reheating** – Reheat to proper internal temperature within 2 hours and serve. Reheat only once to 170°F and repeat chill process or discard food item.

8. **Corrective Action** – Continue to cook to required HACCP temperature for each food. Corrective actions should be listed below:

Daily Equipment Cleaning Chart

ITEM	CLEANING TASK	WHEN
Beverage dispensers	Wipe spills and splashes Take apart, clean and sanitize dispenser spouts Clean drain tray	Upon each occurrence Daily Once per shift
Breath guards	Wipe spills and splashes Clean and sanitize all surfaces	Upon each occurrence Once per shift
Can openers	Clean and sanitize	After every use, and once per shift
Carts, food transport equipment	Wipe spills and splashes Clean and sanitize shelves and racks	Upon each occurrence Daily, after use
Coffee and tea machines	Wipe spills and splashes Rinse baskets, urns and pots Take apart, clean and sanitize spray heads and spouts	Upon each occurrence After each use Daily
Deep fryer	Clean outside surfaces Clean and filter grease	Once per shift Once per shift
Dishwashing machines	Take apart and clean Clean doors, gaskets and surfaces	On a regular basis to remove build-up and ensure clean water Daily
Floors	Wipe spills Sweep Damp mop Sanitize and scrub	Upon each occurrence As needed After each shift Daily
Frozen dessert machines	Wipe spills and splashes Clean drain tray Take apart, clean and sanitize parts, interior surfaces and dispenser spouts	Upon each occurrence Once per shift Daily
Grill, griddle, broiler	Clean and brush grill surfaces Clean surrounding surfaces and grease tray Clean cooking surfaces and backsplash	As needed, or once per shift Once per shift Daily
Hot holding	Wipe spills Clean interior surfaces and racks Clean exterior surfaces	Upon each occurrence Daily Daily

ITEM	CLEANING TASK	WHEN
Ice machine	Clean doors, gaskets and exterior surfaces	Daily
Microwave	Wipe spills Clean and sanitize interior surfaces Clean and sanitize fan shield and tray Clean outside surfaces	Upon each occurrence Once per shift Daily Daily
Mixers, slicers and food processors	Take apart, clean and sanitize parts, surfaces and work tables	After each use, or between each food item change
Ovens	Wipe spills	Upon each occurrence
Range	Wipe spills Clean and sanitize work surfaces	Upon each occurrence Once per shift
Reach-in refrigerators and freezers	Wipe spills Clean outside, doors and gaskets	Upon each occurrence Daily
Scales	Clean and sanitize weighing tray Clean and sanitize exposed surfaces	After each use Daily
Sinks	Clean and sanitize sink interior Clean exterior surfaces and backsplash	After each use Daily, at closing
Steam tables	Drain water and clean wells Clean outside and surrounding surfaces	Once per shift Once per shift
Steamer	Wipe spills Clean and sanitize interior surfaces and racks Clean exterior surfaces	Upon each occurrence Daily Daily
Walk-in refrigerators and freezers	Wipe spills Sweep and damp mop (freezer, sweep only) Clean door surfaces and gaskets Scrub floors	Upon each occurrence Once per shift Daily Daily (except freezer)
Walls	Splashes Wash walls in prep and cooking areas	Upon each occurrence Daily, at closing
Work tables	Clean and sanitize tops and shelves each shift	After each use and after

Weekly & Monthly Equipment Cleaning Chart

Weekly Cleaning

ITEM	CLEANING TASK
Carts and transport equipment	Thoroughly clean and sanitize supports and exterior
Coffee and tea machines	Clean and brush urn, pots and baskets using cleaner specified by manufacturer
Deep fryer	Boil out fryers
Ovens	Clean interior surfaces and racks
Range	Take apart burners, and empty and sanitize catch trays
Reach-in refrigerators	Empty, clean and sanitize
Sinks	Clean legs and supports
Steam tables	De-lime
Walk-in refrigeration and freezer units	Wipe clean and sanitize walls
Work tables	Clean legs and supports; empty, clean and sanitize drawers

Monthly Cleaning

ITEM	CLEANING TASK
Dishwashing machines	De-lime machine
Ice machine	Drain ice, clean and sanitize interior surfaces Flush ice-making unit Defrost and clean
Reach-in freezers	Empty, clean and sanitize
Reach-in refrigeration and freezer units	Defrost
Steamer	De-lime
Walk-in refrigeration and freezer units	Clean fans Empty, clean racks, walls, floors and corners Defrost freezer

Daily Facilities Cleaning Chart

ITEM	CLEANING TASK	WHEN
Carpets	Vacuum	Daily
Chairs	Clean and sanitize seat	After each use
Dining tables	Clean and sanitize	After each use
Display cabinets	Clean and sanitize surfaces	Once per shift
Drains	Scrub covers	Daily
Dry storage areas	Sweep and mop floors	Daily
Employee areas	Clean and sanitize tables used for eating Sweep and mop, if applicable	After each use Once per shift
Floors	Wipe spills Sweep Damp mop Scrub	Upon each occurrence As needed, or between meals Once per shift Daily
Garbage cans	Scrub clean and sanitize cans with hot water or steam and detergent	After emptying, or at closing
Hoods	Clean walls and exposed surfaces of hoods Clean removable filters	Daily Daily
Office areas	Sweep and mop, if applicable Clean work surfaces	Daily Daily
Self-service beverage areas	Wipe spills and splashes Clean and sanitize surfaces	Upon each occurrence Once per shift
Self-service condiment areas	Wipe spills and splashes Clean and sanitize surfaces Take apart, clean and sanitize dispensers	Upon each occurrence Once per shift Daily
Upholstery	Vacuum or brush clean	Daily
Walls	Splashes Wash	As soon as possible Daily (in kitchen and cooking areas)

Weekly & Monthly Facilities Cleaning Chart

Weekly Cleaning

ITEM	CLEANING TASK
Chairs	Clean chair backs, rails and legs
Dining tables	Clean table bases
Display cabinets	Clean cabinet interior
Drains	Flush drains with disinfectant
Dry storage areas	Clean shelves, scrub floors, baseboards and corners
Employee areas	Clean employee lockers and storage areas
Fans	Clean fan guards
Floors	Scrub baseboards and corners
HVAC system	Clean air intake and output ducts
Walls	Wash all walls

Monthly Cleaning

ITEM	CLEANING TASK
Carpets	Steam clean and shampoo, bi-monthly
Ceilings	Wash
Floors	Strip and reseal twice per year
Grease traps	Remove grease and clean
Hoods	Clean and degrease hood system, bi-monthly
HVAC system	Check filters
Light fixtures	Clean shields and fixtures
Upholstery	Steam clean or shampoo, bi-monthly
Walls	Wash all walls

To Prevent Bacterial Growth, Cool Food Rapidly

**140°F–70°F
First 2 Hours**

**70°F–40°F
Next 4 Hours**

TOTAL COOLING = 6 HOURS

COOL FOOD PROPERLY
To Prevent Contamination & Bacterial Growth

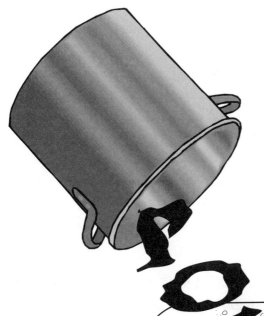

1. Pour food into shallow pan (large pots should not be used to cool food).

2. Food in pan should not be more than 2 inches in depth.

3. Surround with another large container filled with ice.

4. Stir frequently.

Food-Borne Illness Complaint Form

RESTAURANT INFORMATION

Restaurant Name: _____ Date complaint reported:____/____/____

Address: _____

City: _____ State:_____ Zip Code: _____

Phone Number:_____

COMPLAINANT INFORMATION

Name: _____ Date of visit: _____

Address: _____

City: _____ State:_____ Zip Code: _____

Phone Number:_____

Do you have any food allergies? Yes or No List: _____

Number of people dining in your party? 1 2 3 4 5 6 7 8 9 10+

Check items eaten (and write in specific details):   Time meal was eaten: _____ a.m./p.m.

- ☐ Bread/Butter Appetizer _____   ☐ Entrée _____
- ☐ Side Orders _____   ☐ Dessert _____
- ☐ Beverage _____   ☐ Other _____

ILLNESS INFORMATION

Time illness occurred: _____ a.m./p.m.   Length of illness: 1 2 3 4 5 6 7 8 9 10 hours days weeks

Type of illness: (Mark a ✓ next to any the complainant mentions. Do not read off possible symptoms.)

- ☐ Nausea   ☐ Vomiting   ☐ Abdominal Pain   ☐ Diarrhea
- ☐ Lethargy   ☐ Backache   ☐ Rash on _____ ☐ Flushed
- ☐ Dizziness   ☐ Headache   ☐ Chills   ☐ Fever
- ☐ Difficulty Breathing/Swallowing   ☐ Other_____

How was the illness treated? _____

Medical center where treated: _____ Physician: _____

Medical center address and phone:_____

Was an official diagnosis given? Yes or No Explain: _____

Did any other members of your party become ill? Yes or No Explain: _____

Name: _____

Did you eat any of the same items? Yes or No   List: _____

Other items eaten (circle and write in):

- ☐ Bread/Butter Appetizer _____   ☐ Entrée _____
- ☐ Side Orders _____   ☐ Dessert _____
- ☐ Beverage _____   ☐ Other _____

Check with your local Health Department for follow-up procedures regarding handling food-borne illness complaints.
For future reference, attach to this report a list of all food items sold the day of illness.

Title/Name of Person Taking Information: _____

Signature: _____

Allergen-Control Program Worksheet

Name: _____ Inspection Date: _____

Address: _____

Inspector: _____ Firm License #: _____

❑ Y ❑ N   Is an allergen-control program in place at this establishment?

❑ Y ❑ N   Are employees trained in and understand the allergen-control program?

❑ Y ❑ N   To prevent cross-contamination, are all raw ingredients transported and stored properly?

❑ Y ❑ N   If raw materials contain an allergen, are they properly labeled with allergen specifics?

❑ Y ❑ N   Are equipment lockouts, batch sequencing and correct wash procedures used to isolate allergen ingredients?

❑ Y ❑ N   Does food production take place only on dedicated lines using dedicated rooms and equipment?

❑ Y ❑ N   Are single-service items discarded in a sanitary manner after only one use?

❑ Y ❑ N   Are all ingredients clearly listed on the final product label?

❑ Y ❑ N   Are labels checked frequently for accuracy and any obsolete labels discarded?

❑ Y ❑ N   In the event of a recall, is there a complete recordkeeping system or log book to trace back all products?

❑ Y ❑ N   Are standardized procedures for sanitation operations used?

❑ Y ❑ N   Is sanitation effectiveness tested by procedures such as bioluminescence or ELISA testing?

Daily Sanitation Inspection Form

EMPLOYEES

❑ Yes   ❑ No   Employees are wearing clean uniforms or clothing.

❑ Yes   ❑ No   Employees use hair restraints and remove all jewelry.

❑ Yes   ❑ No   Employees are presentable and practice good personal hygiene.

❑ Yes   ❑ No   Eating or drinking is not allowed in food preparation area.

❑ Yes   ❑ No   Ill or infectious employees are not allowed to work.

FOOD HANDLING PRACTICES

❑ Yes   ❑ No   Fresh foods are in good condition and properly labeled and stored.

❑ Yes   ❑ No   Canned goods are sealed and have no dents, bulges, swelling or leaks and rust.

❑ Yes   ❑ No   Cereals, sugar, dried fruits, flour and other dry bulk items are labeled and stored in proper containers and free from insect infestation.

❑ Yes   ❑ No   Refrigeration and freezer units are clean and free of excess ice buildup.

❑ Yes   ❑ No   Refrigerator temperature _____ °F.

❑ Yes   ❑ No   Freezer temperature _____ °F.

❑ Yes   ❑ No   Refrigeration (or other approved method) is used for thawing.

❑ Yes   ❑ No   Milk and milk products are inspected upon delivery, stored in unopened individual containers, and have a temperature of 41°F or lower.

❑ Yes   ❑ No   Cold foods are maintained at 41°F or lower and temperature checked every 2 hours.

❑ Yes   ❑ No   Hot foods are maintained at 140°F or higher and temperature checked every 2 hours.

❑ Yes   ❑ No   Leftovers are properly labeled with time, date and use-by date.

❑ Yes   ❑ No   All foods are properly cooked and/or reheated (165°F).

❑ Yes   ❑ No   All foods are properly cooled (140°F to 70°F within 2 hours; 70°F to 41°F in 4 hours).

FOOD EQUIPMENT AND UTENSILS

❑ Yes   ❑ No   Food contact and work surfaces are constructed of proper materials, installed correctly and in good, workable condition.

❑ Yes   ❑ No   Proper dishwashing facilities are available (a three-compartment sink or dish machine) and used correctly.

❑ Yes   ❑ No   Signs with correct dishwashing procedures (pre-flush, scrape, wash, rinse, sanitize and air-dry) are posted and visible in area.

❑ Yes   ❑ No   Dishwashing machine is clean, free of food particles or residue, uses proper levels of sanitizer and maintains correct water temperature.

❑ Yes   ❑ No   All food service equipment and utensils are cleaned, sanitized and stored correctly to prevent contamination.

❑ Yes   ❑ No   Clean-in-place equipment is adequately cleaned and sanitized, with no left-over food residue.

FACILITY/STRUCTURE

❑ Yes   ❑ No   Floors, walls, ceilings and fixtures are clean and properly constructed.

❑ Yes   ❑ No   Lighting is adequate and well-shielded.

❑ Yes   ❑ No   Water sources are safe, with adequate supplies of pressurized hot and cold water.

❑ Yes   ❑ No   All hand-washing sinks have hot and cold water and are stocked with soap, single-use paper towels and covered waste receptacles.

❑ Yes   ❑ No   Sewage and wastewater is correctly piped for proper disposal.

❑ Yes   ❑ No   Plumbing is installed professionally and maintained with back-flow and back-siphonage devices.

❑ Yes   ❑ No   Ventilation systems are in place and working properly.

GARBAGE/INSECT CONTROL

❑ Yes ❑ No All garbage containers have tight-fitting covers to prevent insect and rodent infestation.

❑ Yes ❑ No There are adequate garbage containers available and they are not overfilled.

❑ Yes ❑ No Garbage containers are cleaned often and no offensive odors exist.

❑ Yes ❑ No Outside refuse storage area is clean and enclosed.

❑ Yes ❑ No Outer openings are protected from insects and rodents, with functional, self-closing doors.

NOTE VIOLATIONS AND CORRECTIVE ACTIONS BELOW:

Safety for All Employees

Employee safety is our first priority. Our goal is to have no employees injured while on the job. Accidents affect everyone involved; they reduce your earnings and cause physical discomfort. We are concerned about your overall health and need your skills on the job!

Management Obligations

- Provide a safe workplace

- Provide training on all equipment prior to employee use

- Provide proper training for any potentially dangerous activities such as cutting or lifting

- Be aware of safety record and make any changes needed for zero injuries

If An Injury Occurs

- Immediately inform your supervisor

- Fill out an employee accident form

- No matter how small—report all cuts and injuries

- Seek medical attention if needed

- Report unsafe conditions to a supervisor immediately

Employee Responsibilities

- Practice safety at all times

- Notify your supervisor if you see other employees acting in a manner which could lead to injury

JOB DESCRIPTION TEMPLATES

Job Title: _____

Company Job Code: _____ FLSA Status: _____

Division/Department: _____ EEO Code: _____

Reports to: _____

Salary Grade/Band: _____ Last Revision Date: _____

SUMMARY

This section provides an overall summary of the job.

PRIMARY RESPONSIBILITIES

This section provides the primary functions of the job. The responsibilities are usually in order of importance and/or time spent. This list may also be used to define "essential functions" for the purposes of the Americans with Disabilities Act. Therefore, duties listed here should be considered "essential." If an applicant cannot perform most, if not all, of the essential functions, the applicant will not be considered for the position.

ADDITIONAL RESPONSIBILITIES

This section provides additional functions of the job. The responsibilities are usually desired but not required. These duties are not "essential functions"; therefore, even if an applicant cannot perform these duties, the applicant will still be considered for the position.

KNOWLEDGE AND SKILL REQUIREMENTS

This section provides specific knowledge and skill requirements such as sales techniques, facilitation skills, generally accepted accounting principles, and physical requirements. The number of years of experience and/or education requirements are also listed here.

WORKING CONDITIONS

This section contains information on working conditions out of the ordinary, such as extensive travel, high noise levels, and frequent lifting of over "x" pounds.

JOB DESCRIPTION: EXECUTIVE CHEF

Job Title: **Executive Chef**

Company Job Code:_____ FLSA Status:_____

Division/Department:_____ EEO Code:_____

Reports to:_____

Salary Grade/Band:_____ Last Revision Date:_____

SUMMARY

Oversees product quality, cleanliness and profitability of all food production for all food outlets and supervises kitchen staff.

PRIMARY RESPONSIBILITIES

1. Coordinates and oversees work of kitchen staff and food production.

2. Directs preparation of meals.

3. Ensures consistency, quality and correct presentation.

4. Schedules kitchen staff employees.

5. Responsible for overseeing that correct food items are purchased and received and maintaining product specs.

6. Responsible for monthly inventory.

7. Plans and develops menus.

8. Ensures standards recipes are followed.

9. Responsible for ensuring all sanitation and safety guidelines are followed in the kitchen.

10. Oversees training for new kitchen employees and development of kitchen staff.

11. Coordinates with sales staff and banquet manager or catering director on production for catered functions.

12. Responsible for effective cost-control management.

13. Maintains a cleaning schedule for all major kitchen equipment on a monthly basis utilizing dishroom employees.

14. Keeps others informed on all information pertaining to receiving, parstocks and pricing.

15. Performs all other duties as assigned.

ADDITIONAL RESPONSIBILITIES

All other duties as assigned.

KNOWLEDGE AND SKILL REQUIREMENTS

1. BA/BS or associate's degree in Hotel/Restaurant Management and/or Culinary Arts.

2. Previous hotel- or kitchen-related experience, knowledge of food and beverage operations, and management experience in food service operations.

3. Requires bending, climbing, reaching, standing, walking, sitting, lifting, carrying, repetitive motions, visual acuity, hearing.

WORKING CONDITIONS

High noise levels, hot, must be able to lift 50+ pounds.

JOB DESCRIPTION: ASSISTANT MANAGER

Job Title: **Assistant Manager**

Company Job Code:_____ FLSA Status: _____

Division/Department: _____ EEO Code: _____

Reports to:_____

Salary Grade/Band: _____ Last Revision Date: _____

SUMMARY

Responsible for the general operation of food service operations. Oversees kitchen and dining room staff. Responsible for operations in the absence of the General Manager. Responsible for promoting good staff/customer relations through consistent implementation of company standards.

PRIMARY RESPONSIBILITIES

1. Manages and oversees general operations on a day-to-day basis.

2. Writes schedules for dining room staff.

3. Performs and analyzes various daily and monthly reports including budgets, sales forecasts and operating reports.

4. Monitors food costs and labor costs and takes corrective actions if necessary.

5. Provides and coordinates training and development program for all staff.

6. Monitors employee performance and participates in annual employee performance reviews.

7. Receives, reviews and acts upon complaints received from guests.

8. Ensures all safety and sanitation guidelines are followed.

ADDITIONAL RESPONSIBILITIES

All other duties as assigned.

KNOWLEDGE AND SKILL REQUIREMENTS

1. College degree in field applicable to hospitality management.

2. Three to five years of restaurant management experience with proven skills in successful cost and labor controls.

3. Requires bending, climbing, reaching, standing, walking, sitting, lifting, carrying, repetitive motions, visual acuity, hearing.

WORKING CONDITIONS

High noise levels, hot, must be able to lift 50+ pounds.

JOB DESCRIPTION: BAKER

Job Title: **Baker**

Company Job Code:_____ FLSA Status: _____

Division/Department: _____ EEO Code: _____

Reports to:_____

Salary Grade/Band: _____ Last Revision Date: _____

SUMMARY

Responsible for the general baking operations.

PRIMARY RESPONSIBILITIES

1. Produces baked goods and desserts in compliance with standard recipes and department procedures.

2. Prepares breads, rolls, muffins and other bakery items.

3. Prepares pies, cakes, tortes and other dessert items.

4. Maintains a sanitary work area.

ADDITIONAL RESPONSIBILITIES

All other duties as assigned.

KNOWLEDGE AND SKILL REQUIREMENTS

1. Degree from a post-secondary culinary arts training program is desirable.

2. A minimum of six months in a baker position.

3. Must be able to stand and walk for long periods of time. Must be able to lift pots, pans, etc., up to 50 pounds in weight. Must be able to read and follow written instructions.

WORKING CONDITIONS

High noise levels, hot, must be able to stand for long periods of time and lift 50+ pounds.

JOB DESCRIPTION: BANQUET MANAGER

Job Title: **Banquet Manager**

Company Job Code:_____ FLSA Status: _____

Division/Department: _____ EEO Code: _____

Reports to:_____

Salary Grade/Band: _____ Last Revision Date: _____

SUMMARY

Responsible for soliciting banquet business and ensuring customer satisfaction for all bookings by making certain functions operate efficiently and customer expectations are met. Supervises all banquet functions and directs and trains all banquet personnel.

PRIMARY RESPONSIBILITIES

1. Coordinates and arranges function for clients. Obtains all necessary information including menu, number of guests, schedule of events, etc.

2. Fills in appropriate paperwork.

3. Coordinates with chef on menu.

4. Staffs all events, including hiring, training and termination.

5. Negotiates prices and draws up contracts.

6. Engages in sales activities, looking for new clients and marketing.

7. Inspects all function areas before event begins, ensuring everything is ready for the guests.

8. Obtains necessary equipment for events.

9. Greets clients upon their arrival and makes self available through the event for any problems arising.

10. Bills client and processes invoice.

11. Supervises event staff and ensures all opening and closing duties are completed.

ADDITIONAL RESPONSIBILITIES

All other duties as assigned.

KNOWLEDGE AND SKILL REQUIREMENTS

1. Two-year associate's degree or a bachelor's degree from a four-year college desired.

2. General knowledge of food and beverage and service procedures.

3. Two years' experience as a server, dining room manager or host/hostess.

4. Ability to bend, squat, and frequently lift 25 pounds and occasionally lift up to 50 pounds.

WORKING CONDITIONS

High noise levels, hot, must be able to stand for long periods of time and lift 50+ pounds.

JOB DESCRIPTION: BARTENDER

Job Title: **Bartender**

Company Job Code: _____ FLSA Status: _____

Division/Department: _____ EEO Code: _____

Reports to: _____

Salary Grade/Band: _____ Last Revision Date: _____

SUMMARY

Responsible for the set-up, maintenance and operation of the bar. Takes drink orders from patrons or waitstaff and prepares and serves alcoholic and non-alcoholic drinks in accordance with standard recipes. Mixes ingredients for cocktails and serves wine and bottled or draught beer. Rings drink orders into register, collects payment and makes change. May also wash and sterilize glassware, prepare garnishes for drinks, as well as prepare and replenish appetizers.

PRIMARY RESPONSIBILITIES

1. Receives drink orders from patrons or waitstaff.

2. Mixes and serves alcoholic and non-alcoholic drinks for patrons of bar and dining room, following standard recipes. Mixes ingredients such as liquor, soda, water, sugar and bitters to prepare cocktails and other drinks. Serves wine and bottled beer or draws draught beer from kegs.

3. Rings drink orders into register, collects money from patrons for drinks served and makes change.

4. Orders or requisitions liquors, other beverages and supplies.

5. Arranges bottles and glasses to make an attractive display and merchandises drinks.

6. Adheres to the basic procedures of personal hygiene such as neat, clean and pressed clothes, styled hair and manicured hands.

7. Always greets customers with a smile and, if possible, by name. Recognizing

new customers is critical; if you are busy, acknowledge her and indicate that you will be with her in a moment. Always place a cocktail napkin in front of the customer to show that he or she has been waited on.

8. When applicable, suggest the house specialty drinks and appetizers or offer the menu for perusing.

9. Make sure the cocktail waiters'/waitresses' tickets are accurate and complete.

10. Do not fill any order until the prices are entered and totaled correctly.

11. Know all the bar prices.

12. Check questionable customers' IDs to ensure they are of legal drinking age.

13. Communicate with coworkers throughout shift.

14. Follow all the health and safety regulations prescribed.

15. Follow all of the restaurant regulations prescribed.

16. Control and limit waste.

17. Communicate problems and ideas to management.

18. Attend all meetings.

19. Fill out all forms as prescribed.

20. Maintain all equipment and tools.

21. Follow all rotation procedures to ensure freshness of all products.

22. Follow management's instructions and suggestions.

ADDITIONAL RESPONSIBILITIES

1. May slice and pit fruit for garnishing drinks.

2. May wash and sterilize glassware.

3. May prepare appetizers, such as pickles, cheese and cold meats and replenish as needed.

4. All other duties as assigned.

KNOWLEDGE AND SKILL REQUIREMENTS

1. High school graduate or equivalent. Must be age 21 or older.

2. Must possess basic math skills and have the ability to handle money.

3. Ability to remain stationary for long periods of time. Able to reach, bend, stoop and frequently lift up to 50 pounds.

WORKING CONDITIONS

High noise levels, hot, must be able to stand for long periods of time and lift 50+ pounds.

JOB DESCRIPTION: BEVERAGE MANAGER

Job Title: **Beverage Manager**

Company Job Code: _____ FLSA Status: _____

Division/Department: _____ EEO Code: _____

Reports to: _____

Salary Grade/Band: _____ Last Revision Date: _____

SUMMARY

Oversees management and profitability of other beverage-related areas of the food service operation. Responsible for supervising and training all beverage personnel and for maintaining cost and labor controls for that department.

PRIMARY RESPONSIBILITIES

1. Develops accurate long- and short-range financial objectives relating to liquor sales.

2. Responsible for the quality, presentation and speed of beverage service.

3. Ensures employees follow proper company procedures.

4. Responsible for scheduling bar personnel.

5. Works closely with banquet manager in preparing banquet functions.

6. Responsible for purchasing beverage-related supplies and maintaining bar inventory.

7. Responsible for generating revenue and providing effective cost controls.

8. Hires and conducts orientation and training of bar personnel.

ADDITIONAL RESPONSIBILITIES

All other duties as assigned.

KNOWLEDGE AND SKILL REQUIREMENTS

1. Minimum of two years' college education.

2. Previous hotel-related experience.

3. Math skills and experience in operating and reading computerized cash register and tape readouts.

4. Requires bending, climbing, reaching, standing, walking, sitting, fingering, grasping, repetitive motions. Requires occasional lifting of up to 60 pounds in weight (kegs and boxes).

WORKING CONDITIONS

High noise levels, hot, must be able to stand for long periods of time and lift 60+ pounds.

JOB DESCRIPTION: BUS PERSON

Job Title: **Bus Person**

Company Job Code: _____ FLSA Status: _____

Division/Department: _____ EEO Code: _____

Reports to: _____

Salary Grade/Band: _____ Last Revision Date: _____

SUMMARY

Assists food servers to maintain service efficiency and ensures guest satisfaction by maintaining cleanliness of the front-of-the-house area.

PRIMARY RESPONSIBILITIES

1. Greets guests appropriately when they are seated.

2. Communicates with host/hostess and waitstaff to maintain service efficiency and ensures guest satisfaction.

3. Maintains cleanliness and sanitation of the front-of-the-house including all tables, chairs, floors, windows and restrooms.

4. Serves water, bread and butter to guests and provides refills as needed.

5. Restocks dining room with china, silverware, glassware, utensils, condiments, and linen, and maintains adequate supplies in the work stations when dining room is opened.

6. Prepares beverages required for service including coffee, iced tea and water.

7. Removes dirty dishes and utensils from tables between courses and clears tables after guests leave.

8. Replaces dishes and utensils for next course and cleans and resets vacated tables.

9. Returns dirty dishes, silverware, glassware and utensils to dishwashing area.

10. May assist waitstaff in serving tables with hot beverages such as coffee or tea.

ADDITIONAL RESPONSIBILITIES

All other duties as assigned

KNOWLEDGE AND SKILL REQUIREMENTS

1. Some high school.

2. No previous food service experience required.

3. Must be able to stand and exert fast-paced mobility for periods of up to four hours in length, and to lift, bend and stoop. Must have the ability to frequently lift and carry bus tubs, trays, and other objects weighing 25 pounds or more.

WORKING CONDITIONS

High noise levels, hot, must be able to lift 25+ pounds.

JOB DESCRIPTION: CASHIER

Job Title: **Cashier**

Company Job Code: _____   FLSA Status: _____

Division/Department: _____   EEO Code: _____

Reports to: _____

Salary Grade/Band: _____   Last Revision Date: _____

SUMMARY

Collects payments of guest checks from servers and/or guests. Ensures accurate accounting of all transactions, collections and disbursements.

PRIMARY RESPONSIBILITIES

1. Receives cash drawer at beginning of work shift and counts money in drawer at beginning and ending of shift to verify its accuracy.

2. Itemizes and totals food and beverage orders or rings food and beverage checks into register. Collects cash, check or credit payment from guest; makes change for cash transactions; checks identification for personal checks; and prepares voucher for credit card purchases.

3. May reconcile checks, cash receipts and charge sales with total sales to verify accuracy of transactions at the end of work shift.

4. Responsibilities may include greeting guests, taking food and beverage orders, and giving them to kitchen staff.

ADDITIONAL RESPONSIBILITIES

All other duties as assigned.

KNOWLEDGE AND SKILL REQUIREMENTS

1. High school graduate or equivalent.

2. Must possess basic math skills and have the ability to handle money accurately.

3. Basic knowledge of the functions of cash registers.

4. Must have ability to remain stationary for periods of up to four hours in length, be able to bend and stoop on occasion, and be able to escort guests to other parts of the facility as circumstances dictate.

WORKING CONDITIONS

High noise levels, hot, must be able to lift 50+ pounds.

JOB DESCRIPTION: COCKTAIL SERVER

Job Title: **Cocktail Server**

Company Job Code:_____ FLSA Status: _____

Division/Department: _____ EEO Code: _____

Reports to:_____

Salary Grade/Band: _____ Last Revision Date: _____

SUMMARY

Primary function is to serve cocktails to the customers in the lounge and dining rooms.

PRIMARY RESPONSIBILITIES

1. Maintain a neat, clean and attractive appearance.

2. Ensure that all customers are relaxed and receptive prior to their meals.

3. Ensure that all customers are served quickly. Always greet customers with a smile and, if possible, by name. Always acknowledge new customers; if you are busy, indicate that you will be with them in a few moments. Place a cocktail napkin in front of each customer; this will indicate that the customer has been waited on.

4. When applicable, suggest the house specialty drinks and appetizers or offer the menu for perusing.

5. Know all bar prices.

6. Write tickets neatly and accurately. Fill in all prices and totals before issuing to the bartender. Make a notation to the bartender when wine is served.

7. Be attentive to your customers. Clean ashtrays and keep the tables and chairs neat and clean. Watch for empty glasses, and politely suggest another drink. Always ask before removing empty glasses.

8. Ensure that all bar tabs are forwarded to the correct dinner check.

9. Always add the cost of cocktails served in the dining room onto the dinner check. It will undoubtedly be an annoyance to the customer to stop eating in order to pay for drinks.

10. Always count out change by repeating the total ticket amount, then "count up": beginning with coins, name each denomination until you reach the amount received.

11. Assist the bartender in any way possible.

12. If age is questionable, check customers' IDs to ensure that they are of legal drinking age.

13. Communicate to coworkers throughout shift.

14. Follow all health and safety regulations prescribed.

15. Follow all restaurant regulations prescribed.

16. Control and limit waste.

17. Communicate problems and ideas to management.

18. Attend all meetings.

19. Fill out all forms as prescribed.

20. Maintain all equipment and tools.

21. Follow all rotation procedures to ensure freshness of products.

22. Follow management's instructions and suggestions.

ADDITIONAL RESPONSIBILITIES

All other duties as assigned.

KNOWLEDGE AND SKILL REQUIREMENTS

1. Must be 21 years of age.

2. Must have at least 1 year of previous serving experience.

WORKING CONDITIONS

High noise levels, must be able to lift 50+ pounds.

JOB DESCRIPTION: COOK

Job Title: **Cook**

Company Job Code: _____ FLSA Status: _____

Division/Department: _____ EEO Code: _____

Reports to: _____

Salary Grade/Band: _____ Last Revision Date: _____

SUMMARY

Primary responsibility is to cook the prepared food items in the prescribed method. Must ensure that all food products have been prepared correctly before cooking.

PRIMARY RESPONSIBILITIES

1. Arrive on time and ready to work.

2. Ensure that proper preparation procedures have been completed.

3. Prepare the cooking areas for the shift.

4. Maintain the highest level of food quality obtainable.

5. Communicate with coworkers, waitstaff and management.

6. Become aware of what is happening in the dining room (e.g., arrival of a large group).

7. Account for every food item used.

8. Maintain a clean and safe kitchen.

9. Follow all health and safety regulations prescribed.

10. Follow all the restaurant regulations prescribed.

11. Control and limit waste.

12. Communicate problems and ideas to management.

13. Attend all meetings.

14. Fill out all forms required.

15. Maintain all kitchen equipment and utensils.

16. Keep every area of the kitchen clean and organized.

17. Follow the proper rotation procedures.

18. Label and date all products used.

ADDITIONAL RESPONSIBILITIES

1. Follow management's instructions and suggestions.

2. All other duties as assigned.

KNOWLEDGE AND SKILL REQUIREMENTS

1. One year of cooking experience and/or associate's degree in culinary arts field.

2. Knife skills.

3. Knowledge of HACCP.

4. Basic cooking knowledge.

WORKING CONDITIONS

High noise levels, hot, must be able to lift 50+ pounds.

JOB DESCRIPTION: COUNTER PERSON

Job Title: **Counter Person**

Company Job Code: _____ FLSA Status: _____

Division/Department: _____ EEO Code: _____

Reports to: _____

Salary Grade/Band: _____ Last Revision Date: _____

SUMMARY

Performs a variety of duties for cafeteria-style service including greeting and serving customers, cold food preparation, stocking counters and steam table.

PRIMARY RESPONSIBILITIES

1. Maintains sanitary standards.

2. Interacts with customers in a friendly and efficient manner.

3. Stocks display refrigerators, salad bar and steam table neatly, accurately and efficiently.

4. Maintains hot or cold temperature conditions as per standards.

5. Maintains appropriate portion control.

6. Cleans tables and chairs, as assigned, by the start of each meal period.

7. Arranges tables and chairs as per diagram.

8. Always checks for salt, pepper and napkins, and stocks accordingly.

9. Cleans equipment, as assigned, thoroughly and in a timely fashion.

10. Keeps floor in work or service area clean and free of debris.

11. Completes shift work, as assigned, timely and thoroughly in accordance with department standards.

ADDITIONAL RESPONSIBILITIES

All other duties as assigned.

KNOWLEDGE AND SKILL REQUIREMENTS

1. High school diploma or equivalent.

2. Demonstrates ability to understand and implement written and verbal instructions.

3. Must be able to lift 25 pounds and stand for periods of up to four hours.

WORKING CONDITIONS

High noise levels, hot, must be able to lift 25+ pounds.

JOB DESCRIPTION: DINING ROOM MANAGER

Job Title: **Dining Room Manager**

Company Job Code: _____   FLSA Status: _____

Division/Department: _____   EEO Code: _____

Reports to: _____

Salary Grade/Band: _____   Last Revision Date: _____

SUMMARY

Oversees dining room and coordinates front-of-the-house food service activities.

PRIMARY RESPONSIBILITIES

1. Maintains operating cost records.

2. Hires, orientates and trains front-of-the-house employees.

3. Conducts performance reviews of front-of-the-house employees.

4. Works with serving staff to ensure quality food and beverage presentation.

5. Ensures proper food-handling procedures.

6. Handles guest complaints.

7. Supervises and trains front-of-the-house employees.

8. Helps plan menus.

9. Monitors budget to ensure efficient operation.

ADDITIONAL RESPONSIBILITIES

All other duties as assigned.

KNOWLEDGE AND SKILL REQUIREMENTS

1. College degree in restaurant/hotel field or equivalent experience.

2. Must be able to speak, read, write and understand the primary language(s) of the work location.

3. Experience in various phases of dining room operation.

4. Must possess a general knowledge of food and beverage procedures and administration.

5. Must be able to lift up to 25 pounds.

6. Highly developed communication skills.

WORKING CONDITIONS

High noise levels, hot, must be able to lift 25+ pounds.

JOB DESCRIPTION: DISHWASHER

Job Title: **Dishwasher**

Company Job Code: _____   FLSA Status: _____

Division/Department: _____   EEO Code: _____

Reports to: _____

Salary Grade/Band: _____   Last Revision Date: _____

SUMMARY

Responsible for supplying spotless, sanitized dishes to the dining room and clean kitchen utensils to the cooks, and for operating dish machine using appropriate supplies and procedures.

PRIMARY RESPONSIBILITIES

1. Correctly operate dish machine.

2. Bus, sort and rack dishes.

3. Place clean dishes in appropriate storage areas.

4. Keep dish area, back kitchen and restrooms clean throughout shift.

5. Empty trash in dish room and kitchen area.

ADDITIONAL RESPONSIBILITIES

All other duties as assigned.

KNOWLEDGE AND SKILL REQUIREMENTS

1. High school diploma.

2. Must be able to speak, read, write and understand the primary language(s) of the work location.

3. Must be able to lift up to 50 pounds.

WORKING CONDITIONS

High noise levels, hot, must be able to lift 50+ pounds.

JOB DESCRIPTION: EXPEDITER

Job Title: **Expediter**

Company Job Code:_____ FLSA Status: _____

Division/Department: _____ EEO Code: _____

Reports to:_____

Salary Grade/Band: _____ Last Revision Date: _____

SUMMARY

Sets the pace and flow in the kitchen. The expediter receives the order ticket from a waiter or waitress or from a printer in the kitchen, and communicates which menu items need to be cooked to the cooking staff.

PRIMARY RESPONSIBILITIES

1. Communicate with everyone in the kitchen.

2. Ensure all food leaving the kitchen is of the level of quality prescribed.

3. Make certain all plates are hot and garnished correctly.

4. Make certain that every food item is accounted for.

5. Safely store all food order tickets for later reference.

6. Fill out all required forms appropriately.

7. Maintain all equipment and utensils.

8. Keep own work area of the kitchen organized.

9. Follow all rotation procedures.

10. Label and date all products used.

11. Follow management's instructions and suggestions.

12. Responsible for laying out and garnishing all the plates.

13. Makes certain that each member of the waitstaff receives the correct plates with the correct items on them.

14. Ensures that every food item that leaves the kitchen has had an order ticket written for it.

ADDITIONAL RESPONSIBILITIES

All other duties as assigned.

KNOWLEDGE AND SKILL REQUIREMENTS

1. Must be able to speak, read, write and understand the primary language(s) of the work location.

2. Must be able to lift up to 50 pounds.

3. At least one year of restaurant kitchen experience.

WORKING CONDITIONS

High noise levels, hot, must be able to lift 50+ pounds.

JOB DESCRIPTION: HOST/HOSTESS

Job Title: **Host/Hostess**

Company Job Code:_____   FLSA Status: _____

Division/Department: _____   EEO Code: _____

Reports to:_____

Salary Grade/Band: _____   Last Revision Date: _____

SUMMARY

Primary responsibilities are to greet and seat guests upon arrival.

PRIMARY RESPONSIBILITIES

1. Assigns service stations to all servers and bus persons.

2. Informs service personnel of menu changes and daily specials.

3. Coordinates the operation of the dining room during meal service periods.

4. Adjusts patron seating flow to balance customers among the various service stations.

5. Graciously greets and seats guests upon arrival.

6. Provides menus to guests.

7. Manages special seating requests of guests consistent with table availability.

8. Relays messages to servers and bus persons as appropriate.

9. Assists with the duties of servers and bus persons as needed.

10. Checks table settings for proper presentation and completeness, and checks service tray stations for adequacy of supplies used for refill or replacement purposes.

ADDITIONAL RESPONSIBILITIES

All other duties as assigned.

KNOWLEDGE AND SKILL REQUIREMENTS

1. High school graduate or equivalent.

2. A minimum of one year of experience in a food service establishment.

3. Ability to stand and walk for periods of up to 4 hours in length.

4. Ability to lift up to 40 pounds.

5. Must be able to speak clearly and listen attentively to guests and other employees.

WORKING CONDITIONS

High noise levels, hot, must be able to lift 40+ pounds.

JOB DESCRIPTION: KITCHEN MANAGER

Job Title: **Kitchen Manager**

Company Job Code:_____   FLSA Status: _____

Division/Department: _____   EEO Code: _____

Reports to:_____

Salary Grade/Band: _____   Last Revision Date: _____

SUMMARY

The primary objective of the kitchen manager is to establish the maximum operational efficiency and food quality of the kitchen. The manager is responsible for all the kitchen personnel and their training. Foremost responsibility is to ensure that all food products are of the highest quality obtainable. Must set an example to other employees through work habits and mannerisms. Must oversee the preparation cooks and ensure that all food products are ordered and accounted for. Also responsible for any breakfast, lunch, brunch or catering functions. Must make certain the kitchen is properly staffed and take any measures needed, including productive shifts, to ensure positive results.

PRIMARY RESPONSIBILITIES

1. Responsible for all personnel in the kitchen.

2. Establishes and delegates work duties in each kitchen area.

3. Responsible for maintaining high food quality.

4. Controls waste and food cost.

5. Ordering, receiving, storing and issuing all food products.

6. Responsible for training of kitchen personnel and maintaining morale of the kitchen staff.

7. Responsible for health and safety regulation enforcement and maintaining a clean and safe kitchen.

8. Communicates possible problem areas to the manager.

9. Schedules all kitchen personnel.

10. Holds kitchen staff meetings.

11. Monitors all food served relative to appearance, temperature, sanitation and quality standards and portion control.

12. Responsible for all meals being served according to the established policies and procedures.

13. Completes all performance evaluations of the employees under the supervision of the position holder.

ADDITIONAL RESPONSIBILITIES

All other duties as assigned.

KNOWLEDGE AND SKILL REQUIREMENTS

1. High school diploma or equivalent.

2. Minimum of two years' experience in the kitchen of a food service facility.

WORKING CONDITIONS

High noise levels, hot, must be able to lift 50+ pounds. Must be able to walk and be on feet for up to 4 hours at a time.

JOB DESCRIPTION: PREP COOK

Job Title: **Prep Cook**

Company Job Code:_____ FLSA Status: _____

Division/Department: _____ EEO Code: _____

Reports to:_____

Salary Grade/Band: _____ Last Revision Date: _____

SUMMARY

Primary responsibility is to prepare food items for cooking in the prescribed method. Must ensure that all food products have been prepared correctly.

PRIMARY RESPONSIBILITIES

1. Prepares all food products according to the prescribed methods.

2. Maintains the highest level of food quality obtainable.

3. Receives and stores all products as prescribed.

4. Maintains a clean and safe kitchen.

5. Follows all health and safety regulations.

6. Follows all restaurant regulations.

7. Controls waste.

8. Communicates all problems and ideas for improvement to management.

9. Communicates and works together with coworkers as a team.

10. Arrives on time and ready to work.

11. Attends all meetings.

12. Fills out all forms as prescribed.

13. Maintains all equipment and utensils.

14. Organizes all areas of the kitchen.

15. Follows proper rotation procedures.

16. Labels and dates all products prepared.

17. Follows management's instructions and suggestions.

ADDITIONAL RESPONSIBILITIES

All other duties as assigned.

KNOWLEDGE AND SKILL REQUIREMENTS

1. High school diploma.

WORKING CONDITIONS

High noise levels, hot, must be able to lift 50+ pounds.

JOB DESCRIPTION: PANTRY COOK

Job Title: **Pantry Cook**

Company Job Code:_____ FLSA Status: _____

Division/Department: _____ EEO Code: _____

Reports to:_____

Salary Grade/Band: _____ Last Revision Date: _____

SUMMARY

Responsible for all cold food item preparation.

PRIMARY RESPONSIBILITIES

1. Portion and prepare cold food items including salads, salad dressings, appetizers and sandwiches using standardized recipes.

2. Maintains a sanitary and clean work area.

3. Washes, peels, slices and mixes vegetables, fruits or other ingredients for salads, cold plates and garnishes.

4. Distributes food to waiters/waitresses to serve to customers.

5. Assists pastry chef when necessary.

ADDITIONAL RESPONSIBILITIES

Performs all other duties as assigned.

KNOWLEDGE AND SKILL REQUIREMENTS

1. High school diploma desired but not essential.

2. Must be able to follow directions for equipment and recipe production.

3. Six months of kitchen experience preferred.

4. Must be able to lift up to 20 pounds and be able to stand and walk for extended periods of time.

WORKING CONDITIONS

High noise levels, hot, must be able to lift 20+ pounds.

JOB DESCRIPTION: SERVER

Job Title: **Server**

Company Job Code:_____ FLSA Status: _____

Division/Department: _____ EEO Code: _____

Reports to:_____

Salary Grade/Band: _____ Last Revision Date: _____

SUMMARY

Responsible for coordinating serving stations and providing customers with quality service.

PRIMARY RESPONSIBILITIES

1. Greet guests and provide them with menu information, including preparation techniques, specials and wine pairings.

2. Communicate with dining room and kitchen personnel.

3. Take food and drink orders using appropriate procedures.

4. Ensure all items are prepared and served accurately.

5. Process guest orders in a timely and accurate fashion.

6. Observe customers to ensure satisfaction.

7. Serve food and beverages according to standard procedures.

8. Total bill and accept payment.

9. Assist bus people and host/hostess.

10. Stock station and perform assigned side duties.

ADDITIONAL RESPONSIBILITIES

All other duties as assigned.

KNOWLEDGE AND SKILL REQUIREMENTS

1. Prefer at least one year of fine-dining serving experience.

2. Must be able to speak, read and understand primary language(s) of work place.

3. Must be able to perform simple math calculations.

4. Must be able to move quickly and stand for up to 4 hours at a time.

5. Must be able to lift trays of up to 25 pounds.

6. Must have customer service experience.

WORKING CONDITIONS

High noise levels, hot, must be able to lift 25+ pounds.

WEAR FOOD-SAFETY EQUIPMENT PROVIDED

LLEVE el EQUIPO de la SEGURIDAD de ALIMENTO PROPORCIONADO

PROPER FOOD STORAGE

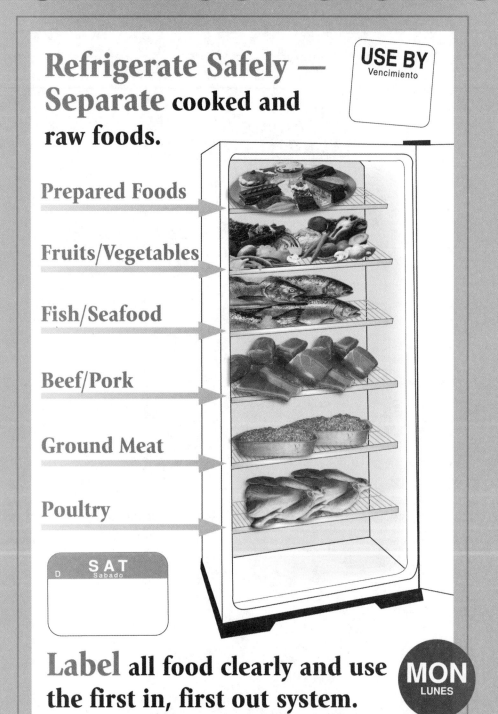

**Refrigerate Safely —
Separate cooked and
raw foods.**

USE BY
Vencimiento

Prepared Foods

Fruits/Vegetables

Fish/Seafood

Beef/Pork

Ground Meat

Poultry

SAT
D Sabado

Label all food clearly and use
the first in, first out system.

MON
LUNES

Call DayMark Food Safety Systems at **1-800-847-0101** for all your
food-safety label needs or visit their Web site at www.dissolveaway.com

ALMACENE ALIMENTO APROPIADAMENTE

COOKING TEMPERATURES

Hold at specified temperature for 15 seconds to kill bacteria.

Poultry 165°F

- Includes chicken, turkey, duck, goose—whole, parts or ground
- Soups, stews, stuffing, casseroles
- Stuffed meat, poultry, fish and pasta
- Leftovers (to reheat)

Ground Beef 155°F

- Hamburger, meatloaf and other ground meats; ground fish
- Fresh shell eggs—cooked and held for service (such as scrambled)

Pork & Fish 145°F

- Pork, ham, beef, corned beef, roasts (hold 4 minutes)
- Beef, lamb, veal, pork (steaks or chops)
- Fish, shellfish
- Fresh shell eggs—broken, cooked and served immediately

Wash and sanitize your thermometer after each use.

Las TEMPERATURAS que COCINAN

DISHWASHING

The correct procedure for manual dishwashing. Use a 3-compartment sink:

1 **Sort** and **Scrape** dishes.

2 **Wash** with detergent in hot water at least 110°F.

3 **Rinse** in clean water to remove detergent.

4 **Sanitize** in hot water 171°F for at least 30 seconds or chemical sanitizer 75°F.

5 **Air Dry.** Do not towel dry.

LAVAR de PLATO

DON'T CONTAMINATE

Use separate cutting boards for raw meats and vegetables.

Store raw meat below all cooked and non-cooked food.

Use different utensils for each type of food. Wash and sanitize after every use.

NO CONTAMINE

Fill glass with finely crushed ice. Add clean tap water to top and stir well.

· · · · · · · · · · · · · · ·

Immerse stem into glass, without touching sides or glass bottom.

· · · · · · · · · · · · · · ·

Wait a minimum of 30 seconds. Check temp.

· · · · · · · · · · · · · · ·

Thermometer should read 32°F. If not, it needs to be adjusted.

· · · · · · · · · · · · · · ·

To adjust, hold the nut under the head of the thermometer with a suitable tool and turn the head so the pointer reads 32°F.

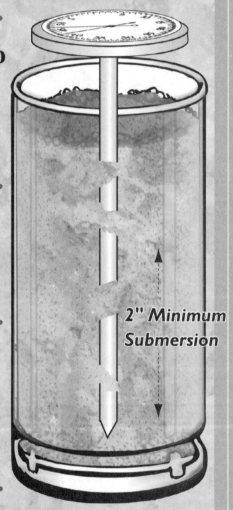

2" Minimum Submersion

FIRST IN, FIRST OUT

Rotate food to prevent food-borne illness and reduce spoilage.

Label the day food was received and when it should be used.

MON
LUNES

SAT
Sabado

Store foods so labels are clearly visible and use products expiring first.

Check food expiration dates and throw away at or before expiration.

ITEM: _____
DATE: _____ QTY: _____
TIME IN: _____ ☐AM USE BY: _____ ☐AM
☐PM ☐PM
START TEMP: _____ 2 HR TEMP: _____
4 HR TEMP: _____ CORRECTIVE ACTION: _____
FRI
Viernes

Call DayMark Food Safety Systems at 1-800-847-0101 for all your food-safety label needs or visit their Web site at www.dissolveaway.com

PRIMERO EN, PRIMERO FUERA

1 **Analyze Hazards.**
Analice los Peligros.

2 **Identify Critical Control Points.** Identifique los Puntos Críticos del Control.

3 **Establish Critical Limits.**
Establezca los Límites Críticos.

4 **Monitor CCPs.**
Controle CCPs.

5 **Establish Corrective Action.**
Establezca la Accione Correctiva.

6 **Keep Records.**
Lleve Registros.

7 **Verify HACCP System.**
Verifique HACCP Sistema.

STEP-BY-STEP HANDWASHING

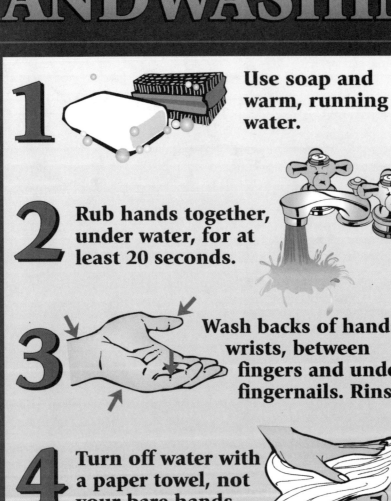

1 Use soap and warm, running water.

2 Rub hands together, under water, for at least 20 seconds.

3 Wash backs of hands, wrists, between fingers and under fingernails. Rinse.

4 Turn off water with a paper towel, not your bare hands.

5 Dry hands with an air dryer or paper towel.

El PASO POR PASO MANO LAVANDO

PERSONAL HYGIENE

Wear hair restraints at all times.

Remove all jewelry including rings, watches, necklaces and earrings.

Uniforms must be neat and clean.

La HIGIENE PERSONAL

KEEP IT CLEAN

1 **Rough Clean.**
Aspero Limpio.

2 **Soap.**
El jabón.

3 **Sanitize.**
Desinfecte.

DISINFECTANT

MANTÉNGALO LIMPIA

SEPARATE, DON'T CONTAMINATE

Keep hot foods

140°F

HOT

41°F

and cold foods

COLD

SEPARADO, NO CONTAMINA

CLEAN UP SPILLS

LIMPIE ROCIE

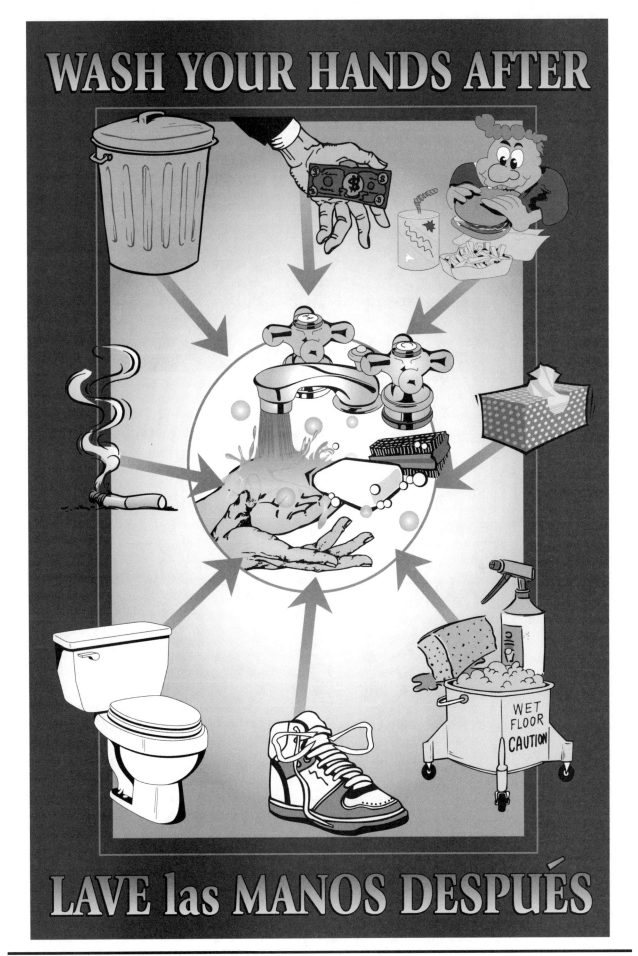

WASH YOUR HANDS AFTER

LAVE las MANOS DESPUÉS

KEEP DOORS & WINDOWS CLOSED

MANTENGA PUERTAS & VENTANAS CERRARON

HACCP PRODUCTS

This section contains a variety of products designed to make implementing an HACCP program easier. They will also help reduce the risk of food-borne illness and contamination. The products are divided into the following categories:

THE SERVSAFE® PROGRAM

The ServSafe® program provides the resources to help keep food safety as an essential ingredient in every meal. ServSafe® training is the one commitment to food safety implementation that we should all share every day.

Atlantic Publishing now carries the complete line of ServSafe® products including instructor guides, answer sheets, instructor slides, manager training and food-safety CD-ROMs and instructor tool kits. Many of the products are available in English and Spanish. Please call 1-800-814-1132 or visit our Web site at **www .atlantic-pub.com** for a complete listing.

ServSafe® Coursebook and Exam Sheet *Third Edition*

Prepare for the ServSafe® Food Protection Manager Certification Exam. This all-inclusive text supplies functional guidance on food quality, maximum storage periods, crisis management, plus helpful resource lists.

English Item # SSC-03 $89.95

ServSafe® Essentials Third Edition

This text covers principles necessary to maintain food safety within your operation and prepares participants for the ServSafe® Food Protection Manager Certification Exam. Content is activity-based, exercise-intensive, and visually engaging. Adapts to one or multiple-day training formats.

English Item # SSE-03 $73.95
Spanish Item # SSE-SP $73.95

Successfully complete the ServSafe® course and receive your industry-recognized certificate!

6-Video or DVD Set: ServSafe® Steps to Food Safety

Video 1: Starting Out with Food Safety

Defines food-borne illness, how foods become unsafe, and what safety practices to follow. *(12 minutes)*

Video 2: Ensuring Proper Personal Hygiene

Introduces employees to ways they might contaminate and thorough hand washing. *(10 minutes)*

Video 3: Purchasing, Receiving and Storage

Explains how to choose a supplier, calibrate and use a thermometer properly, deliveries, and food storage. *(12 minutes)*

Video 4: Preparing, Cooking and Serving

Identifies proper practices for thawing, cooking, holding, serving, cooling and reheating food. *(11 minutes)*

Video 5: Cleaning and Sanitizing

Describes the proper procedures for cleaning and sanitizing. *(10 minutes)*

Video 6: Take the Food Safety Challenge

Identify good and bad practices presented in five short scenarios from different industry segments. *(45 minutes)*

DVD—English & Spanish Item # SSS-DVD $580.00 (Both versions on one DVD)
VHS Video—English & Spanish Item # SSS-V1 $580.00 (Both versions on one)

KITCHEN SAFETY LABELS

SAFETY & SANITATION LABELS

These self-adhesive, pressure-sensitive and washable labels will further enforce your food safety program. Each comes as a set of five labels. Labels contain both English and Spanish.

Wash Hands Before Handling Food	Item # WHB-LB (Set of Five)	$9.95	No Smoking	Item # NS-LB (Set of Five)	$9.95
Wash, Rinse, Sanitize Label	Item # WRS-LB (Set of Five)	$9.95	Caution HOT	Item # HOT-LB (Set of Five)	$9.95

HAND WASHING

GloGerm Sanitation Training Kit

Use this NEW training kit to train employees in proper hand-washing techniques. The kit includes a lotion and powder which contain "plastic germs" that glow when exposed to UV light. Demonstrate proper hand-washing techniques by applying the lotion to employees' hands. After normal hand washing, expose their hands to the UV light; it will expose the areas the employees missed. Use the powder to demonstrate proper surface cleaning. Each kit includes GloGerm oil, GloGerm powder, battery-operated UV light stick, batteries and carrying case.

GloGerm Sanitation Training Kit Item # GLO-03 $47.95
GloGerm Replacement Lotion 8 oz. Item # GGO-03 $16.95
GloGerm Replacement Powder Item # GGP-03 $14.95

Hand & Nailbrush Kit

Works better than soap and water alone for cleaning under fingernails where bacteria, dirt and other contaminants can become trapped. Promotes vital cleansing of hands for food service personnel. Includes a 5" x 2" brush, cord to secure the brush in place, hanging hook, and an adhesive-backed hand-washing instruction decal in English and Spanish.

Item #	Description	Price
HNK-03	Brush Kit	$13.95
HNB-03	Brush w/ Polyester Bristles	$7.95
HNL-03	36" Coiled Security Line	$3.95
HNH-03	Brush Hook Only	$3.95

To order call 1-800-814-1132, or shop online at atlantic-pub.com

SOFTWARE

The Food and Drug Administration's (FDA) Food Code CD-ROM 2004-2005

This is a compendium of model food safety guidelines for food service operations based on the latest science. The Food Code, endorsed by the USDA's Food Safety and Inspection Service and the CDC, contains the latest FDA advice on preventing food-borne disease in restaurants. It has requirements for safeguarding public health to ensure that consumers' food is safe. The model is used as a reference by the more than 3,000 state and local regulatory agencies. The CD-ROM also contains two manuals not found in the printed version: Draft for Managing Food Safety: A HACCP Principles Guide for Operators of Food Service; and the Plan Review Manual (Adobe Acrobat Reader is included to view and search the CD-ROM). PC-compatible: Windows 3.1 or higher, Windows NT; Macintosh: System 7; 4.5MB hard disk space required and a CD-ROM drive.

Item # FC-CS $99.95

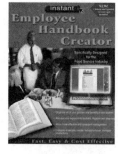

Employee Handbook Creator Guide

A cost-effective solution for developing your own employee handbook. Simply review the 100+ policies already written, and insert your own information when prompted. Complete with table of contents, introduction and a form for each employee to sign. Topics on the companion CD-ROM include federal labor laws, non-discrimination, age requirements, orientation period, training, evaluations, schedules, overtime, standards of conduct, harassment, absences, tardiness, resignations, payment procedures, tip reporting, benefits, vacations, holidays, workers' compensation, employee meals, employee safety, management/employee relations, sanitation, dress code, accidents and emergencies, alcohol serving policy, confidential information, solicitation, and more. Use with Windows and any word processor, IBM-compatible.

Item # EHB-CS SALE $59.95

VIDEOS

CertiSafe Food Safety Training Videos

Developed from a chef's perspective, this training program is designed as an introductory program for new employees and as a refresher course. Contains detailed instructions on hand washing, cross-contamination, heating and cooling of foods, temperature danger zones, thawing, storage, and cleaning procedures. Includes on-screen questions and a companion test and study guide. 35 minutes. English and Spanish versions available.

English with companion materials Item # CSV-V1 $69.95
Spanish with companion materials Item # CSV-SP $69.95

Changing the Future of Food Safety!

This training kit covers the basics of food protection in a retail food service kitchen with a humorous approach that engages the workers. The core of the program is a five-part videotape (10 minutes each), set in an actual commercial kitchen. The modules follow the staff as they learn how food-borne illness is caused and how to prevent it. Includes a guide for trainers, handouts for workers, posters for the kitchen, and tests for each module.

English Item # FSF-V1 $149.95 • Spanish Item # FSP-V1 $149.95

KITCHEN SAFETY

Kolor-Cutting Board System

A food-safety cutting board system focused on reducing cross-contamination. Never gamble on the safety or durability of another cutting board. Select new and improved Kolor-Cut Extra, featuring improved durability and heat resistance while reducing cross-contamination with dedicated color-coded cutting boards. Features added toughness against cut-grooving, marring, scarring; will not dull knives; heat resistant to 185°F without warpage; cold resistant to -40°F; steam-cleanable, dishwasher safe; non-porous; non-absorbent boards carry NSF logo emboss for all to see; helpful "kitchen-proof" wall chart FREE with each 6-board combo set.

12 x 18 set of six boards/Chart: White - Dairy; Green - Fruits & Vegetables; Yellow - Poultry; Blue - Cooked Foods; Red - Meat; Beige - Fish. Includes wall chart. **Item # CB-1218-KC $99.95**

18 x 24 set of six boards/Chart: White - Dairy; Green - Fruits & Vegetables; Yellow - Poultry; Blue - Cooked Foods; Red - Meat; Beige - Fish. Includes wall chart. **Item # CB-1824-KC $199.00**

Heavy-Duty Storage Stand **Item # KLR-ST $59.95**

Litmus Paper Test Kit (Chlorine)

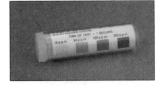

Simply use the chemically treated paper strips as a quick and easy test for sanitizer strength. Strips and color chart come supplied in a waterproof plastic vial. 100 test strips per vial. Sold in a set of three vials per pack (three test kits, 300 strips total).

Item # LPT-03 $9.95

Cool Cooked Foods Fast!

Drops temperature fast to prevent bacterial growth. Just fill with water and freeze! Quickly cools sauces, soups and stews for safer storage in your freezer or cooler. Wide mouth for easy filling. Includes 2 heavy-duty caps. Easy-to-clean, dishwasher safe, NSF-listed.

(2-Liter) Item # FLC-02 $27.95
(4-Liter) Item # FLC-04 $37.95

Gloves

This new cut-resistant glove provides outstanding protection against cuts and lacerations. Utilizes a high-tensile stainless steel core, encapsulated to prevent fractures and breakage. All materials are USDA-accepted. Easy to launder (single glove).

Small **Item # CRG-SM $19.95**		Large **Item # CRG-LG $19.95**	
Medium **Item # CRG-MD $19.95**		X-Large **Item # CRG-XL $19.95**	

Cutting Board Scraper

This new tool is an easy, convenient way to remove cuts from plastic cutting boards. Keep boards in perfect shape by removing bacteria harboring scratches and cuts. Dishwasher safe, one-piece plastic handle. Replaceable blade available.

Item #	Description	Price
CBS-03	Cutting Board Scraper	$29.95
CBR-03	Cutting Board Replacement Blade	$9.95

SAF-T-ICE Scoop Caddie

Keep the ice scoop safe from bacteria, dirt and ice burial — designed to meet Board of Health guidelines everywhere. Features ribbed bottom to keep scoop edge dry; convenient hinged lid that covers scoop and allows for easy access. Easy-to-install bracket mounts with self-adhesive strips for screws. Dishwasher safe. Tough HDPE plastic construction. **Item # SI-2000 $23.95**

SAF-T-ICE Funnel

Loads ice bucket faster, safer and with less mess. Saf-T-Ice Funnel provides a fast, safe, efficient way to fill Saf-T-Ice Totes. Made of tough, dishwasher-safe, high-density plastic. Fits easily over Saf-T-Totes. **Item # SI-3000 $49.95**

SAF-T-ICE Tote

Saf-T-Ice Totes helps you control ice transfer cross-contamination! Made of tough, transparent, durable polycarbonate. Will not nest, keeping dirt and bacteria from being transmitted by stacking. Six-gallon size keeps the carrying weight at safe levels. Features a stainless steel bail handle for easy carrying/emptying. Meets health department requirements for dedicated food service containers. Dishwasher-safe.

Item # SI-6000 (pack of 2) $79.95

Scoops

The easy-to-grip-and-hold sanitary plastic handle transfers less cold to hands. Features a hole for connecting to ice machine. Durable polycarbonate material. The 6-oz scoop is tapered to make pouring of ice into glasses easy and eliminate glass chipping.

6-oz Scoop	Item # SC6-06	$4.25
32-oz Scoop	Item # SC32-32	$7.99
64-oz Scoop	Item # SC64-64	$8.99

Shortening Monitor Kit (Deep Fryer)

The convenient, objective test for determining fryer oil breakdown. Now you will know exactly when to replace or discard fryer oil. Simply dip the paper test strip into heated fryer oil for 2 seconds, and 15 seconds later, the strip can be evaluated with the accompanying guide. Contains 40 test kit strips. **Item # SMK-03 $49.95**

Fridge-Kare

Control and improve air quality of walk-in/reach-in coolers with Fridge-Kare. The self-contained power of Fridge-Kare cleanses cooler air, improves operating efficiency, lowers relative humidity, lowers average cooler temperature, reduces energy consumption, reduces mold and bacteria generation, eliminates or greatly reduces odor transfer, and extends food shelf life of all perishables. One Fridge-Kare effectively treats 250 cubic feet for up to six months. **Fridge-Kare (1) Item # FK-1000 $24.50**

To order call 1-800-814-1132, or shop online at atlantic-pub.com

THERMOMETERS

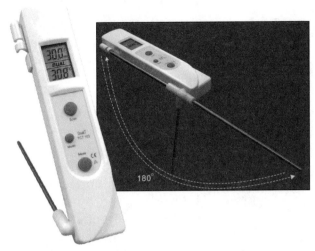

ThermaTwin Infrared Thermometer

Our ThermaTwin is the ultimate tool for temperature measurements. This one thermometer contains both the Non-Contact Infrared Sensor (Micro Machining Thermopile) and the tough Teflon-coated thermocouple probe. Now one thermometer does the job of two for a price lower than any infrared thermometer. Easy to use and carry, point-and-shoot instant results allow you to quickly access temperature information. Features FDA Class II laser with 4:1 optics and 7-second temperature hold. Durable and compact. Battery included. NIST traceable; certificate of calibration; max, min and lock modes (infrared); compact (designed to fit into shirt pocket); lightweight (uses an inexpensive watch battery); auto power off.   **Item # TTT-03 $99.95**

Hanging Dial Thermometers

Hangs or stands in refrigerator, freezer, holding oven or oven.

Refrigerator/Freezer -20°F to 80°F	Item # RF-TM	$7.95
Oven 200°F to 600°F	Item # OV-TM	$7.95
Holding Oven 100°F to 175°F	Item # HO-TM	$7.95

Digital Pen-Style Thermometer

Makes quick temperature checks simple. Pen-style digital test thermometer has a built-in shirt clip and easy-to-read display. Probe cover can be used as an extended handle. -40°F to 390°F. Uses 1.5-volt battery (included).   **Item # DPT-TM $29.95**

Dishwasher Thermometer

Designed to read and hold the highest temperature to which it is exposed. Will hold its temperature until mercury is shaken down. 0°F to 220°F (-17°C to 104°C). **Item # DWT-TM $34.95**

Cooling Thermometer

The 18" stem reaches deep into large pots recording center temperatures. HACCP guidelines are indicated on the dial for easy reference and instructions. The vessel clip frees hands for stirring. 2-1/2" dial. Range of 30°F to 165°F.   **Item # CTC-TM $29.95**

T-Stick Disposable Thermometers

Disposable sensors give accurate reads in 5 seconds. Recordable with time, date and initial space on back of each stick. Use T-Stick 160 for testing dishwasher rinse water. Simply place on a fork as shown at right. For states requiring 170°F, use T-Stick 170.

Item #	Count	Description	Price
TST-9342	500 Cnt.	140°F Tub	$89.95
TST-9344	500 Cnt.	160°F Tub	$89.95
TST-9346	500 Cnt.	170°F Tub	$89.95

To order call 1-800-814-1132, or shop online at atlantic-pub.com

SANITATION & SAFETY POSTERS

These eye-catching posters help you ensure compliance with FDA/USDA regulations and best food safety practices. Now you can make sure your employees are aware of critical regulatory requirements and best practices with this high-quality, affordable poster series. Display these posters in key work areas and important food-safety messages will be continually reinforced, even when your quality manager is not in the work area. Posters include a message in both English and Spanish so critical safety concepts can be understood by more employees. Each 11" W x 27" L, easy-to-read poster is built to last, featuring heavy, 3-mil lamination with sealed edges to protect against damage from the work environment. Set of 16.   **Item # FSP-PS $99.95**

SEPARATE, DON'T CONTAMINATE

Stresses the proper temperatures for both hot and cold foods.

Item # FSP13-PS $8.95

KEEP IT CLEAN

Shows employees the three basic steps to maintaining a sanitary workplace.

Item # FSP14-PS $8.95

7 PRINCIPLES OF HACCP

An excellent reference for the seven main HACCP points.

Item # FSP15-PS $8.95

PROPER FOOD STORAGE

Illustrates correct refrigeration techniques and proper labeling and food rotation.

Item # FSP16-PS $8.95

WASH YOUR HANDS

Illustrated to show handwashing essentials.

Item # FSP1-PS $8.95

STEP-BY-STEP HANDWASHING

Demonstrates the five essential handwashing steps.

Item # FSP2-PS $8.95

WASH YOUR HANDS AFTER

Shows employees eight key activities to wash hands after.

Item # FSP3-PS $8.95

DON'T CONTAMINATE

Features crucial tips on avoiding contamination and food-borne illness.

Item # FSP4-PS $8.95

PERSONAL HYGIENE

Focuses on hair restraints, removing jewelry and cleanliness.

Item # FSP5-PS $8.95

CALIBRATE THERMOMETERS

Easy-to-understand instructions for keeping thermometers accurate.

Item # FSP6-PS $8.95

COOKING TEMPERATURES

For various types of food.

Item # FSP7-PS $8.95

DISHWASHING

Illustrates the proper technique for manual dishwashing.

Item # FSP8-PS $8.95

WEAR FOOD SAFETY EQUIPMENT

Reminds employees to utilize safety items.

Item # FSP9-PS $8.95

FIRST IN, FIRST OUT

Focuses on proper labeling and food rotation.

Item # FSP10-PS $8.95

CLEAN UP SPILLS

Emphasizes the importance of sanitation and cleanliness.

Item # FSP11-PS $8.95

KEEP DOORS & WINDOWS CLOSED

Helps maintain a safe working environment.

Item # FSP12-PS $8.95

To order call 1-800-814-1132, or shop online at atlantic-pub.com

WORKPLACE SAFETY POSTERS

Communicate important information to your employees by posting these colorful, four-color informative Safety and Human Resource posters throughout your workplace. Each poster is 11" x 17" and is laminated for long-term protection. Buy individually or the full set and save. Posters are available in English or Spanish.

Topics include: First Aid For Burns, First Aid For Cuts & Wounds, First Aid For Choking, Proper Lifting, Emergency Phone Numbers, Drug-Free Workplace, Fire Extinguisher Use, CPR Guidelines, Falling, and Sexual Harassment.

English (All 10 Posters) • Item # WPP-PS $79.95   Spanish (All 10 Posters) • Item # WPPSP-PS $79.95

ENGLISH

First Aid For Burns...Item # FAB-PS $8.98
First Aid For Cuts & Wounds ....Item # FAC-PS $8.98
First Aid For Choking ....Item # FACH-PS $8.98
Safety - Lift It Properly...Item # SLP-PS $8.98
Safety - First Aid Emergency Phone #s..................Item # SFA-PS $8.98
Safety - Drug-Free Workplace...............................Item # SDF-PS $8.98
Safety - Fire Extinguisher Poster...........................Item # SFE-PS $8.98
Safety - CPR Guidelines...Item # SCP-PS $8.98
Safety - Slip, Trip & Fall ....Item # SST-PS $8.98
Sexual Harassment...Item # SX-PS $8.98

SPANISH

First Aid For Burns...Item # FABSP-PS $8.98
First Aid For Cuts & Wounds ....Item # FACSP-PS $8.98
First Aid For Choking ....Item # FACHSP-PS $8.98
Safety - Lift It Properly...Item # SLPSP-PS $8.98
Safety - First Aid Emergency Phone #s..................Item # SFASP-PS $8.98
Safety - Drug-Free Workplace...............................Item # SDFSP-PS $8.98
Safety - Fire Extinguisher Poster...........................Item # SFESP-PS $8.98
Safety - CPR Guidelines...Item # SCPSP-PS $8.98
Safety - Slip, Trip & Fall ....Item # SSTSP-PS $8.98
Sexual Harassment...Item # SXSP-PS $8.98

2005 Federal Law Poster

Newly Revised! The most comprehensive Federal Labor Laws Poster available, including new 2004 overtime laws. The poster provides coverage for all five mandatory federal labor law posting requirements. Posters are laminated to reduce wear and tear and measure 17" x 25".

English Item # FLLEN-PS $29.95
Spanish Item # FLLSP-PS $29.95

DISSOLVE-A-WAY® LABELS

Labels Dissolve In Water In Less Than 30 Seconds!

Before water is
applied

5-12 seconds after
water is applied

12-30 seconds
after water is
applied

Features:

- Labels dissolve in any water temperature in under 30 seconds.

- Labels will not leave any sticky residue, which can harbor harmful bacteria.

- Labels are biodegradable.

- FDA-compliant for indirect food contact.

Benefits:

- Labels adhere to plastic and stainless steel containers, yet easily

rinse away when pans are washed.

- Great for prep pans—no more scrubbing!

DISSOLVE-A-WAY® LABELS

2.5"

#110062 (Specify Day)
125 labels/roll

1" x 1.5"

#110081 (Specify Day)
250 labels/roll

1"

Use By #110073
(Specify Day)
500 labels/roll

7/8 x 1 1/4"

Economy #110029 (Specify Day)
1,000 labels/roll

2"

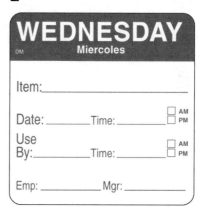

#110053 (Specify Day)
250 labels/roll

DISSOLVE-A-WAY® SHELF LIFE LABELS

2"

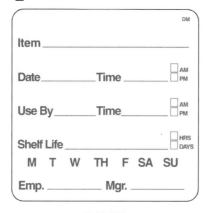

#112437
250 labels/roll

2" x 4"

Item		
Date	Time	☐ AM ☐ PM
Use By	Time	☐ AM ☐ PM
Shelf Life	Days	☐ HRS ☐ DAYS
M	T	W	TH	F	SA	SU
Emp.	Mgr.	

#110084 • *125 labels/roll*

HACCP PRODUCTS

MOVEMARK® REMOVABLE LABELS

2"
Item #0035 500 labels/roll

Best Used For:

Use MoveMark™ Removable Day-of-the-Week and Shelf Life labels in your kitchen when you need to easily and cleanly remove labels from metal and/or plastic containers.

Features:

- No residue after removal (remove before washing).

- Works well in walk-in coolers and freezers.

- Great for food containers in coolers, freezers and dry storage.

- Aggressive in the freezer, yet removes easily at room temperature.

- Minimum application range of 15°F (-10°C).

- Working temperature range of -20°F to 160°F (-29°C to -71°C).

3" Circle
Item #0108 500 labels/roll

Benefits:

- Reduce labor time spent in removing old label residue.

- Improve your bottom line by preventing food waste.

Available Sizes:

- 3/4"
- 1" x 2"
- 2.5"
- 3" x 4.5"
- 1"
- 2"
- 3" Circle

2.5" Item #0061 250 labels/roll

To order call 1-800-847-0101 or online at www.daymark.biz

REMARK® REPOSITIONABLE LABELS

How To Use:

Label prepped items with product name, prep date and employee initials. Re-label products once removed from original containers or packaging. Indicate the preparation, thaw or use-by date on ready-to-eat foods. Remove label before washing container or pan.

Features:

- Can be repositioned on the same pan or put on another pan when transferring food.

- Excellent for HACCP records.

- Remove the label from the old container.

- Place it on the new container.

- Pour food from the old container to the new container.

Benefits:

- Safe alternative to masking tape— no sticky residue!

- Specially designed for food safety.

Available In:

- 1" x 3" Food Safety Labels
- 1" x 3" Day-of-the-Week Labels
- 1" x 3" Use-By Labels
- 2" x 3" Label
- 2" x 4" Label
- 3" x 5" Label

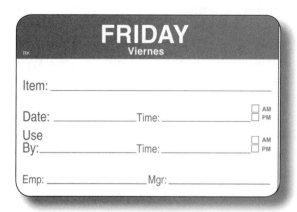

2" x 3"   **Item #2467**
500 labels/roll

Remove...

Place...

Pour

To order call 1-800-847-0101 or online at www.daymark.biz

DATE CODING MARKERS–MACHINE-APPLIED LABELS

Best Used For:

Marking item and date information on high volumes of prepared, pre-portioned product.

Features:

- Fast and efficient date coding.

- Instantly print labels where you need them—dry storage, produce, prep, cooler, freezer.

- Many label colors, styles, sizes and adhesives.

Benefits:

- No more hard-to-read handwritten tapes and labels.

- DayMark® Date Coding Markers pay for themselves in just one week.

- Writing on masking tape and labels wastes 520 hours a year.

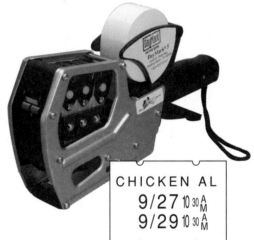

Available In:

- 1 Line Marker (DM3)
- 2 Line Marker (DM4)
- 3 Line Marker (DM5)
- Prep/Use-By Marker (DM4.5)
- XL 2-Line Marker

Machine-applied labels are available in the following adhesives:

- DissolveMark™ (Dissolve-A-Way®)
- MoveMark™ (Removable)
- DuraMark™ (Permanent)
- CoolMark™ (Freezable)

To order call 1-800-847-0101 or online at www.daymark.biz

COOLMARK® FREEZABLE LABELS

Features:

- Aggressive adhesive sticks to any packaging surface.

- Working temperature range of -65°F to 160°F (-54°C to 72°C).

- CoolMark™ solves the common problem of using labels that do not stick after being frozen.

- Labels can be applied to frozen packaging.

- Available in both hand-applied and machine-applied labels.

Benefits:

- Adheres to all frozen food packaging.

- Great for frozen containers, boxes and cryovac bags.

- No ice "barrier" between the label and the packaging surface.

- CoolMark™ labels feature easy-to-read, pre-printed text.

- Marks dates and times for pulling, thawing and use-by dates.

Available Sizes:

- 2"
- 1" x 2"
- 2" x 3"
- DM3 (1-Line) date coding marker labels

Available in both hand-applied and machine-applied labels.

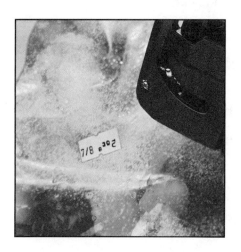

TIMESTRIP™ LABELS

Features:

- Disposable "visual alarm clock."

- Color advances to show expiration.

- Stand-alone removable adhesive strip can be applied right on food packages.

- Comes in 2-, 3- and 5-day time progression strips.

Benefits:

- New way to monitor food freshness.

- Hi-tech yet simple.

- No more confusion about use by date.

- Saves money—food used before its expiration date.

- Prevent illness—food is discarded when it is not safe for consumption.

- Perfect for use on costly, perishable items.

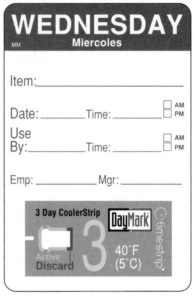

Companion labels also available
2" x 3"   #112862   *500 labels/roll*

Actual size labels (1.5" x .75")

2 Day	#112770	*100 per pack*
3 Day	#112771	*100 per pack*
5 Day	#112772	*100 per pack*

To order call 1-800-847-0101 or online at www.daymark.biz

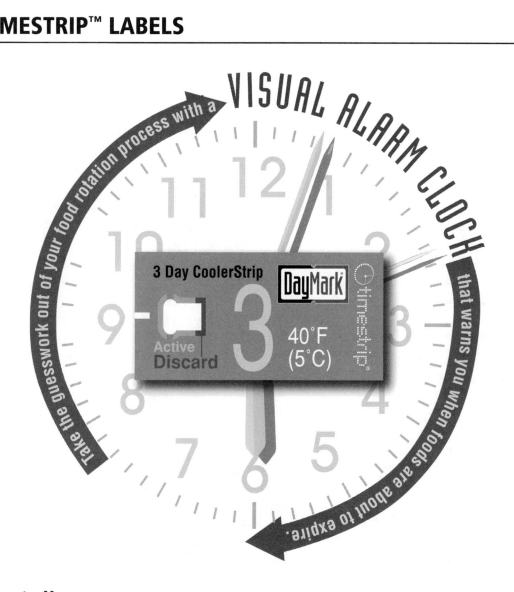

How to Use

- Peel off the backing paper.

- Squeeze the bubble on the back. Red will appear to show that the coolerstrip is activated.

- Apply TimeStrip to the companion label or directly to the packaged food.

- The first window will show that its activated.

- The red band of color will gradually travel across the white space as time elapses.

- When the red band completely covers the white area, discard the food.

To order call 1-800-847-0101 or online at www.daymark.biz

PORTION BAGS

How To Use:

Measure exact amount of food and place in pre-portion bag. Streamline the process by using a saddle-pack dispenser. Mark bag with the date of pre-portioning. Include weight or size of portion when appropriate. Store pre-portioned items close to workstations for increased worker efficiency.

Benefits:

* Heat-resistant ink.

* Micowaveable and freezable.

* High-density polyethylene (HDPE) bags can withstand moist heat up to 220°F.

* Saddle-pack dispensing.

* White writing area (Day-of-the Week and UseBy bags only).

* Proper rotation is ensured.

* Facilitates exact portioning and measurement.

* Easy-to-close, flip-lock top.

* Safe for use in the microwave, boiling water and steamer.

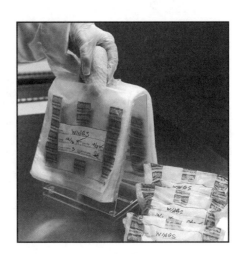

Features:

* Pre-portioning controls food costs and saves time during peak business hours.

* Ideal for seafood, poultry, meats and cut or prepared vegetables.

* Portion bags are saddle-packed for dispensing.

HACCP TEST

The following questions can be used to test employees on HACCP competency. The answer key follows along with a certifcate for successfully completing the HACCP exam.

MULTIPLE CHOICE

1. Most disease-causing bacteria grow between the temperatures of _____.
   a. 32°F and 65°F
   b. 41°F and 140°F
   c. 70°F and 135°F
   d. 100°F and 155°F

2. Bacteria only need _____ to reproduce enough cells to cause a food-borne illness.
   a. 2 hours
   b. 4 hours
   c. 6 hours
   d. 8 hours

3. CCP is short for _____.
   a. crucial control point
   b. critical control place
   c. critical counter point
   d. critical control point

4. The four growth phases of bacteria are:
   a. rapid, stationary and death
   b. lag, log and death
   c. lag, log, stationary and death
   d. lag, rapid, stationary and death

5. Approximately every _____ the bacteria count will double under optimal conditions.
   a. 15 minutes
   b. 45 minutes
   c. 60 minutes
   d. 75 minutes

6. Which of the following is not a symptom of a food-borne illness?
   a. nausea
   b. diarrhea
   c. fever
   d. sneezing

7. Which agency is responsible for inspecting domestic and imported meats, poultry and processed meats?
   a. USDA
   b. FDA
   c. EPA
   d. CDC

8. Which agency enforces health standards and work-related safety regulations?
    a. EPA
    b. U.S. Department of Commerce
    c. OSHA
    d. CDC

9. The health department will inspect a food operation at least once _____.
    a. every week
    b. every month
    c. every 6 months
    d. every year

10. Most potentially hazardous foods should be kept at a temperature of _____ or below when received.
    a. 32°F
    b. 41°F
    c. 65°F

11. All shelving units should be kept _____ from floors and walls.
    a. 4 inches
    b. 6 inches
    c. 8 inches
    d. 12 inches

12. Hot food must be held at _____.
    a. 120°F
    b. 135°F
    c. 155°F
    d. 165°F

13. Reheated foods must be reheated to _____.
    a. 120°F
    b. 135°F
    c. 155°F
    d. 165°F

14. Potentially hazardous foods must finish the cooling process within _____.
    a. 2 hours
    b. 4 hours
    c. 6 hours
    d. 8 hours

15. Food should be discarded if it exceeds _____ during cold prep or serving.
    a. 41°F
    b. 55°F
    c. 65°F
    d. 70°F

16. An estimated _____ cases of food-borne disease occur each year in the United States.
    a. 1 million
    b. 9 million
    c. 34 million
    d. 76 million

17. Which of the following is not a measurement for monitoring critical control points?
    a. visual
    b. taste
    c. time
    d. temperature

18. HACCP is a _____ system.
    a. reactive
    b. preventive
    c. ineffective

19. What is the proper method of rotation of stored food called?
    a. HACCP
    b. CCP
    c. FIFO

20. What is the temperature range of fresh meat and poultry?
    a. 31°–35°F
    b. 33°–38°F
    c. 40°–60°F
    d. 45°–55°F

21. Bacteria grow best in foods that are in the pH range of _____.
    a. 0.0–4.6
    b. 2.6–8.0
    c. 4.6–7.0
    d. 5.0–9.6

22. Shell stock tags must be kept on-site for _____.
    a. 1 week
    b. 30 days
    c. 60 days
    d. 90 days

FILL IN THE BLANK

23. List the seven principles of HACCP.

    1. _____

    2. _____

    3. _____

    4. _____

    5. _____

    6. _____

    7. _____

24. FATTOM is an acronym for _____ _____.

25. List at least five factors contributing to food-borne illness.

    1. _____

    2. _____

    3. _____

    4. _____

    5. _____

26. What are the two types of thermometer calibration methods?

    1. _____

    2. _____

27. List at least three activities after which employees should wash their hands.

    1. _____

    2. _____

    3. _____

28. List at least three methods of cooling foods.

1. _____

2. _____

3. _____

29. What does MSDS stand for?

_____

TRUE/FALSE

30. Raising the pH in foods may render them non-potentially hazardous.
True
False

31. Only kitchen staff needs to be trained in HACCP principles.
True
False

32. Anaerobic bacteria must have oxygen in order to grow.
True
False

33. Choosing a reputable pest-control operator is an essential component of a HACCP plan.
True
False

34. CCPs are points in the process where bacteria or other harmful organisms may grow or food may become contaminated.
True
False

35. HACCP involves eight principles.
True
False

MATCHING

Match with correct definition. List the letter of the correct definition next to the word below.

Bacteria _____

Contamination _____

Cross-Contamination _____

Corrective Action _____

Critical Control Point _____

Critical Limit _____

Food-Borne Illness _____

Food-Borne Outbreak _____

HACCP Plan _____

HACCP System _____

Hazard _____

Microorganism _____

Monitoring _____

Operational Step _____

Parasite _____

Pathogen _____

Record _____

Risk _____

Toxin _____

Virus _____

a.   Living single-cell organisms.

b.   A measurable limit at a CCP that can be monitored to control the identified hazard to a safe level in the food.

c.   The unintended presence of potentially harmful substances, including microorganisms, chemicals and physical objects in food.

d.   An activity that is taken by a person whenever a critical limit is not met.

e.   A protein-wrapped genetic material which is the smallest and simplest life-form known.

f.   A biological, physical or chemical property that may cause a food to be unsafe for human consumption.

g.   The occurrence of two or more people experiencing the same illness after eating the same food.

h.   The transfer of harmful substances or disease-causing microorganisms to food by hands, food-contact surfaces, sponges, cloth towels and utensils that touch raw food, are not cleaned, and then touch ready-to-eat foods.

i.   A poisonous substance that may be found in food.

j.   The result of implementing the HACCP principles in an operation that has a foundational, comprehensive, prerequisite program in place.

k. A form of life that can be seen only with a microscope; including bacteria, viruses, yeast and single-celled animals.

l. The act of observing and making measurements to help determine if critical limits are being met and maintained.

m. An operational step or procedure in a process, production method, or recipe, at which control can be applied to prevent, reduce or eliminate a food safety hazard.

n. A documentation of monitoring observation and verification activities.

o. A written document which is based on the principles of HACCP and which describes the procedures to be followed to ensure the control of a specific process or procedure.

p. An organism that grows, feeds and is sheltered on or in a different organism and contributes to its host.

q. A microorganism that is infectious and causes disease.

r. An estimate of the likely occurrence of a hazard.

s. Sickness resulting from acquiring a disease that is carried or trans-

mitted to humans by food containing harmful substances.

t. An activity in a food establishment, such as receiving, storage, preparation, cooking, etc.

HACCP TEST ANSWER KEY

MULTIPLE CHOICE

1. Most disease-causing bacteria grow between the temperatures of _____.
    a. 32°F and 65°F
    b. 41°F and 140°F
    c. 70°F and 135°F
    d. 100°F and 155°F

2. Bacteria only need _____ to reproduce enough cells to cause a food-borne illness.
    a. 2 hours
    b. 4 hours
    c. 6 hours
    d. 8 hours

3. CCP is short for _____
    a. crucial control point
    b. critical control place
    c. critical counter point
    d. critical control point

4. The four growth phases of bacteria are:
    a. rapid, stationary and death
    b. lag, log and death
    c. lag, log, stationary and death
    d. lag, rapid, stationary and death

5. Approximately every _____ the bacteria count will double under optimal conditions.
    a. 15 minutes
    b. 45 minutes
    c. 60 minutes
    d. 75 minutes

6. Which of the following is not a symptom of a food-borne illness?
    a. nausea
    b. diarrhea
    c. fever
    d. sneezing

7. Which agency is responsible for inspecting domestic and imported meats, poultry and processed meats?
    a. USDA
    b. FDA
    c. EPA
    d. CDC

8. Which agency enforces health standards and work-related safety regulations?
    a. EPA
    b. U.S. Department of Commerce
    c. OSHA
    d. CDC

9. The health department will inspect a food operation at least once _____.
    a. every week
    b. every month
    c. every 6 months
    d. every year

10. Most potentially hazardous foods should be kept at a temperature of _____ or below when received.
    a. 32°F
    b. 41°F
    c. 65°F

11. All shelving units should be kept _____ from floors and walls.
    a. 4 inches
    b. 6 inches
    c. 8 inches
    d. 12 inches

12. Hot food must be held at _____.
    a. 120°F
    b. 135°F
    c. 155°F
    d. 165°F

13. Reheated foods must be reheated to _____.
    a. 120°F
    b. 135°F
    c. 155°F
    d. 165°F

14. Potentially hazardous foods must finish the cooling process within _____.
    a. 2 hours
    b. 4 hours
    c. 6 hours
    d. 8 hours

15. Food should be discarded if it exceeds _____ during cold prep or serving.
    a. 41°F
    b. 55°F
    c. 65°F
    d. 70°F

16. An estimated _____ cases of food-borne disease occur each year in the United States.
    a. 1 million
    b. 9 million
    c. 34 million
    d. 76 million

17. Which of the following is not a measurement for monitoring critical control points?
    a. visual
    b. taste
    c. time
    d. temperature

18. HACCP is a _____ system.
    a. reactive
    b. preventive
    c. ineffective

19. What is the proper method of rotation of stored food called?
    a. HACCP
    b. CCP
    c. FIFO

20. What is the temperature range of fresh meat and poultry?
    a. 31°–35°F
    b. 33°–38°F
    c. 40°–60°F
    d. 45°–55°F

21. Bacteria grow best in foods that are in the pH range of _____.
    a. 0.0–4.6
    b. 2.6–8.0
    c. 4.6–7.0
    d. 5.0–9.6

22. Shell stock tags must be kept on-site for _____.
    a. 1 week
    b. 30 days
    c. 60 days
    d. 90 days

FILL IN THE BLANK

23. List the seven principles of HACCP.

1. Analyze hazards.

2. Identify critical control points.

3. Establish preventative measures.

4. Establish monitoring procedures.

5. Establish corrective actions.

6. Establish procedures to verify system is working properly.

7. Establish effective recordkeeping.

24. FATTOM is an acronym for

Food

Acid

Temperature

Time

Oxygen

Moisture

25. List at least five factors contributing to food-borne illness.

1.   Use of leftovers

2.   Improper cleaning

3.   Cross-contamination

4.   Contaminated raw food

5.   Inadequate reheating

6.   Improper hot storage

7.   Inadequate cooking

8.   Infected people touching food

9.   Time between preparing and serving

10.   Improper cooling

26. What are the two types of thermometer calibration methods?

1.   Ice point method

2.   Boil point method

27. List at least three activities after which employees should wash their hands.

1.   Smoking

2.   Eating

3.   Using the restroom

4.   Handling money

5.   Touching raw food

6.   Touching or combing their hair

7.   Taking a break

8.   Handling anything dirty

28. List at least three methods of cooling foods.

1. **Cool in small batches**

2. **Use shallow pan**

3. **Stir frequently**

4. **Ice-water bath**

5. **Blast chill**

6. **Add cool water as ingredient**

29. What does MSDS stand for?

Material safety data sheet

TRUE/FALSE

30. Raising the pH in foods may render them non-potentially hazardous.
    True
    False

31. Only kitchen staff needs to be trained in HACCP principles.
    True
    False

32. Anaerobic bacteria must have oxygen in order to grow.
    True
    False

33. Choosing a reputable pest-control operator is an essential component of a HACCP plan.
    True
    False

34. CCPs are points in the process where bacteria or other harmful organisms may grow or food may become contaminated.
    True
    False

35. HACCP involves eight principles.
    True
    False

MATCHING

Match with correct definition. List the letter of the correct definition next to the word below.

Bacteria: **a** *Living single-cell organisms.*

Contamination: **c** *The unintended presence of potentially harmful substances, including microorganisms, chemicals and physical objects in food.*

Cross-Contamination: **h** *The transfer of harmful substances or disease-causing microorganisms to food by hands, food-contact surfaces, sponges, cloth towels and utensils that touch raw food, are not cleaned, and then touch ready-to-eat foods.*

Corrective Action **d** *An activity that is taken by a person whenever a critical limit is not met.*

Critical Control Point **m** *An operational step or procedure in a process, production method, or recipe, at which control* can be applied to prevent, reduce or eliminate a food safety hazard.

Critical Limit **b** *A measurable limit at a CCP that can be monitored to control the identified hazard to a safe level in the food.*

Food-Borne Illness **s** Sickness resulting from acquiring a disease that is carried or transmitted to humans by food containing harmful substances.

Food-Borne Outbreak **g** *The occurrence of two or more people experiencing the same illness after eating the same food.*

HACCP Plan **o** A written document which is based on the principles of HACCP and which describes the procedures to be followed to ensure the control of a specific process or procedure.

HACCP System **j** The result of implementing the HACCP principles in an operation that has a foundational, comprehensive, prerequisite program in place.

Hazard **f** A biological, physical or chemical property that may cause a food to be unsafe for human consumption.

Microorganism **k** A form of life that can be seen only with a microscope; including bacteria, viruses, yeast, and single-celled animals.

Monitoring **l** The act of observing and making measurements to help determine if critical limits are being met and maintained.

Operational Step **t** An activity in a food establishment, such as receiving, storage, preparation, cooking, etc.

Parasite **p** An organism that grows, feeds and is sheltered on or in a different organism and contributes to its host.

Pathogen **q** A microorganism that is infectious and causes disease.

Risk **r** An estimate of the likely occurrence of a hazard.

Record **n** *A documentation of monitoring observation and verification activities.*

Toxin **i** A poisonous substance that may be found in food.

Virus **e** A protein-wrapped genetic material which is the smallest and simplest life-form known.

Certificate of Completion

This hereby certifies that

_____

has satisfactorily completed HACCP Food Sanitation and Safety Training and passed all required examinations

on this _____ day of _____, 20____ .

_____
Signature of Manager

FOOD SANITATION HACCP

INDEX

A

B

D

I

J

K

L

P

W

walk-in coolers 411

walls 252

waste removal 303

water 117, 134, 295

wiping cloths 131

wood 280

Y

yersiniosis 26, 27

yield 177, 351

COMPANION CD RÓM INCLUDED

THE ENCYCLOPEDIA OF RESTAURANT FORMS

A Complete Kit of Ready-To-Use
Checklists, Worksheets and Training Aids
for a Successful Food Service Operation

Douglas Robert Brown

Item # ERF-02 $79.95
500 Pages Hardbound
ISBN 0910627-29-0
Publication Date: 2004

The Encyclopedia of Restaurant Forms: A Complete Kit of Ready-to-Use Checklists, Worksheets and Training Aids for a Successful Food Service Operation

If you're in the process of starting a new restaurant or are managing an existing food service operation, you need this book to do it right. Included in this book are hundreds of easy-to-implement tools, forms, checklists, posters, templates and training aids to help you get your operation organized and easier to manage while building your bottom line! The material may be used "as is" or readily adapted for any food service application. For example, you'll find a practical form to use when interviewing employees, a template for developing an employee schedule, and checklists for examining the food service operation and preparing a budget.

Expertly organized, this unique book takes you step by step through each department of a restaurant, caterer, hotel and non-commercial operation. Among the topics covered are management principles of planning, organizing, coordinating, staffing, directing, controlling and evaluation; product purchasing, receiving, storing and issuing, preparation and service; employment and personnel practices; and management of equipment and money. All of this tested, ready-to-use help is organized for quick access into 11 sections with a companion CD-ROM.

This manual will arm you with the right information to help you do your job. Keep it on your desk for continual reference. The many valuable forms contained in this work may be easily printed out and customized from the companion CD-ROM. There are over 488 ready-to-use business forms, checklists, training aids, contracts and agreements!

Timed HACCP Checklist — Ch 1

Incident Report — Ch 4

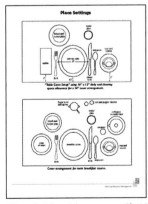

Place Setting Diagram — Ch 10

To order call toll-free 800-814-1132 or visit www.atlantic-pub.com

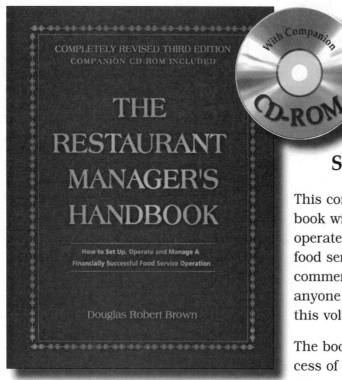

COMPLETELY REVISED THIRD EDITION
COMPANION CD ROM INCLUDED

THE RESTAURANT MANAGER'S HANDBOOK

How to Set Up, Operate and Manage A
Financially Successful Food Service Operation

Douglas Robert Brown

Item # RMH-02 $79.95
600 Pages Hardbound
ISBN 0-910627-09-6
Publication Date: 2003

The Restaurant Manager's Handbook: How to Set Up, Operate and Manage a Financially Successful Food Service Operation

This comprehensive and massive 600-page book will show you step by step how to set up, operate and manage a financially successful food service operation. Operators in the non-commercial segment as well as caterers, and anyone in the food service industry, will find this volume very useful.

The book's 19 chapters cover the entire process of a restaurant start-up and ongoing management in an easy-to-understand way, pointing out methods to increase your chances of success and showing how to avoid the many common mistakes. The companion CD-ROM contains all the forms demonstrated in the book for easy use in a PDF format.

While providing detailed instruction and examples, the author leads you through finding a location that will bring success, learn how to write a winning business plan, how to buy and sell a restaurant, franchising, basic cost-control systems, profitable menu planning, sample restaurant floor plans and diagrams, successful kitchen management, equipment layout and planning, food safety and HACCP, successful beverage management, learn how to set up computer systems to save time and money, learn how to hire and keep a qualified professional staff, IRS tip-reporting requirements, managing and training employees, generate high-profile public relations and publicity, learn low-cost internal marketing ideas, low- and no-cost ways to satisfy customers and build sales, learn how to keep bringing customers back, accounting and bookkeeping procedures, auditing, budgeting and profit planning, as well as thousands of great tips and useful guidelines.

The extensive resource guide details over 7,000 suppliers to the industry; this directory could be a separate book on its own. This *Restaurant Manager's Handbook* covers everything for which many companies pay consultants thousands of dollars.

There are literally hundreds of innovative ways demonstrated to streamline your restaurant business. Learn new ways to make the kitchen, bars, dining room and front office run smoother and increase performance. Shut down waste, reduce costs and increase profits. In addition, operators will appreciate this valuable resource and reference in their daily activities and as a source of ready-to-use forms, Web sites, operating and cost-cutting ideas and mathematical formulas that can be easily applied to their operations. Highly recommended!

To order call toll-free 800-814-1132 or visit www.atlantic-pub.com

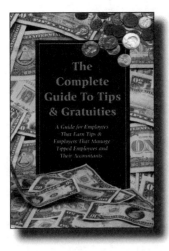

The Complete Guide to Tips & Gratuities: A Guide for Employees Who Earn Tips & Employers Who Manage Tipped Employees and Their Accountants

There are millions of workers in the United States that rely on tips for most of their income, and there are well over two million businesses where the employers rely on tipped employees. According to recent statistics from the U.S. Department of Labor, food and beverage service-related workers held 6.5 million jobs in 2000 alone. The U.S. Department of Labor estimated in a 2001 study that tips and gratuities accounted for well over $5 billion per year being left on plates and tip trays, financed on credit cards and handed directly into happy, open palms.

For the first time, this new book deals with all aspects of tips and gratuities. For the employee or self-employed, learn how to earn more tips and how to properly account for and pay taxes on them. For the employer, learn how to manage and properly account for the taxes on tipped employees. For the bookkeeper and accountant, get the latest on tax and withholding laws. Apart from all the great and practical advice in the book, it has to be remembered that tips have to be earned; thus, there are literally hundreds of little tricks, hints and suggestions to help tipped employees, well, make more tips!

Item # CGT-02 $19.95
144 Pages • ISBN 0910627-38-X

The Waiter & Waitress and Waitstaff Training Handbook: A Complete Guide to the Proper Steps in Service for Food & Beverage Employees

This training handbook was designed for use by all food service serving staff members and all types of service including French, American, English, Russian, Family-Style and Banquet. It covers every aspect of restaurant customer service for the positions of host, waiter or waitress, head waiter, captain and bus person. Step-by-step instructions on hosting, seating guests, taking/filling orders, loading/unloading trays, table side service, setting an elegant table, folding napkins, promoting specials and side orders, handling problems, difficult customers, managing tips, handling the check and money, and more.

Plus, learn advanced serving techniques such as flambé and carving meats, fish, and fruits. It also features a chapter devoted exclusively to food safety and sanitation. Food service managers will find this an excellent foundation for your organization's training program.

Item # WWT-TH $29.95
288 pages • ISBN 091062747-9

This Title Also Available in Spanish
Item # WWT-SP • $29.95
288 pages • ISBN 0910627-48-7

How to Open a Financially Successful Specialty Retail and Gourmet Foods Shop

If you plan to open a specialty retail store, or small store inside an existing retail space, then this book is a must. It shows how, with minimal effort and a small investment compared to other food businesses, you can start your own specialty retail store and be highly profitable!

This is the A-to-Z guide to making it in your own store. Learn the expert tips, tricks and a vast gold mine of crucial how-to information. This is an ideal guide for newcomers to the business, as well as experienced operators. In addition to basic operational practices, this book will demonstrate how to increase impulse sales and improve presentation, utilize merchandising fixtures and techniques, cross-merchandising, point-of-purchase materials, and develop a product sampling program. Never before has so much practical information about the specialty store business been offered in one book.

The CD-ROM contains a complete, editable business plan in MS Word format as well as comprehensive supply lists to help you stock your start-up gourmet store.

Item # SRG-02 $39.95
288 pages • ISBN 0910627-32-0

How to Open a Financially Successful Bakery

The small bakeries that are popping up everywhere in this country can be started with a low investment compared to other food business, and can be highly profitable! If your dream is to own and operate a bakery, this book will help you transform making bread into making profits. From bagels to zucchini muffins, your offerings are virtually endless, but your job is to make the choices that will bring customers to your door and leave with a smile on their face.

This detailed text contains all the information you will ever need to start, operate and manage a highly profitable bakery. Twenty-four comprehensive chapters cover all the bases, from purchasing equipment to controlling labor costs. This is a perfect book for entrepreneurs, schools, colleges and technical training centers.

Item # FSB-02 $39.95
288 Pages • ISBN 0910627-33-9

The CD-ROM contains a complete, editable business plan in MS Word format as well as comprehensive supply lists to help you stock your bakery.

To order call toll-free 800-814-1132 or visit www.atlantic-pub.com

Other great books available from Atlantic Publishing:

15 BOOKS AVAILABLE!

This 15-book series from the editors of the *Food Service Professional Magazine* are the best and most-comprehensive books for serious food service operators available today. These step-by-step guides on specific management subjects are easy to read, easy to understand and will take the mystery out of the subject. The information is "boiled down" to the essence. They are filled to the brim with up-to-date and pertinent information. These books cover all the bases, providing clear explanations and helpful, specific information. All titles in the series include the phone numbers and Web sites of all companies discussed.

1-800-814-1132 Call toll-free 24 hours a day, 7 days a week. Or fax completed form to **1-352-622-5836**. Order Online! Just go to **www.atlantic-pub.com** for fast, easy, secure ordering.

SOFTWARE GUIDE

SAVE 40%
EMPLOYEE HANDBOOK CREATOR GUIDE
Finally, a cost-effective solution for developing your own employee handbook. Simply review the 100-plus policies already written for you and insert your own information when prompted. Complete with table of contents, introduction and a form for each employee to sign. Use with Windows or any word processor.

Item # EHB-CS ~~$99.95~~ **Sale $59.95**

Qty	Order Code	Book Title	Price	Total
	Item # EHB-CS	Employee Handbook Creator Guide	$59.95	
	Item # FS1-01	Restaurant Site Location	$19.95	
	Item # FS2-01	Buying & Selling a Restaurant Business	$19.95	
	Item # FS3-01	Restaurant Marketing & Advertising	$19.95	
	Item # FS4-01	Restaurant Promotion & Publicity	$19.95	
	Item # FS5-01	Controlling Operating Costs	$19.95	
	Item # FS6-01	Controlling Food Costs	$19.95	
	Item # FS7-01	Controlling Labor Costs	$19.95	
	Item # FS8-01	Controlling Liquor Wine & Beverage Costs	$19.95	
	Item # FS9-01	Building Restaurant Profits	$19.95	
	Item # FS10-01	Waiter & Waitress Training	$19.95	
	Item # FS11-01	Bar & Beverage Operation	$19.95	
	Item # FS12-01	Successful Catering	$19.95	
	Item # FS13-01	Food Service Menus	$19.95	
	Item # FS14-01	Restaurant Design	$19.95	
	Item # FS15-01	Increasing Rest. Sales	$19.95	
	Item # FSALL-01	**Entire 15-Book Series**	**$199.95**	

Best Deal! **SAVE 33%**

15 GUIDE-TO SERIES books for $199.95

Subtotal	
Shipping & Handling	
Florida 6% Sales Tax	
TOTAL	

SHIP TO:

Name_____ Phone(____) _____

Company Name_____

Mailing Address _____

City _____ State _____ Zip _____

FAX (____) _____ E-mail _____

❏ My check or money order is enclosed ❏ Please send my order COD ❏ My authorized purchase order is attached

❏ Please charge my: ❏ MasterCard ❏ VISA ❏ American Express ❏ Discover

Card # ☐☐☐☐-☐☐☐☐-☐☐☐☐-☐☐☐☐ Expires ☐☐-☐☐

Please make checks payable to: **Atlantic Publishing Company** • 1210 SW 23rd Place • Ocala, FL 34474-7014
USPS Shipping/Handling: add $5.00 first item, $2.50 each additional or $15.00 for the whole set. Florida residents PLEASE add the appropriate county sales tax.

DID YOU BORROW THIS COPY?

Have you been borrowing a copy of *HACCP & Sanitation in Restaurants and Food Service Operations: A Practical Guide Based on the FDA Food Code* from a friend, colleague or library? Don't you wish you had your own copy for quick and easy reference? To make it easy for you to order, please photocopy the order from below and send to:

Atlantic Publishing Company • 1210 SW 23rd Place • Ocala, FL 34474-7014

YES! Send me____copy(ies) of HACCP & Sanitation in Restaurants and Food Service Operations: A Practical Guide Based on the FDA Food Code (Item # HSR-02) for $79.95 + $5.00 for USPS shipping and handling.

Atlantic Publishing Company
1210 SW 23rd Place
Ocala, FL 34474-7014

Add $5.00 for USPS shipping and handling. Florida residents PLEASE add the appropriate sales tax for your county.

Please Print

_____
Name

_____
Organization Name

_____
Address

_____
City, State, Zip

Order toll-free 800-814-1132
FAX 352-622-5836

❏ My check or money order is enclosed. *Please make checks payable to Atlantic Publishing Company.*

❏ My purchase order is attached. *PO #_____*

www.atlantic-pub.com • e-mail: sales@atlantic-pub.com

DID YOU BORROW THIS COPY?

Have you been borrowing a copy of *HACCP & Sanitation in Restaurants and Food Service Operations: A Practical Guide Based on the FDA Food Code* from a friend, colleague or library? Don't you wish you had your own copy for quick and easy reference? To make it easy for you to order, please photocopy the order from below and send to:

Atlantic Publishing Company • 1210 SW 23rd Place • Ocala, FL 34474-7014

YES! Send me____copy(ies) of HACCP & Sanitation in Restaurants and Food Service Operations: A Practical Guide Based on the FDA Food Code (Item # HSR-02) for $79.95 + $5.00 for USPS shipping and handling.

Atlantic Publishing Company
1210 SW 23rd Place
Ocala, FL 34474-7014

Add $5.00 for USPS shipping and handling. Florida residents PLEASE add the appropriate sales tax for your county.

Please Print

_____
Name

_____
Organization Name

_____
Address

_____
City, State, Zip

Order toll-free 800-814-1132
FAX 352-622-5836

❏ My check or money order is enclosed. *Please make checks payable to Atlantic Publishing Company.*

❏ My purchase order is attached. *PO #_____*

www.atlantic-pub.com • e-mail: sales@atlantic-pub.com

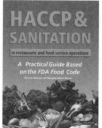

DID YOU BORROW THIS COPY?

Have you been borrowing a copy of *HACCP & Sanitation in Restaurants and Food Service Operations: A Practical Guide Based on the FDA Food Code* from a friend, colleague or library? Don't you wish you had your own copy for quick and easy reference? To make it easy for you to order, please photocopy the order from below and send to:

Atlantic Publishing Company • 1210 SW 23rd Place • Ocala, FL 34474-7014

YES!

Send me_____copy(ies) of HACCP & Sanitation in Restaurants and Food Service Operations: A Practical Guide Based on the FDA Food Code (Item # HSR-02) for $79.95 + $5.00 for USPS shipping and handling.

Atlantic Publishing Company
1210 SW 23rd Place
Ocala, FL 34474-7014

Add $5.00 for USPS shipping and handling. Florida residents PLEASE add the appropriate sales tax for your county.

Please Print

_____
Name

_____
Organization Name

_____
Address

_____
City, State, Zip

Order toll-free
800-814-1132
FAX 352-622-5836

❏ My check or money order is enclosed. *Please make checks payable to Atlantic Publishing Company.*

❏ My purchase order is attached. *PO #* _____

www.atlantic-pub.com • e-mail: sales@atlantic-pub.com

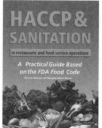

DID YOU BORROW THIS COPY?

Have you been borrowing a copy of *HACCP & Sanitation in Restaurants and Food Service Operations: A Practical Guide Based on the FDA Food Code* from a friend, colleague or library? Don't you wish you had your own copy for quick and easy reference? To make it easy for you to order, please photocopy the order from below and send to:

Atlantic Publishing Company • 1210 SW 23rd Place • Ocala, FL 34474-7014

YES!

Send me_____copy(ies) of HACCP & Sanitation in Restaurants and Food Service Operations: A Practical Guide Based on the FDA Food Code (Item # HSR-02) for $79.95 + $5.00 for USPS shipping and handling.

Atlantic Publishing Company
1210 SW 23rd Place
Ocala, FL 34474-7014

Add $5.00 for USPS shipping and handling. Florida residents PLEASE add the appropriate sales tax for your county.

Please Print

_____
Name

_____
Organization Name

_____
Address

_____
City, State, Zip

Order toll-free
800-814-1132
FAX 352-622-5836

❏ My check or money order is enclosed. *Please make checks payable to Atlantic Publishing Company.*

❏ My purchase order is attached. *PO #* _____

www.atlantic-pub.com • e-mail: sales@atlantic-pub.com